AMERICA: A PORTRAIT IN HISTORY

PRENTICE-HALL, INC. ENGLEWOOD CLIFFS, NEW JERSEY 07632

DAVID BURNER
State University of New York at Stony Brook

ROBERT D. MARCUS
State University of New York at Stony Brook

EMILY S. ROSENBERG
Macalester College

second edition

AMERICA

A PORTRAIT IN HISTORY

VOLUME II—Many Americans

Library of Congress Cataloging in Publication Data

Burner, David (date)
    America: a portrait in history.

    Includes bibliographical references.
    CONTENTS: v. 1. A new people.—v. 2. Many Americans.
    1. United States—History. I. Marcus, Robert D.,
(date) joint author. II. Rosenberg, Emily S.,
(date) joint author. III. Title.
E178.1.B92–1978b   973   78–742
ISBN 0–13–024232–2 (v. 1)
ISBN 0–13–024240–3 (v. 2)

AMERICA: A Portrait in History

second edition   *David Burner* / *Robert D. Marcus* / *Emily S. Rosenberg*

VOLUME 2

*Maps on pages 362, 428, 454, and 670 are from
Hofstdater, Miller, Aaron and Jordan,* The United States, *4th edition,
by permission of Prentice-Hall, Inc.*

Printed in the United States of America
10   9   8   7   6   5   4   3   2   1

Prentice-Hall International, Inc., *London*
Prentice-Hall of Australia Pty. Limited, *Sydney*
Prentice-Hall of Canada, Ltd., *Toronto*
Prentice-Hall of India Private Limited, *New Delhi*
Prentice-Hall of Japan, Inc., *Tokyo*
Prentice-Hall of Southeast Asia Pte. Ltd., *Singapore*
Whitehall Books Limited, *Wellington, New Zealand*

to
William Arthur and Beatrice Bird Burner
Leonard Roger and Dorothy Zimmerman Marcus
Albert Arthur and Helen Griggs Schlaht

CONTENTS

PREFACE

As the history of the United States lengthens and its influence spreads, textbooks that introduce students to the subject keep getting shorter. This is less of a paradox than it seems. Teachers of American history have never deliberately beguiled their students into the comfortable illusion that any one book could summarize the nation's complex past. Most students, however, after a few months of handling a thousand-page, double-column, four-pound book, which posed every question he or she found on the examinations, easily drifted into the security-blanket conception of the textbook. Introductory courses in other disciplines with more conceptual structure, such as the sciences, where a textbook actually could communicate nearly everything a first-year student had to know, reinforced this impression. And often the backgrounds of any historical interpretations they encountered—the documents, the key scholarly articles—proved not easily accessible to students, driving both instructors and their classes back to the all-important textbook.

Clearly all this has changed. The instructor can put paperbacks into his students' hands and major collections of reprinted documents and monographs into his college or university library. He also can draw on imaginative collections of documents and of historical interpretations packaged for student use. Even beyond that, modern methods of photo-duplication make it possible to reproduce the most arcane materials out of an instructor's own research if he thinks it will strike a chord of student interest. In short, there are now a few feet of smooth path into the tangled thicket of inquiry into the past—enough to encourage students to begin the journey. The task of a modern textbook is to facilitate that journey—not to convince students that they have already reached their destination.

There are many reasons to make this journey. Americans are a historically minded people. All over the country they invest money and energy in preserving the remains of a rapidly vanishing past. They designate buildings historic landmarks, restore old villages, collect "Americana." More important, in every national crisis arguments hinge on which precedent offers the best guide to present policy. Statesmen debate interpretations of the Constitution, a document nearly two hundred years old. Few people have ever believed more firmly in the moot doctrine that history has direct lessons to teach the present.

This, however, is not the principal justification for studying the history of the United States. Historical study benefits us less as a guide to politics than as a goad to imagination. More than any other subject, history extends our vision of American life. With eyes fixed only on the present, we become slaves to our era. With our gaze ranging more widely through time, we develop a sense of the multiple possibilities of experience and of our institutions. History, paradoxically, sharpens our vision of the present by stripping away its inevitability, by suggesting all the possibilities for making a different life. To the present-bound American, automobiles are the mode of transportation, television the media for communication, ballpoint pens the way to write, Norman Mailer the reigning literary giant, Jimmy Carter the only President we have. The past is larger than this, crowded with people, and styles, and ideas. The hard journey through it returns the traveler to a present he did not fully see before his trip.

America: A Portrait in History aims to meet the needs of the present generation of students and teachers. Its title, we hope, describes it with precision. This history of the American past attempts to project images that will linger in students' minds. The biographies that begin each chapter introduce people from the past who did things that most students thought typical only of the present: a political balladeer of the 1930s, an eighteenth-century agitator and iconoclast, a famous gangster of the 1920s.

A record, included in the book, offers the angry denunciations of Tom Paine's *Common Sense;* the experience of slavery as narrated by ex-slave Frederick Douglass; the poignant demands of a black woman, Sojourner Truth, at the Women's Rights Convention at Seneca Falls, New York, in 1848; the smug assurance of steel magnate and philanthropist Andrew Carnegie; William Jennings Bryan's "Cross of Gold" speech at the 1896 Democratic National Convention;

Charlotte Gillman's "Are Women Human Beings?"; Franklin D. Roosevelt's First Inaugural; Martin Luther King's "I Have a Dream"; and José Gutiérrez on the dreams of his own Chicano ethnic group.

The illustrations offer an unusually active vision of Americans doing things with force and energy. Most of all, the text aims at telling the story of past Americans with clarity and, we hope, in a way that will transmit to students some of the excitement that the authors have found in their own study of American history.

ACKNOWLEDGMENTS

Indispensable help in the composition of this book has come to us from Norman L. Rosenberg of Central Michigan University. We also wish to thank for capable assistance Terry Cooney, James Moore, Steve Stowe, Susan Strasser, Timothy Patterson, and Marian Wilson; our able typists have been Marian Wilson, Patricia Flannery, and Barbara Engels.

We did not act on every suggestion, and responsibility for the final manuscript, its strengths and its shortcomings, is ours alone.

AMERICA: A PORTRAIT IN HISTORY

The poetry of Walt Whitman portrays the American spirit of the era.
Culver Pictures.

7

WAR AND PEACE
1860-1876

ROBERT E. LEE

The Confederacy was one of the great gambles of American history. Pitting its nine million inhabitants (over one-third of them black slaves who might or might not be loyal) against the 22 million from which the Union could draw, its weakness in manpower was matched by weakness in its railroad network, its industrial plant, its banking system, its navy, and its new and untested government. Less tangible, but perhaps as important, it suffered a deep moral isolation from a world civilization struggling to end slavery.

Robert E. Lee was no enthuasiast for secession. Family tradition opposed it: his father "Lighthorse Harry" Lee had been a Revolutionary War Hero, and his mother's family, the Carters, had also played an honorable role in the founding of the United States. Lee's wife was the great granddaughter of Martha Washington, and Lee had grown up in Alexandria surrounded by momentoes of George Washington, upon whom he modeled his life. Lee had received his education from the United States government at West Point and had served all his adult life in the United States Army, distinguishing himself in the Mexican

War, serving for a time as the superintendent of West Point, and achieving some eminence as an army engineer. When secession came, the Lincoln administration sounded him out about taking command of the Union army. Yet Lee, who had only days before accepted promotion to colonel (despite having been offered the highest rank in the Confederate army, brigadier general), saw no choice but to resign his commission rather than to face the responsibility of leading troops against his native state. Lee in the end was a Virginian.

Lee, forced to make a choice in 1861, could only choose to defend his native state. Assuming direction of the Confederacy's forces was merely a later extension of his role in Virginia. When, after 1865, the Confederacy was no more, he found it easy to resume his loyalty to the Union and to urge other southerners to follow his lead. He was never a southern nativist, only a Virginian in a bad season.

Most of Lee's role as a general was in defending his home state. He had to keep the Union armies from Richmond, the Confederate capital, while seeking to strike the dramatic blow that would either destroy the Union's will to continue the battle or would bring in the European powers on the southern side. Several times he came close, but always he lacked the manpower to follow up his victories and rout the Union army. His most daring campaign ended at Gettysburg when the Union lines only barely held and his armies took losses they would never replenish. To appreciate the daring of this campaign, one need only glance at a map. Gettysburg is far from the Virginia peninsulas that Lee had to defend. It is north of the District of Columbia, north even of Baltimore, very much in the enemy's country. Lee's associate, General James Longstreet, noted the "subdued excitement" that ran through the generally calm Lee when he went over to daring attack. Like his hero, Washington, Lee had to retreat even though his instinct was to attack. He usually kept a reasonable balance between the two approaches—as Washington had—but he had no French alliance, no reliable navy (Yorktown had been partially a French naval victory), and his enemy's supply line did not stretch across an ocean. Eventually his army could be worn down, and once he had an opponent willing to suffer the casualties that victory would cost, he had to lose. By 1865 Grant's earlier victories in the West and Sherman's march through Georgia had isolated Lee's Virginia army from most of its supplies. Then Grant steadily threw in his troops, took his losses, and fought inch by inch until what had once been Lee's army was but a mass of starving men. On Palm Sunday 1865 Lee surrendered the Army of Northern Virginia.

Lee is not an easy figure for twentieth-century Americans to understand. Handsome, heroic, a brilliant commander and tactician, beloved of his men, respected by his adversaries, always humble, always responsible, removed from all politics and self-interest in his role as commander, he seems too perfect for an age that prefers its heroes flawed. Especially are we uncomfortable with having so peerless a leader in such a morally dubious cause as defending a nation based on slavery. But Lee's age believed in heroism and virtue, and Lee molded his great—but surely not unique—inner strengths to an ideal of behavior which his society supported and applauded. His culture—North and South after the war—accepted and expected his disinterested moralism much as ours insists upon the human foibles that our great men and women display. Lee epitomized an aristocratic ideal vanishing even then but which the Confederacy was supposed to revive. He was not a man of the people—whatever that means; and he was very much on the losing side.

The dreaded encounter

SECESSION AND THE FAILURE OF COMPROMISE

Even before Abraham Lincoln began his long journey from Springfield to Washington, seven states of the Lower South had left the Union to form the Confederate States of America. The founders of the Confederacy claimed to be protecting traditional liberties and a settled way of life against the assaults of a hostile central government. The election of Lincoln and the "Black Republicans," argued secessionists, demonstrated the corruption of the American electorate and reflected the South's minority status; in such a situation, southerners must not innocently await the greater oppression which would surely follow. Only through separation could white southerners control their own destiny and enjoy the benefits, as they understood them, of republican government. Secessionists were not rejecting the American experiment; they believed that they were preserving it in its true, original form. They could leave the Union proclaiming that the North had trampled upon the Constitution, abandoning the cause of limited government and menacing the property rights of slaveholders. The Confederacy represented a revolution to conserve traditional values, not to change them.

Seventy-year-old James Buchanan sadly watched the southerners go, hoping that time and a new administration might reunite the nation. The Democratic president proclaimed secession illegal and declared the Union "perpetual." After bringing several pro-Union Democrats into a reorganized cabinet, he also refused southern demands to surrender several military installations, including Fort Sumter in Charleston harbor. But Buchanan qualified this nationalism with the claim that the central government possessed no authority to coerce wayward states back into the "perpetual" Union. And even if the Constitution allowed the power of coercion, he feared that a forceful response would set off the larger conflict everyone wished to avoid. Long considered prosouthern, the aging president believed that abolitionists' fanaticism and the free-soil Republicans' menacing statements had pushed the South into a corner. In time, Buchanan hoped, northern extremists might temper their stands and permit some new compromisers to solve the difficulties as in 1820 and 1850.

But the "compromise of 1860" never came, even though a number of individuals and groups did seek some peaceful means of restoring the Union. A House "Committee of Thirty-Three" and a Senate "Committee of Thirteen" discussed compromise plans, and a conference of elder statesmen, chaired by former President John Tyler, gathered in Washington in early 1861. Neither this Washington Peace Convention nor Congress could resolve the crucial issue: the matter of slavery in the territories. The most widely discussed compromise proposal, championed by Senator John J. Crittenden of Kentucky, called for extension of the Missouri Compromise line to the Pacific and for adoption of an irrevocable constitutional amendment which guaranteed protection of slavery wherever it existed. These and other "peace" proposals were futile. The extremist fire-eaters, then dominating politics in the cotton states, probably would have rejected the Missouri Compromise solution; more important, Lincoln and the Republican party rejected any concession on the territorial issue. "Free-soil" had been one of the party's founding principles, not an electoral slogan which Republicans would concede to secessionists. Any agreement which permitted slavery to expand south of 36°30', Lincoln believed, would only encourage the slave powers' designs upon Mexico or other Latin American territory. The nation must take a firm stand against slavery's expansion.

Although Lincoln and the Republicans rejected compromise on the free-soil question, they did not consider their stand a necessary commitment to war. Throughout the secession crisis, many Republicans still believed in the possibility of a peaceful solution to sectional differences. Secession seemed a

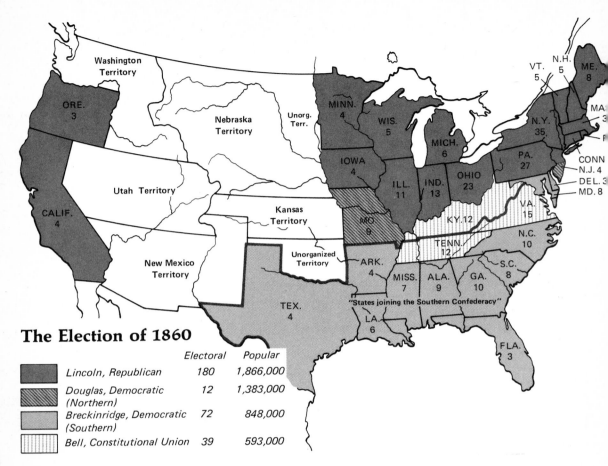

The Election of 1860

	Electoral	Popular
Lincoln, Republican	180	1,866,000
Douglas, Democratic (Northern)	12	1,383,000
Breckinridge, Democratic (Southern)	72	848,000
Bell, Constitutional Union	39	593,000

short-term aberration, not a permanent fact of national politics. But Republicans differed on how to achieve reconciliation. Immediately after slipping into Washington to avoid a rumored assassination plot, Lincoln began conferences with leading Republicans, especially William Seward of New York. Many Republicans considered the New Yorker their party's real leader, and, as secretary of state, Seward probably expected to dominate the less-experienced man from Illinois. But Lincoln quickly proved to be his own man.

THE PROBLEM OF THE FORTS

After taking the oath of office, Lincoln announced his position. Facing a raw March wind and reading in his high-pitched voice, the president assured the South that Republicans harbored no designs upon slavery in the slave-holding states. They would favor a constitutional amendment to protect slavery and would enforce the Fugitive Slave Law. But he made no concession of free soil, severely condemned secession as "anarchy," and pledged to "hold, occupy and possess" all Union property within the Confederate zone.

The most immediate problem was Confederate pressure upon federal facilities and military installations, especially Fort Sumter in South Carolina and Fort Pickens in Florida. Sumter, an important symbol of Union authority within the Lower South, provided the first test of Lincoln's policy and leadership. Faced with a decision on resupplying Sumter and several other forts, Lincoln carefully polled cabinet members and other important leaders. During these deliberations, Seward lost much of the president's respect by suggesting that the administration might provoke a war with European powers to unite the country against a common enemy. After great soul-searching, Lincoln took the calculated risk of sending a relief squadron to Fort Sumter. On April 4, 1861, he publicly announced the dispatch of several vessels.

Did Lincoln lure the South into firing the first shot? Persistent charges that he deliberately maneuvered the South into the aggressor's role seemed strained. No longer as confident of peace as he had once been, Lincoln certainly realized that his actions raised at least the *probability* of setting off hostilities. But Lincoln still believed that there was a *possibility* that the resupply mission might reach Sumter without a fight. The new Confederate government, however, believed it could not risk the humiliation of a successful relief expedition and decided to take the fort immediately. On April 13, a bloodless bombardment forced surrender of the garrison and began the most bloody conflict in American history.

Upon hearing news of Sumter's surrender, Lincoln acted swiftly. Without waiting for Congress to reconvene, he issued a proclamation calling for seventy-five thousand volunteers to put down "combinations too powerful to be suppressed by the ordinary course of judicial proceedings." When Congress reassembled on July 4, 1861, it legitimized this and several other quasi-military decisions.

AND THE WAR CAME

Since Confederate guns had resolved the issue of the forts, the status of the slaveholding states of the Upper South became the president's next dilemma. When he took the oath of office, eight of the fifteen slave states remained outside the Confederacy, and the president worked to keep as many as possible in the Union. In all of these states Unionist sentiment existed, but the Sumter incident forced immediate decisions. Virginia, Arkansas, Tennessee, and North Carolina quickly opted for secession. From seven the Confederacy had become eleven.

The sectional tug-of-war then shifted to the border states, and through a variety of stratagems the administration prevented the four remaining slave

Fort Sumter, South Carolina—the beginning of the war between the States.
Harper's Weekly, April 1861

states from leaving the Union. After anti-Union mobs attacked federal troops and cut the critical rail line between Baltimore and Washington, Lincoln sent troops into Maryland. Although Kentucky boldly defied the president's call for volunteers by declaring its "neutrality," Lincoln played a more cautious game there. He considered Kentucky—ironically, both his birthplace and that of the Confederacy's Jefferson Davis—the key area. "I hope to have God on my side," Lincoln reportedly said, "but I must have Kentucky." He delayed a decision to send troops to the Blue Grass State, preferring to dispatch a shipment of "Lincoln Rifles" to Unionists in the western part of the state and to wait. In the end, the president's policies succeeded: Kentucky, Maryland, Delaware, and Missouri remained in the Union. In addition, western Virginia broke off from the rest of the state and entered the Union as West Virginia in 1863. The war had come, and the new president surprised his critics and boldly took command.

Another new nation

CONFEDERATE GOVERNMENT

The Confederate constitution demonstrated secessionists' basic agreement with American institutions. The delegates who assembled at Montgomery, Alabama, in February 1861 were generally moderate rather than fire-eating secessionists, and they selected Howell Cobb, a respected Georgian, as president of the constitutional convention. The constitution, largely drafted by Alexander Stephens of Georgia, followed the general outlines of the federal Constitiution of 1787. In a few instances the southern constitution departed from the Union document: in the incorporation of a bill of rights into the constitution itself, in a six-year term for the president, and in a specific-item veto for the chief executive. It differed most radically from the original, of course, in providing specific guarantees for slavery. And unlike the Constitution of 1787, the Confederate document contained the word *slave* rather than some euphemism such as *persons bound to labor or service*.

After accepting the constitution, delegates selected Jefferson Davis of Mississippi as provisional president. Davis had left Kentucky for Mississippi at an early age, attended West Point, served with some distinction in the Mexican War, and married into a wealthy planter family. Probably the best-known southern politician since Calhoun, Davis served as a United States senator and as Franklin Pierce's secretary of war during the 1850s. Acutely aware of the great burdens which secession thrust upon him, Davis labored hard—probably too hard—to make the Confederacy a success. He proved reluctant to delegate power and spent too much time on small details. One of his cabinet officers complained that the president had a tendency "to slide away from the chief points to episodical questions" and that cabinet meetings "would exhaust four or five hours without determining anything." Davis clashed with other officials, especially Vice-President Alexander Stephens, Calhoun's heir as the South's expert in constitutional metaphysics. Although shy and reserved, Davis did provide a symbol of integrity and purpose which, at least initially, compared more than favorably with the awkward and inexperienced Lincoln.

PROBLEMS OF THE CONFEDERACY

The Confederacy could easily adapt the Union's governmental structure; translating form into reality proved more difficult. Traditional southern fears of centralized authority frustrated Davis's administration. Governor Joseph Brown of Georgia, for example, consistently denounced outside interference in his state's affairs, even when such "meddling" involved crucial military arrangements. A few state courts issued writs of *habeas corpus* (a court order requiring authorities to bring a prisoner before a judge) to release men who were attempting to evade the Confederacy's unpopular draft law. And in the hills of North Carolina and Georgia, "moonshiners" strongly resisted the efforts of Confederate officials seeking copper coils from homemade stills.

Political disorganization always plagued the Confederate government. Lacking the lever of party loyalty—the Confederacy never developed a two-party system—Davis found it more difficult than Lincoln to control his cabinet. Davis went through no less than six secretaries of war, five attorneys general, and four secretaries of state. Unlike Lincoln, Davis possessed no party machinery with which to fight obstructive state leaders, and he simply had to suffer the opposition and abuse from independent state chieftains such as Brown and Robert Toombs in Georgia. Finally, the lack of party organization impeded efforts to inform and mobilize the Confederate electorate. Lacking the party hoopla which had surrounded Jacksonian politics, Confederate elections apparently generated little excitement and failed to stimulate voter interest.

The absence of available resources and lack of time to develop alternatives also hampered the Confederacy. A sectional balance sheet clearly reveals the Confederacy's inferior position: only one-fifth of the nation's manufacturing, less than half of the population, an acute shortage of hard coin and bullion. The South's chaotic railroad system consisted of mostly short lines, eleven different track gauges, and too little rolling stock. Largely devoted to agriculture, the Confederacy lacked the technology and the skilled labor to undertake rapid industrial expansion. Richmond was the only significant industrial center, and the Confederate government soon left tiny Montgomery to make that city its capital.

Unlike the Lincoln administration, Confederate leaders never overcame obstacles to wartime organization. After initially relying upon supplies from Europe, Josiah Gorgas, chief of ordnance for the Confederate states, built up a series of arsenals throughout the South. Both the administration in Richmond and state governments encouraged development of enterprises such as textile mills, mining operations, shoe factories, and ironworks. But the South never approached the North's industrial output, and war destroyed most of the gains. Unfortunately for the "lost cause," the Confederate industrial spurt came too late and produced too little. Lack of materials forced some manufacturers to resort to bizarre expedients—such as using lard as a lubricant and cloths soaked in linseed oil as machine belts.

The Confederacy always faced serious money problems. Neither taxes nor loans provided enough revenue to run the war or to meet other pressing needs. The central government finally resorted to "tithing-in-kind," requiring farmers to give the government one-tenth of their output of wheat, corn, peas, beans, and other crops. Officials also resorted to the printing press, issuing vast quantities of paper money. This unstable paper (which was not legal tender) quickly drove all other currency out of circulation, and merchants resorted to various expedients to compensate for the lack of small coins. Counterfeiters enjoyed a thriving trade. The Confederacy's harried treasurer, struggling to run his own presses fast enough, even suggested a plan by which the government would take in bogus bills, affix a "valid" stamp, and reissue them as legitimate currency. The currency problem undercut public confidence in the Richmond government and produced dangerous inflation. The price of flour in Richmond more than doubled between 1860 and 1862; soap went from ten cents to a dollar a pound; and coffee shot up from fifty cents to twenty dollars per four pounds. And although it was no comfort to Virginians, coffee was even more expensive in Texas at seven dollars per pound.

SOUTHERN SOCIETY AT WAR

Within a few years food shortages plagued many areas of the agrarian South. Cities, magnets for ever-greater numbers of poor farmers seeking work and war refugees seeking protection, faced the most severe problems. In April 1863 some Richmond women, led by one of their number brandishing a six-shooter and a bowie knife, started a bread riot which escalated into a scramble for any type of food from anywhere. Richmond's City Hospital alone lost over three hundred pounds of beef during the looting. Only the intervention of Virginia's governor, a detachment of troops, and Jefferson Davis himself calmed the mob and stopped the pillaging. Richmond's expe-

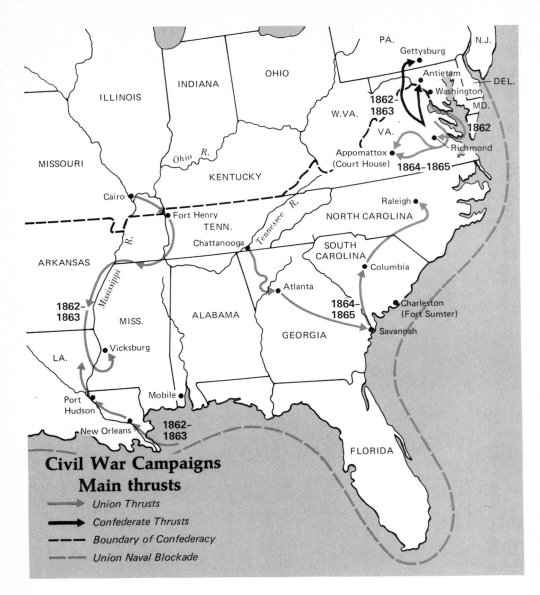

Civil War Campaigns
Main thrusts

→ Union Thrusts
→ Confederate Thrusts
– – – Boundary of Confederacy
– – – Union Naval Blockade

rience was not unique; similar uprisings beset Atlanta, Macon, and Mobile, where marchers demanded "Bread or Peace." As always, the poor suffered most but the wealthy also discovered shortages of the amenities of cultured living. Southerners began substituting water for whiskey, and "cold-water parties" became the fad—even in fashionable old Charleston. One Carolina host judged his Christmas party a great success and concluded that the cold-water punch "answered admirably. We danced until 2 o'clock. There were plenty of young ladies in town."

U.S. Grant: a better general than Robert E. Lee?
UPI

The war disrupted more than the drinking habits of Charleston's social-ites; the conflict produced significant social adjustments for women. Many plantation ladies began to work as nurses for the wounded or to run plantations in their husbands' absence. A few served the cause as spies and smugglers. And many women from the growing urban slums and impoverished rural areas labored, far less gloriously but just as effectively, in the new factories and ammunition plants. With the disruption of normal family life among soldiers, women also found the "world's oldest profession" a profitable enterprise.

Secession changed the ways in which whites exploited black labor, but the totality of the conflict also demonstrated black people's crucial place in southern society. On some plantations, where the white males had donned the gray, black slave "drivers" assumed greater responsibilities. In order to free more whites for military service, manufacturers used greater numbers of black laborers; in one Alabama factory black people provided more than three-quarters of the work force. In Virginia, which had more highly diversified and developed industries than most other slave states, black workers performed almost every service imaginable. Blacks labored on defense structures, unloaded ships, performed skilled crafts, and tended to wounded whites in overcrowded hospital facilities. The army used blacks as labor troops, and in the last desperate days of the conflict the Confederate Congress authorized recruitment of slaves and free blacks to serve in the armed forces. Some black units were formed, but the war ended before they joined the regular Confederate armies. While many blacks thus played a significant role in the struggle for southern independence, many others, seeing the opportunity to escape bondage, fled to Union lines.

The war's effect on race relations is hard to measure. Some historians have suggested that the war produced gradual changes in the slave system which would have "reformed it to death." The war itself informally loosened the chains of slavery, and some state legislatures did enact laws extending the civil and legal rights of black persons. But the fearful reaction to President Lincoln's Emancipation Proclamation and the tragic history of Reconstruction suggest that white southerners were still committed to maintaining their area as a "white man's country."

The civil war

THE WAR IN PERSPECTIVE

Writers have probably devoted more words to the American Civil War than to any other conflict in human history. The war coincided with significant modern innovations in journalism, particularly more effective use of the telegraph and greater reliance upon "on-the-spot" reporters. The press bom-barded the public with accounts of the war's progress. In some instances battle plans or other classified information fell into the hands of scoop-hungry journalists who passed the news along to readers. And there was always the inevitable second-guessing of wartime strategy and tactics. In addition, more serious writers churned out endless pages of what one critic has called "patriotic gore." Lee's final surrender at Appomattox hardly interrupted these chronicles, which reached epidemic proportions during the centennial observances of the 1960s.

Much of the older writing concentrated upon the leading military heroes. Robert E. Lee, the quiet Virginian who turned down command of the Union armies to serve his beloved state, still dominates the literature. Scion of a distinguished Virginia family, Lee struggled against heavy odds to defend his native land and to keep his army in the field. And no account of the war omits Thomas J. Jackson, a devoutly religious man who left Virginia Military Academy to become Lee's trusted "right hand." When "Stonewall" Jackson fell at Chancellorsville, a victim of his own troops' misdirected fire, the Confederacy lost their most skillful tactician, a general who consistently befuddled Union commanders with his lightning moves. In older accounts of the campaigns, Confederate leaders generally came off better than their Yankee counterparts, but recent writers have stressed the innovative tactics of Union commanders, particularly hard-drinking, tough Ulysses S. Grant. Lacking the dignified charm and fine breeding of Lee, Grant proved to be a skillful planner who, much better than Lee, understood the nature of this first "modern" war. "If men make war in slavish observance of rules," Grant wrote, "they will fail. . . . War is progressive because all the instruments and elements of war are progressive."

Gaining President Lincoln's confidence in the underpublicized western campaigns of 1862–63, Grant later exploited the Union's superior resources to force Lee's surrender in the East. Generally the villain in magnolia-scented accounts, fierce William T. Sherman did lay waste a sixty-mile strip in Georgia, but he also was a resourceful field commander, outmaneuvering Confederate forces protecting Atlanta and the Deep South. Like Grant, Sherman recognized the need for innovative military strategies, such as striking at the enemy's economic rather than military strength.

The Civil War took a frightful toll in human lives. Submarines, ironclad ships, and torpedoes made their first appearance. More important to the average soldier, new designs in firepower also changed land warfare. Whereas the old smoothbore musket was a hit-or-miss type of weapon, the new rifles propelled a much more accurate, much deadlier missile. Although rifled cannons were not so much in evidence as infantry rifles, the old smoothbore cannons fired murderous cannisters filled with lead slugs, producing the same effect as gigantic sawed-off shotguns. Commanders adjusted slowly to

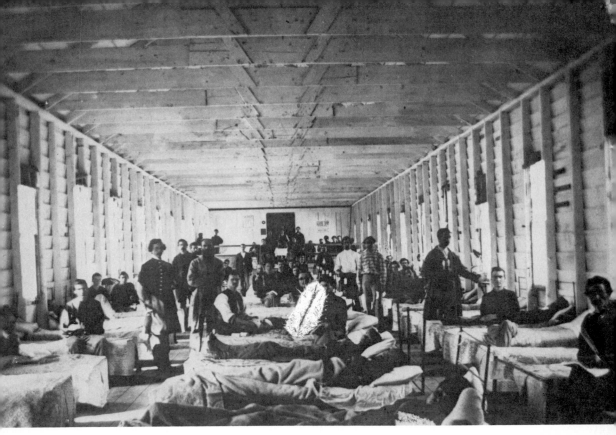

Convalescent hospital in Alexandria, Virginia.
Brady Collection, National Archives

these and other types of new military technology. Close formations and straightforward charges too often proved suicidal to the men in the ranks. Even in our age of bombers and missiles, Civil War casualty figures seem staggering. During a single day of fighting at Antietam, the North had almost twelve thousand dead and wounded and the South about an equal number. And other battles which lasted two or three days proved proportionately bloody.

Even if a soldier were not killed at once, his chances for survival were not good. Camps offered only the most primitive sanitary facilities, and smallpox, dysentery, and typhoid could prove as fatal as the new weaponry. That conditions were not worse owes much to philanthropic organizations—such as Clara Barton's and the U.S. Sanitary Commission—which were organized to improve the life of the ordinary Union soldier. Because of the lack of money, conditions in the southern ranks were worse and relief efforts less extensive. Little could have been done to improve medical facilities in any case; doctors simply had not yet unraveled the mysteries of treating infections nor discovered the need for sterilizing surgical instruments. Ambulance facilities were also primitive, and when a wounded soldier reached a medical tent he was often left in the hands of a tired surgeon working under extremely difficult conditions. Perhaps the most unfortunate men of all were those who rotted away in barbaric prison camps. Although commanders probably never carried on deliberate extermination policies, the fatality rate from disease and malnutrition reached three thousand per month in the stockade at Andersonville, Georgia. And Union prison camps were better only by comparison; nearly as many Confederates died in Union installations as Yankees perished in southern camps. Writing of the centennial "celebrations" of the 1960s, southern author Robert Penn Warren suggested that a day of national mourning would be the most appropriate memorial.

The casualties of war.
Nebraska Historical Society

General William Tecumseh Sherman (1820–91). This photograph was taken in 1865, the year of final Union victory.

THE COURSE OF BATTLE

For most participants, the war's first battle, Bull Run (Manassas), killed the initial burst of enthusiasm. Although "Old Fuss and Feathers" Winfield Scott was too infirm to command troops, this hero of the Mexican War joined others in warning against an ill-prepared Union advance into Virginia. But war is propelled by political as much as by military considerations; believing that the Union cause needed a quick victory, Lincoln ordered a thrust against Richmond. Fashionable Washingtonians followed in their carriages, hoping to enjoy the action. Considering their lack of preparation, troops from both sides fought bravely, but General Thomas Jackson's forces held like a "stonewall," and the South claimed the war's first victory. Caught in the jam of onlookers, servants, and carriages, Union troops became confused; a fairly orderly retreat turned into a rout. Union forces had entered battle amid cries of "On to Richmond" and poems such as:

> A hundred thousand Northmen
>   In glittering war array
> Shout, "Onward now to Richmond!
>   We'll brook no more delay;
> Why give the traitors time and means
>   To fortify the way
> With stolen guns, in ambuscades?
>   Oh! Answer us, we pray."

After Bull Run, Confederates gleefully sang:

> Yankee Doodle, near Bull Run,
>   Met his Adversary,
> First he thought the fight he'd won,
>   Fact proved quite contrary
>
> Panic-struck he fled, with speed
>   Of lightning glib with unction,
> Of slippery grease, in full stampede
>   From famed Manassas Junction.

Neither side could rejoice for long; the war became a sobering and brutal business, four long years of suffering and bloodshed.

The overall Confederate strategy seemed clear: to stave off defeat until foreign powers extended recognition and assistance or until time forced the Union to recognize southern independence. Southern armies, however, could not remain totally defensive, waiting for the fumbling Union giant to find its strength; whenever possible, Confederate forces assumed the offensive, hoping to keep the larger Union armies off balance and to undermine morale in the free states. This strategy of an "offensive defense" was similar

W. Homer, The Army of the Potomac—A Sharp-Shooter on picket Duty.
Library of Congress

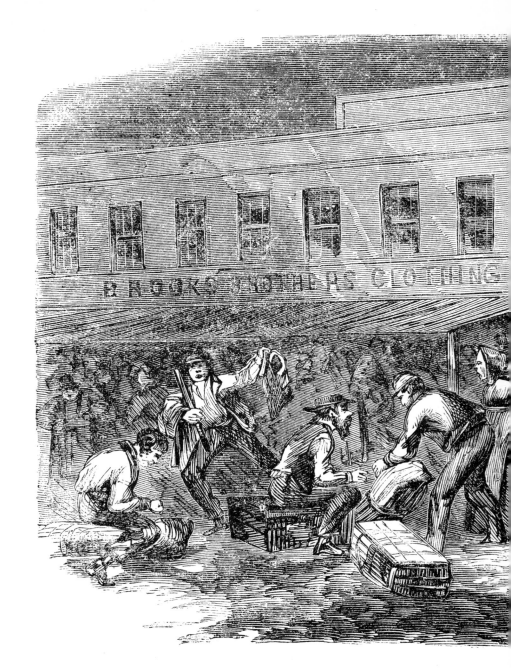

Draft riots in New York City.
Culver Pictures

to the one employed by General Washington during the American Revolution, but the Confederacy did not always carry it off. Too often gray-clad troops were chewed up in inconclusive engagements with larger Union armies.

Gradually, Union strategists devised a plan of their own. After the initial stabs at Richmond, Union armies attacked on a broad front, in the western areas of the Confederacy as well as into Virginia. Following Grant's promotion to general commander in the spring of 1864, he and Lincoln followed a strategy of keeping maximum pressure on the Confederate armies. Their aim was less to conquer territory than to grind down southern manpower with the Union war machine.

WAR WEARINESS AND VICTORY

By 1863 war weariness became apparent in both the North and South. Jefferson Davis faced continual sniping from his political opposition, and, for a time, Lincoln feared that he might not defeat Democratic presidential candidate General George B. McClellan in 1864. Running under the "Union" rather than the Republican party label, Lincoln capitalized upon nationalist sentiment and, in an effort to attract wider support, selected Andrew Johnson, a war Democrat from Tennessee, as a running mate. These political moves and union battlefield victories contributed to the president's reelection. Lincoln eventually outpolled McClellan by a wide margin, but his early electoral problems revealed the depths of popular frustration over the war.

Although the supply of army volunteers never dried up (partly because the Union offered a sizeable bounty to enlistees), both sides resorted to the first forced drafts in American history. Neither southerners nor northerners appreciated the innovation, but the Union law, which permitted draftees to buy their way out of the service, proved particularly unpopular. Antidraft riots broke out in New York City in 1863, forcing the government to send in federal troops. In the Confederacy, troop morale suffered because of the continual tardiness of paychecks.

In the end, the Union proved too strong for the outproduced, outgunned, and outmanned Confederacy. Initially Lee's forces did well in the Virginia campaigns, but in the bloody one-day Battle of Antietam (September 17, 1862) a larger Union army stopped a Confederate thrust northward. Antietam was an important turning point: it convinced England to postpone recognition of the Confederacy and encouraged President Lincoln to issue his Emancipation Proclamation. Despite the more publicized eastern campaigns, however, Union armies achieved their first great successes in the West. Here they employed their naval superiority in the Gulf of Mexico and along the Mississippi. With the surrender of Vicksburg on July 4, 1863,

Antietam; Twenty-five thousand men dead or wounded in a day.
Alexander Gardner, photographer

the Union gained control of the Mississippi River and split the Confederacy in half. At almost the same hour, another Union army threw back Lee's forces at a small college town in Pennsylvania —Gettysburg. Lee had hoped that his Pennsylvania campaign would compensate for the expected defeats in the West, but the Confederacy's deepest penetration into Union territory ended in disaster. Lee's troops suffered heavy casualties, and the defeat killed any chance of British recognition. Hard fighting lay ahead, and the Union strategy involved considerable time and manpower. But by April 1865 Lee's army had dwindled to twenty-five thousand ragged, tired, and hungry soldiers. Shortly after the dramatic meeting between Lee and Grant at Appomattox Courthouse, the other large Confederate army surrendered to General Sherman in North Carolina. The war was over. Southern legends of the "lost cause" began to take shape.

BLACK YANKEES

As the war dragged on, the Union began to use black troops against the South. Initially the Lincoln administration refused black volunteers; they feared that the appearance of black Yankees on the battlefield might suggest that the war had purposes in addition to restoration of the Union. Some northern officials also doubted the black man's fighting ability and feared racial friction within the military. But black leaders and white abolitionists continued to press the issue, hoping that military service would strengthen the case for emancipation and national protection of black peoples' liberties. Black abolitionist Frederick Douglass complained that blacks "were good enough to help win American independence, but they are not good enough to help preserve that independence against treason and rebellion." Eventually, northern war weariness and pressure from abolitionists led to acceptance of blacks in 1862. By the end of the war, almost one hundred eighty thousand blacks served in the army—about 10 percent of the total enlistees—and nearly fifty thousand—or about 25 percent—sailed with the navy.

Black soldiers faced even greater hardships than their white counterparts. Some commanders never altered their prejudices against blacks and relegated them to labor battalions. Because of discriminatory promotion policies, few blacks gained officers' commissions or even attained the rank of sergeant. And throughout most of the conflict, the War Department even discriminated at the pay line: black privates received three dollars a month less than whites. Southerners, too, singled out black Yankees. Some Confederate commanders announced a policy of killing even those black soldiers who surrendered or of forcing them into slavery. Such action only encour-

Sailors on the deck of the U. S. S. Monitor, James River, Va., July 9, 1862.

J. F. Gibson, photographer, Library of Congress

aged blacks to fight harder. After observing two black regiments, General N. P. Banks reported that "whatever doubt may have existed heretofore as to the efficiency of organizations of this character, the history of this day proves conclusively to those who were in a condition to observe the conduct of these regiments, that the Government will find in this class of troops effective supporters and defenders."

Politics and policy in the north

ECONOMIC LEGISLATION

The War for the Union dominated northern attention between 1861 and 1865, but it did not prevent politicians from enacting legislation designed to encourage commerce and industry. The voluntary exodus of slave-state representatives removed some agrarian opponents of aid to business and, more important, reduced the number of sectional interests which Congress had to balance. Since the Republican party dominated Congress during the war years, the general thrust of economic programs represented the application of their old free-soil, free-labor principles. With assistance from the national government, Republican leaders believed, the nation could develop a modern political economy, a commercial-industrial one which would stand in sharp contrast to the plantation-based slave system of the South. The result, however, was not a simple victory for northeastern businessmen over agricultural representatives. Instead, a number of conflicting interest groups—occupational as well as sectional—lobbied in the wartime Congresses. Congressmen ultimately enacted a series of laws directed at the needs of the manufacturing and commercial sectors as well as at the dreams of free-soil agriculturalists.

Congress faced long-standing disputes over tariffs and national banking legislation. In the Morrill Tariff of 1861, passed shortly before Lincoln took office, Congress raised duties to 1846 levels. And during later sessions protectionists secured additional levies which boosted rates higher than they had ever been before. Congress also revised the country's banking structure. Ever since Andrew Jackson slew the "Monster"—the second Bank of the United States—the country had lacked a central banking system. The National Banking Acts of 1863 and 1864 created a series of national institutions which were to invest one-third of their capital in federal bonds. The banks could then issue paper money—national bank notes—in amounts up to 90 percent of the market value of these securities. In order to discourage the circulation of state bank notes, Congress later imposed a 10 percent tax on the issues of all institutions which did not join the national banking system. The new measures provided a more stable, national currency.

The wartime Congresses also extended federal aid for internal improvements. Competing sectional and commercial groups scuttled proposals to improve the Illinois Ship Canal and to construct a new waterway from Lake Michigan to the Mississippi River, but Congress did approve the long-delayed transcontinental railway. Plans called for the new road to run across the middle of the country from Omaha to Utah and then on to California. In addition to removing slave-state congressmen who desired a southern route, the war gave the project the justification of military necessity. In a series of acts during the 1860s, Congress granted private railroad developers thirty million acres of public land and extended generous loans. Once sectional obstacles were eliminated, most representatives approved the railway proposal, a measure in line with the nineteenth-century policy, extending to this day, of using government to promote transportation projects.

The national government also offered assistance for other economic purposes. The Homestead Act, similar to a bill vetoed by President Buchanan in 1860, followed the old Jeffersonians' vision of a continent of independent yeoman farmers. Under the 1862 act, settlers could file a claim to one hundred and sixty acres of public land, live on this quarter-section for five years, and then receive title upon payment of a small fee. Republican congressmen, especially those from the Middle West, considered the Homestead Act a vital piece of party legislation, but the results proved disappointing. Many more settlers obtained cheap tracts from railroads or private land companies than from the government. And in some areas, land transferred under the Homestead Act actually involved fraudulent claims by stooges for large lumber and mining corporations. (One timber company employee fulfilled the requirement of building a homestead by raising a tiny cabin—eighteen by thirty inches.) Reacting to unfounded fears that the Homestead Act would drain workers from the East and hoping to counter the inevitable wartime labor shortage, Congress then authorized immigration of contract laborers from Europe and the Orient and permitted employers to deduct the costs of passage from the immigrants' paychecks.

The Morrill Land Grant Act of 1862 secured broader geographical support. In return for federal land grants, states would finance colleges devoted to education in agriculture, engineering, and military science (the forerunner of present-day ROTC programs). Sometimes considered a western-oriented measure because of its agricultural features, the Morrill Act actually drew significant support from eastern representatives who believed that their most populated states would gain the most from the land grants.

When the war came, some critics expressed fears about the strength of the national government. The extension of authority during the war, whether viewed as a return to the Hamiltonian vision of national power or as a new assertion of federal supremacy, represented a substantial victory for those interest groups who sought to expand the power of the central government over the economy.

LINCOLN AND CIVIL LIBERTIES

The Civil War raised grave constitutional problems involving the powers of the national government versus the rights of individuals. In 1860 federal courts possessed few guidelines for civil liberties cases, particularly for those involving the limits of dissent. To many lawyers, the infamous Sedition Act of 1798 always stood as a stark symbol of governmental repression. But the Supreme Court had never determined its constitutionality, and many legal authorities considered the Sedition Law perfectly valid. Although American Indians, Mexicans, and fugitive black slaves felt the brunt of federal coercion, during the first five decades of the nineteenth century legal disputes between the federal government and individual white citizens were rare. Requiring the extension of federal power, the Civil War forced development of some clearer standards in civil liberties cases.

Although faced with widespread criticism of the war and its conduct, Lincoln sought no new sedition law and mounted no systematic drive against protesters. A lawyer himself, Lincoln always agonized over civil liberties questions; more important, he wished to avoid political and constitutional imbroglios. Spectacular legal prosecutions, he believed, would only rebound against his administration. And even if he had wanted to conduct a reign of terror against dissenters, he lacked the prerequisites. There was no extensive federal apparatus to investigate and prosecute critics, and the Lincoln administration did not enjoy enough popular support to risk the backlash against such a crusade.

But Lincoln did not permit dissent to go unchecked. Instead of instituting judicial proceedings, the president suspended the writ of *habeas corpus* and he ordered the State Department to arrest individuals under his executive power. Such procedures, which bypassed the courts and ignored congressional authority over *habeas corpus*, produced numerous protests. Despite the criticism, in the fall of 1862 Lincoln issued a general proclamation which declared that anyone discouraging enlistments, resisting conscription, or committing any disloyal act was subject to martial law and trial in military tribunals. The War Department enforced Lincoln's proclamation and arrested at least thirteen thousand persons, most of whom the government never brought to trial.

The most notorious example of military justice involved an out-spoken Ohio politician, Clement Vallandigham. One of a noisy group of self-styled "Peace Democrats" (called "Copperheads" by Republicans and prowar Democrats), Vallandigham denounced the conflict. Speaking for many midwestern Democrats, he claimed that the war endangered civil liberties, the traditional Democratic doctrine of limited government, and the interests of agriculture. As a congressman from 1860 to 1863, Vallandigham trumpeted all these themes and also stoutly opposed moves toward emancipation of blacks. "We are in the throes of a revolution," he argued, "and I cannot see what the issue is yet, but I dread the worst." Vallandigham's platform became "the Constitution as it is, the Union as it was." Defeated for reelection in 1862, he escalated his attacks, and in 1863 General Ambrose Burnside (most famous for giving side-whiskers their name) arrested the fiery Ohioan for his criticism of the war.

Burnside's ill-advised action permitted Vallandigham to play the martyr role he long coveted and gave Lincoln what he did not want—a hero for the antiwar movement. A military tribunal convicted Vallandigham and confined him to prison for the duration of the war. Protests quickly developed across the country, forcing Lincoln to find a way of blunting the Vallandigham issue. Using his executive power once again, Lincoln changed the sentence to banishment to the Confederacy, but even this failed to eliminate his determined adversary. Fleeing the South for Canada, Vallandigham ultimately returned to Dayton and renewed his verbal assaults on the Lincoln administration and the war. The president now wisely ignored him. The United States Supreme Court refused even to hear the Ohioan's claim that his arrest and trial were unconstitutional. Adroitly ducking the issue, the Court ruled that it possessed no jurisdiction over the proceedings of military tribunals (ex parte Vallandigham, 1864.)

After the war was safely over, however, the High Court rejected the methods employed by Lincoln. In ex parte Milligan (1866), the justices ruled that martial law and military trials for civilians "can never exist where the civil courts are open, and in the proper and unobstructed exercise of their jurisdiction." Written by one of Lincoln's closest political associates, David Davis of Illinois, the Milligan decision represented belated vindication for persons such as Clement Vallandigham and provided some firmer legal protection for the right of dissent.

How should one judge Lincoln's record on civil liberties? Most constitutional experts have argued that the law courts must sometimes balance individual freedoms against the needs of the entire community. Lincoln himself believed that the chief executive should use his power to protect the nation in times of serious peril. He also claimed that his moves were not "vindictive" but "preventive"; they were undertaken "not so much for what has been done, as for what probably would be done." But some libertarians have claimed that balancing individual freedoms and societal "needs" inevitably dilutes personal liberties. Lincoln's actions presaged more serious violations of individual freedoms during World Wars I and II. And if the Great Emancipator did not adopt the sweeping measures of Woodrow Wilson and Franklin Roosevelt, it may have only been because he lacked the means of coercion and the popular support these later wartime presidents enjoyed. Any final assessment of Lincoln's record largely depends upon how we weigh the conflicting values of personal liberty and national security.

INDIAN POLICY

The national government also embarked on a new phase of its Indian policy during the Civil War era. After Union forces evacuated Indian Territory in Oklahoma to fight the South, Confederate negotiators moved in to coax Indian nations into joining their cause. Despite serious dissent within the tribes, a number did support the Confederacy. Citing these defections as justification, the United States government ultimately renegotiated new, less favorable treaties with the Indian nations. The Seminole Treaty of 1866 was typical. The tribe relinquished for fifteen cents an acre the two million acres it had received only ten years earlier and was forced to resettle on a smaller tract for which the Seminoles paid fifty cents an acre. In addition, the tribe granted railway rights through its territory and made other concessions as well. Surprisingly, Indian nations who remained loyal to the Union often came out worse than those who joined the Confederacy. Trapped by the North-South conflict, the once-mighty tribes could do little to save their lands; and though Indian Territory never became a major front during the Civil War, years of raids and skirmishes eventually took a heavy toll in lives and property.

Further to the north, in Minnesota, an uprising by the Santee Sioux in 1862 prompted a vigorous counterstrike by Union forces. Troops under General John Pope, formerly Lincoln's chief commander in the eastern theater of the war, finally crushed the Minnesota Sioux and moved them, together with other tribes, off their traditional lands. But the fighting in Minnesota soon spilled over into other areas, and by the end of the Civil War the entire Great Plains was a battlefield. A report by a special Peace Commission blamed the United States government for the violence.

> The best possible way . . . to avoid war is to do no act of injustice. When we learn that the same rule holds good with Indians, the chief difficulty is removed. But it is said our wars with them have been almost constant. Have we been uniformly unjust? We answer unhesitatingly, yes.

The Civil War was a critical period in the history of the Indian nations. Government policies, inaugurated then, set the style for two decades of warfare. Pursuing contradictory aims, such as pledging the sanctity of Indian lands while promoting expansion of settlers and railroads, and setting impossible goals, such as assigning the army to protect settlements scattered throughout the Great Plains, the policy satisfied no one. Humanitarians condemned it as too harsh, westerners as too lenient, and most army officers, charged with keeping the peace, as simply stupid. If the Civil War era inaugurated a tragic period for the defeated South, it brought no less disaster to Native Americans on the Great Plains.

The civil war and the race question

THE WAR AND RACIAL JUSTICE

The North first envisioned the war as one to save the Union. Lincoln maintained that the nation was indivisible and that "no State, upon its own mere motion, can lawfully get out of the Union." Soon after hostilities began, Congress adopted a resolution which announced the limited purpose of the northern war effort: it was "not waged . . . in any spirit of oppression or for . . . overthrowing or interfering with the rights or established institutions of those states." This statement committed the government only to an effort "to defend and maintain the supremacy of the Constitution." In short, the administration's task was to put down the illegal insurrection without abolishing slavery or affecting the status of black people.

As the conflict dragged on, however, the question of war goals became more complicated. A small group of Republicans championed the theory that the seceding states had committed constitutional "suicide" and reverted to territorial status. They were no longer members of the indivisible Union, as Lincoln maintained. Such constitutional arguments were not mere hairsplitting; if the secessionist areas were territories, then Congress could exercise greater authority in "reconstructing" them after the war. Some Republicans envisioned not only emancipation but legal, political, and economic gains for the former slaves. Other congressional Republicans supported more moderate goals, and some conservatives joined Democrats in opposing any change in the South's pattern of race relations. Alignments shifted according to precise issues, but gradually a small, ill-defined group of "radical" Republicans emerged as the champions of abolishing slavery and protecting the rights of black people.

Wartime pressures and events pushed northern racial policies in a libertarian direction. To be sure, white racism remained strong—New York City's antidraft rioters lynched several blacks and burned an Afro-American orphanage in 1863—but abolitionists and black civil rights leaders achieved some successes during the war. The national government made a number of symbolic gestures which repudiated the racist position of the Supreme Court in the *Dred Scott* decision. For the first time, blacks sat in the congressional visitors' gallery, attended lectures at the Smithsonian Museum, and marched in a presidential parade. More important, Congress repealed an 1825 law which prohibited blacks from carrying the mail, abolished slavery in the territories, enacted a plan of compensated emancipation for the District of Columbia, and ended the ban against black witnesses testifying in federal courts. And some states, under pressure from civil rights forces, passed statutes desegregating public transportation facilities and repealed other discriminatory laws. Black people still did not enjoy all the rights and privileges of whites, but some progress toward racial justice occurred during the Civil War.

THE CRUSADE FOR EMANCIPATION

White abolitionists and black leaders pressed for emancipation, but President Lincoln feared that any early move would alienate Unionists within the slave states and undermine support for the war effort in the North. Early in the war, the president modified General John C. Fremont's order freeing all slaves in Missouri. By 1862 Lincoln altered his views somewhat; he asked Congress to grant federal funds to any state which would adopt a program of gradual emancipation. Although Congress failed to act on this suggestion, the Second Confiscation Act (1862) declared that all slaves of rebel masters would be free as soon as they came within the Union army's lines. Appeals from abolitionist groups and Congress's piecemeal attacks on slavery provided two reasons for Lincoln to issue his Emancipation Proclamation; concern that European nations might recognize the Confederacy also influenced the president's decision. "I cannot imagine that any European power would dare recognize and aid the Southern Confederacy," he wrote, "if it became clear that the Confederacy stands for slavery and the Union for freedom."

In September 1862, following the Union victory at Antietam, Lincoln issued a preliminary Emancipation Proclamation. Drafted with great care, the proclamation applied only to areas of the Confederacy still in rebellion on January 1, 1863; it exempted the border states and all parts of the South which were then in Union hands. Secretary of State Seward reportedly observed that the administration emancipated slaves "where we cannot reach them" and held them "in bondage where we can set them free." Employing no ringing phrases on behalf of human liberty, Lincoln justified qualified emancipation as "a fit and necessary war measure for suppressing the rebellion." Lincoln further suggested that Congress should provide a system of gradual, compensated emancipation under state control. The president's actions were limited—in many respects the Emancipation Proclamation added little to the Second Confiscation Act—but they were not without significance. Most northern blacks applauded the president, viewing his moves as important first steps toward total emancipation. Following announcement of the preliminary Emancipation Proclamation, army recruiters began enrolling black volunteers, long a goal of Afro-American leaders. And in January 1865 Congress, with the support of the president, submitted the Thirteenth Amendment—outlawing slavery throughout the nation—to the states for ratification.

The problem of reconstruction

LINCOLN, CONGRESS, AND RECONSTRUCTION

Emancipation did not end the problems involved in restoring the Union; it made them more difficult. Lincoln originally hoped for a speedy end to the war and a rapid resumption of antebellum political ties. Although events on the battlefield made these goals impossible, the president continued to advocate a flexible, moderate approach to postwar Reconstruction. Lincoln had never been an abolitionist or a supporter of the broad libertarian goals of some antislavery Republicans. He always approached racial issues cautiously. Even after supporting emancipation, he hoped that the process would be gradual and largely under the direction of state officials in the former slave areas. Colonization of blacks outside the United States, he thought, was the ideal, though certainly not immediate, solution to America's racial problems. And Lincoln was always a cagey politician. He had spent most of his political life in the now-defunct Whig party, and he undoubtedly wished to shape moderate policies which would attract former Whigs in both the North and the South.

In late 1863 Lincoln outlined a formal plan for Confederate areas coming under Union control. He offered a relatively easy Reconstruction for whites and minimal changes for blacks. Under his "10 percent plan," whenever a total of white voters equal to one-tenth of those who had voted in 1860 took an oath of future loyalty to the Union and its laws, they could form a new state government. Before the war ended, Lincoln recognized "10 percent" governments in Arkansas, Tennessee, and Louisiana, and he organized Unionist regimes in other areas of the South. But Congress refused to admit representatives from these states, and their electoral votes were not counted in the presidential contest of 1864. Lincoln agreed that Congress should play some role in the Reconstruction process, but he always sought to maximize presidential leadership and minimize congressional participation.

Abolitionists, black leaders, and radical Republicans urged congressmen to demand more fundamental changes in the South, particularly firm guarantees for the civil and political rights of blacks. The radicals did not control Congress, but even moderates supported a more thoroughgoing program than the president's 10 percent plan. The Wade-Davis Bill of 1864 required 50 percent of white adult males to take loyalty oaths before southerners could form new state governments; furthermore, before persons could vote for delegates to state constitutional conventions, they would have to take "ironclad" oaths, swearing that they had never supported the secessionist cause. Despite pressure for guaranteeing suffrage to blacks in the South,

Congress, like the president, limited the vote to whites. But Lincoln saw the Wade-Davis Bill (which unlike his own plan would not be operative until after the war) as too harsh and as a challenge to presidential leadership. To the surprise of many Republicans, he pocket-vetoed the bill.

Lincoln and many other Republicans differed over the details of Reconstruction, but they agreed on a number of fundamental issues: the importance of Republican party unity; the need for the national government's participation in the Reconstruction process; and the requirement of some minimal guarantees for the rights of newly freed slaves. On the crucial suffrage question, Lincoln seemed to offer hope of compromise with even the radicals. Shortly before his death, the president endorsed at least qualified suffrage for "very intelligent" blacks and former black soldiers in the Union army. Throughout the war, Lincoln and Republican congressional leaders settled a number of difficult issues, and Lincoln's whole political career revealed that he knew the value of flexibility. But on April 14, 1965, Lincoln fell victim to an assassination plot hatched by a small group of prosouthern diehards. While the president watched a performance of *Our American Cousin*, John Wilkes Booth shot him at close range with a small pistol. By morning Lincoln was dead; an unknown, Andrew Johnson of Tennessee, was president.

THE FIRST PRESIDENT JOHNSON

Andrew Johnson puzzled his contemporaries, and historians have done little better explaining this complicated man. Rising to prominence as a Jacksonian Democrat in Tennessee, Johnson received the second spot on the 1864 ticket because of his strong pro-Union views. He himself was an intended target of the plot which struck down the president, but Johnson's rum-soaked would-be assassin lost his courage. Thrust into power at a crucial point in the nation's history, Johnson was a politician without a party, a former slaveowner presiding over emancipation, and a racist confronting strong pressures to extend civil rights to black Americans. Johnson sometimes seemed all too aware of his humble origins and his limited qualifications for high office. But like any president succeeding a fallen leader, he enjoyed initial goodwill, even from many radical Republicans. The break with Congress, which would lead to his impeachment, came gradually and was largely Johnson's own doing.

Johnson's failure stemmed from his inability to appreciate the mood of most congressmen and the majority of northern voters. He wanted a lenient "restoration" process, and he hoped to carry it out quickly and present Congress with a *fait accompli*. Such a course was obviously bound to alienate congressional Republicans, particularly when it turned out that the so-called

Johnson governments in the southern states contained a number of former Confederate leaders and adopted laws placing blacks in a position of quasi-slavery. These "black codes" restricted the rights of blacks in a number of ways, but the most ominous sections required them to work and provided stiff penalties for unemployment or lack of a permanent residence. The Civil War had deeply touched many northerners, and the unmistakable gray tinge of the "restored" governments and the black codes seemed to indicate that southerners remained rebels at heart. Northerners began to insist that the South acknowledge defeat, and changing the status of blacks seemed an appropriate sign. Growing numbers of Republicans demanded that emancipation mean something more than slavery under a different name.

Rejecting representatives from the "Johnson governments," Congress challenged the president's attempt to dictate Reconstruction policy. Congress created the Freedmen's Bureau, a federal agency designed to provide economic and social assistance to blacks, and passed the Civil Rights Act of 1866, a measure which conferred citizenship on the freedmen and guaranteed a number of their civil and political rights. When Johnson vetoed both of these measures, he separated himself from Republican moderates and from many northern voters. Republican congressmen quickly overrode his veto of the Civil Rights Bill and then created a second version of the Freedmen's Bureau, again over a presidential veto. Relations between the White House and Capitol Hill grew ever more bitter, and the battle climaxed in February 1868 when Johnson's Republican opponents obtained a vote for impeachment from the House of Representatives. From March 30 to May 16, 1868, the impeachment trial of Andrew Johnson dragged through the United States Senate.

Most Republicans believed that the president had a constitutional role to play in Reconstruction and refused to bypass the executive branch by permitting Congress to administer the process. These Republicans were not attacking the office of the presidency; they sought to remove its occupant, Johnson, because they felt he had failed to perform his constitutional duties. Invoking the narrow argument that another beleaguered president, Richard Nixon, would revive more than a century later, Johnson and his defenders claimed that governmental officials could be impeached only for violation of criminal laws. The president's Republican opponents took the broader, and probably sounder, line of argument. They contended that Johnson's actions, particularly his removal (in violation of a congressional statute) of Secretary of War Edwin M. Stanton, violated his presidential authority and therefore provided adequate grounds for impeachment. Complex legal arguments became entangled in even more complicated political maneuvering, ultimately dividing Senate Republicans. In the end, seven Republicans broke with their colleagues and voted with Democrats and several independents against impeachment. As a result of these defections, the Senate fell a single ballot short of the two-thirds majority required for impeachment.

Why did Johnson misread the situation? Historians have proposed numerous explanations. Johnson, a political outsider, failed to understand congressional politics and isolated himself from the Republican majority. Raised in the states' rights tradition of Andrew Jackson, Johnson perhaps truly believed that Congress possessed no constitutional power to pass the Freedmen's Bill and the Civil Rights Act; certainly he relied upon constitutional limitations in justifying his vetoes. An insecure man with little formal education, he may have felt inadequate and outclassed in the presence of the southern belles and plantation gentlemen who argued their cases at the White House. And his own racism could have blinded him to many northerners' desires to protect the civil and political rights of former slaves. The president appeared to feel that an antiblack stance would prove politically advantageous, appealing to his natural Democratic constituency as well as to conservative and moderate Republicans. Whatever Johnson's motives, his miscalculations ended presidential influence over Reconstruction; the initiative passed to Congress, and "Radical Reconstruction" began.

RADICAL RECONSTRUCTION

For over a century, writers have examined Radical Reconstruction. Even writers whose views differ widely have generally agreed that the years between 1867 and 1876 were a tragic period, an agonizing story of prejudice, politics, and unfulfilled promises.

The earliest critics of Reconstruction condemned it as a cynical and brutal rape of southern society. Political opportunism and hatred of the South, it was claimed, motivated the radical Republicans' policies: military rule under the four Reconstruction Acts (enacted in 1867 and 1868); black suffrage; and violation of the spirit, if not the letter, of the Constitution. Prosouthern accounts stressed the alleged corruption of Reconstruction regimes, the unruliness of former slaves, the greed of northern "carpetbaggers," and the treachery of southern "scalawags." Reconstruction was a dark epoch, a perversion of America's liberal tradition. In this view, the lifting of radical rule by the white "redeemers" represented a return to constitutional government and to proper racial relations in the South.

Although the exaggerated condemnations of Radical Reconstruction persisted, during the 1930s interpreters began to see other motives. These writers claimed that the radical Republicans really represented northeastern business interests, greedy capitalists who feared that a speedily reconstructed South might regain its political power and overturn northern businessmen's control of the national government. Idealistic rhetoric and moral platitudes, it was implied, masked the sordid economic motives of the business-domi-nated Republican party: exploitation of the South and advancement of in-dustrial over agrarian interests. Reconstruction was a tragedy because it so-lidified predatory capitalists' hold upon American government.

More recently, a new generation, influenced by the civil rights struggles of the 1950s and 1960s, has viewed Reconstruction as another phase in black Americans' search for justice. To these authors, radical Republicanism repre-sented the last burst of abolitionist idealism; the radicals tried to provide na-tional protection for the rights of the freedmen and to extend some measure of social and economic assistance. Not particularly vindictive and not the tools of a capitalist conspiracy, congressional Republicans, moderates as well as radicals, undertook their actions only after they realized the extent of southern intransigence and presidential obstructionism. And their measures were not unusually severe, particularly when compared to the postwar poli-cies of other victorious nations. The national government committed only a small number of troops to military Reconstruction, and the entire process lasted only a few years in most states. From this perspective, the tragedy of Reconstruction came not from its harshness but from its relative mildness. Northern efforts did not bring enough change in the status of black people; Reconstruction only temporarily interrupted white supremacy in the South.

The reconstructed union

RECONSTRUCTION AND THE SOUTH

Reconstruction did represent an attempt to achieve a degree of racial equal-ity for blacks. Two important additions to the Constitution, the Fourteenth and Fifteenth Amendments, laid the basis for greater federal protection of civil and political liberties. The Fourteenth Amendment, ratified in 1868, offered a definition of national citizenship which included black people; it prohibited states from denying any person "life, liberty, or property without due process of law"; and it warned that no state could "deny to any person within its jurisdiction the equal protection of the laws." Although during the late nineteenth and early twentieth centuries the Supreme Court used the Fourteenth Amendment to shield business corporations from state regu-lation, there is little evidence to suggest a business conspiracy behind the amendment. Its framers saw it as a constitutional bulwark not only for newly freed blacks but for all citizens; it was intended to be "Everyman's Constitution."

Two years later the Fifteenth Amendment declared that a citizen's right to vote "shall not be denied or abridged . . . on account of race, color, or pre-vious condition of servitude." Applying to male blacks in the North as well

Charles Sumner, one of the leading radicals in Congress.
Brown Brothers

as to former slaves in the South, the amendment had nationwide political implications. Some northern supporters of the amendment may have been concerned with protecting crucial black votes in key districts, but others risked a white backlash to guarantee suffrage to the black man.

In the South, contrary to postwar propaganda and historical legend, ignorant and corrupt blacks under the thumb of evil whites did not dominate Reconstruction governments. Blacks occupied some state and numerous local offices, but they never controlled any southern state. And black officials were not particularly dishonest or incompetent. Undoubtedly corruption existed, but the chicanery of Reconstruction governments must be measured against the records of previous white southern administrations and against the sorry reputation of many northern governments during this era. On the whole, Reconstruction governments made substantial progress toward postwar recovery. They drafted progressive new constitutions, expanded social services, improved roads, encouraged railway construction, promoted investment, and established the South's first public school systems. Much of the so-called extravagance of Reconstruction legislators merely represented expenditures for needed, sometimes long-delayed, public projects.

During the Reconstruction years, the national government provided only limited assistance for the freedmen in the South. The Freedmen's Bureau coordinated relief activities and tried to ease the difficult transition from slavery to freedom. The bureau found employment opportunities, supervised labor contracts, and tried to safeguard black peoples' legal and political rights. But although the bureau's contemporary critics generally indicted it for doing too much to assist blacks, later historians have emphasized the agency's ambivalent record. Many well-meaning officials were overly paternalistic; others displayed outright prejudice toward black people; some encouraged blacks to enter into exploitative sharecropping contracts; most did too little to enlarge opportunities for the former slaves. A few radicals, notably Thaddeus Stevens of Pennsylvania, advocated confiscation of some plantations and redistribution of the land to the former slaves. But most congressmen and northern citizens recoiled in horror at expropriation and extensive federal aid. Freedmen's hopes of obtaining "forty acres and a mule" quickly faded.

Private philanthropic and religious groups also tried to aid freedmen. Various sectarian groups, especially the Congregational Church, sent both money and representatives to the South. Church-related educational institutions gave many black children their first opportunity to learn to read and write. Blacks rushed to use the new schools, and many teachers commented upon the enthusiasm of the former slaves. Church groups also helped establish black colleges and industrial schools, and the Freedmen's Bureau extended some financial assistance to missionary schools, including Howard University in Washington, D.C.

Frederick Douglass wrote a fascinating autobiography about his rise from slavery.
Blanche K. Bruce, Frederick Douglass, Hiram R. Revels.
Culver Pictures

America's first black members of Congress.
Culver Pictures

THE END OF RECONSTRUCTION

The idealism and commitment initially associated with congressional Reconstruction and the first crusade for racial justice gradually faded into opportunism and indifference. Congress failed to renew the Freedmen's Bureau in 1869; white terrorist organizations, such as the Ku Klux Klan, intimidated blacks in the South; southern whites who had once accepted Reconstruction governments began to withdraw their support; and increasing numbers of northern citizens lost interest in the whole Reconstruction process. To be sure, Reconstruction did not collapse overnight. During the early 1870s Congress passed several Force Acts aimed at the KKK and other night-riding bands. And the Republican administration of Ulysses S. Grant mustered sufficient manpower to put the first Klan out of business by the end of 1871. In 1875 Congress approved a Civil Rights Act which guaranteed equal rights in public places and forbade exclusion of blacks from jury duty. (In 1883 the Supreme Court declared the act unconstitutional.) As late as 1876 a few federal troops remained in South Carolina, Florida, and Louisiana. But the zeal for reform had largely vanished, and the Republican party, once the catalyst for social change, became less a force for racial justice and more a bulwark for the status quo.

Republicans faced a renewed challenge from the Democratic party as well as divisions within their own ranks. In 1868 General Grant, who captured the Republican presidential nomination without much opposition, won a comfortable victory over his Democratic rival, Horatio Seymour of New York. But the strength of the Democrats, traditionally the antiblack party, slowly revived. While Republicans waved the "bloody shirt," denouncing Democrats as traitors to the Union, their opponents concentrated on the race issue, indicting Republicans for their problack policies. "I say that we are not of the same race; we are so different that we ought not to compose one political community," announced a prominent Indiana Democrat: "I say . . . this is a white man's Government, made by the white man for the white man." Some Republicans also began to question their party's southern strategy, and intraparty dissatisfaction diluted Republican enthusiasm for Reconstruction. In 1872 Grant easily turned back a challenge from a coalition of Democrats and "Liberal Republicans," who offered newspaper editor Horace Greeley, a well-known reformer, as their candidate. But in 1874, beset by political and financial scandals within the Grant administration, the party surrendered control of the House of Representatives to the Democrats and nearly lost its majority in the Senate.

Faced with serious political pressures, the Grant administration began to back away from an active Reconstruction policy. In contrast to its earlier action against the KKK, it offered little federal resistance to a new southern offensive against blacks—the "Mississippi plan." As described by a Mis-

The first Ku Klux Klan.
Culver Pictures

sissippi editor, the plan was simple: "Carry the election peaceably if we can, forcibly if we must." White Democrats armed themselves, formed paramilitary units, disrupted Republican meetings, and terrorized blacks. Between 1874 and 1876 the strategy spread, and a series of "race riots" swept across the South. In reality most of these were simply pogroms against blacks, part of white redeemers' efforts to break the radicals' control and end the crusade for black equality. The national government generally failed to oppose the Mississippi plan. When Mississippi's last radical governor appealed to Grant's attorney general for protection of black voters in 1875, he received a negative reply. The attorney general curtly informed the governor that northern citizens were "tired of these annual autumnal outbreaks in the South."

Reconstruction ended in the aftermath of the bizarre presidential election of 1876. Ohio Republican Rutherford B. Hayes and New York Democrat Samuel J. Tilden were both conservative gentlemen and experienced governors of large states. Both stood for honesty in government, civil service reform, sound money, and both planned to withdraw federal troops from the South. The range of disagreement between them was slight indeed. Yet the November election began one of the more tense episodes in American political history.

On election night grave robbers broke into the tomb of Abraham Lincoln and attempted to steal his corpse, lending a tone to what followed. Tilden distanced Hayes in the popular vote and apparently in the electoral college as well. But irregularities in three southern states threw nineteen electoral votes in doubt, leading the Republicans to contest the outcome. The Democrats countered with a challenge to one Republican electoral vote in Oregon (all that Tilden needed for victory), and the election quickly escalated into a major constitutional crisis. Angry Democrats threatened a renewed Civil War. Sinister men plotted to assassinate officials involved in the electoral imbroglio—one in Louisiana was shot and wounded. A Democratic editor went to jail for an editorial which invited Hayes's assassination if he were made president.

After a long winter of threats, maneuvers, and negotiations, southern Democrats abandoned Tilden when Hayes agreed to remove the last federal troops, to grant patronage and recognition to white southerners, and to support economic legislation for the region. This compromise of 1877 was a major step in the reconciliation of the two recently warring sections, and in the North's abandonment of southern blacks. It signaled the formal end of Radical Reconstruction.

Things to think about: 1860–1876

Why, after Lincoln's election, did southern states secede? Why did secession lead to war? See David M. Potter, *Lincoln and His Party in the Secession Crisis* (rev. ed., 1962); Kenneth M. Stampp, *And the War Came* (1950); Richard N. Current, *Lincoln and the First Shot* (1962); Stephen Channing, *Crisis of Fear* (1970); and William L. Barney, *The Road to Secession* (1974).

What advantages did the North have during the war? What handicaps did the South labor under? How did the war affect society in both sections? See David Donald, ed., *Why the North Won the Civil War* (1960); Bruce Catton, *Centennial History of the Civil War* (3 vols., 1961-65); Frank Vandiver, *Their Tattered Flags* (1970); Emory M. Thomas, *The Confederacy as a Revolutionary Experience* (1971); and Allan Nevins, *The War for the Union* (3 vols., 1959-70). Two books by Bell I. Wiley treat the life of ordinary soldiers: *The Life of Johnny Reb* (1943) and *The Life of Billy Yank* (1952). George M. Frederickson treats intellectual developments in the North in *The Inner Civil War* (1965); Daniel Aaron, *The Unwritten War* (1973), is a superior work. The role of black people is discussed in Benjamin Quarles, *The Negro in the Civil War* (1953), and James M. McPherson, *The Negro's Civil War* (1965). The struggle for emancipation is discussed in James M. McPherson, *The Struggle for Equality* (1962), and John Hope Franklin, *The Emancipation Proclamation* (1963).

Why did black Americans fail to achieve real equality during the era of Reconstruction? What changes did the war make in race relations? General accounts include Kenneth M. Stampp, *The Era of Reconstruction* (1965); John Hope Franklin, *Reconstruction After the Civil War* (1961); Rembert W. Patrick, *The Reconstruction of the Nation* (1969); Forrest G. Wood, *The Era of Reconstruction* (1975); and W. E. B. DuBois's classic account, *Black Reconstruction in America, 1860-1880* (1935). Excellent specialized studies are Eric L. McKitrick, *Andrew Johnson and Reconstruction* (1960); John H. and LaWanda Cox, *Politics, Principle, and Prejudice, 1865-1866* (1963); Joel Williamson, *After Slavery: The Negro in South Carolina During Reconstruction, 1861-1877* (1965); Robert Cruden, *The Negro in Reconstruction* (1969); Michael Les Benedict, *A Compromise of Principle* (1974); and Lawrence Grossman, *The Democratic Party and the Negro* (1976). Another excellent monograph is Willie Lee Rose's *Rehearsal for Reconstruction* (1964). C. Vann Woodward's *Reunion and Reaction* (1951) explains the process by which Reconstruction was liquidated.

Rutherford B. Hayes: Winner in
the electoral college.
Culver Pictures

Samuel J. Tilden: Winner of the
popular vote. *Culver Pictures*

8

AN AGE OF CONFIDENCE 1876-1890

CHIEF JOSEPH

The Nez Percé of the far Northwest contradicted almost every stereotype of the Indian. Ensconced in the narrow valleys between the Cascade and Bitterroot mountains (lands now parts of Idaho, Washington, and Oregon), they apparently never attacked settlers before their great war with the whites in 1877. They had aided Lewis and Clark in 1805. In 1831 they sent a delegation to St. Louis to discover the source of the white man's "medicine." The Nez Percé welcomed outsiders and were quick to learn from and trade with them. They even survived a gold rush into their lands in the sixties, remaining at peace despite numerous outrages by the miners. Nonetheless, friction sharpened in the 1860s as cattle ranchers eyed lands on which Indian horses grazed. In 1863 the federal government negotiated a treaty to delimit Indian land titles, but a group of braves, loosely led by Old Joseph, the father of a more famous Joseph, rejected it. Turning away from the Christianity they had learned from missionaries, they began a peaceful but determined resistance to the white man's designs on their ancestral lands. "My son," Old Joseph whispered as he lay dy-

ing, "you are the chief. . . . You must stop your ears whenever you are asked to sign a treaty selling your home. . . . This country holds your father's body. Never sell the bones of your father and your mother."

Chief Joseph was ever true to this stern injunction. Although he struggled to avoid conflict, his people's fate was all too typical: rapacious settlers pressing for land, unfeeling Indian agents, bungling in governmental departments, an unsympathetic general, a forced and hurried evacuation of their lands, and finally young braves driven to fury and terrible violence. Once at war, Joseph and his tribe enacted one of the great feats of military prowess and human endurance (for this army traveled with its women and children, its sick and aged). A United States Army ROTC instruction manual describes Joseph's achievement: "In 11 weeks, he had moved his tribe 1600 miles, engaged 10 separate U.S. commands in 13 battles and skirmishes, and in nearly every instance had either defeated them or fought them to a stand-still." Joseph and fewer than two hundred braves withstood an army. The effort, of course, was doomed to failure, and with its failure, the Nez Percé would no longer exist as an independent people. Chief Joseph surrendered on October 5, 1877. His memorable speech gave all the reasons:

> I am tired of fighting. Our chiefs are killed. . . . The old men are all killed. It is the young men who say yes or no. He who led the young men is dead. It is cold and we have no blankets. The little children are freezing to death. My people, some of them, have run away to the hills and have no blankets, no food; no one knows where they are, perhaps freezing to death. I want time to look for my children and see how many of them I can find. Maybe I shall find them among the dead. Hear me, my chiefs, I am tired; my heart is sick and sad. From where the sun now stands, I will fight no more forever.

The Nez Percé's fighting days were over.

For all his fame as a guerrilla leader, Chief Joseph was essentially a diplomat. When the United States government immediately reneged on the terms under which he had surrendered, shipping the tribe to Indian Territory (the present state of Oklahoma), Joseph began a careful and patient campaign to return his people to their mountain home. While he never succeeded in regaining his beloved Wallowa Valley—Old Joseph's gravesite—after five years of direct interviews with the president, the secretary of the interior, and numerous congressmen, and by enlisting the editorial support of several eastern journals, he did get his dispirited and rapidly decreasing tribe back to the mountains where they could thrive again. In his new home in western Washington, Joseph became an Indian elder statesman, a national symbol of courage and freedom. He returned to the Wallowa Valley but once, in 1900, an old man. There he found only the consolation that a settler—a man with, as he said, "a spirit too rare among his kind"—had enclosed and cared for his father's grave.

1876–1890

1876	*Custer's last stand, June 26*
1877	*Chief Joseph surrenders*
	Munn v. *Illinois*
	Railroad strikes
1878	*Joseph Pulitzer begins* St. Louis Post-Dispatch
1879	*Henry George,* Progress and Poverty
	Thomas Alva Edison invents incandescent lightbulb
1880	*James A. Garfield (Republican) elected president, defeating Winfield S. Hancock*
1881	*Helen Hunt Jackson,* A Century of Dishonor
	Garfield is assassinated; Chester A. Arthur becomes president
1882	*Chinese Exclusion Act*
1883	*Pendleton Civil Service Act*
1884	*Grover Cleveland (Democrat) elected president, defeating James G. Blaine*
1885	*Josiah Strong,* Our Country
1886	*Henry W. Grady, "The New South"*
	Haymarket Massacre, May 4
	American Federation of Labor (AFL) organized
	Wabash case
1887	*Interstate Commerce Act*
	Dawes Severalty Act
	Edward Bellamy, Looking Backward: 2000–1887
1888	*Benjamin Harrison (Republican) elected president, defeating Cleveland*
1890	*Battle of Wounded Knee, December 29*

The depression of the 1870s

Americans glimpsed a threatening future in the long depression of the 1870s. The collapse of Jay Cooke & Co., the nation's best-known banking house, in September 1873 marked the beginning of six lean years. At first it had seemed unreal: when a newsboy shouted the headline *"All About the Failure of Jay Cooke"* a policeman promptly arrested him. No one could believe that Jay Cooke, who had sold bonds for the Union during the Civil War, who had befriended presidents and supported churches, could be bankrupt. But soon the dismal economic reality sank in: the orgy of railroad building in the sixties and early seventies which had spanned the continent and doubled the nation's tracks was over. Europe, with its own financial troubles, would not invest large sums in America to build railroads before

358

settlement and commerce caught up with mileage already constructed. The expansion of heavy industry ceased and the nation struggled with the problems of depression.

Workers suffered most from the unstable economy. When groups of the unemployed called for a public works program to provide jobs, their negotiators met only scorn and their meetings were brutally suppressed. Seven thousand laborers jammed a New York City park to demonstrate in 1874 and the police moved in. "It was the most glorious sight I ever saw," exulted the commissioner, "the way the police broke and drove the crowd. Their order was perfect as they charged with their clubs uplifted." Samuel Gompers, future leader of the American Federation of Labor, remembered how he had "barely saved [his] head from being cracked by jumping down a cellarway." Labor violence peaked in the great railroad strikes of 1877. Workers took control of Pittsburgh until President Hayes called in the United States Army. Dozens of men died; millions in property was destroyed; leading journals dreamed nightmares of social revolution.

Other kinds of disorder—some new, some long familiar—disturbed the American dream of progress. Roving gangs of young toughs in San Francisco gave the language a new word: "hoodlum." Their New York counterparts were "street rats": the Baxter Street Dudes, the Little Dead Rabbits, the Hudson Dusters. The Daybreak Boys, thieving from the piers at dawn, were under twelve years old. The New York Society for the Reformation of Juvenile Delinquents reported its business "largely on the increase."

On the West Coast, rioting unemployed workmen shouting "The Chinese must go!" burned dozens of buildings in San Francisco's Chinatown, and for months afterward no Chinese could walk the streets in safety. The outbreak came after twenty-five years of anti-Chinese propaganda in California. Chinese immigrants, at first welcomed as a source of cheap labor, soon were despised for undercutting American workmen and for being strange and "un-American" in their ways. California law invalidated their testimony in courts, barred them from public employment, and forbade them from intermarrying with whites. Segregated schools became common, as did informal vigilante groups keeping them off the gold fields and from other favored kinds of work. California's campaign against the "coolies" received national endorsement in 1882 when Congress, in the Chinese Exclusion Act, made them the first national group forbidden entry into the country.

THE RETURN OF CONFIDENCE

Yet the mood of 1877 was short-lived. Americans had peered into the abyss and drawn back. After all the threats of renewed civil war, a compromise solved the election dispute between Hayes and Tilden, and the North forgot the atrocities that persisted in the South. The two parties emerged untarnished from the electoral conflict with the renewed loyalty of millions of Americans who voted more consistently and followed their parties more faithfully than at any other time in our history.

Late in the decade the economy swung upward. The middle class had sustained but the slightest economic damage from the long depression; although it was a slow time for heavy industry and fresh long-term investment, commerce nevertheless paced briskly as prices dropped and induced sales. As a result, real income—the amount people can buy with the money they receive—rose spectacularly in the depression decade. Despite wage cuts, even factory workers gained in purchasing power. As the seventies ended, the nation—its farthest reaches being settled, immigrants pouring onto its shores, its cities growing, and its influence gaining in the markets of the world— looked confidently ahead. Americans envisioned a future that would be, if not pure gold, at least gilded by the prospect of economic advance. Fastening on the title of a popular novel by Mark Twain and Charles Dudley Warner published in 1873, they accepted the term "Gilded Age" for the generation of industrialization and expansion that followed the Civil War.

The wild west

By the late nineteenth century the West was settling into the familiar checkerboards of farms and range. But this last frontier also contained the "Wild West" of ten-gallon heroes and villains famous in song, story, and advertisement. Legends grew about the mining frontier, the cattle towns, and the Indian wars. From the late forties into the eighties, the West experienced one mining boom after another: California in '49, then Pike's Peak and Virginia City, Oro Fine Creek, Helena, Leadville, the Black Hills, Virginia City again, Leadville again, and so it went. In the same era the cowboys brought millions of cattle to the railroads for shipment to eastern markets. First they came on "long drives" from Texas up the famous trails—the Chisholm, the Goodnight-Loving, the Western, and the Shawnee—then from open-range ranches farther north where a few watering places on the dry grasslands allowed free grazing over miles of government-owned land. And the Indians were essential to the legend—driven west, herded into reservations, coerced into treaties and then betrayed, attacked, and defeated. The Wild West was a scene of exploitation and violence, one whose largeness of scale gave it a mythical and poetic dimension.

Behind the tales lurked many paradoxes. Mining gold and silver held glamour for nineteenth-century Americans—fanatics for bright, hard, heavy, "real" currency, and distrustful of paper credit. But the work was little different from mining coal or iron ore. For all the grizzly and venturesome prospectors, large eastern-financed corporations—with cumbersome equipment,

REWARD
($5,000.00)
Reward for the capture, dead or alive,
of one Wm. Wright, better known as
"BILLY THE KID"
Age, 18. Height, 5 feet, 3 inches.
Weight, 125 lbs. Light hair, blue
eyes and even features. He is
the leader of the worst band of
desperadoes the Territory has
ever had to deal with. The above
reward will be paid for his capture
or positive proof of his death.
JIM DALTON, Sheriff.
DEAD OR ALIVE!
"BILLY THE KID"

lots of capital, railroads, and a labor supply—underwrote the extractions and reaped the rewards.

The cowboy is a glamourous figure, the ideal of the historic American: strong, silent, masculine, independent, rude but honorable, the conqueror of nature and the lesser breeds. In reality, it was a dirty, rough, lonely, and often ill-paid job for men who because of character or background had rejected their society or been rejected by it. Large numbers of them—perhaps 25 percent—were black. When time and distance transformed cowboys into national folk heroes, the black cowpunchers disappeared from view until the 1960s.

SOLDIERS AND INDIANS

And the Indian wars—source for a thousand films with interchangeable red targets falling before the white man's guns—also differed from their appearance in legend. When white men pushed west of the Mississippi they met perhaps a quarter-million Indians on the plains and in the mountains— Sioux, Blackfeet, Crow, Cheyenne, Arapaho, Apache, Comanche, Osage, and Pawnee, as well as Nez Percé, Ute, and Shoshone in the mountain valleys. Government policy traditionally treated these tribes, somewhat contradictorily, as independent nations capable of negotiating treaties with the United States and as wards of the "Great White Father" in Washington. Old promises of a frontier dividing Indians and settlers gave way in the later 1860s to the realities of tribes herded onto reservations. And settlers ignored the fiction of tribal independence as they found old treaties standing in their way.

By the seventies the Plains Indians were reaching the end of their independent existence. Most of the tribes were nomadic, traveling with the massive herds of buffalo, or bison, which provided them with food as well as materials for their tepees, blankets, and clothing. Encroachments on the land would have taken their final toll in any case, but the wanton slaughter of

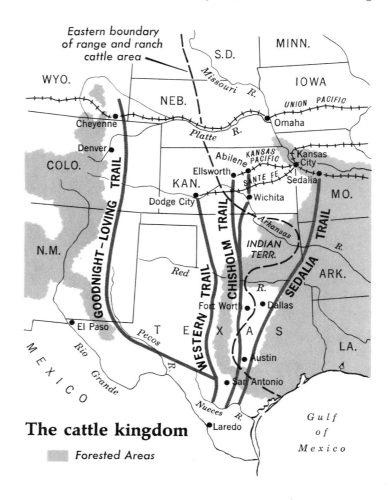

The cattle kingdom
Forested Areas

buffalo for food, sport, or hides virtually extinguished them as a species in scarcely ten years after the Civil War and doomed the Indian civilization dependent on hunting them.

The Indians responded to the white advance in many ways, but none led to any but a disastrous outcome. Most bowed to superior force and accepted the reservations provided them, but some made high tragedy of the pursuit of freedom. Bands of Sioux, for example, skirmished for years to remain on their hunting grounds. In 1876 the army sought to drive the last renegades onto reservations. Colonel George A. Custer was one of several officers giving chase to Chief Crazy Horse and his braves. Just before the two armies met, the Sioux medicine man, Sitting Bull, had a vision during the Sun Dance ceremonies of white soldiers falling into the Indian camp upside down. His vision became prophecy when Custer led his small force of two hundred fifty men to their death in a head-on encounter with thousands of braves at the Little Big Horn in Montana Territory.

Such Indian victories were short-lived. The Sioux lost their land before the year's end, and with their defeat substantial Indian resistance to the white advance was over. Skirmishes, some earning the title of "wars," continued through the 1880s as Indians forced onto barren lands and threatened with starvation struck out in hopeless defiance of the onrushing settlers and the United States Army. Most tribes, however, accepted the bleak reservations which became synonymous with despair among both Indians and concerned whites.

WOUNDED KNEE

Then in 1888 a new religion arose among the Paiute Indians of Nevada—based on the so-called ghost dance which promised a return to the order existing before the white man had destroyed the Indians' homelands. The religion, essentially pacifist and otherworldly, spread rapidly across the desert and Great Plains; in the hands of Sitting Bull, still defiant although long confined to Sioux reservations in the Dakotas, it became more worldly and belligerent. Indian agents and the army moved to forbid the dancing and to disarm the Sioux warriors who had begun to believe that by wearing garments painted with sacred symbols, the white man's bullets would be rendered harmless. This attempt led to a largely predictable disaster, a skirmish in which several on both sides, including Sitting Bull, were killed. Then the tragedy deepened beyond anyone's power of prediction. Troops of the Seventh Cavalry—Custer's old regiment—initiated a search for arms in an Indian village at Wounded Knee Creek; a shot rang out and the troops began indiscriminately killing the largely disarmed and already surrendered braves, while cannon raked the tepees occupied by women and children. Then the army slaughtered every Indian in sight. Bodies of women and children were

Sitting Bull.
Culver Pictures

later found as far as three miles away from the village. Yet throughout the ghost-dance excitement, and even after Wounded Knee, there was not a single raid on a white settlement.

THE DAWES ACT

Destruction of the Indians' potential to resist led to a general softening of tensions between them and the whites. A number of books—Helen Hunt Jackson's *A Century of Dishonor* (1881) was the most famous—presented their case. The solution to the Indians' plight, upon which virtually everyone except the western frontiersmen and the Indians (who were not consulted) agreed, was the eventual breakup of the reservations; individual Indians could then become "civilized" private property-owning farmers. An

Villa of Brule, Sioux Indian encampment.
Library of Congress

Indian Bureau agent in charge of a Sioux reservation envisioned a brave now going out to his own fields singing:

> We'll have a little farm, a horse, a pig, and cow,
> And she will mind the dairy and I will guide the plow.

This policy was embodied in the Dawes Severalty Act (also called the General Allotment Act) of 1887. Theodore Roosevelt later described the act as "a mighty pulverizing engine to break up the tribal mass." The century of dishonor gave way to a half-century of cultural disintegration; Indians suffered both the material loss of millions of acres of reservation land and the spiritual loss of much of their culture. Generally the attempt to make Indians into property-owning farmers failed. Even if the policy had fitted well with Indian culture (it often did not), this was scarcely an era to establish farms: hundreds of thousands of experienced white and black farmers were also losing their land as droughts, declining farm prices, and advancing agricultural technology made the traditional family farm an economic impossibility. Only in the 1930s did the Hoover administration and particularly Franklin Roosevelt's New Deal shift Indian policy back toward encouraging tribalism; but by then the Indian civilizations had suffered an irremediable blow.

Agriculture and industry

Farming was still the nation's leading industry. Its growth continued to finance America's startling industrial expansion. Farm products accounted for about three-quarters of American exports. Acreage increased enormously as the farming frontier filled out the continental United States. Crop specialization, new machinery and scientific techniques, and improved transportation raised the yield of expanding farmlands. Burgeoning cities and industry here and abroad created a growing market for this bounteous production. The early 1880s were boom times. Prices for farm commodities remained high, land values climbed steeply, and huge wheat-growing "bonanza farms" used giant combines to make fabled profits.

This expansion, however, exceeded market conditions. Improved transportation opened new and competitive foreign farmlands even more rapidly than it created fresh markets. And the innovative techniques meant heavier capital investment than the relatively primitive credit system could provide, raising interest rates to painful levels. Farm tenancy rose throughout the country, as did such onerous mechanisms for financing farms as crop liens and sharecropping, especially in the South. By the mid-eighties the ever-larger crops forced farm prices down, making fixed charges like mortgages a

Harvey Dunn, Dakota Woman
Friends of the Middle Border Museum, Mitchell, South Dakota

progressively larger burden. Still, optimism survived until 1887, when a severe drought in the Kansas wheatfields ushered in a lengthy period of reduced rainfall across the Great Plains. A precipitous drop in land values foreshadowed a general depression in agriculture that would trouble American farmers for more than a decade.

Despite the problems which American farmers faced, the capital base for industrialism paradoxically came mostly from the land. It is easy to forget that nineteenth-century men—like all men before them—thought of wealth largely as land. The growth of a vast agricultural kingdom and great mineral resources constituted the nation's fundamental material capital. Spreading agriculture provided food, population surpluses to support growing cities, markets for manufactured goods, and over three-fourths of our foreign exchange. From this came European tools, goods, and capital. Agriculture directly supported the great initial burst of industrial activity in America, the building of a vast railroad network to carry farm products. Railroads, mining, and land absorbed the bulk of foreign investment, and all of these depended on the riches of the soil and the population spreading over it. No wonder that farmers late in the century could not understand their failure to profit from industrialization. In the words of a favorite farm protest song:

> When the farmer comes to town,
> With his wagon broken down,
> O, the farmer is the man who feeds them all!
> If you'll only look and see,
> I think you will agree
> That the farmer is the man who feeds them all.

Refrain:
> The farmer is the man,
> The farmer is the man,
> Buys on credit till the fall;
> Then they take him by the hand,
> And they lead him to the land,
> And the merchant is the man who gets it all.

ECONOMIC ATTITUDES

In little more than a generation, America had changed from an agricultural nation to the industrial giant of the world. Families moved westward, population grew everywhere, buildings climbed upward, cities spread outward. The world Americans entered so rapidly—of whirring machinery, sprawling cities, exotic new neighbors—seemed a vast juggernaut which no man controlled. Even businessmen, who seemed more attuned to industry than anyone else, did not fully understand it, but the promised benefits were too vast to reject.

Americans pursued economic growth with single-minded devotion. Perennial shortages of skilled labor in a rapidly growing country had created a tradition in which both workers and managers were receptive to new technology, to faster ways of getting a job done. Consumers as well would accept new products, even dangerous new devices such as electric lights, with remarkably little hesitation. Businessmen had no serious rivals in government, the professions, or the church for the acclaim of society; a legend of upward mobility encouraged virtually all classes to perceive a personal interest in the progress of industry. And the desire for physical comforts and material signs of social advancement—traits that Alexis de Tocqueville had noted in the 1830s—induced a powerful work ethic. "I cannot be idle," one representative businessman wrote in his diary; "to me, idleness is the most terrible punishment."

Government as well, responding to this urge, dedicated itself not so much to laissez-faire as to what one writer has called "entrepreneurial liberty": the opening of opportunity to men of business. Subsidies to railroads, a free-wheeling national banking system, a generous land policy, protective tariffs, and an endless array of state and local legislation and judicial decisions cleared the way for industry and thwarted the hopes of all opponents, including the fledgling labor movement.

POPULATION

A fast-growing population was another vital base for economic growth. Here were labor, markets for goods, promises for a larger future to fire the enthusiasm of investors and the daring of entrepreneurs. Immigration provided a goodly part of the increase: 2½ million immigrants in the seventies, 5 million in the eighties, 25 million in the whole period from the Civil War to World War I. Yet the domestic population increase exceeded the European influx as a source of manpower: native-born groups more than doubled between the end of the Civil War and the close of the century. Rural folk, still a majority of the nation, maintained high birth rates and sent an army of young men and women into the cities seeking excitement and opportunity and often finding instead a place in the swelling battalions of labor. While urban birth rates declined throughout the period, life expectancy increased. Investment in such public health facilities as improved water supply and sewers paid striking social dividends. A growing, healthier, better-educated, and more skillful labor force was, according to the most recent calculations, the main multiplier of economic growth in the period, exceeding the importance of either capital investment or invention.

INVESTMENT CAPITAL

"Confidence" is the businessman's magic word. Where it exists money appears, and when it vanishes so does capital. Nineteenth-century Americans took money terribly seriously just because capital was both scarce and skittish. Most came from overseas, and the long-term success in acquiring this foreign gold makes it easy to forget what an achievement this represented. European willingness to invest in land, transportation, and industry required either something near a certainty of substantial profit or strong hopes for fabulous riches. The network of world communications was not what it would become in the twentieth century. A German or English investor required special inducements to send his money to America, where he could scarcely follow its progress. Even an investor in an eastern city might find difficulty in checking on an enterprise in the West. Thus the confusion and irregularity of American economic expansion becomes understandable. A

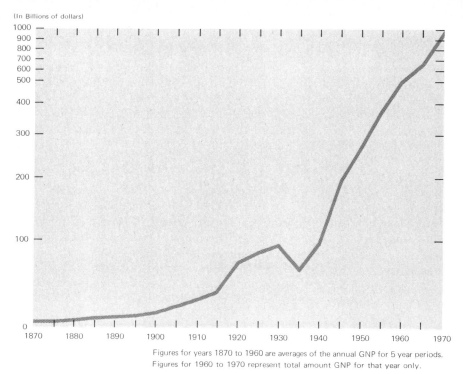

(In Billions of dollars)

Figures for years 1870 to 1960 are averages of the annual GNP for 5 year periods.
Figures for 1960 to 1970 represent total amount GNP for that year only.

Growth of the American economy since 1870.

"boom" psychology, bonanza profits, subsidies to guarantee investments or insure profits—all had a certain cockeyed logic in coaxing some $3 billion out of foreign investors during the nineteenth century. A large portion of this money went into railroads, where these processes can be viewed on a gargantuan scale.

"Maine to California"

RAILROADS AND AMERICAN
BUSINESS LIFE

"The generation," wrote Henry Adams, ". . . was mortgaged to the railroads." Between the 1830s, when the American railroad network began, and the mid-1890s, when it was more or less complete, over 166,000 miles of track crisscrossed the land, creating national markets and shaping the economy for generations.

The railroads grew in phenomenal spurts of construction: 28,000 miles in the sixties and early seventies, 73,000 in the boom times of the eighties, another 20,000 during the nineties. Independent short lines rapidly consolidated into giant unified systems: the Pennsylvania, the Erie, the New York Central, and the Baltimore and Ohio in the East; the Southern and the Atlantic Coast Line to the South; the Illinois Central, the Chicago and Northwestern, the Missouri Pacific, and the Chicago, Burlington, and Quincy in the Middle West. Even more spectacular to the railroad-conscious public of the Gilded Age were the five transcontinental roads pushed through between 1869 and 1893. Four of these—the Union Pacific–Central Pacific system; the Southern Pacific; the Atchison, Topeka, and Santa Fe; and the Northern Pacific—profited from generous federal, state, and even local subsidies. Only James J. Hill's Great Northern line, the last to be completed,

The Golden Spike
Courtesy Union Pacific Corporation

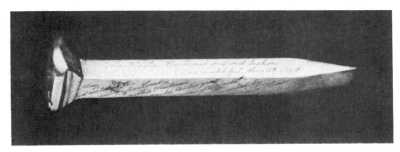

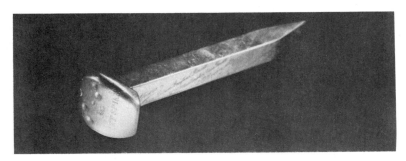

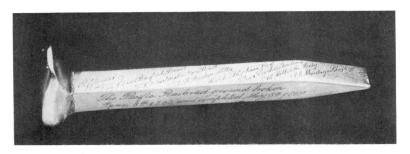

arose solely from private funds. Americans took enormous pride in the trans-continentals, considering them as much their own property as that of bankers and railroadmen.

Contemporary financial machinery could scarcely cope with investments of this magnitude. In an economy where an industrial facility like an up-to-date oil refinery cost fifty thousand dollars, railroads worth tens of millions were already common. A double-barreled attack coaxed investment in this wholly new kind of enterprise. Promoters offered investors bonds with assured interest, sometimes directly or indirectly guaranteed by government subsidies, and common stock as well. The bonds protected their investment in almost any circumstances; the stock offered the chance of huge profits if all went well. The result, of course, was overcapitalized railroads loaded down with large interest payments and "watered" stock far in excess of a road's potential.

Normal profits could not service such debts. Railroads avoided bankruptcy by creating the illusion of prosperity: the railroad promoter sold not just railroads, but expectations. The best way to keep up such expectations was through rapid expansion and high dividends. Railroads raced for new markets, building parallel to each other and stealing each others' freight business by general rate cuts or special rebates to large customers. At the

N. H. Trotter, Held Up.
The Smithsonian Institution

same time they exploited the markets they monopolized by charging high rates. Often builders skimped on construction costs to meet their debts and pay their dividends and milked capital out of their lines by organizing separate construction companies, so that, for instance, Jay Gould the railroad president could overpay Jay Gould the railroad builder with his investors' money. The process built a lot of railroads, but at the cost of financial chaos, periodic depression when the boom psychology collapsed, and the growing insecurity of virtually every segment of society. Railroads became a symbol of industrial disruption, attractive at first—Whitman wrote of the locomotive's "fierce-throated beauty"—but finally feared and hated.

WHOSE RAILROADS?

The railroads moved steadily toward completing a national market. The entire country celebrated when technical improvements such as the air brake, automatic signaling devices, telegraphic communications, Pullman sleeping cars, magnificent iron and steel bridges, standard track gauges, and uniform time zones tightened the transportation and communications network. But the vast financial organization and the railroads' obvious power over government frightened the public. Competition gave way, first to informal trusts and then to holding companies setting rates and parceling out markets. "Competition don't work well in the transportation business," said one railroadman. Large shippers had competing railroads at their mercy: John D. Rockefeller not only received secret discounts on his oil shipments, he even forced railroads to "rebate" to him part of what they charged his rivals. And the little men, if they were not served by more than one railroad, paid for it all.

Attempts to control the railroads began in the Middle West. The National Grange of the Patrons of Husbandry, founded in 1867 to provide social life for farm families, turned to politics after the depression of 1873 began. By the mid-seventies, Granger-dominated legislatures in Illinois, Iowa, Minnesota, and Wisconsin passed laws establishing state commissions with powers to regulate railroads, grain elevators, and warehouses. The Supreme Court in the so-called Granger cases, of which *Munn* v. *Illinois* was the most important, upheld this legislation in 1877, asserting that states could constitutionally regulate businesses "clothed with a public interest—enterprises such as railroads and grain elevators that affected a large part of the community. But the railroads fought a dogged legal battle against the state commissions and finally in the *Wabash* case (1886) the Court, now with several new justices, threw out state regulation of interstate lines on the grounds that the regulation of interstate commerce was a power only Congress could exercise.

By that time, numerous shippers and even some railroadmen tired of cutthroat competition had joined the farmers in a drive for national regulation.

Congress responded in 1887 with the Interstate Commerce Act. This law forbade some discriminatory practices and followed the precedent of the Granger laws in establishing a commission to police the railroads. The Interstate Commerce Commission, hampered by adverse court decisions, failed to exercise serious control over the railroads for nearly a generation. Its precise legal powers would only emerge after numerous court cases and further legislation in the twentieth century. Nevertheless, it provided an important precedent for a number of independent regulatory agencies which, still fraught with controversy, persist into the present.

A national economy

Where railroads led, industry followed. Each major industry took a similar route toward national markets, technical improvements, and increased central control. And all saw vast production at lower prices. The steel industry grew out of a single technological advance: the Bessemer process for turning brittle iron into harder, more flexible steel by blowing air through molten iron to burn out its impurities. The oil industry arose suddenly in the sixties as scientists and entrepreneurs demonstrated the use of oil as an illuminant and lubricant. The refrigerated railroad car, the growth of city populations, and a large cattle-range industry on the Great Plains transformed meatpacking from a local butcher's trade to a centralized national industry. The same process occurred in numerous other fields: electricity, textiles, shoes, liquor, agricultural machinery, prepared foods. All were helped by innovations in communication: the typewriter, the large-scale use of the telegraph, the telephone, cash register, adding machine, electric light, electric engine, linotype machine. On this technological base, astute men created new means of centralizing decision making, processing information, controlling far-flung operations, monitoring prices and products. From it rose a typical modern class—the white-collar worker; a characteristic modern form of organization—the bureaucracy; and a characteristic modern hero (and villain)—the great industrialist. Of the three, the first two were the most important, but the "captain of industry" caught the imagination of contemporaries and of historians.

HEROES OF BUSINESS

American society had always admired businessmen, but never more so than in the period between the Civil War and the Great Crash of 1929. The dramatic spread of railroad and manufacturing with its inevitable effect on day-to-day life was a running advertisement for the captain of industry. The great railroadmen, manufacturers, and bankers became national heroes,

John D. Rockefeller: industrial statesman or robber baron?
Brown Brothers

their names famous everywhere, their stories inspirations for young men. The public watched as Cornelius Vanderbilt and Jay Gould battled for control of the Erie Railroad; as California's "big four"—Leland Stanford, Charles Crocker, Collis P. Huntington, and Mark Hopkins—pushed the Central Pacific east in competition with the Union Pacific moving west. John D. Rockefeller's piety and financier Jim Fiske's extravagant ways both aroused wonder. The great meatpackers, Philip Armour, Gustavus Swift, Nelson Morris, and Michael Cudahy became literally household words, their names staring forth from the shelves at every American housewife. Similarly, the word *cigarette* would immediately suggest the name of James B. Duke; mention of copper brought the Guggenheims to mind; J. P. Morgan was virtually a synonym for banking, Andrew Carnegie for steel, Henry O. Havemeyer for the sugar industry. None of this was literally true: it was never that easy to monopolize a huge industry. But these men's careers, with their titanic struggles for control of great companies, seemed apt symbols of the growth and concentration that the era experienced.

America harbored as well an antibusiness tradition, attacking economic man for his materialism, business leadership for its undemocratic character, and commercial ethics for their cautious avoidance of the "strenuous life." A

Pennsylvania oil fields.
Culver Pictures

few reformers delivered this message to the Gilded Age public, but the ex-tollers of business like Andrew Carnegie, who identified enterprise with "Triumphant Democracy," drowned them out. Late-nineteenth-century America squared the ideas of business leadership and of democracy by view-ing industrialists as common men risen from the ranks. Horatio Alger, Jr., in numerous popular success novels, sublimated his sexual interest in boys into a legend of how industrious lads rose to become important businessmen. Serious analysts assumed that great men came from poor rural families. This myth, reborn anew each generation, generalizes the atypical experiences of a few to a whole social class. Statistical studies have repeatedly shown that most people climb to dominant positions in the American economy from a start relatively high up, with advantages of money, education, social con-nections, good marriages, and the like. For every Andrew Carnegie who started from poverty, about six began with status, and in each succeeding generation still fewer rose from the masses to the elite.

THE ACHIEVEMENT

The successful businessmen of the nineteenth century were not inventors or technicians. They organized men, commandeered resources and capital, drove down production costs, and put the pieces together in a national mar-ket. They gambled, expecting both high profits for reinvestment and re-duced risks in their future operations. Representative men like Andrew Car-negie and John D. Rockefeller dealt in basic commodities—steel and oil—and devoted their energies to producing them cheaply and selling them widely. This required larger plants, more reliable transportation, and beating competitors to markets—mostly by lowering prices. Sometimes the age de-manded more sinister methods: deliberate price wars, cutting off raw mate-rials and transportation, intimidating suppliers and customers. None of these businessmen was responsible for the kind of technological improve-ment that we associate with Henry Ford. Their efforts, however, allowed their customers to buy, for example, the same oil sent through similar pipe-lines and railroad cars and marketed by the same means in the same contain-ers all over the country. Multiplied through numerous industries, these ad-vantages created the framework of a national economy, facilitating the mobility of millions of Americans from place to place and the expansion of hundreds of secondary industries.

Most of all, the great industrialists offered a semblance of form and con-trol to an otherwise chaotic development in human history. They were the heroes of an age desperately searching for order. For the measure of order they could bring amid the threatening excitement of industrial growth, they were most handsomely rewarded.

Labor

UNORGANIZED WORKERS

The great strikes of 1877 forced middle-class Americans into sudden aware-ness of the discontented workers in their midst. While factory life was far from new in the seventies, the idea of a permanent and essentially separate industrial working class was both novel and difficult to accept. America's im-age of itself made no provision for this: a land of opportunity could not have a class without room for advancement. Workers themselves hesitated to view their status as unchanging—and who could blame them. Many had but recently left the farm or Europe in an effort to improve their circumstances. And enormous numbers of workers moved from place to place seeking the security that always seemed to elude them. Fluctuations in the economy made the laborer's lot uncertain, while new high-speed machinery made work increasingly tiresome, nerve-racking, dangerous, and personally unre-warding. Tangible evidence of this decline in the status of labor seemed present as women and children performed more and more previously male functions.

This alienation of the worker grew despite nearly full employment and wages which, thanks to shrinking prices, brought a better standard of living throughout the eighties. The industrial labor force had expanded rapidly, from under 1 million in 1860 to over 3 million in 1890. But workers felt con-trol over their lives slipping from them, thought they got too little of the gains of industrialism, and found themselves baffled by their own middle-class aspirations as the possibility of living up to them seemed to recede with each passing year.

Deep fault lines ran through the working class. White laborers rarely ac-cepted blacks. Native-born workers resented new arrivals from Europe (and even more so Asians) and consistently championed restrictive immigration policies. Skilled workers generally held aloof from unskilled, and well-settled workers distrusted the newcomers from other towns who might again vanish tomorrow. Workers who lived in small industrial towns might be an ac-cepted part of a community, identifying with the interests of other local people, but residence patterns in large cities separated factory workers from the middle class. Loyalty to political party frequently collided with com-mitment to a labor union. Bigoted foremen and craft unions often kept an informal monopoly on the best jobs. "That job is not a hunky's job," one ambitious immigrant heard, "and you can't have it." No wonder that labor spoke with no single voice, but instead drifted with the winds of opinion on "the labor question," clinging to individualist ideologies and dreams of a middle-class future while toying with collectivist utopias and complicated reform schemes. Workingmen said little, even when asked, and labor leaders blew an uncertain trumpet. They were not alone in their confusion about the implications of the onrushing industrial system. Neither businessmen nor the government officials and academic experts who began collecting statistics in this era showed much insight into the world of the factory. Labor leaders simply paid more harshly for their uncertainties, since their constituency bore the brunt of industrialism.

THE KNIGHTS OF LABOR

Labor organization remained local and largely confined to a few skilled crafts such as printing and cigarmaking until the prosperous years of the late sixties and early seventies stirred workers to organize. About three hundred thousand joined unions, but hard times after an unsuccessful attempt at forming a labor party decimated their ranks. A second upsurge came in the 1880s with returning prosperity and an unprecedented number of strikes, most local and many quite informal. A remarkable national organization, the Noble Order of the Knights of Labor, was the beneficiary—not the instigator—of this new labor militancy.

The Knights defy any standard classification. Founded as a secret society in 1869, they were partly a fraternal organization, partly a political reform agency, and partly a federation of unions. Ten years later, under the leadership of Terence V. Powderly, they threw off their secrecy, dropped their fraternal rituals, and came out for the eight-hour day. The organization began to grow: from less than ten thousand members in 1879, it rose to forty-two thousand in 1882. Then in mid-decade the economy weathered a brief downturn. This dip, which scarcely affected the middle class, aroused an unprecedented militancy among workingmen. Workers flocked to the Knights' banner: one hundred ten thousand in 1885, over seven hundred thousand a year later. More men struck than ever before—first to avoid wage cuts during the depression, then to gain increases or shorter hours. A nationwide movement for the eight-hour day did in fact force a small decline in the average workday.

The Knights were an awkward vehicle for workers seeking immediate gains. Opposed to strikes, craft unionism, and even collective bargaining, the movement's main appeal was its utopian promise of a brotherhood of labor. Nor was this mere rhetoric. Sixty thousand black workers flocked to its banner. Women joined. So did unskilled laborers. Yet skilled workers came, too. Despite the Knights' ideology, which looked toward cooperative ventures to turn workers into middle-class Americans, it expressed the solidarity of workers quite as vividly as it expressed their confusion about their role in society. Utopian, decentralized, and probably as democratic as any organization in American history, it floated forth on a sea of optimism.

HAYMARKET!

This inchoate militancy built toward a tragic climax. At a demonstration in Chicago's Haymarket Square, as a few anarchists harangued an apathetic crowd of workmen, one hundred and eighty policemen charged, some man unknown to history threw a dynamite bomb, and the police opened fire on the crowd. Seven policemen died and dozens of people were injured. The episode resulted from hysteria building up over labor activity, and the bombing led to yet further hysteria: a court returned a guilty verdict in the case of eight anarchists, none ever linked to the actual bombing, and four of them were hanged. The labor movement—which had no part at all in the terrible Haymarket affair—was the great loser. Coming just when the Knights' strike activities had ceased to achieve results, it destroyed the "spirit of 1886" of labor optimism and militancy in an instant. The Knights went into a decline almost as precipitous as their rise.

The collapse of the Knights of Labor in the aftermath of the Haymarket Riot perhaps symbolized the darkening mood of the late eighties better than any other single event. Workingmen and the forces of middle-class humanitarianism would remain separated for a half-century of industrial organization, while a new organization formed that year, the American Federation of Labor, advanced the interests of a thin segment of skilled workers, rejecting any larger role in the organization of industrial society.

This new organization was devoted to what its leading spirit, Samuel Gompers, a Dutch-Jewish immigrant who had been a founder of the cigarmaker's union, called "pure and simple unionism." The AFL sought to organize skilled workers along separate craft lines rather than to create a single large union. It also rejected alliances with political groups and the development of specific reform proposals such as workers' cooperatives or wages and hours legislation, seeking instead only higher wages and shorter hours. With these more limited goals, which reflected a realistic accommodation with a capitalist-industrial society, the AFL succeeded in dominating the organization of American labor for the next half-century, holding skilled workers largely aloof from the currents of socialism, anarchism, and political reform that influenced the labor movements of other industrialized countries.

Cities

"HOW YA' GONNA KEEP 'EM DOWN ON THE FARM AFTER THEY'VE SEEN BROADWAY?"

Popular singers crooned "Carry Me Back to Ole Virginny" and sighed to be "Down by the Old Mill Stream." Churchmen and reformers denounced the city as a hotbed of vice and crime. Rural politicians artfully drew district boundaries and apportioned legislatures to control its power. Yet the streams of humanity flooding the urban centers were larger even than the western migration; millions of Americans joined millions of European immigrants in the emerging cities. And the products of the city, both its goods and its culture, washed back across the land, eroding folk cultures and creating an urban mentality which made the city the natural goal of young men and women everywhere.

The cities grew enormously. In the decade of the eighties Chicago doubled in population; St. Paul, Minneapolis, Kansas City, and Denver nearly tripled. American cities were unlike most others in the world's history. The religious, strategic, and governmental forces behind urbanization in much of the rest of the world were weak in America. Our cities were organized almost exclusively on commercial principles. They lacked the public vistas of palace, church, plaza. Instead we carved them into gridlike patterns and then sliced them into standard lots of about twenty-five by one hundred feet to maximize real estate profits. Most services were left to private enterprise. For a time, people—their eyes still on the rural past—simply failed to realize their needs. Garbage disposal is no problem out in the country, and health care can be left to the family. So too with food supply, transportation, even fire prevention. Children reared outside cities need few special provisions. Even most of the mentally ill can be cared for at home. The city environment changed all this. Health care was everyone's concern when epidemic threatened. Water supply and sewage were early recognized as the indispensible urban public services. Other urban needs such as transportation and food could yield profits and with minor controls stayed in private hands.

MAKING CITIES HABITABLE

The late-nineteenth-century city was an uncomfortable place for most of its inhabitants. Contemporary accounts dwell on filth, stench, disease, and fear of the poor rootless denizens of the slums. No one could miss noticing the traffic in vice, the lack of "wholesome recreation," the narrow, mean lives of overcrowded residents, the animosity and violence among the various races and nationalities of the city. And the contrasts between the extremes of wealth visible in the rows of the mansions and the poverty of the tenements offended American visions of a classless democracy.

One solution to urban problems was technical; new inventions could make life more comfortable. Cities encouraged inventions, both because they offered large markets and because among the population were the technical knowledge and skills that a creative mind could exploit to develop a practical device. Inventors, typically, were city people, not the country tinkers of legend, and their neighbors eagerly adopted whatever was new. Electric lights, the electric trolley, elevated railroads, the telephone—all were developed and quickly applied en masse to the cities. And all made fortunes for those who controlled them. New York City streets in the late nineteenth century were dark with wires and pipes. People threaded their way through poorly understood electrical installations and murderous machinery. The American rate of industrial accidents rose to the highest of any nation in the world. Yet people flocked into cities, accepting new devices and delighting in each novelty though it slay them. They thoroughly learned the lesson of technological solutions to social problems: Americans began to think it their peculiar genius.

"Yankee Ingenuity" became a cliché, and men like Thomas Alva Edison national idols. Edison, the "Wizard of Menlo Park" (an early site of his New Jersey research laboratory), was an apt symbol. Inventor—or improver—of the phonograph, incandescent lightbulb, motion picture projector, and many other devices, Edison earned almost all of his thousand or more patents in collaboration with numerous assistants. Last of the great tinkerers, Edison was also the nation's first director of a research laboratory devoted to invention.

This faith in technology, even if it could extend too far, rested on hard accomplishment. Ingenious and massive engineering solved municipal water and sewage problems. The crucial problem of internal transportation gave way dramatically late in the eighties with the introduction of the electrically powered trolley. This multiplied enormously the area available to city workers, relieving housing problems by initiating the mass suburban exodus that has continued to the present. Further aid came from new steel-girder construction and the elevator. Cities could now build both up and out. As a consequence, the range of people who could afford adequate housing dipped deep into the lower middle class. Older center-city areas continued to decay, but the more skilled workers could at least begin to hope for access to decent quarters outside the factory districts. While poor laborers bounced about from slum to slum or from city to city looking for jobs, a narrow stratum of workers—printers, construction workers, and the like—might, with the help of working wives and children, buy a small house in closeby suburban districts, join a burial society, and save a few hundred dollars in a savings bank. This small elite of labor formed the core of organized workers, especially in the American Federation of Labor, while the shifting masses beneath them remained too transient for either organization or political power.

CITY CIVICS

The cities were arenas of suspicion and mistrust rather than integrated communities. Civic consciousness remained weak among people who moved often or were new to the city. The philosophy of social Darwinism, which held that society evolved naturally as a vast organism with no rational control,

The Tweed Ring. "Let Us Prey."
Culver Pictures

suited the urban scene well. In the Gilded Age it was essentially the philosophy of the city. The battles of nature, red in tooth and claw, seemed to be duplicated in the counting rooms and on the pavement. Men in despair of controlling their environment took refuge in such fatalism.

The city was on every tongue and in almost every book. Reform-minded Americans saw it as a political failure. Churchmen and women's groups considered it a moral disaster area. Social scientists and novelists viewed it as the home of emerging class distinctions, of extremes of wealth and poverty which they could not square with their ideals. Especially, they saw that normal commerical ethics met their nemesis in the city. Everywhere the supplying of urban services—public or private—carried the stigma of corruption, much as railroad building had. Electric lights, trolleys, telephones, and subways did not lend themselves to various and competing efforts: they simply worked better as single enterprises. Monopolies, called franchises, became the standard means of providing for these services. This public sale of economic opportunity inevitably trailed bribery and theft in its wake. And outright public expenditures worked no better: a squat little County Court House cost the New York City taxpayers $13 million, about $9 million of it going into the pockets of city "boss" William Marcy Tweed and his friends.

THE CITY MACHINE

The politics of the city symbolized all that was new and uncomfortable about this strange and novel environment, and people automatically thought the worst. Traditional methods constantly failed to provide services, and new procedures inevitably outraged moral sensibilities formed in a simpler world. Most outrageous of all, according to reformers, were the political "machines," informal organizations of lower-class voters held together by jobs, favors, and bargains. Party leaders like Tweed, acidly depicted in the Thomas Nast cartoon (see p. 383), were the cities' "bosses," financing their political organizations on funds extracted from businessmen in exchange for franchises and other privileges and securing the loyalties of their voters by distributing municipal jobs, small charities, informal legal aid (even to swaying a judge's decision), and similar assistance.

The machines, rather than the official organs of government, seemed to run the cities. Reformers condemned these "rings" for turning elections into contests over favors instead of tests of public opinion. They saw these organizations as a bar to efficiency and to the improvement of public services, as pirates taking their levy on the public. Naturally, they blamed them for the many and obvious ills of city life.

This attack was not wholly false. Corruption was rife, and the expectation of it made taxpayers unwilling to invest public funds in needed municipal services. On the other hand, the political machines performed useful services in adjusting the new immigrants and the new arrivals from the countryside to city ways. They helped the bewildered new citydwellers pick their way through the hazards of urban life, finding them jobs, getting them out of legal tangles, and giving them some scrap of pride in the fragile neighborhood communities they managed to create. Stressing ethnic identity, the machine politicians ratified the preference of the first generation for retaining the religion and something of the culture of their forefathers. And it introduced them to an interest-group politics in some ways more modern and serviceable than the official civic ideals of Yankee reformers.

Yet the machines were products of the urban evils from which the immigrant and everyone else suffered, and they offered no way out. Public health services could benefit the poor more than having the block captain occasionally pay for a doctor's services. Welfare agencies could give more help than the occasional basket of coal or the Thanksgiving turkey that might come from the boss. Businessmen would invest more in cities with honest and efficient governments than they would where they had to purchase franchises from corrupt mayors or aldermen. The machines offered the cities no future, and their reformer enemies, so arrogant and wrong in the short run with their condescension toward immigrants and their condemnation of "favors," were surely right in the end. Eventually—for good or ill—rational and bureaucratic methods would replace the clan loyalties and political favors of the machine.

TOWARD URBAN AMERICA

For all their condemnation of the cities, Gilded Age Americans seemed to move steadily to them, indicating a popular view far less negative than the hue and cry about vice and corruption might suggest. Here and there one could even glimpse a developing sense of urban community. A startling array of associations—clubs, settlements, religious and secular self-help and study organizations—gave shape to people's lives. Groups of middle-class women struggled to help their poorer neighbors. Newspapers replaced gossip over the back fence, keeping people in touch with their new world. Spectator sports, especially baseball, gave city people a focus for their new pride in being New Yorkers or Chicagoans or San Franciscans.

WOMEN IN THE CITIES

Women especially found new freedoms in the cities. While the first successes of the movement for women's suffrage occurred in the female-scarce Rocky Mountain states, the major focus of the movement was in the cities. The two major women's rights associations, Susan B. Anthony's National Woman Suffrage Association and Lucy Stone's American Woman Suffrage Association, were centered in New York and Boston respectively. Women formed associations to purify society, to alleviate the lot of the poor, to fight for temperance or against prostitution, to spread new knowledge about childrearing, to protect women when they traveled or worked in factories, and to improve American education.

Many of these activities reflected women's growing role in the economy. In the last thirty years of the nineteenth century the number of women employed for wages tripled. About 20 percent of American women were paid for their work by 1900, many of them in the most rapidly growing parts of the labor force. The proportion of female workers in domestic service was declining while their role in manufacturing and the professions was increasing sharply. The most spectacular growth of all came in the new white-collar occupations—salespeople, typists, secretaries, bookkeepers, and accountants—with over a half-million women in these occupations in 1900. Of course, one must set against these evidences of change the recognition that in virtually every field women were concentrated in the lowest-paid occupations. Many were teachers and nurses, few lawyers or doctors; many were unskilled and few skilled workers. Yet this growing role in the economy was the essential base for the struggle toward equality that continues into the present.

The new south

In 1886 Henry W. Grady, a leading southern newspaper editor, addressed a New York mercantile audience on the "The New South." This oration, which made him a national figure and a regional hero, refuted the traditional antebellum image point by point. It pictured a New South with factories instead of plantations, business in place of politics, thrift rather than luxury; a region with an effective, inexpensive, and docile labor force, not the shiftless "Sambo" that Northerners envisioned. Part boast, principally a promise about the future to northern investors, this assertion rested on a substantial economic recovery in the late seventies and early eighties from the acute devastation of the Civil War. The South built more miles of railroad in the eighties than in all its previous history. Birmingham, Alabama, an exhausted cornfield at the beginning of the seventies, was well on its way to leadership in American production of pig iron. A "cotton mill crusade" to "bring the factories to the fields" swept the South as investment in this industry became virtually a civic mission. Production of raw materials and crude industrial goods—turpentine, lumber, iron, coal, cotton yarn, cottonseed oil, fertilizer, and tobacco products—all grew impressively. And by the late seventies southern agriculture had regained ground lost in the wartime and postwar disorders: in the next years cotton, sugar, and tobacco production forged ahead of the prewar crop size. All this offered some substance for

Grady's vision of a New South "less splendid on the surface, but stronger at the core [with] a hundred farms for every plantation, fifty homes for every palace; and a diversified industry that meets the complex need of this complex age."

The 1880 census had revealed a vast increase in the number of southern farms, which Americans gratefully accepted as proof of the death of the old plantations. Americans did not notice or want to notice that the demise of the plantation system was as mythical as the glories with which they now invested its past. For on closer examination, the "fifty homes" that replaced the "palace" were the miserable cabins of ex-slaves, and the "hundred farms" did not belong to the poor tenants who worked them under an onerous system of sharecropping which reduced its victims to peonage only a shade above the slavery of old. Desperate for credit—always a necessity for farmers—the ex-slaves had to mortgage their future crops for supplies. This placed them in bondage to the storekeepers who furnished them with food, tools, and seed. In a capital-scarce economy the storekeeper himself paid high interest rates, and he more than passed them on to his credit customers, who, being in his debt, could not go elsewhere.

The system was vicious: many farmers ended the year in debt, necessitating the same arrangement for the next year—and at worse terms. In addition, the merchant, to make sure he got paid, demanded the cropper devote every possible acre to the "cash crop," cotton. Even more than before the war, the South suffered from a one-crop economy. These credit conditions, added to the chronically depressed cotton prices of the late nineteenth century, gave the farm protest of the nineties more support in the South than in any other part of the nation.

For all the "New South" rhetoric, the area had only begun to industrialize. The South remained overwhelmingly rural, and despite the undeniable economic progress of the eighties, it was by far the poorest part of the country. The growth that did occur profited northern capital more than the South. The most lucrative southern industries, such as lumbering and mining, were largely in northern hands. Discriminatory freight rates encouraged the production of raw materials or crudely processed goods and discouraged the more profitable manufacture of finished products. Industrialism brought little in the way of increased markets to southern farmers, nor did the jobs it created significantly improve the life of poor southerners, black or white. In fact, the great inducement to bring capital to the South was shockingly low wages. Southern promoters boasted of the "family wage," requiring full-time labor of entire families for survival. Profits from such manufactures averaged 22 percent of investment in a typical year, with well-managed firms earning as high as 75 percent annually. And this was white man's work—or more strictly, white folks' work, since two-thirds of the operatives were women and children. Cotton mills were off-limits to blacks.

BLACKS

Black Americans were the poorest people in a poor land. For a half-century after emancipation they remained largely in the South and on land they did not own. They worked for wages, or on shares, or as tenants. Some moved into the towns; many migrated from the southern Atlantic states toward richer bottomlands in Alabama, Mississippi, Louisiana, and Texas. But only a few found opportunity. Sharecropping, harsh labor-contract laws, and imprisonment for minor crimes—which meant working under the most deplorable conditions as convict labor leased to the large coal, lumber, or railroad-building corporations—left most blacks in conditions only slightly improved from slavery. The political promise of Reconstruction had given way to cruel disappointment. The federal government's support for their civil rights had vanished with the abandonment of Reconstruction and the Supreme Court's refusal to sustain civil rights legislation.

Yet the picture was not wholly bleak. Small but vital gains created the institutions and encouraged the men and women on which black hopes for the future would rest. A few black farmers became landowners in the prosperous early eighties; some urban blacks rose into a precarious middle class of storekeepers, caterers, sleeping-car porters, and skilled craftsmen. A more solid stratum of leaders rose out of the schools and churches. Education offered the best hope. Supported first by the Freedmen's Bureau, then by northern philanthropists, industrial education in particular allowed blacks to progress with the least opposition and often with the positive support of white Americans, northern and southern. The industrial-education movement grew throughout the seventies and eighties, well before Booker T. Washington gave it national publicity and leadership—and long before its limitations became clear to thoughtful black leaders. In the eighties, with vocational-training schools like Hampton and Tuskegee blossoming, it seemed a major ground for optimism.

The industrial-education movement was part of a general strategy of coalition with prosperous whites, which had replaced the old and obviously exhausted radical alliance of Reconstruction. Booker T. Washington, the talented, wily, and energetic president of Tuskegee Institute, rose from slavery to dominance of black political life preaching a doctrine of industrial training, black self-improvement, accommodation to white prejudices, and cooperation with southern Democrats and northern Republicans. This conservative strategy brought philanthropic support for black education, federal patronage and behind-the-scenes power (Washington held tight rein over both), and some leverage in southern politics.

Blacks continued to vote in fairly large numbers in the eighties, to hold minor offices as well as a few seats in Congress, and to receive some share of the limited services that poverty-stricken southern governments offered. One result of this was a measure of integration, especially for middle-class blacks.

This strategy also restricted violence against poorer blacks by providing powerful and respected political allies. Conservative southern Democratic leaders like L. Q. C. Lamar in Mississippi and Wade Hampton in South Carolina worked to maintain decency toward blacks and a limited but real political role for them. This was without doubt political exploitation, a strategy to use poor blacks to rule over lower-class whites; and it condescended to blacks, who were herded to the polls to vote as instructed. Yet it ended most of the slaughters of the mid-seventies and was mildness itself compared to the horrors that would come in the nineties in the organized system of intimidation, segregation, and disenfranchisement known as Jim Crow. Black leaders knew that they had made a retreat after Reconstruction; they would soon learn to their horror that it had turned into a rout. Like all strategies for black-white cooperation in American history, this one was a makeshift, bore some fruit for several years, raised high hopes, and ended in violent disappointment.

Political life

The Gilded Age enjoyed its public life. Politics played a larger, if not a more important, part in American life than ever before. A greater proportion of eligible voters went to the polls, and more voted according to party preference than at any other time in our history. Before the age of mass spectator sports and mass media, politics provided entertainment, information, and social life. More important, in a period of rapid change and disintegration of old communities, it offered a familiar cast of friends and enemies. It addressed immediate loyalties rather than larger national perspectives.

Chautauqua meetings drew thousands of culture-hungry Americans.
Brown Brothers

Throughout most of the country, local politics held an intense popular interest. Contests often pitted ethnic and cultural groups against one another. Arguments over school laws, Sunday closings, or prohibition were often intense struggles over which social group would determine customs and values as well as who would gain the offices, franchises, and other rewards of local power. And the residue of passion of the Civil War gave an added edge to public life. Americans found a decided pleasure in refighting the war from a safe distance. If the old Americans were Republicans, the new immigrants would be Democrats; in western states, the stream of northern immigrants carried their Republicanism with them and southern settlers their loyalty to the Democrats.

Virtually the whole flow of information about public affairs came through the channel of party: newspapers were party organs; social clubs, like the Union League Clubs growing out of the war, had party labels attached to them; even the run of daily conversation in the barbershop, saloon, or grocery came from the same source, for no self-respecting Republican would have his beard trimmed in a "rebel" Democratic barbershop any more than a Democrat would trade with a "Black Republican." Politics was one way of establishing identity, a source of community. Just as a present-day American might identify himself by length of hair, brand of beer, or model of car, so men of that day (in most states women could not vote) used political loyalties as a means of saying who they were.

NATIONAL ISSUES

National politics, far removed from this fierce localism, was pallid by comparison. The main issues of style and culture that divided ethnic groups on the local level had no clear expression in national affairs, for the federal government had not yet entered everyday American life as it would in the twentieth century. Little of importance rested on the resolution of the principal national issues. The problem of civil rights for the freedman had turned into stale recrimination even before the collapse of Radical Reconstruction. Republican promises to protect blacks' voting rights in the South and to aid their education with federal funds failed because Republicans cared more about tariff and currency policy while Democrats, fiercely racist, deeply opposed any federal intervention in the South. The parties spoke differently about tariff protection, with Republicans favoring the highest rates, but when it came to legislation, serious efforts at reforming the tariff vanished into a set of particular interests. The tariff indeed was, as one bewildered Democratic candidate had lamely asserted, "a local issue," affecting different areas and industries in different ways. On the currency question (discussed in Chapter 00), neither party could unite sufficiently to enact a consistent program. Some economists think that the resulting instability in financial arrangements itself hampered the economy. Finally, the question of civil service affected only a limited number of people, and here positive accomplishment proved possible.

A small but vigorous reform movement led by college-educated men in the cities championed the idea of a federal bureaucracy appointed on the basis of competitive examination rather than political connections. Presidents Hayes, Garfield, Arthur, and Cleveland all supported this goal of a "merit system" to strengthen the presidency, which since the impeachment trial of Andrew Johnson had been scarcely a match for Congress. Nevertheless, progress was slow until Garfield's assassination in 1881 by a crazed political office seeker stirred public outrage. Then Congress with backing from Garfield's successor, Chester A. Arthur, at last responded with the Pendleton Act of 1883 which initiated the merit system for some federal employees.

DEAD CENTER

The Gilded Age is the classic case of "dead-center" politics. When people are not sure where they are going they may either gamble on strange directions or, more often, they will simply cling to the familiar and see that nothing very much is allowed to change. In the confident eighties, this latter approach dominated. The parties remained poised in an amazingly even balance: presidential elections were close, party divisions in Congress narrow, and most of the time no party controlled all branches of government at once. In the 1880 campaign the Republican candidate, James A. Garfield, defeated the Democrat Winfield Scott Hancock by a popular majority in the entire nation of under ten thousand votes. In 1884 Grover Cleveland defeated his Republican rival, James G. Blaine, in a particularly dirty campaign marked largely by discussions of Cleveland's alleged illegitimate child and Blaine's alleged illegitimately gained railroad bonds. Cleveland's victory in the electoral college depended on an extremely narrow victory—by under twelve hundred popular votes—in New York. And in 1888 Republican Benjamin Harrison defeated Cleveland in the electoral college despite Cleveland's hundred-thousand-popular-vote plurality.

With parties so closely balanced, innovation became a risk. In any case it was unnecessary. Even the "out" party felt no need for new appeals, since the old ones were probably good enough to win the next election. Nor did the parties need strong leaders to woo the electorate. Better to take someone safe and available. And so we have the men who dominated Gilded Age politics: respectable, able, even dedicated, but faceless—our forgotten presidents: Rutherford B. Hayes (1877–1881), James A. Garfield (1881), Chester A. Arthur (1881–1885), Grover Cleveland (1885–1889), Benjamin Harrison (1889–1893). Only the one Democratic president of the era, Grover Cleveland, lives in party tradition, and most of his historical importance comes from the events of his troubled second administration in the nineties.

Thomas Wolfe, a major American novelist of the 1930s, looked in amused wonder at his father's passionate devotion to such heroes. This was the age of the "four lost men":

> For who was Garfield, martyred man, and who had seen him in the streets of life? Who could believe his footfalls ever sounded on a lonely pavement? Who had heard the casual and familiar tones of Chester Arthur? And where was Harrison? Where was Hayes? Which had the whiskers, which the burnsides: which was which? Were they not lost?

Yes, they were: lost when pressing problems in the late eighties and the nineties made their kind of politics suddenly an anachronism.

Intellectual responses

The Gilded Age was a bewildering time: the political system ignored many obvious needs and with few exceptions the era's social thought was either confused or evasive. Most Americans fronted the world with a personal Christian faith that said little about social problems. These were often left to the "laws" of political economy, which assured progress only if men avoided too much collective effort to direct change. Analogies drawn from science buttressed these beliefs. Some used Charles Darwin's picture of nature—a struggle for existence in which the fittest survived—to support the classical economists' views of society, although most businessmen simply considered themselves as the Christian stewards of society's wealth. Most reformers looked for ways to solve specific problems within the laissez-faire framework: increase credit through some scheme for greenback or silver currency, or upgrade government through civil service reform, or raise wages through producer cooperatives or private bargaining between workers and employers.

Henry George, a California journalist, explored more profoundly the ills of industrial society. In 1879, his *Progress and Poverty* asked why poverty endured amid vastly increased wealth. Reflecting on his experience of western land booms, George noted that where men gathered to work, the value of land rose. One man's labor turned into his neighbor's "unearned increment" in the form of increasing land prices and rent, making landlords wealthy and workers poor. A "single tax" on land, consuming this profit earned from other men's efforts, would remove all other tax burdens while preventing the growth of damaging social classes—millionaires and paupers. George's analysis, which tied the new and elusive industrial wealth to land—a familiar form of property—offered an easier way to understand changes in American life than did the more orthodox economics of the period. Two million people bought his books in a quarter-century, and his theory, spread by hundreds of Single Tax Clubs, influenced a generation of reformers.

Everywhere one looked men were building pieces of a new institutional structure with strengthened capacities to attack social problems. The vigorously growing Protestant churches soon responded to the new age. A "social gospel" movement, heralded by Josiah Strong's best-selling polemic *Our Country* (1885), sought to return the churches to the social role they had exercised in the heroic antislavery days. A humanitarian impulse, sparked by religious enthusiasms, turned hundreds and soon thousands of men and women to active engagement in an early war on urban poverty. In this era, charity began its transformation into organized philanthropy: what began as sentimental pathos toward the "deserving poor" (with its accompanying vicious hostility toward the "depraved classes") began to turn into the empirical study of poverty and the profession of social work. Despite misunderstanding, condescension, and formidable ethnic barriers, middle-class Americans opened settlement houses in poor neighborhoods and began to understand the victims of industrial society.

PUBLIC EDUCATION

People who might despair of answers to the economic and political questions of the age turned to education. Booker T. Washington was anything but isolated in his belief that only the right kind of education could solve major social problems. The public school became an object of nearly mystical faith: it would Americanize the immigrant, urbanize the farmboy, tame the radical, and make the worker temperate and industrious while teaching him basic skills. These dreams, mixing spiritual uplift, industrial education, and social control, were beyond any institution's capacities. But in the last thirty years of the century, school enrolments increased over 250 percent and illiteracy rates dropped by half. Kindergartens and public high school systems were among the innovations beginning to spread in the period. And above them towered the new universities, monuments of an age of cultural growth.

HIGHER EDUCATION

While men like Andrew Carnegie and John D. Rockefeller built the country's basic industries, other men nearly as famous in their time built the great universities. The transformation they wrought in higher education was almost as great as what the captains of industry did in steel and oil. Earlier in the nineteenth century American colleges had been ministerial preserves for their faculty and administrators and gentlemen's clubs for their students. Most instructors dished out a routine classical curriculum, emphasizing recitation and rote memory. All this began to change after the Civil War. The Morrill Act of 1862 offered a public subsidy for the state schools. Wealthy industrialists made the founding or extension of private universities a fashionable philanthropy. The founding of Johns Hopkins in 1876 and the reforming of Harvard under President Charles W. Eliot, beginning in 1869, were major examples of the new university. The emphasis was on science and research. Instead of a fixed classical curriculum, Eliot's elective system allowed students to follow their own interests and faculties to offer instruction in their own wide-ranging fields of inquiry.

The clerical hold on education broke: Harvard abolished compulsory chapel in 1886, and large secular universities—Wisconsin, Michigan, MIT, Cornell, Johns Hopkins, Harvard, and Columbia—began to dominate educational philosophy. Faculty were better trained (many in German universities), better paid, and more independent. They soon gathered together in professional organizations to protect and extend their new-found status and to enforce professional standards in their field. Thus the American Historical Association was founded in 1884, the American Economic Association in 1885; the psychologists organized in 1892, and the sociologists in 1905. In many cases they were creating a public role for their expertise that would eventually take them beyond the reaches of the university into government, industry, and organized philanthropy. They were a new class, the organized intelligentsia, whose influence would soon be noticed in the progressive era.

The important academic statesmen of the period—Daniel Coit Gilman of Johns Hopkins, Eliot of Harvard, James B. Angell of Michigan, and William Rainey Harper of the University of Chicago (which began in the nineties with a large bequest from John D. Rockefeller)—were among the most clear-sighted men of the age. They brought together organized scientific knowledge, traditional culture, the patronage of industry, and the children of successful Americans. Their aim was to create the rudiments of an elite, disciplined, cultured, yet up-to-date and scientific-minded leadership for an essentially leaderless and confused society. Eliot, who made his social goals particularly explicit, argued that universities "should exert a unifying social influence." They should draw students from a large area (he instituted entrance examinations in fifty cities to undo Harvard's inbreeding of students from father to son). This would enable Harvard to rise above "political discussions and divisions" and become "a school of public spirit, . . . patriotic in the best sense." In an age with a largely sterile official politics, this was a more sensible and in the long run more influential politics. It would soon be the age of the expert.

POPULAR EDUCATION

This concern for learning did not end with the school-aged population: adult education mixed artfully with entertainment in the Chautauqua summer schools and traveling lecturers; public libraries multiplied under the patronage of Andrew Carnegie and others; popular newspapers and magazines found audiences among the millions of Americans with elementary educations. Joseph Pulitzer, publisher of the *St. Louis Post-Dispatch* and the *New York World*, showed how a "people's newspaper," as he called it, could be built on bold headlines, pictures, sensations, comics, sports stories, first-rate political and financial reporting, and crusading exposures of corruption. This was the age of the reporter: people wanted "the news," not editorial opinion. Newspapers were the city equivalent of the small town's back-fence gossip: everything a little racier than in reality. With news of events came news of new products: behind the newspaper and magazine revolution was a new industry, advertising—another institution shaping the emerging society.

Toward a new age

In the late eighties the serious problems of industrialism surfaced again as they had in 1877. The uprising of labor shattered the age's complacent attitudes. Henry George, the celebrated reformer, provoked national attention when he ran for mayor of New York City in 1886 as the candidate of a new Labor party. Against the opposition of Republicans, Democrats, and the Catholic Church, and probably losing thousands of votes in the Tammany-controlled electoral count, he nonetheless received a recorded vote of nearly seventy thousand—almost one-third of the total. In the same year (and in spite of the Haymarket bombing) a labor party in Chicago succeeded in electing several state legislators and judges and came within a whisker of electing a congressman. Men talked of a new labor party in the near future, perhaps with Henry George as its presidential candidate. These hopes would not be realized, but the assumption behind them—that old political loyalties were at last weakening and new ones might soon emerge—proved true.

Farmers became as restless as workers. The Southern Alliance, a farmers' organization, suddenly in 1886 began to mushroom much as the Knights of Labor had done. Soon after, with the collapse of the agricultural land boom in Kansas and the onset of drought and farm depression, a Northern Alliance began a similar, if less spectacular, growth. In the 1890s these two groups would merge into the People's party, or Populists, the greatest agrarian radical movement in American history.

Popular interest in reform ideas quickened in the late eighties and early nineties. The great upheaval of labor in 1886 inspired Edward Bellamy, an unsuccessful lawyer, editor, and author who had brooded for years over society's injustices, to write *Looking Backward: 2000–1887*, a utopian fantasy describing an ideal society set safely in the future. Bellamy dubbed its socialist economy "Nationalism," made its citizens staunchly religious, and blessed them with peace, justice, and a charming array of gadgets. The book sold a half-million copies within a few years, inspired fifty other authors to publish utopian romances, and gave rise to one hundred and sixty-five Nationalist Clubs. Dozens of organizations promoted the book. The Theosophists endorsed it. So did the Women's Christian Temperance Union and the Grangers; it influenced the Populists and various forms of American socialism. *Looking Backward* expressed the vague and unconscious socialism of the heart for which millions of respectable Americans yearned, a society transfigured by grace—not by class conflict or social revolution.

Fresh hopes jostled against old fears. The churches, no longer complacent, worried about the "social problem." Reform had widened its vision while conservatives prepared to defend the society which industry had created. Public debate turned to great abstractions: the "trust question," the "labor question," the "immigrant question," the "currency question." The confident eighties rapidly slid into the anxious nineties.

Things to think about: 1876–1890

How could the ambitions of white American settlers and the needs of Indians both have been met in the nineteenth century? On the western movement see first Frederick Jackson Turner's classic essay "The Significance of the Frontier in American History" (a paper originally delivered in 1893), in Turner, *The Frontier in American History* (many current editions); Ray Allen Billington's comprehensive *Westward Expansion* (1967); and specifically on the Plains area, Walter Prescott Webb, *The Great Plains* (1931). Good general histories of American Indians are Wilcomb E. Washburn, *The Indian in America* (1975), and Angie Debo, *A History of the Indians of the United States* (1970). To see the story from an Indian viewpoint, read Dee Brown, *Bury My Heart at Wounded Knee* (1971), and to envision the conflict from the perspective of a commander of the U.S. Army, see Richard N. Ellis, *General Pope and U.S. Indian Policy* (1970).

How did industrialism affect American life? Robert H. Wiebe, *The Search for Order, 1877-1920* (1967), and John A. Garraty, *The New Commonwealth, 1877-1890* (1968), are important attempts to describe the impact of industrialism. Thomas C. Cochran and William Miller, *The Age of Enterprise* (1942), remains a useful introduction to economic history. H. J. Habakkuk, *American and British Technology in the Nineteenth Century: The Search for Labour-saving Inventions* (1962), and Robert

Higgs, *The Transformation of the American Economy, 1865-1914: An Essay in Interpretation* (1971), attempt to determine what made the machinery hum.

What kind of men became "captains of industry"? William Miller, *Men in Business* (1952), studies the backgrounds of successful businessmen; Edward C. Kirkland, *Dream and Thought in the Business Community, 1860-1900* (1956), studies their attitudes; Sigmund Diamond, *The Reputation of the American Businessman* (1955), studies what people thought about them. Matthew Josephson, *The Robber Barons* (1934), gives a hostile view of their activities. Allen Nevins, *Study in Power: John D. Rockfeller* (2 vols., 1953), is more sympathetic. John G. Cawelti, *Apostles of the Self-Made Man* (1965), deals with the myths surrounding this subject. The example on which many of these myths are based has been carefully studied in Joseph Frazier Wall, *Andrew Carnegie* (1970).

How did workers respond to industrialism, and how did American society respond to the workers in their midst? Herbert G. Gutman, *Work, Culture, and Society in Industrializing America: Essays in American Working-class and Social History* (1976), is an essential book for viewing industrialism from the bottom up. Stephan Thernstrom, *Poverty and Progress: Social Mobility in a Nineteenth Century City* (1964), gives striking examples of the life of workers and of their aspirations. Phillip Taft, *Organized Labor in the United States* (1964), is a convenient summary. For studies of particular strikes, see Robert V. Bruce, *1877: Year of Violence* (1959); Henry David, *The History of the Haymarket Affair* (1936); and Donald L. McMurry, *The Great Burlington Strike of 1888* (1956).

Why did Americans consider the governance of cities their greatest civic failure? On urbanization see Sam Bass Warner, Jr., *The Urban Wilderness* (1972), and Constance M. Green, *The Rise of Urban America* (1965). On city government see Alexander B. Callow, Jr., *The Tweed Ring* (1965), and Seymour Mandelbaum, *Boss Tweed's New York* (1965), as well as Zane L. Miller's *Boss Cox's Cincinnati* (1967). The view of charity workers is carefully analyzed in Nathan Irvin Huggins, *Protestants Against Poverty: Boston's Charities, 1870–1900* (1971). For an overview of immigrants in the cities see Oscar Handlin's graphic *The Uprooted* (1951). For the movement to the suburbs, Sam Bass Warner, Jr.'s *Streetcar Suburbs: The Process of Growth in Boston, 1870–1900* (1962) is excellent.

After Reconstruction ended, did the South revert to its old prewar patterns or was it a "New South" as Henry Grady said? Two books by C. Vann Woodward, *Origins of the New South, 1877–1913* (1951) and *The Strange Career of Jim Crow* (2nd rev. ed. 1966), are indispensable. W. J. Cash, *The Mind of the South* (1941), has heavily influenced our view of all the South's history. Anne Firor Scott, *The Southern Lady: From Pedestal to Politics, 1830–1930* (1970), deals with a neglected subject. Michael Schwartz, *Radical Protest and Social Structure: The Southern Farmers Alliance and Cotton Tenancy, 1880–1890* (1976), offers a vivid description of the economic system that replaced the antebellum plantation.

How did blacks respond to the end of Reconstruction? August Meier, *Negro Thought in America, 1885–1915* (1963), carefully analyzes the debates among black leaders. Rayford W. Logan, *The Negro in American Life and Thought: The Nadir, 1887–1901* (1954), exam-

ines opinions in the press. George B. Tindall, *South Carolina Negroes, 1877–1900* (1952), and Vernon Lane Wharton, *The Negro in Mississippi, 1865–1890* (1961), are superior state studies. Louis R. Harlan, *Booker T. Washington: The Making of a Black Leader, 1865–1901* (1972), is the first volume of a major biography. Students should read Washington's own *Up From Slavery*, originally published in 1901 (numerous editions). A major study of black social history extending into this period is Herbert G. Gutman's *The Black Family in Slavery and Freedom, 1750–1925* (1976).

How did Americans understand the changes their society was undergoing? Were they equipped to deal with it? Eric Goldman, *Rendez-vous with Destiny* (1952), Richard Hofstadter, *Social Darwinism in American Thought* (1940), and Sidney Fine, *Laissez-Faire and the General-Welfare State* (1956), all deal with the emergence of reform ideas. George A. Barker, *Henry George* (1955), is a thorough study, as is Arthur E. Morgan, *Edward Bellamy* (1944). Henry F. May, *The Protestant Churches and Industrial America* (1949), describes the religious response. David J. Pivar, *Purity Crusade* (1973), analyzes a reform movement in which women were particularly active. See Eleanor Flexner, *Century of Struggle* (1970), for the women's rights movement.

What was all the tumult and shouting about in Gilded Age politics? Matthew Josephson, *The Politicos, 1865–1896* (1938), is readable and acerbic; H. Wayne Morgan, *From Hayes to McKinley* (1969), is readable and admiring of its subject. Allan Nevins, *Grover Cleveland* (1932), is an excellent biography. Thomas C. Reeves, *Gentleman Boss: The Life of Chester Alan Arthur* (1975), is a good account of a representative politician who became president. Ari Hoogenboom, *Outlawing the Spoils* (1961), deals with one of the era's successes, civil service reform. Woodrow Wilson's contemporary account, *Congressional Government* (1885), remains worth reading as does James Bryce, *The American Commonwealth*, originally published in 1888 (several editions).

9

THE ANXIOUS NINETIES

1890-1900

JACOB S. COXEY

The depression of the mid-nineties was a blockbuster. Most of the nation's railroads went into bankruptcy; banks closed by the hundreds, businesses by the tens of thousands; millions of workers lost their jobs. Thousands of workers, especially in the Far West, banded together into so-called armies of the unemployed to seek work, to commandeer free rides on trains to move toward employment, even to keep from starvation by pooling what they could beg. Jacob S. Coxey's inspiration was to transform these aimless unfortunates into a "petition with boots on."

Coxey was a successful businessman, a pillar of the community of Massillon, Ohio. In rimless glasses and a well-cut business suit, this forty-year-old man of medium height and build, brown hair, small mustache, and earnest but undramatic speech hardly seemed a terrifying figure. Nonetheless, "J. S. Coxey's Good Roads Association of the United States and Commonweal of Christ," better known as Coxey's Army, dominated the newspapers for weeks during 1894, forcing prosperous readers, as one journalist noted, to listen to "the in-

398

articulate clamor for work for the workless'' angrily buzzing across the nation.

Coxey offered his followers a program: ''Good Roads and the Non-Interest Bearing Bonds.'' Both would have authorized the secretary of the treasury to issue legal tender notes (Coxey's answer to the currency question). Under the Good Roads Bill, the federal government would use the notes to hire workmen at a dollar and fifty cents per eight-hour day. Under the Bonds Bill, local and state governments could deposit special bonds in the treasury in return for legal tender notes which they would use in the same way to employ men on municipal improvement projects. Something like this plan, condemned as madness in the nineties, would become government policy in the great depression of the 1930s. Coxey illustrated the sincerity of his belief in this panacea by christening his son Legal Tender Coxey and bringing him and his mother on the great march from Massillon to Washington, D.C.

Coxey laid the groundwork for his enterprise with some care. He secured the cooperation of leading Populists and of numerous labor groups. He also spent two thousand dollars advertising the venture until the press itself descended to provide unlimited free publicity. Although most of the marchers were genuinely unemployed workmen, the charlatans and publicity seekers of the age did not pass up this opportunity. One, in fact, was at Coxey's right hand: Carl Browne, known familiarly as ''Old Greasy'' for his presumed hostility to bathwater. Huge, bearded, and unkempt, Browne was always dressed in a Wild West costume, complete with Mexican silver half-dollars for buttons. Soon to join them was a man quickly dubbed ''the great unknown.'' A born leader who rapidly gained an important place in the army, he refused to reveal his identity, giving reporters a running story with which to flummox their readers. He was ''Captain Livingstone, late of the British army'' by one account; ''Jensen, a Swede employed by the Pinkerton detective agency'' according to another. A woman—the wife of the Great Unknown?—swarthed in heavy veils would appear and disappear. Then there was Cyclone Kirtland, the Pittsburgh astrologer; Honore Jaxon, half-breed Indian dressed in feathers and hired by the *Chicago Times* to make the march eating nothing but oatmeal; and snappily dressed Douglas McCallum, author of ''Dogs and Fleas, by One of the Dogs.''

The march was full of strange happenings. Browne fought the Unknown, who separated from Coxey and formed his own little army after at last identifying himself as the man who had made and sold ''the great Kickapoo Indian Blood Medicine'' at the recent Chicago World's Fair. Coxey and his associates put up at good hotels every night while the men slept on straw. He even went off periodically to confer with Populist leaders, attend to his sand business, or sell a few of his horses. Coxey's daughter by an earlier marriage ran away from home to join her father in Washington and led the hosts as the "Goddess of Peace" dressed in white robes with flowing blonde hair on a prancing stallion. In Washington only twelve hundred others converged with Coxey's group of a mere five hundred, and instead of Congress enacting his program under the irresistible pressure of soul force, police arrested Coxey and Browne for stepping "upon certain plants, shrubs, and turf then and there being and growing" on the Capitol grounds—in short, for disobeying a Keep Off the Grass sign.

Contemporaries scarcely knew what to make of the Coxey episode. Most newspapers held it up to ridicule. Congress shrugged it off, although not without angry speeches from Populists who objected to the treatment Coxey had received. Yet tens of thousands lining the streets through which the ragged army tramped had shown sympathy with its aims. "The Coxeyites," wrote a perceptive English journalist who observed them, "ridiculed by the classes, have the sympathy of the masses." Coxey and the other industrial armies roaming the West and seeking to join him had made some points difficult to ignore: that men, unemployed, even destitute, could nonetheless display their power by means outside the ordinary channels of politics; that new pressures on American institutions could no longer be ignored; and that the operation of the economy, even a private-enterprise economy, was no private matter.

Then there were other points that almost no one got. The age of media politics had arrived. Coxey's real achievement was in forcing the newspapers to do his work for him. The charlatanism, the comedies, the sensations had performed a function: while publicizing the trivial, the newspapers had carried the serious message of want and need as well. Eventually, the nation would learn that media exposure, the manufacture of events, even the soul force that Carl Browne espoused could have serious political meaning. Coxey's march was a beginning for an important strain in twentieth-century public life. And Coxey never changed: in 1928, shortly before his death, he was still good copy, as he again urged a march of the unemployed on Washington. Few took such unemployment seriously in 1928, but they would soon see their error. Before long, men would be marching again, and for much the same reasons that Coxey had led his Commonwealers.

1890 Sherman Antitrust Act — *some ideas applied by Roosevelt & Taft*
Sherman Silver Purchase Act
McKinley Tariff
1892 *Agricultural* Populist party nominates General James Baird Weaver for president
Cleveland again elected president defeating Harrison and Weaver
1893 Repeal of Sherman Silver Purchase Act
1894 Coxey's Army — *read 398*
Pullman strike
Wilson-Gorman Tariff
Republican sweep in congressional elections
1895 Venezuela boundary dispute
Cuban revolution — *Spanish American War — Teller Amendment*
1896 William Jennings Bryan delivers "Cross of Gold" speech to Democratic convention and later is endorsed by Populist party
William McKinley (Republican) elected president, defeating Bryan
Plessy v. Ferguson
1897 Bradley Martin Ball, February 10
1898 Sinking of Maine in Havana harbor
—Spanish-American War, 20 April—10 December
Annexation of Hawaii
1899 Thorstein Veblen, The Theory of the Leisure Class
First Open Door notes — *yes*
1900 Foraker Act
McKinley reelected president, defeating Bryan
Second Open Door notes
1901 Platt Amendment

Billion-dollar politics

American politics during the Gilded Age had seemed singularly incapable of confronting the problems created by rapid industrialization. But even the most hidebound leaders began to sense the rising discontent and tried to respond. Grover Cleveland's State of the Union message in 1887 was a novel call to action. The only such message ever devoted to a single topic, it demanded reductions in tariffs in order to end a troublesome government surplus, to lower the price of such necessities as textiles, sugar, and coffee, and—so he asserted—to strike a blow at the "trusts." Cleveland succeeded in defining the terms of debate both in Congress and in the presidential campaign of 1888. He failed, however, either to push tariff reduction through the Republican-controlled Senate or to gain reelection (although he topped his Republican rival, Benjamin Harrison, in the popular vote).

The Republicans now controlled the White House and both houses of Congress. Party leaders, sensing the voters' new restlessness, eagerly sought to do something positive. Harrison, a conscientious Presbyterian elder, must have liked the biblical text about casting one's bread upon the water; he had Congress spend most of the surplus on an improved navy, a subsidy to the American merchant marine, coastal defenses, and improved rivers and harbors. Nor did this ex–Civil War general forget his old army comrades. "It is no time now," he intoned, "to use an apothecary's scale to weigh the rewards of the men who saved the country." In four years he doubled the number of pensioners. This busy Congress also passed the McKinley Tariff, which lowered revenues by raising rates to prohibitive levels; cut excise taxes on tobacco and alcohol; and passed two important pieces of legislation bearing the name of the long-time Republican senatorial expert on economic questions, John Sherman of Ohio—the Sherman Antitrust Act and the Sherman Silver Purchase Act.

NEW DIRECTIONS

This Congress, the first to appropriate more than a billion dollars ("This is a billion-dollar country" was House Speaker Thomas B. Reed's bland explanation), was a confusing signpost pointing down many crisscrossing roads. Speaker Reed had autocratically modernized procedures in the House of Representatives in order to push through this large legislative program. The problem of a treasury surplus that had plagued the nation since the late sixties disappeared, replaced in 1894 by the problem of a deficit in the national accounts. (An unspent government surplus injured the economy by removing money from circulation.) The McKinley Tariff established a national economic policy that encouraged the growth of manufacturing establishments by protecting them from foreign competition, while the Sherman Antitrust Act discouraged their growth by holding them liable to prosecution for limiting competition. Businessmen did not appear upset. The large investment in things nautical, which built on efforts that had begun earnestly in the eighties, shaped modern American naval power and offered a potent inducement for overseas imperialism.

Prophetic in another way was the failure of two bills that had been on the Republican agenda for a generation. One provided federal funds for education and the other national control of elections. Aimed at defending or augmenting the rights of blacks, both lost in the shuffle of Republican economic legislation. Henceforth, the Republicans would protect business, not blacks, while Democratic state governments in the South were free at last to institute one of the world's harsher racial regimes.

JIM CROW

Once the Republican Congress failed to act, southern governments moved swiftly to disenfranchise and segregate blacks. Mississippi led the way in 1890, revising its constitution to require poll taxes, residence requirements, and difficult literacy tests which removed thousands of whites from the voting rolls along with virtually all blacks. Other states quickly adopted this "Mississippi Plan." Segregation ("Jim Crow")—the physical separation of the races—was already a powerful institution supported by custom. However, as long as blacks retained some political force, it was a far from total system. Now the southern states (and some border and western ones as well) moved to give it the force of law, requiring separate "white" and "colored" facilities in transportation, schools, churches, courts, post offices, and almost everywhere else. The urge to isolate, exploit, and degrade blacks, an urge previously held in check by fears of stirring the old abolitionist sentiments of the North, now had free rein. The United States Supreme Court confirmed this national consensus in *Plessy* v. *Ferguson* (1896), which declared that "separate but equal" accommodations in public facilities were constitutional. A series of cases in ensuing years upheld most restrictions on voting and extended the "separate but equal" doctrine to education and other activities. Jim Crow and disenfranchisement remained legal institutions for more than half a century until a second Reconstruction overturned them in the 1950s and 1960s.

MONEY AND BANKING

The Sherman Silver Purchase Act reflected the deepest confusions of all. Republican congressmen voted solidly for it, yet almost no one liked the bill. Sherman himself was "ready to repeal it" the day it became law, but feared worse in its stead. People always feared something worse on the "currency question," the great conundrum of the age, endlessly dull and technical yet endlessly debated—perhaps the key to some great door to prosperity and equality. James A. Garfield years before had recorded in his diary the sad story of David Batcheller Mellish, a New York congressman who "devoted himself almost exclusively to the study of the currency, became fully entangled with the theories of the subject and became insane," dying in an asylum.

Money and banking had ever been potent issues in American politics because the nation had always lacked a satisfactory banking system. Hamilton and Jefferson divided over the Bank of the United States and the issues of funding the national debt. Andrew Jackson found his enemy in the second Bank of the United States. The Civil War saw a new banking system that tied bank notes to government bonds, and the federal government printed hundreds of millions of "greenback" dollars. In the postwar era, then, money was a genuinely complicated subject: by the time of the Sherman Act, the government had issued nine different kinds of currency. In addition, banknotes circulated that were backed by government bond holdings. Somewhere in this tangle, most people believed, was the source of the economy's ills: the periodic panics and depressions and especially the steadily declining prices, so painful to farmers.

In the sixties and seventies, those who wished to halt the decline in prices and the shrinking of the money supply had rallied to the standard of the greenbacks, the paper money issued during the war. Conservatives responded with an attempt to contract the currency by removing from circulation this fiat money, backed only by the government's word. The issue ended in a compromise, with $300 million in greenbacks retained, but given gold backing. This assured their value, and few were ever turned in for coin.

Keppler's "The Bosses of the Senate."
Library of Congress

THE BOSSES OF THE SENATE.

THE "CRIME OF '73"

Farmers and manufacturers who wanted more money in circulation next turned to silver. Gold and silver had been the joint standard of currency throughout national history, but silver, long overpriced in comparison to gold, had not circulated as coin for years. People would not spend as currency silver dollars worth about $1.03 for their metallic content. In the early seventies, the situation threatened to change as great silver-mining deposits in the West began to pay out their treasure. Financiers and their representatives in Congress, worried over the inflationary possibilities of this new source of currency, inserted into a 1873 coinage act a clause removing the silver dollar from the list of official coins. Most inflationists unthinkingly let through this apparently minor amendment. Soon, silver flooded the market and its price dropped to a level where coining it paid. At that point, its new-found political friends, realizing that it was no longer a legal monetary standard, cried foul. The Currency Act of 1873 became the "Crime of '73," part of a vast conspiracy against the people by politicians like John Sherman, bondholders, bankers, and sinister British and Jewish agents of international finance.

There was a germ of truth in these exaggerated charges. Men had knowingly demonetized silver, and while they had not conspired in the dark of night, neither had they shared their expert knowledge of the silver market with others in Congress. This act had clearly profited those who held government bonds and long-term debts—eastern bankers and rentiers and their western allies. And these people were, just as the silverites claimed, closely tied to international financiers and foreign governments. They were part of a worldwide economy whose reliance on gold currency caused prices to decline steadily, benefiting creditors and hurting debtors.

The advanced commercial nations, led by Great Britain, had already eliminated silver from their currency, creating a system of international finances based on gold that assured uniformity of price levels throughout most of the world. This expedited international markets in agricultural staples, simplified the commercial activities of England's merchants, and provided a uniform standard which gave investors some assurance about their foreign holdings. American industry built on a capital base of European investment, and payment on that investment was expected to be in gold. Naturally, in a world undergoing rapid economic expansion but whose gold supply increased more slowly, the stock of gold never kept up with this economic activity. In terms of gold, prices of other goods throughout the world constantly declined.

While the linking of a gold standard and declining prices was not just the imaginings of conspiracy-minded farmers, the stories, endlessly repeated in the West, of bags of gold and secret agents with vaguely Jewish names corrupting the American Congress came straight from overheated imaginations. John Sherman did not need to be bought; conservatives like him simply saw America's economic future in maintaining the flow of gold from overseas. In this he could scarcely be called incorrect. Nor was he deceived about its implications, although he dared express them only in private:

> *Undoubtedly [he wrote] the tendency of all civilizations is to make the rich richer and the poor poorer. . . . Labor becomes more abundant and cheaper, property increases and the fortunate few enjoy the greater share of the blessings of life. He would be a wise man who could change this course of civilization, and a very bold one to try to do it.*

SILVER LEGISLATION

The outraged cries of silver men in the seventies brought yet another compromise, the Bland-Allison Act of 1878. This committed the government to purchasing at least $2 million worth of silver per month to be made into coins. Much of it never went into circulation, and the act had little effect on the currency supply. Yet the compromise survived until 1890, when a shift in the balance of power in the Senate lent new force to the desires of silver miners and inflation-minded farmers.

The entrance of six western states into the Union created a "silver bloc" which forced passage of the Sherman Silver Purchase Act in 1890. The silver senators wanted still more than the 4.5 million ounces of silver that the new law required the government to purchase each month. They argued for the free coinage of whatever silver anyone brought to the mint. Conservatives wanted far less, fearing that this unsettling of the government's finances would disturb trade and bring on depression. The Sherman Act was an unstable compromise. It survived only until 1893, when Grover Cleveland fronted down the silverites to repeal it, splitting his party in the process.

Later generations have generally looked down on the idealistic cure-alls and political jockeying that went into the currency question. Yet this effort at public education deserves respect, however limited its results. A reasonable modern parallel would be the issue of nuclear-arms limitations. Everyone agrees that the fate of the world hangs on this question. Most people understand that it is an elaborate, technical issue of strategies and diplomacy, although a few believe that there are simple and immediate unilateral solutions. Up to this point the parallel is quite exact. The great divergence comes in the political uses of the issue: disarmament has never been the issue of a presidential election or the subject of sustained and intense public debate in Congress and the press. Generally it has been left to experts and soldiers. The great currency debate was a monument to nineteenth-century democracy: strident and sometimes uninformed, but usually public and often at a high level. Even the cries of conspiracy bespoke the common assumption that this was everyone's business, a belief that has too rarely applied to public issues in the twentieth century.

Agricultural discontent

THE AGRARIAN IDEAL

Most of the soldiers in the Revolutionary and Civil wars were farmers; so were most of the men who supported our national heroes—Jefferson, Jackson, Lincoln, and Grant. This was as it should be according to nineteenth-century thought: democracy rested on a sturdy and independent yeomanry, men close to the soil, capable of running their own affairs. Politicians and journalists extolled the virtues of agricultural pursuits. The growth of cities confirmed these assumptions: cities were sores on the body politic, corrupt enemies of democracy. The nation showed its feelings by granting rural areas a disproportionate number of seats in state legislatures. Farmers could be secure knowing that their representatives sat squarely on the fulcrums of power.

Yet increasingly through the post–Civil War period, farmers learned to fear that others had their hands on the levers. The theoretical power of "the people"—which farmers took to be themselves—had ceased to be the real force directing their lives. Farmers in the new or underdeveloped areas—Illinois and Iowa in the seventies, Kansas, Nebraska, and the Dakotas in the late eighties and nineties, and many parts of the southern backcountry—experienced this most directly. Burdensome mortgages threatened their land,

Barn raising c. 1895.
Minnesota Historical Society

declining agricultural prices suddenly made their crops less valuable, and profit margins shrank as freight rates took a larger share of their crop prices (despite a steady decline in the rates themselves). The farmers' political strength, as well, somehow evaporated as it flowed from the local courthouse to the state legislature to the halls of Congress.

AGRARIAN PROTEST

Sporadic protest movements suddenly turned into an angry political revival in the late eighties as drought in the West, sagging prices for cotton and wheat, and tighter money turned frustration into fury. Farm groups, active in the eighties in various local efforts such as cooperative purchasing, rounding up stray cattle, or dealing with horse thieves, turned to politics in the 1890 elections.

In the West the revival took the form of third parties and agricultural alliances; in the South it was mainly such alliances struggling to capture the Democratic party. Everywhere three-party politics created odd coalitions or "fusions," so that when the outcome became known it was still hard to tell just how much the alliances had won. Contemporaries usually credited them with victory. By that standard eight southern legislatures plus Kansas and Nebraska were in alliance hands, three senators and forty-four congressmen receptive to their wishes were on their way to the capital, and they had done well enough in two other northern states to hold the balance of power. Such a showing was more than encouraging, it was intoxicating. Alliance leaders immediately began making overtures to representatives of labor, hoping to create a new national party to replace one of the old ones, much as the Republicans had displaced the Whigs in the 1850s.

THE POPULISTS

In February 1892 a meeting of eight hundred farm leaders, reformers, and a few labor leaders organized the People's party, quickly to become known as the Populists. They called for a national convention to meet in Omaha on July 4, and there, besides nominating a presidential ticket, adopted a party platform with the most far-reaching reforms in American political history. An elaborate preamble offered an apocalyptical vision of a nation "brought to the verge of moral, political, and material ruin" by a conspiracy of greedy private interest. The new People's party would do what neither the Republicans nor the Democrats had even done: expand the power of government "as rapidly and as far as the good sense of an intelligent people and the teachings of experience shall justify, to the end that oppression, injustice, and poverty shall eventually cease in this land." In this pledge lies much of the history of twentieth-century American politics, at least the history of its aspiration and rhetoric: the new century's liberalism would be in large part a scramble by people very different from the Populists to meet some of the Populists' demands without major disruptions of the social order.

POPULISM AND
TWENTIETH-CENTURY REFORM

The more concrete aims of the Populist platform also influenced the future: their call for a graduated income tax; a postal savings system (post office savings accounts such as immigrants had known and trusted in Europe); some form of government financing of farm credit; the direct election of senators; the enforcement of laws against importing labor by contract; and steps toward achieving the eight-hour day for industrial workers. All these eventually came to pass. The Populists' general objective of using government control of the money supply to improve business and agricultural conditions has become financial orthodoxy, although their particular nostrum—the free and unlimited coinage of silver at a ratio of sixteen to one with gold—never got a trial. But none of these accomplishments came under the leadership of Populists; and some items on their list never became law—the public ownership of railroads and of telephone and telegraph companies, the prohibition of alien land ownership or the one-term presidency. Those parts of the Populist platform that were finally enacted bore the mark of the corporate and urban world which put them through and have, perhaps, ended being very different from anything the Populists envisioned. For the Populists, leaders as well as followers, were, as the founder of the party in Oklahoma said, "ordinary folk," not the "better classes," and what people do for themselves is by that fact different from what their betters do for them.

The Populists, who could get but 8 percent of the presidential vote in 1892 and then merged with the renovated Democratic party in 1896, succeeded principally in frightening the other parties and injecting new notes into political argument. They commanded hard support only in a few rural areas; the older, more settled regions rejected their apparently radical appeal. The expansion of government under more conservative auspices over the next half-century reflected their program rather than their ideas, which were deeply embedded in the nineteenth century. They sought, perhaps paradoxically, to use government to return initiative to individuals and the local community. For example, their "subtreasury plan" would have provided government financial instruments and warehousing to make farmers their own bankers, able to use their own nonperishable stored produce to generate their own credit. The Populists also believed in government by party, not by experts, and in revivalistic public debate heavy with moral overtones.

They sought to impose their view of righteousness on others, not by sly manipulation but by open debate and exhortation. In this sense, they may well have been out of place in an increasingly heterogeneous nation. They were somewhere between the old image of the farmer as "the people" and the new realities; soon the farmer would pass into a minority of the population and have to advance as a special-interest group, as self-interested as all the rest. The Populists resisted this, eternally to their credit. What became of their dreams in the twentieth century would have seemed as tarnished to them as their silver standard does to us.

The second Cleveland presidency

The election of 1892 offered few surprises and, outside the strongly Populist areas, even less excitement. President Harrison stood on the record of the billion-dollar Congress, former President Cleveland on his performance in the White House from 1885 to 1889. Except for the Democrat Cleveland's promise of modest tariff reform, the two men had the same credentials: a proven capacity to run the nation's business in sound, conservative, if unimaginative fashion. When Cleveland and his party gained a clear-cut victory, few solid citizens anticipated serious change. Even strongly Republican and protection-minded businessmen might echo Andrew Carnegie's estimate of Cleveland as "a pretty good fellow." The previous year, at the height of the national currency debate, Cleveland had delighted bankers with a public letter denouncing the free coinage of silver as "a reckless and dangerous experiment." Many thought his moderate views on tariff reform and his remarks against the growth of trusts would allay discontent without upsetting anyone's interest: "People will now think the Protected Manfrs. are attended to and quit agitating," commented Carnegie on the election outcome.

Yet Cleveland raised very different hopes as well. Heady words like "liberal" and "reform" had already attached themselves to his first administration: reforms of civil service, the tariff, pensions, Indian policy, trusts, railroads. He had found support in 1892 from men with ideas very different from the cautious businessmen who financed his presidential campaign. Populist leaders quietly backed him in exchange for Democratic endorsement of their local candidates. Henry George campaigned actively for Cleveland, as did Eugene V. Debs, then a Terre Haute labor leader and soon to be America's leading socialist. Cleveland, despite his contemporary reputation for bluntness, had in fact maintained a delicate political balance over the years. He was confident that it would continue in his second administration.

THE DEPRESSION OF THE NINETIES

He was proved wrong: economic depression led his party to disaster. Only weeks after he took office a stock market panic ushered in major collapse. Statistics show that the depression of the seventies was sharper and the Great Depression of the 1930s longer and more costly, but in human terms this was the worst depression in American history. It came after large parts of the population were locked in cities and before generations of effort at social welfare had softened the blow that fell on the urban poor during a depression. And like the next great depression, it landed hard upon farmers, who had already suffered years of bad times. In the depression's deepest trough, the winter of 1893–94, more than 2½ million men walked the streets and rode the rails seeking work. Charities and a few local governments offered scant aid. Beliefs about the damaging effects on character of relief, even when given in exchange for work on public projects, stymied any large-scale assistance. Government officials and publicists as well as reformers and welfare workers repeated Cleveland's famous statement during his first administration that "though the people support the Government the Government should not support the people." Meanwhile people died from cold and hunger. Many survived through the largesse of saloonkeepers connected with the political machines. "Hinky Dink" Kenna, one of the more corrupt of the "gray wolves" on Chicago's Board of Aldermen, in a single week fed eight thousand destitute men in his First Ward saloon. When one of his employees demanded a nickel from an unfortunate with too much appetite, Hinky Dink promptly fired the offending bartender. Few voters forgot such things on election day.

SILVER REPEAL

Grover Cleveland's solution to the problems of depression was rather more theoretical than Hinky Dink's. He, like so many of his contemporaries, saw the answer in the currency question. The problem was to restore the confidence of businessmen, and the issue that worried them most was clearly silver. Forthright action in favor of gold would, Cleveland and his advisers believed, loosen the paralysis that had fallen upon American industry, offering the only permanent relief for the unemployed.

Cleveland proceeded with a presidential vigor unparalleled since Lincoln's wartime leadership. Fresh from a dramatic, secret, and life-endangering operation aboard a friend's yacht in which a cancer on the roof of his mouth was removed, he called a special session of Congress. He then staked his entire political capital on forcing through repeal of the Sherman Silver Purchase Act over the objections of a large part of his own party. Had the economy then swung upward, he would have earned an overwhelming triumph. Instead it sagged to its nadir and Cleveland was left with popular hatred, a divided party, little support in Congress, and a long term as president stretching before him. "Think of it!," Cleveland lamented: "Not a man in the Senate with whom I can be on terms of absolute confidence."

GROVER CLEVELAND VERSUS HIS PARTY

As late as 1892 only Cleveland had seemed capable of holding together the disparate elements making up the Democratic party; the conservative bankers and merchants, the low-tariff railroadmen, and the southern business leaders along with the urban immigrants and workmen and the thousands of poor and middling Democratic farmers in the South and West. After 1893 the party crumbled at his every touch. As the depression shrank tax receipts and treasury balances, Cleveland had to go to Wall Street, virtually hat in hand, to float the bonds that would save the United States government from bankruptcy. An undersecretary of the treasury wrote in distress (and of course in secret) of the "curious spectacle of the U.S. finances being controlled by a committee, of which J. P. Morgan is Chairman, and the majority of whom are Hebrews, while the Secretary of the Treasury sits, practically powerless in his office." Cleveland's western and southern enemies understandably thought the worst. "When Judas betrayed Christ," one-eyed Ben Tillman told the angry farmers he led in South Carolina, "his heart was not blacker than this scoundrel, Cleveland, in deceiving the Democracy."

Nor could Cleveland gain any lost ground by turning to other issues. He failed to control Congress's efforts at tariff reduction and got five months of party-destroying argument in the Senate and a bad bill in the bargain. The main provision of the Wilson-Gorman Tariff that was palatable to his western and southern enemies, a small tax on large incomes, died almost instantly at the unsympathetic hands of the Supreme Court. This in fact climaxed a series of unpopular decisions protecting manufacturers from the new antitrust law and holding labor unions and their leaders liable to penalties under vague and comprehensive "blanket" injunctions against collective activities—including, of course, strikes.

1894: CRISIS YEAR

Class antagonism far beyond anything seen before in America surfaced in 1894. Coxey's Army was a symptom of deep conflict. The great Pullman strike, arriving on the heels of numerous labor disturbances, looked to many like the long-awaited social revolution. Eugene V. Debs, the brilliant and energetic leader of the American Railway Union, led a massive boycott against the Pullman Palace Car Company of Pullman, Illinois; the railroad

Edward Steichen, J. P. Morgan, 1903—"I'm not in Wall Street for my health."
Collection, The Museum of Modern Art, New York. Gift of the photographer

owners retaliated by stopping all trains into Chicago, and with the help of a compliant judge, an eager United States attorney general, and an obstinate president, fearing disorder and insistent on moving the mails through Chicago, succeeded in getting federal troops to break the strike. Grover Cleveland had added another clutch of enemies, including Governor John Peter Altgeld of Illinois, who engaged in public recriminations with Cleveland for sending federal troops in the absence of any request from the state. Public opinion supported the president, but Altgeld would have his revenge two years later in leading Cleveland's enemies at the Democratic national convention.

The congressional elections of 1894, coming at the trough of the depression, gave a clear reading of society's tensions. The administration suffered the greatest political defeat in American history. From a commanding 218 representatives in the House, the Democrats shrank to 105, giving the Republicans a majority of 140. The Populists gained another four hundred thousand votes, but their geographical base of support had shrunk rather than increased and their larger totals came mostly from fusion arrangements. The older parties were stealing their issues and some of their support. For all the discontent in the land, the Republicans, not any radical group, had profited from the distress of the decade. But the results also illustrated the popularity of the silver issue. Democrats, trapped by Cleveland's currency policy and the tariff fiasco, did not elect a single congressman anywhere between Ohio and California. After 1894 it appeared that the Democrats were already split on the currency question and that western Republicans were pushing toward a disruption in their party. The 1896 election would be the most important in decades.

The election of 1896

The results of 1894 set the political tone for 1896. The dominant note was Republican confidence. Men began actively to seek the nomination as soon as the congressional results came in, and by early 1896 the contest had largely ended. William McKinley of Ohio, champion of high tariffs, with a fuzzy record on currency, popular with workingmen, and a solid favorite in the Middle West, easily outdistanced the other candidates. The party met in St. Louis in June to nominate him, placating his eastern rivals with a firm declaration in the platform to maintain the "existing gold standard." A small bolt of western silver Republicans bothered the Republican leadership not at all. McKinley's hometown band mockingly played "Silver Threads Among the Gold" as the leader of the Republican silver forces, Senator Henry M. Teller of Colorado, delivered as emotion-laden speech of farewell to the party he had helped found forty years before. Mark Hanna, McKinley's campaign manager, happily shouted "Go! Go!" A correspondent for the *Omaha World-Herald*, scrambling over the reporters' desks to view the scene more closely, was equally excited: ex-congressman William Jennings Bryan, a Nebraska Democrat, had worked for a moment like this all of the past three years.

ENTER WILLIAM JENNINGS BRYAN

The Democratic convention, meeting in Chicago in July, was among the most dramatic national party conclaves in American history. Administration Democrats put up a hard fight for gold, but three years of intense debate and organization and the obvious political need to repudiate the unpopular Cleveland gave the silver forces a huge majority. Bryan's brilliant speech defending the silverites' platform gave them a candidate as well.

Thirty-six years old and with a national political experience of only two terms in Congress, the young Nebraskan seemed an unlikely presidential candidate. But he had labored assiduously to combine the silver forces—Democratic, Populist, and Republican—and was a true representative, even an embodiment, of western small-town and rural culture, a genuine man of the people. Most of all, he was a great orator in an age that valued oratory above all else. Generations of western schoolchildren would later declaim his famous convention speech. His cry of defiance against the eastern world of banks and merchants and railroadmen: "We beg no longer, we entreat no more; we petition no more; We defy them!" rung across the prairies for generations. His stately conclusion—"You shall not press down upon the brow of labor this crown of thorns, you shall not crucify mankind upon a cross of gold"—although widely denounced by his enemies in 1896 as blasphemous (especially since he accompanied it with the appropriate gesture of pressing his hands against his brow), remains a permanent part of the folklore of American politics.

The convention, badly in need of a viable silver candidate, accepted him on the fifth ballot the next afternoon. The Populists, meeting afterward, had no real choice but to accept him as their candidate as well: he had maintained excellent relations with their leaders and stood for their most popular if not for the full range of their goals. If they had refused and he had come anywhere near election, they would have been considered betrayers of the cause.

BRYAN'S PLATFORM

Bryan launched the first modern barnstorming campaign, covering eighteen thousand miles, making six hundred speeches, and reaching perhaps five million people. He talked mostly about silver, not because he was a fanatic but

William Jennings Bryan,
the peerless leader.
Library of Congress

because this was the only issue that held together his supporters and because the other major issue, the tariff, could only cost him votes by reminding voters of his party's failure to win reform. Also, he recognized that silver, whatever the technical virtues or demerits it had as a monetary standard, had come to symbolize economic reform. Bryan advocated a federal income tax, wanted to limit severely the note-issuing role of private banks, opposed the kind of injunctions that had been issued during the Pullman strike, and was devoted to tariff reform. He argued that until silver won there was "no other reform that can be accomplished." Opponents who sensed that there were more reforms to come if Bryan became president were surely correct.

On the other hand, Bryan's Populist followers who thought he would do less than they wished were correct as well. Bryan was the first national exem-

417

plar of a new kind of liberalism that would soon be called progressivism—devoted to active reform of existing economic institutions without, however, destroying or fundamentally altering them. Silver, because it lacked appeal to workingmen who saw that inflation would hurt their standard of living, was an unfortunate issue on which to argue the need for reform. But it was the only possible issue at the time, and Bryan gave it the best defense he could. He fought for a reform movement that would both meet modern needs and preserve intact the agrarian world of his childhood—a gallant, impossible program.

BRYAN VERSUS MCKINLEY

Aside from Bryan, the Democrats had practically nothing else. Many Democratic organizations in the East and Midwest abandoned him. When they did not openly support the opposition, they backed a "gold Democrat" ticket fielded to draw votes away from Bryan. Worse yet, every major business interest except a few silver-mine owners turned against the Democrat's apparently radical platform. Where previously most contributions came from individual businessmen and were more or less evenly divided between the parties, suddenly, with no Democratic directors objecting, corporations could support the Republicans straight out of their treasuries. Businessmen sooned gained confidence in the Republican manager, Marcus Alonzo Hanna, a Cleveland millionaire industrialist turned politician. There were virtually no bars to what they could give. Hanna raised several million dollars to blanket the nation with 250 million pieces of campaign literature and paid speakers to orate for McKinley and newspapers to support him. A scrawled note from Hanna would move hundreds of the party faithful over the rails to Canton, where McKinley, flanked by his aging mother and invalid wife, could deliver set little speeches for national distribution through the newspapers. At Hanna's word, banks threatened to foreclose mortgages or deny credit if McKinley were not elected. Hanna became a legend.

"Dollar Mark," the great "national boss," embodied as much legend as his adversary, the "boy orator of the Platte." (The Platte River in Nebraska, Easterners joked, was six inches deep and six miles wide at the mouth.) Hanna had performed a function much like other businessmen in the Republican party in the past. But he had performed it somewhat better and in more fortunate circumstances. He was an apt symbol of the marriage of business and politics which the Republican party consummated in 1896. It would be a lasting arrangement. For the next generation, Republicans would be the numerical majority in the nation, and leaders of large-scale business and finance would dominate party councils. Hanna was the Gilded

Age's appointment with the twentieth century. Americans, as Henry Adams recognized, had declared themselves "once for all, in favor of the capitalistic system with all its necessary machinery."

THE OUTCOME

The electoral outcome was obvious by early fall. McKinley collected 271 electoral votes, Bryan only 176. A higher proportion of eligible voters turned out than in any other national election before or since. Bryan, who lost by half a million votes, nevertheless had a higher popular-vote total than any candidate prior to that year. Cries of foul play rent the air, and there is no question that they reflected a reality: economic coercion was rampant and corruption common. But the charge that the Republicans won only by these tactics is untrue, for subsequent elections in which such allegations were rare confirmed the results of 1896. It was the decision not merely of a moment but of a generation. Until the next great swing of the political wheel in the 1930s, Republican majorities, high tariffs, and sound money would be the rule. The last, ironically, proved least important of all. Late in the decade, the economy—and prices—began to swing upward in a long economic spiral that would endure until 1929. And suddenly currency was abundant—not from silver, but from the gold that angry farmers had so despised. A new way of extracting the metal from low-grade ores, the cyanide process, together with fresh discoveries of ore in Australia, Alaska, and South Africa at last made gold an adequate base for the international monetary system. The silverites had essentially been correct about the inadequacy of the world's gold stock in the early nineties to meet economic needs. Bryan, one might say, had won his point by losing his issue. The next reform movement, progressivism, would consist of urban as well as rural people, and they would worry about inflation, not falling prices. And Bryan would be there, having lost what he immediately called "The First Battle" but fighting on.

The gay nineties

THE BRADLEY MARTIN BALL

Not everyone went hungry or felt anxious in the nineties. Wealthy Americans remembered the "gay" nineties. The gayest event of all was the Bradley Martin Ball. This unparalleled extravaganza took place at the Waldorf Hotel in New York on the night of February 10, 1897, after weeks of preparation by New York society and of anticipation in newspapers all over the country.

Mrs. Bradley Martin, daughter of a New York banker and wife of a wealthy lawyer, while reading the newspapers one winter morning of how the poor were suffering from the depression, decided to cheer people up and "give an impetus to trade" with a costume ball. Requiring her guests to dress in accurately rendered court costume from the "most lavish periods of history," Mrs. Bradley Martin quickly precipitated a massive contest in ostentation: preparations for the hall alone cost one hundred twenty-five thousand dollars, and Mrs. Bradley Martin's Mary Queen of Scots costume—black velvet and white satin with a jeweled stomacher and a ruby necklace—made its intended impression. However, some observers were more struck with Mrs. Astor's uncanny ability to find places on her dark blue velvet gown for two hundred thousand dollars' worth of diamonds. The banker August Belmont was clearly the most gallantly dressed man in a ten-thousand-dollar suit of gold-inlaid steel armor. The real losers were the fifty women who dressed as Marie Antoinette: "It was painful to contemplate," reported one

European objets d'art grace the Fifth Avenue home of John Jacob Astor.
Brown Brothers

society editor, "the future of all these young women who were to lose their heads."

The ball was both a triumph and a disaster. "It may not be surpassed in another hundred years," oozed one society reporter: "It was a gorgeous, superb, and wonderful spectacle." Yet a prominent Episcopal rector had warned that such an occasion in a time of depression and social tension was "ill-advised." He proved correct. Newspapers condemned the Bradley Martins for their extravagance. Clergymen preached sermons against them. College debating societies resolved their iniquity. The New York assessor wreaked a more practical vengeance by doubling their taxes. The Bradley Martins surrendered their hopes of becoming the royalty of New York society, permanently retreating to England.

The Bradley Martin Ball ended neither social extravagance nor its fascination for the public. But "society" began to fear the whip of the press, especially when journalists combined reports of such orgies of big spending with muckraking accounts of the business practices that had created these fortunes. Eight years later, the dandy James Hazen Hyde had to flee the country after spending two hundred thousand dollars on a masked ball. He should have known better: daddy's company, Equitable Life, was under heavy political attack in 1905. Nor did public opinion respond any more favorably to Harry Lehr's "dog dinner," at which his friends' dogs dined on paté. Rich people began to learn that what titillated the public did not necessarily win its approval. Since "society" has learned that lesson, Americans have found it far less interesting.

CULTURE—HIGH AND LOW

A new popular culture—one critic dubbed it the "chromo-civilization"— dominates our image of the late nineteenth century: the "yellow press," dime novels, McGuffey readers, Chautauqua, humor magazines like *Frank Leslie's Jolly Joker*, Horatio Alger novels, houses built in grotesque imitation of medieval fortresses with turrets and curlicues and cast-iron deer on the lawn, immigrants with heavy accents, and rich men and women draping their overweight bodies with every kind of ostentatious display.

This picture is not false—only one-sided. It was a time of cultural growth as well. The Gilded Age got its name from Mark Twain's book of that title. And while contemporaries thought of Twain primarily as a humorist and the author of children's books, Ernest Hemingway cited *Huckleberry Finn* as the one great American novel. Twentieth-century critics rejected the age's writing as anemic and "genteel" and only later discovered that Henry James was our major novelist and William Dean Howells a central figure in American literary history.

All three of these major writers illustrate the complexity of the early industrial age. Twain denounced business morals but sought the society of ty-

*Mark Twain—Samuel Langhorne Clemens (1835–1910), dressed in
academic robe.*
Mark Twain Memorial, Hartford, Connecticut

coons. He played at being a funnyman—an eccentric dressed in a white suit—while pillorying the shallow sensationalism of the newspapers. Henry James wrote dozens of carefully crafted novels and stories pitting American innocence against European corruption and rapacity. Yet he found the decadent Continent a far more comfortable home than his native land. And Howells, editor, critic, and novelist, maintained his position atop the pantheon of genteel American letters while calling for an end to laissez-faire capitalism in *A Traveller from Altruria* (1894) and publicly denouncing the hanging of the Haymarket martyrs.

Thorstein Veblen in *The Theory of the Leisure Class* (1899) burlesqued the American plutocracy's "conspicuous consumption" of every "honoric" commodity, such as the masterpieces of European culture. New American millionaires did at times buy paintings by the yard along with titled husbands for their daughters—in both cases ignorant of the product they were receiving. Nevertheless, many a collector who began by wasting huge sums on worthless paintings eventually acquired expert guidance and purchased the art treasures now on view in the great American museums. And this same age produced several important American painters: Thomas Eakins and Winslow Homer, realists largely free from the sterile conventions of nineteenth-century academic art; Albert Pinkham Ryder, whose eerie canvases were intensely romantic yet wholly unsentimental; and the expatriates, James A. McNeill Whistler and Mary Cassatt, whose absorption in European art styles would eventually influence post–World War I art in this country.

The isolated empire

The United States had always been an imperial nation, gathering new territories, settling new lands, brushing aside those who stood in its path. Through most of the nineteenth century Americans purchased, fought for, or took from the willing hands of settlers a western empire carved largely from the old Spanish conquests.

The Civil War added a new dimension to American expansion, for the conflict created not only a larger and more ambitious central government, but a powerful navy as well. William H. Seward, the aggressive secretary of state during Reconstruction, actively sought overseas expansion. In addition to purchasing Alaska—on the continent but separated from the rest of American territory—Seward seized the unclaimed Midway Islands far out in the Pacific and tried to buy Denmark's possessions in the West Indies. Both Denmark and the islands' inhabitants were willing, but the United States Senate was not.

President Grant had similar ambitions and they met a comparable fate. With Cuba in revolt against Spain after 1868, he looked longingly for an

The Gulf Stream, *Winslow Homer.*
The Metropolitan Museum of Art, Wolfe Fund, 1906

American role in the West Indies, but Secretary of State Hamilton Fish thought it unwise. Grant especially wanted to annex Santo Domingo, but even the most heavy-handed presidential pressure could not overcome the Senate's opposition. A treaty that would have gained us a naval station in Pago Pago in Samoa foundered on the same shoal. Despite a healthy measure of ambition for overseas expansion, the weight of American thinking was still against foreign adventures. As if to remove temptation, Congress allowed the Civil War navy to decay to a point where the English wit Oscar Wilde called it the chief romantic ruin that America could offer the tourist.

The American people before the nineties based their rejection of an overseas empire on arguments which by this time had the force of tradition. The Founding Fathers, especially Washington and Jefferson, had told them to look resolutely westward both to advance their interests and preserve their freedoms. American institutions could accommodate a vast continental empire divided into new sovereign states with populations similar in race and culture to the older areas. But the Constitution would not tolerate rule over foreign populations, people with strange tongues and political habits. This would mean an enlarged federal government, standing armies, ccrps of dip-

424

lomats, and sinister alliances with the corrupt nations of Europe. And in the "uncivilized" world, expansion presented fresh racial dilemmas, a major objection to the Santo Domingan adventure. Who needed these problems when in the West opportunity beckoned and to the east the Atlantic Ocean provided security without armies, navies, or alliances?

VOICES FOR EXPANSION

This traditional rationale for isolation remained a bulwark against most foreign adventure until the nineties, but fresh events, needs, and ambitions chipped away at it. By the end of the century, we were the foremost industrial power. Adventurous souls saw that this offered opportunities for glory on the world's stage; practical ones sensed, especially during depressions, the need for world markets; religious leaders discovered a moral duty to spread American institutions and Christian missions. New intellectual currents, especially social Darwinism, emphasized the conflict of races and cultures in the world and with it the need to compete for markets and power. The theories of Captain Alfred T. Mahan, asserting that naval power determines the course of history, powerfully influenced leaders of opinion in government, the military, and to a lesser extent businessmen.

ISLANDS IN THE PACIFIC

Foreign policy, however, is more the result of specific events than of grand theories, and events everywhere were pulling America into the vortex of world affairs. Fresh experience reversed the old aphorism of trade following the flag: the flag followed private enterprise. For example, American merchant ships in the Pacific had long made stopovers in Hawaii and Samoa. A few countrymen, seeing opportunities there, settled, creating economic involvements and attracting missionaries. Transcontinental railroads in the United States and the advance of steam transport across the Pacific increased their economic importance. With the European nations hungrily gobbling up the unclaimed areas of the world, settlers looked to the American government for security, while American administrators eyed sites for naval stations such as Pearl Harbor in Hawaii. Once European penetration of these areas began, American prestige was at stake, and private adventures became diplomatic, even military concerns.

In Samoa conflicting German, English, and American interests in the South Pacific archipelago produced a decade of intrigue leading to a naval confrontation in 1889. Fortunately, a hurricane dispersed fleets, and a conference created a tripartite protectorate over the islands. The arrangement, abandoned ten years later, marked a turn in American policy from its traditional isolationism.

HAWAII

Hawaii blossomed into a far more important outpost of the American economy. Missionaries there advertised the islands' economic possibilities in the religious press, attracting settlers who organized the native sugar industry. A reciprocity treaty in 1875 admitted their produce duty-free, booming the Hawaiian economy and tying it tightly to that of the American mainland. The American navy moved into Pearl Harbor, gaining treaty rights to this great natural basin in 1887.

Then in the nineties disaster struck. The McKinley Tariff removed the duty on sugar, wiping out the Hawaiian advantage in the American market. A year later political trouble followed hard on the economic problems. A new monarch ascended the throne of this American-run but nominally Polynesian kingdom. Queen Liliuokalani, a genuine nationalist, was determined to return power to the natives, now threatened not only by American domination but also by competition from tens of thousands of Chinese, Japanese, and Portuguese imported to work on the sugar plantations. Early in 1893 she proclaimed a new constitution eliminating the white-controlled legislature. The new regime survived but three days. American planters, with the aid of an enthusiastic United States minister and a detachment of sailors and marines placed to threaten the Royal Palace, staged a bloodless coup d'etat. They raised the Stars and Stripes and declared Hawaii an American protectorate.

The successful revolutionists raced to Washington and within two weeks had signed a treaty of annexation with the eager State Department. Still they had not been fast enough. With the Harrison regime about to end, the Senate delayed and the new secretary of state withdrew the treaty. Cleveland investigated, objected to the skullduggery of the planters and the minister, and tried to reinstate the queen. The Americans, firmly in control, would have none of it and finally forced Cleveland to recognize their government. Once the Republicans returned to power, they annexed Hawaii (1898) by joint resolution of the two houses of Congress, avoiding a treaty fight in the Senate.

LATIN AMERICA

American interests in Latin America were at least as great. Americans saw economic possibilities and hungered for a canal across Central America linking their Atlantic and Pacific maritime interests. Secretary of State James G. Blaine, who served both in the brief Garfield administration and in most of Harrison's, looked for ways to assert American leadership in the hemisphere. He organized a Pan-American Conference in 1889 and sought unsuccessfully for trade and arbitration agreements. A minor incident in Valparaiso, which angered President Harrison, almost led to open conflict between the United States and Chile in 1891. Americans seemed anxious for a chance to flex their muscles.

THE VENEZUELA BOUNDARY DISPUTE

The chance came in 1895. Cleveland, his popularity at a low point, seized on an old dispute between Great Britain and Venezuela over the latter's border with British Guiana. Championing the cause of small nations, his secretary of state demanded that England submit to American wishes and gratuitously proclaimed that the United States was "practically sovereign on this continent." England at first ignored the American threats, but when Cleveland persisted in his belligerent posture and received enthusiastic popular support in the press and in Congress, the British government began to worry. They were threatened by a rising Germany and faced incipient revolt in South Africa. To add the United States, with its huge potential strength, to the list of enemies was, said the British colonial secretary, "an absurdity as well as a crime." The English agreed to arbitration, winning most of the disputed territory that way. The result, paradoxically, was a marked improvement in Anglo-American relations. Having been to the brink, the two nations, recognizing their economic and diplomatic need for each other, embarked on their course of close friendship in the twentieth century.

The cuban revolution

Americans had coveted Cuba for most of the nineteenth century, and only northern fears of new slave states prevented an attempt at annexation before the Civil War. Along with Puerto Rico, Cuba comprised all that remained of the once-great Spanish Empire in the New World. Revolution broke out there in 1868 and continued for a decade. During those years Americans watched the brutal conflict raging close to their shores, and in at least one instance our government cautiously declined an excuse for intervention.

Much had changed when the rebels renewed the conflict in 1895. The second Cuban revolution was a shocker. The rebels deliberately laid waste the island, burning crops in order to push out their rulers and, by damaging American interests, to force the United States to intervene. The Spanish, under a new commander, Valeriano Weyler, adopted a policy of herding the population into camps to separate them from the rebels. In a world not yet accustomed to concentration camps, the results—about two hundred thousand dead of starvation and epidemic—horrified millions.

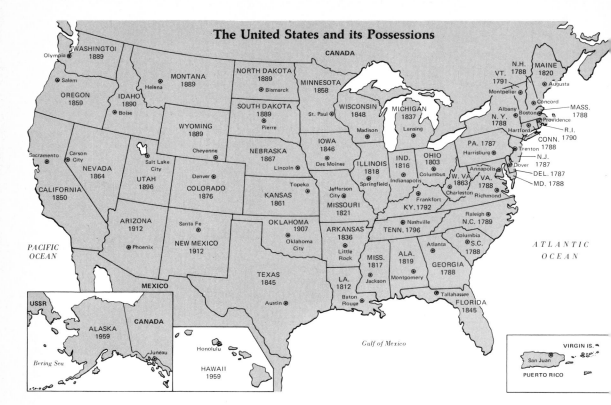

The United States and its Possessions

WASHINGTON 1889 · Olympia · Salem

OREGON 1859

MONTANA 1889 · Helena

IDAHO 1890 · Boise

NORTH DAKOTA 1889 · Bismarck

MINNESOTA 1858 · St. Paul

CANADA

WISCONSIN 1848 · Madison

MICHIGAN 1837 · Lansing

N.H. 1788 · Concord

VT. 1791 · Montpelier

MAINE 1820 · Augusta

MASS. 1788

R.I. · Providence

N.Y. 1788 · Albany · Boston

CONN. 1790 · Hartford

SOUTH DAKOTA 1889 · Pierre

WYOMING 1889 · Cheyenne

NEBRASKA 1867 · Lincoln

IOWA 1846 · Des Moines

ILLINOIS 1818 · Springfield

IND. 1816 · Indianapolis

OHIO 1803 · Columbus

PA. 1787 · Harrisburg

N.J. 1787 · Trenton · Dover

DEL. 1787 · MD. 1788

Sacramento · Carson City

NEVADA 1864

Salt Lake City

UTAH 1896

COLORADO 1876 · Denver

KANSAS 1861 · Topeka

MISSOURI 1821 · Jefferson City

KY. 1792 · Frankfort

W. VA. 1863 · Charleston

VA. 1788 · Richmond

N.C. 1789 · Raleigh

CALIFORNIA 1850

ARIZONA 1912 · Phoenix

NEW MEXICO 1912 · Santa Fe

OKLAHOMA 1907 · Oklahoma City

ARKANSAS 1836 · Little Rock

TENN. 1796 · Nashville

Atlanta

S.C. 1788 · Columbia

PACIFIC OCEAN

TEXAS 1845 · Austin

LA. 1812 · Baton Rouge

MISS. 1817 · Jackson

ALA. 1819 · Montgomery

GEORGIA 1788

ATLANTIC OCEAN

MEXICO

Gulf of Mexico

FLORIDA 1845 · Tallahassee

USSR

ALASKA 1959 · Juneau

CANADA

Bering Sea

Honolulu

HAWAII 1959

VIRGIN IS.

San Juan

PUERTO RICO

THE YELLOW PRESS

A new journalism spread word of these atrocities throughout the country. Two rival New York papers, Joseph Pulitzer's *World* and William Randolph Hearst's *Journal,* made dashing reporters and sensational articles a national craze. When news was lacking, they were not above creating it. Spanish policy was just made for these "yellow press" tactics: heart-rending scenes for reporters to present, shocking sights for artists to capture, outrages for editors to exaggerate. Spanish soldiers got the full treatment: they were murderers, torturers, sex fiends. Expansionist-minded political leaders, anti-Catholic clergymen, and Cuban propagandists vouched for the truth of these stories. The public, which had already demonstrated its jingoistic mood in the Venezuela incident, absorbed these stories for three years with ever-rising demands that something be done.

STEPS TOWARD WAR

McKinley, who genuinely sympathized with Cuba's agony, was scarcely the man to resist these pressures. A popular joke went: "Why is McKinley's mind like a bed?" "Because it has to be made up for him every time he wants to use it." Still, businessmen, just recovering from their own agony

428

during the long depression, objected to fresh upsets that might damage the economy, and many leaders of opinion repeated the traditional arguments against entanglement. McKinley moved cautiously. A strong but carefully worded protest brought a softening of Spanish policy, and with the rebels weakening during 1897, chances of war diminished.

Then two dramatic events in February 1898 shoved Americans toward conflict. One was the de Lôme letter—the private thoughts of Dupuy de Lôme, Spanish minister in Washington, written to a friend, stolen, and purchased by William Randolph Hearst. In this note, the minister had contemptuously expressed the current opinion of McKinley: that he was "weak and a bidder for the admiration of the crowd." De Lôme resigned as soon as the letter appeared, but the American public was furious and the wavering McKinley edged one step closer to war.

Destruction of the U.S. Battleship Maine.
Culver Pictures

$50,000 REWARD.—WHO DESTROYED THE MAINE?—$50,000 REWARD.

The Journal will give $50,000 for information, furnished to it exclusively, that will convict the person or persons who sank the Maine.

EDITION FOR GREATER NEW YORK

NEW YORK JOURNAL
AND ADVERTISER.

The Journal will give $50,000 for information, furnished to it exclusively, that will convict the person or persons who sank the Maine.

NO. 5,572.   Copyright, 1898, by W. R. Hearst—NEW YORK, THURSDAY, FEBRUARY 17, 1898.—16 PAGES.   PRICE ONE CENT in Greater New York. Elsewhere TWO CENTS

DESTRUCTION OF THE WAR SHIP MAINE WAS THE WORK OF AN ENEMY.

$50,000!

$50,000 REWARD!
For the Detection of the Perpetrator of the Maine Outrage!

The New York Journal hereby offers a reward of $50,000 CASH for information, FURNISHED TO IT EXCLUSIVELY, which shall lead to the detection and conviction of the person, persons or government criminally responsible for the explosion which resulted in the destruction at Havana, of the United States war ship Maine and the loss of 258 lives of American sailors.

The $50,000 CASH offered for the above information is on deposit with Wells, Fargo & Co.

No one is barred, be he the humble but misguided seaman acting as a spy, or the attache of a government secret service, plotting, by any devilish means, to revenge fancied insults or cripple menacing countries.

This offer has been cabled to Europe and will be made public in every capital of the Continent and in London this morning.

The Journal believes that any man who can be bought to commit murder can also be bought to betray his comrades. FOR THE PERPETRATOR OF THIS OUTRAGE HAD ACCOMPLICES.

W. R. HEARST.

Assistant Secretary Roosevelt Convinced the Explosion of the War Ship Was Not an Accident.

The Journal Offers $50,000 Reward for the Conviction of the Criminals Who Sent 258 American Sailors to Their Death. Naval Officers Unanimous That the Ship Was Destroyed on Purpose.

$50,000!

$50,000 REWARD!
For the Detection of the Perpetrator of the Maine Outrage!

The New York Journal hereby offers a reward of $50,000 CASH for information, FURNISHED TO IT EXCLUSIVELY, which shall lead to the detection and conviction of the person, persons or government criminally responsible for the explosion which resulted in the destruction at Havana, of the United States war ship Maine and the loss of 258 lives of American sailors.

The $50,000 CASH offered for the above information is on deposit with Wells, Fargo & Co.

No one is barred, be he the humble but misguided seaman, acting not a few miserable dollars by acting as a spy or the attache of a government secret service, plotting by any devilish means, to revenge fancied insults or cripple menacing countries.

This offer has been cabled to Europe and will be made public in every capital of the Continent and in London this morning.

The Journal believes that any man who can be bought to commit murder can also be bought to betray his comrades. FOR THE PERPETRATOR OF THIS OUTRAGE HAD ACCOMPLICES.

W. R. HEARST.

POWDER MAGAZINE

NAVAL OFFICERS THINK THE MAINE WAS DESTROYED BY A SPANISH MINE.

George Eugene Bryson, the Journal's special correspondent at Havana, cables, that it is the secret opinion of many Spaniards in the Cuban capital that the Maine was destroyed and 258 of her men killed by means of a submarine mine, or fixed torpedo. This is the opinion of several American naval authorities. The Spaniards, it is believed, arranged to have the Maine anchored over one of the harbor mines. Wires connected the mine with a powder magazine, and it is thought the explosion was caused by sending an electric current through the wire. If this can be proven, the brutal nature of the Spaniards will be shown by the fact that they waited to spring the mine until after all the men had retired for the night. The Maltese cross in the picture shows where the mine may have been fired.

Hidden Mine or a Sunken Torpedo Believed to Have Been the Weapon Used Against the American Man-of-War---Officers and Men Tell Thrilling Stories of Being Blown Into the Air Amid a Mass of Shattered Steel and Exploding Shells---Survivors Brought to Key West Scout the Idea of Accident---Spanish Officials Protest Too Much---Our Cabinet Orders a Searching Inquiry---Journal Sends Divers to Havana to Report Upon the Condition of the Wreck.
Was the Vessel Anchored Over a Mine?

BY CAPTAIN E. L. ZALINSKI, U. S. A.

(Captain Zalinski is the inventor of the famous dynamite gun, which would be the principal factor in our coast defence in case of war.)

Assistant Secretary of the Navy Theodore Roosevelt says he is convinced that the destruction of the Maine in Havana Harbor was not an accident. The Journal offers a reward of $50,000 for exclusive evidence that will convict the person, persons or Government criminally responsible for the destruction of the American battle ship and the death of 258 of its crew.

The suspicion that the Maine was deliberately blown up grows stronger every hour. Not a single fact to the contrary has been produced.

Captain Sigsbee, of the Maine, and Consul-General Lee both urge that public opinion be suspended until they have completed their investigation.

They are taking the course of tactful men who are convinced that there has been treachery.

Washington reports very late that Captain Sigsbee had feared some such event as a hidden mine. The English cipher code was used all day yesterday by the naval officers in cabling instead of the usual American code.

William Randolph Hearst reports the calamity in his New York Journal, February 17, 1898

In the midst of this furor, the American battleship *Maine*, sent to Havana to protect American lives and property, exploded in Havana harbor, killing 264 men on board. The newspapers instantly blamed Spain: "Remember the *Maine!* To hell with Spain!" became the cry. Actually only the Cuban rebels stood to gain from the atrocity, but no proof has ever come to light about who planted the mine that exploded the ship's power magazines.

Hopes for peace sank with the *Maine*. Still, American policymakers managed to pave the road to war with blunders. The administration made a set of demands—an armistice, American mediation, and an immediate end to the concentration camps. Spain agreed. In fact, it agreed to everything but Cuban independence. McKinley ended up in the ridiculous position of requesting a declaration of war against Spain in the same message in which he informed Congress that the enemy had capitulated to every American demand. The president had not, in fact, made the needs of the moment sufficiently clear: without independence, the Cubans would not cease fighting, nor would the American jingos be satisfied. McKinley could control neither the rebels nor his own Congress. The war resolution contained the Teller Amendment, promising "to leave the government and control of the Island to its people." The nation had pledged a war against the Spanish Empire, not an adventure in American imperialism.

WAR IN THE PHILIPPINES

The conflict, fortunately for the United States which had a modern fleet but a poorly equipped army, was fought largely at sea. Assistant Secretary of the Navy Theodore Roosevelt had already sent a secret order to Commodore George Dewey, commander of the Asiatic Squadron, to prepare an attack on the Spanish fleet at Manila in the Philippines. Once word of the declaration reached the Orient, Dewey steamed toward Manila. On May 1 his modern fleet sailed against the decrepit Spanish ships under Admiral Montojo. Dewey made the remark "You may fire when ready, Gridley" that so entranced his compatriots; and seven hours later the Spanish fleet was no more. Not a single American died in the battle. Dewey asked for troops, and on August 13 a combined force of Americans and Philippine nationalists under the leadership of Emilio Aguinaldo captured Manila. America, fighting for Cuban freedom, had gained a Pacific empire, one they would soon regret having.

WAR IN CUBA

In Cuba the end came more quickly. The Atlantic Squadron blockoded the island, holding the Spanish fleet in Santiago harbor. A ragtag American army of a few regulars and many thousand volunteers, with few supplies and itchy woolen uniforms for the tropical heat, gathered at Tampa, Florida. Seventeen thousand men, including Lieutenant Colonel Theodore Roosevelt and his informal regiment of "Rough Riders," invaded Cuba in June. On July 1, with Roosevelt's men and some black troops leading the way, the army stormed up San Juan Hill, making Teddy a national hero and persuading the Spanish that Santiago was lost. This was an error, since the army, Rough Riders and all, was too ridden with dysentery to advance, and the navy (remembering the *Maine*) feared to engage the enemy in the heavily mined harbor. Nevertheless, the brave Spanish Admiral Pascual Cervera, acting on orders, sailed his antique fleet out of the harbor to the complete destruction he anticipated. With an American army occupying Puerto Rico and the Spanish army trapped without transport, the Spanish commander surrendered on July 16. Spain sued for peace and the armistice took effect on August 12. John Hay, soon to be secretary of state, voiced the American mood when he remarked that it had been a "splendid little war."

War in the Philippines.
The World, *May 8, 1898*

The World's Greatest Circulation Record!
1,011,068
PER WEEK-DAY APRIL AVERAGE.
GAIN in One Year · · · 338,748

The World.

" *Circulation Books Open to All.*"

The World's Greatest Circulation Record!
1,011,068
PER WEEK-DAY APRIL AVERAGE.
GAIN in Three Years · · · 461,205

VOL. XXXVIII. NO. 13,410.   PRICE **FIVE** CENTS.   NEW YORK, SUNDAY, MAY 8, 1898.   (Copyright, 1898, by the Press Publishing Co., New York World.)   PRICE **FIVE** CENTS.

DEWEY'S MARVELLOUS NAVAL ACHIEVEMENT----
Spanish killed and disabled, 618—one-third their fighting force. Americans killed, none.

American Flag now flying over Spain's two greatest forts in the Philippines.

THE WORLD'S SPLENDID NEWS VICTORY.

Eleven Spanish Ships Destroyed, 300 Spaniards Killed Outright; No American Ships Disabled, No American Sailors Killed; Only Six Injured---Capt. Mahan, the Pre-Eminent Strategist, to The World: "Commodore Dewey Has Fought the Greatest Naval Battle on Record"---All Spanish Forts Destroyed; Dewey Now Has Manila at His Mercy.

AMERICAN SHIPS, CONSTANTLY IN MOTION, FOUGHT AT RANGE OF ABOUT ONE MILE; THE SPANISH TORPEDO BOATS WERE SUNK AS THEY ADVANCED TO STRIKE.

By The World's War Correspondent, E. W. Harden, who was on the United States Gunboat McCulloch throughout the Battle.

(*Copyright, 1898, by the Press Publishing Company, New York.*)   (*Special Cable Despatch to The World.*)

HONG KONG, May 7.—At daybreak on Sunday morning, May 1, Commodore Dewey's Asiatic squadron, six fighting ships, the Olympia, Baltimore, Boston, Concord, Raleigh and Petrel, annihilated the Spanish fleet of the Philippines.

Dewey captured the naval arsenal and the forts at Cavite, Manila Bay.

ELEVEN SPANISH WARSHIPS DESTROYED.

Dewey's fleet sunk seven cruisers, four gunboats and two transports, and captured one transport, several tugs and a small steamer.   Among the cruisers and gunboats sunk were the flagship Reina Maria Cristina, Castilla, Velasco, Don Juan de Austria, the Isla de Cuba, General Lezo, Marquez del Duero, Mindanao and Ulloa.

The Spaniards lost three hundred killed.   Four hundred of them were wounded.

The Governor-General of the Philippines officially reported that the Spanish squadron lost in killed and disabled six hundred and eighteen—about one-third of their fighting force.

Not one American was killed, although the battle was hard fought and lasted three and a half hours.

The American gunners and American guns were infinitely better than the Spanish.

The war had been quick and relatively painless. Fewer than five hundred Americans died in combat, and the war did not damage the economy as businessmen had feared. The divisions in American society, so visible in mid-decade, seemed to vanish in an orgy of nationalism. Americans fell in love with the idea of empire. Popular opinion was all in favor of holding the "Phillipines" (as Americans misspelled them at first); businessmen, changing their minds, now saw the islands as a route to increased Asian trade. Missionaries and humanitarians saw new fields for their labors.

THE ANTI-IMPERIALISTS

An influential group of citizens, however, sensed that the realities of empire might be less pleasing than the glow produced by patches of American yellow on the world map set against the English pink and the French green. These anti-imperialists were a mixed lot. Ex-Presidents Harrison and Cleveland opposed annexing overseas territory, as did William Jennings Bryan. Many prominent Democrats wanted no part of the Philippines, but neither did such respected Republicans as Speaker Reed and John Sherman. College presidents, intellectuals, writers, and reformers, as well as some labor leaders, joined the anti-imperialist crusade.

These opponents of imperialism argued that holding colonies went against the Constitution and that governing foreign territories without their consent violated American ideals. But less benevolent motives intruded as well. Southern Democrats frankly wanted no more dark-skinned Americans. Samuel Gompers, too, feared an influx of "Negritos" willing to work at low wages. Few of these anti-imperialists opposed American economic penetration abroad. They simply thought that taking colonies was the wrong way to proceed, and this argument, rejected at first, would eventually prevail.

THE PEACE TREATY

In 1898 McKinley saw that most Americans favored holding the islands. Public opinion would not tolerate returning them to Spain and feared their falling into the hands of another power. The American peace commissioners drove a hard bargain during the negotiations in Paris. They bought the Philippines for $20 million from an unwilling but helpless Spain. In addition, Spain granted Cuban independence, assumed Cuba's debt, and ceded Puerto Rico and the island of Guam in the Pacific. With the annexation of Hawaii coming in the same year, we were indeed an empire.

Still, there was the Senate, always a more difficult adversary for McKinley than the Spanish. Anticolonial feeling and Democratic manipulations almost defeated the Treaty of Paris, but McKinley found support from an unexpected quarter. Bryan, opposed to annexing the islands but thinking to make anti-imperialism his theme for 1900, did not urge his Senate followers to oppose ratification. Even so, the treaty barely won the needed two-thirds. Bryan then proceeded to obscure the issue during the campaign by polishing up the free-silver question once again. The contest did not become the referendum on empire which Bryan had promised, but his overwhelming defeat nevertheless destroyed anti-imperialism as a national issue. McKinley won a second term with the ardent imperialist and war hero Theodore Roosevelt as his vice-president.

GOVERNING AN EMPIRE

The course of empire moved smoothly for Americans everywhere but in the Philippines. In Cuba enlightened military rule stamped out yellow fever, built schools, and modernized the economy and public administration. Under limitations imposed by the Platt Amendment, which gave the United States the right to intervene militarily and a naval base at Guantanamo Bay, Cuba became quasi-independent in 1902. It would remain essentially an American satellite until 1959.

Puerto Rico accepted American rule with equanimity. In 1900 Congress by the Foraker Act established a civil government, denied Puerto Ricans American citizenship (they finally got it in 1917), and fixed some tariffs on their exports to the mainland. A challenge to the tariff provisions on the grounds that Puerto Rico was part of the United States lost in the Supreme Court. This case, *Downes* v. *Bidwell* (1901), was one of the so-called Insular Cases in which the Court, through the most involuted logic, ruled that the Constitution followed the flag only as closely as Congress allowed. Within rather broad limits, we could do what we would with the new possessions.

THE PHILIPPINE INSURRECTION

The Philippines, source of the most serious domestic arguments, also proved the most difficult area to govern. Until the Spanish defeat, American commanders in the area had encouraged the independence movement under Aguinaldo. When the Filipinos realized that they were changing masters, not gaining independence, large-scale revolt broke out, giving Americans their first taste of putting down a nationalist rebellion. This war was neither little nor splendid. It took three years and forty-three hundred American lives; it required, ironically, American use of concentration camps—better equipped versions of what we had condemned in Cuba—and was marked by atrocities on both sides. As the war petered out, a commission headed by William Howard Taft, then an Ohio judge, worked successfully to improve relations with the Filipinos. Taft, showing both genuine sympathy and delicate tact, succeeded in getting natives to join in a new political beginning. Military rule gave way in 1901 to a civilian government with Taft as appointed governor.

THE OPEN DOOR

The Philippines taught an important lesson. Even Theodore Roosevelt, who more than any other man had been responsible for the events leading to our acquisition of this Pacific archipelago, soon wanted to drop the burden of rule. Americans began to see the merits of an informal empire, thinking to gain the profits and the strategic values of other lands without the responsibilities of owning and running them. This new, noncolonial imperialism achieved its best statement and first important triumph in the "Open Door" notes which Secretary of State John Hay sent to the major powers in 1899 and 1900.

The United States, suddenly a Pacific power, faced an immediate need for a policy in the area. Like the Spanish Empire, China had collapsed before a new and aggressive naval power during the brief Sino-Japanese war of 1894–95. European powers, fearing that Japan would acquire all China's commerce, rushed forward to carve out their own pieces of the tottering empire. This left Secretary Hay in a dilemma. Anti-imperialist sentiment at home made it impossible for America to join the feast or even to combine with a willing Great Britain to put a stop to it. But American businessmen demanded the State Department do something to prevent their being shut out of a potentially lucrative market.

Hay found the answer in a clever bit of diplomacy. He sent a circular letter to all the powers asking them to respect the trading rights of others and not to impose discriminatory duties within their spheres of influence, but rather to allow Chinese officials to continue collecting the Chinese tariffs. This was something like an invitation not to sin: too vigorous an assent suggested that one had erred and was mending his ways, but to reject the note was a confession of guilt. Consequently, most of the replies were ambiguous. Nevertheless, Hay announced in 1900 that the powers had all "accepted" his proposals. Again, who could contradict him? Hay had bought diplomatic advantage on the cheap: Japan, Russia, France, Germany, and Great Britain did not carve up all China only because they feared falling into war with each other in the process. Meanwhile, Hay took credit for saving China. A nationalist uprising, the "Boxer Rebellion" which broke out in China the next year, gave Hay the chance to reinforce this impression. Worried that the occurrence might serve as an excuse for further dismembering China, he issued another round of notes which went even a step further in their promise to maintain Chinese sovereignty.

The "Open Door" notes were a sensation in the United States. Henry Adams wrote that "Hay put Europe aside and set the Washington Government at the head of civilization." This was an exaggeration. We were not a power in Asia, and the China market remained more a mirage than an economic reality. The door to China had opened but a crack.

The "Open Door" notes did, however, throw wide the gates for an American president to make his entrance onto the world stage unhampered by arguments over imperialism. The notes provided a legal and moral formula for asserting American interests in the absence of military force. Hay knew that no nation was prepared to upset the balance of force in China. When the day came that some power—Japan, for example—felt strong enough to do so, then the United States would have to apply a heavy shoulder to keep that door open. And no one, not even Hay's bellicose friend Theodore Roosevelt, believed that the American public was ready for that. Hay had made us an Asian interest without being an Asian power. The dangers and confusions inherent in this policy reverberated through the twentieth century and are not yet stilled.

Things to think about: 1890–1900

Why did the public find the currency question so exciting? On the political background of the issue see Irwin Unger, *The Greenback Era* (1964), Walter T. K. Nugent, *Money and American Society* (1968), and Allen Weinstein, *Prelude To Populism* (1970). For the economic backgrounds see Milton Friedman and Anna J. Schwartz, *A Monetary History of the United States* (1970). The flavor of debate is best caught in William H. Harvey, *Coin's Financial School* (1895), available in modern editions.

What place did populism have in the American reform tradition? John D. Hicks, *The Populist Revolt* (1931), is still the best general account. Richard Hofstadter, *The Age of Reform* (1955), poses important questions about populism. Norman Pollack, *The Populist Response to Industrial America* (1962), Walter Nugent, *The Tolerant Populists* (1963), and C. Vann Woodward, "The Populist Heritage and the Intellectual," *American Scholar* 59 (1959): 55–72 (frequently reprinted), try to answer Hofstadter's questions. Michael Schwartz, *Radical Protest and Social Structure: The Southern Farmers Alliance and Cotton Tenancy, 1880–1890* (1976), provides essential background for southern populism.

Were Grover Cleveland's actions in his second term an indication of courage, cunning, or stupidity? Allan Nevins, *Grover Cleveland* (1932), is a sympathetic account. Horace S.

Merrill, *Bourbon Leader: Grover Cleveland* (1957), votes against Cleveland as does J. Rogers Hollingsworth, *The Whirligig of Politics* (1963). Geoffrey Blodgett, *The Gentle Reformers* (1966), portrays with great insight one group of Cleveland's supporters. Francis B. Simkin, *Pitchfork Ben Tillman* (1944), describes one of Cleveland's enemies.

Why after a generation of "dead center" politics did the Republicans emerge as the dominant party in 1894? Three important studies examine in detail voting patterns in the nineties: Paul Kleppner, *The Cross of Culture* (1970), Richard Jensen, *The Winning of the Midwest* (1971), and Samuel T. McSeveney, *The Politics of Depression* (1972). Elmer E. Schattschneider, *The Semi-Sovereign People* (1960), offers a suggestive approach to the meaning of these changes.

What was at issue in the "Battle of the Standards" in 1896? Robert Durden, *The Climax of Populism* (1965), analyzes the Populists' stake. Paul W. Glad, *McKinley, Bryan, and the People* (1964), is a graceful and perceptive account of the election. Stanley L. Jones, *The Presidential Election of 1896* (1964), is thorough. For pictures of the major figures, see Paolo E. Coletta, *William Jennings Bryan* (3 vols., 1964-69)—everything you always wanted to know about Bryan; H. Wayne Morgan, *William McKinley and His America* (1963)—a sympathetic biography; C. Vann Woodward, *Tom Watson; Agrarian Rebel* (1938)—brilliant portrait of an important southern Populist.

How did Americans react to the depression of the 1890s? Donald L. McMurry, *Coxey's Army* (1930), is the standard work on that episode. Almont Lindsey, *The Pullman Strike* (1942), and Stanley Buder, *Pullman: An Experiment in Industrial Order* (1967), cover the era's greatest upheaval. Charles Hoffman, "The Depression of the Nineties," *Journal of Economic History* 16 (1956): 137-64, and Samuel Rezneck, "Unemployment, Unrest, Relief . . . during the Depression of 1893-1897," *Journal of Political Economy* 61 (1953): 324-45, give some measure of the depression's impact. John Higham, *Strangers in the Land: Patterns of American Nativism, 1860-1925* (1955), and Donald E. Kinzer, *An Episode in Anti-Catholicism* (1964), show some of the less savory reactions. Arnold M. Paul, *Conservative Crisis and the Rule of Law* (1960), superbly analyzes the courts' reactions to the tensions of the nineties. For the Bradley Martin Ball and other pleasures of the "gay nineties" read Dixon Wecter's entertaining work, *The Saga of American Society* (1937), and John Higham, "The Reorientation of American Culture in the 1890's," in *Writing American History* (1970).

Why did the United States build an overseas empire at the end of the nineteenth century? David M. Pletcher, *The Awkward Years* (1962), deals with the early eighties. Walter LaFeber presents a tightly reasoned argument for the economic basis of expansion in *The New Empire* (1963); Ernest R. May, *American Imperialism: A Speculative Essay* (1968), is suggestive. William A. Williams, *The Tragedy of American Diplomacy* (1959), and George Kennan, *American Diplomacy, 1900-1950* (1951),

sharply define two approaches to American foreign policy that have divided diplomatic historians.

Why did the United States go to war with Spain over Cuba? Richard Hofstadter, "Manifest Destiny and the Philippines," in *America in Crisis*, edited by Daniel Aaron (1952), offers an explanation applying social psychology. H. Wayne Morgan, *America's Road to Empire* (1965), Ernest R. May, *Imperial Democracy* (1961), and Philip S. Foner, *The Spanish-Cuban-American War* (1972), examine the Cuban crisis. Joseph E. Wisan, *The Cuban Crisis as Reflected in the New York Press* (1934), argues the importance of "yellow journalism." On the war itself see Frank Friedel, *The Splendid Little War* (1958).

Why did the United States keep the Philippines? Leon Wolff, *Little Brown Brother* (1961), describes the Philippine insurrection. Robert L. Beisner, *Twelve Against Empire* (1968), is a well-written account of a number of leading opponents of imperialism. Williams, cited above, is shrewd on the meaning of the argument over imperialism. On the rest of the American Empire see David F. Healy, *The United States in Cuba, 1898-1902* (1963), Merz Tate, *The United States and the Hawaiian Kingdom* (1965), and Edward Berbusse, *The United States in Puerto Rico, 1898-1900* (1966).

Which was the Open Door policy: Realistic economic diplomacy or pointless idealism? George Kennan's and W. A. Williams's works cited above argue the issues vigorously. See also Thomas J. McCormick, *China Market* (1967), A. Whitney Griswold, *The Far Eastern Policy of the United States* (1938), and Tyler Dennet, *John Hay* (1933).

10

PROGRESSIVE AMERICA
1900-1918

JANE ADDAMS OF THE NINETEENTH WARD

When twenty-nine-year-old Jane Addams opened Hull House on the corner of Polk and Halsted Streets in Chicago, this settlement house joined the Nineteenth Ward's other institutions—nine churches and two hundred and fifty saloons—in ministering to the needs of a densely packed neighborhood of Italian, German, Jewish, Bohemian, and French-Canadian immigrants. Jane Addams vividly recorded the scene that greeted her in 1889:

> The streets are inexpressibly dirty, the number of schools inadequate, sanitary legislation unenforced, the street lighting bad, the paving miserable and altogether lacking in the alleys and smaller streets, and the stables foul beyond description. . . . Rear tenements flourish; many houses have no water supply save the faucet in the back yard.

At Hull House she provided a social and cultural center for the urban poor, offering them friendship when they wanted it and charity when they needed it, and forcing an unwilling city to provide them with so-

438

cial services such as garbage collection, improved schools, and playgrounds.

Her great competitor in service to the ward was one of the saloonkeepers, Johnny Powers, the district's alderman. On election day he drove about tossing nickels to the children and cigars to the men. Whenever one of his constituents died, Johnny was there with flowers and baskets of food—kosher food if the family was Jewish. They called him "The Chief Mourner." And, by Addams's own testimony, "one out of five voters in the Nineteenth Ward held a job dependent on the good will of the alderman," working for the city or for the telephone or streetcar companies that purchased valuable franchises from Powers and his friends. The upright Jane Addams and the thoroughly corrupt Johnny Powers were political enemies, and Powers won all the elections in the ward. Yet the future was on Addams's side. The private charities of Hull House would become the municipal social services of the future, and these welfare services would put men like Johnny largely out of business.

How did the well-bred daughter of a state legislator from a neat village in northern Illinois find herself among the poor of the Nineteenth Ward? Jane Addams inherited a tradition of concern for the downtrodden. Her father, a Quaker, an abolitionist, and a Republican legislator who exchanged letters with Abraham Lincoln, instilled in her a sense of mission and a stern morality. At college in the 1870s she defended "the woman's cause" and showed a gift for public speaking. Representing her school in a statewide oratorical contest, she placed fifth out of ten in a fierce competition: William Jennings Bryan only finished second!

After college, Jane Addams attempted to go to medical school, but her health, never too strong, prevented her. She had a slight curvature of the spine from birth which necessitated four major operations during her lifetime and persuaded her that marriage was not a possibility. Now she was face to face with the problem of finding what she should do in life. For eight years she struggled with "the snare of preparation"—studying, writing, traveling, worrying, and feeling hemmed in by the restrictions of being a "lady." Finally in 1888 she found her answer at Toynbee Hall, London. Inspired by this pioneer social settlement, she and a friend, Ellen Gates Starr, bravely set forth on a new adventure at Hull House, understanding only their own need to find useful work. But in their big house amid all the little and miserable hovels, they could learn as well the needs of a city.

Hull House was as much an intellectual as a social center. Writers like John Dewey, Henry Demarest Lloyd, and W. E. B. Du Bois came to lecture and argue. Most important of all, Miss Addams and her co-workers studied their own city, writing a steady stream of books and papers mapping the human geography of this portion of urban America. A generation of pioneers in social work and dozens of vital precedents for social services emerged from over forty years of work.

From 1915 to the end of her life in 1935, Jane Addams added to her life's mission an ardent opposition to war. She helped found a number of women's groups opposing war, some of which are still active. During and immediately after World War I, she took part in efforts to feed "enemy women and children" and was bitterly attacked for it. The Daughters of the American Revolution expelled her for refusing to support the war effort. But years later, in 1931, she was corecipient of the Nobel Peace Prize. As always Jane Addams, the noblest progressive of them all, flourished in unpopular causes.

Mrs. Blaney, Mrs. Wilmarth, and Miss Addams
Culver Pictures

1901	Assassination of McKinley (September 6); Theodore Roosevelt becomes president
1902	Newlands Reclamation Act
	Anthracite Coal Strike
1903	Departments of Commerce and Labor established; Elkins Antirebate Act
1904	Roosevelt Corollary to Monroe Doctrine
	Roosevelt reelected president, defeating Alton B. Parker
1905	Portsmouth Peace Conference
1906	Hepburn Act
	Pure Food and Drug Act
	Meat Inspection Act
1907	Gentlemen's Agreement with Japan
1908	White House Conservation Conference
	Muller v. Oregon
	William Howard Taft (Republican) elected president, defeating Bryan
1910	Mann-Elkins Act
1912	Socialists nominate Eugene Debs for president; progressives nominate Theodore Roosevelt on Bull-Moose ticket
	Woodrow Wilson (Democrat) elected president, defeating Taft, Roosevelt, and Debs
1913	Sixteenth Amendment, the income tax
	Seventeenth Amendment, popular election of United States senators
	Federal Reserve Act
	New York Armory art show
1914	Federal Trade Commission Act
	Clayton Antitrust Act
1915	Sinking of the Lusitania, May 7
1916	Adamson Act
	Federal Farm Loan Act
	Wilson reelected president; defeats Charles Evans Hughes
1917	United States enters World War I, April 6
	Espionage Act
1918	Republicans gain control of Congress, November 5
	Armistice Day, November 11

The first years of the twentieth century, the "progressive era," recall Teddy Roosevelt and Woodrow Wilson, "trustbusting" and campaigns against corrupt bosses and tainted beef, horseless carriages, Greenwich Village, and the first World Series. Its flavor of high moralism and exuberance comes from a richly various group of reformers. They sought many of the goals that have ever since been identified with reform in this century: regulation of large corporations, rooting out corruption in government, alleviating urban poverty, improving labor conditions, and eliminating waste and inefficiency in the use of natural resources. Many also spearheaded "reform" movements which would seem very unprogressive today: immigrant restriction, racial segregation, and prohibition were all justified as measures to raise moral tone and eliminate political corruption. Progressives injected a special urgency into political and intellectual life that marked off their times from the less vivid age of dead-center politics that preceded them.

A NEW GENERATION

The sharp change in public mood came from a new generation moving onto the national scene. Typically, progressives were young, native-born, Protestant, and college-educated, although as the movement advanced, more Americans of immigrant stock influenced progressivism. Most were small businessmen or members of a profession, people with influence in the local community. Many had toyed with advanced ideas and new forms of political action in the late eighties and early nineties. They read Edward Bellamy and Henry George, adopted the message of the social gospel, and engaged in the eternal battle against municipal corruption. But the anxieties of the mid-nineties had driven most into firm support of McKinley against Bryan's apparently dangerous ideas.

These young reformers were not radicals but fiercely patriotic Americans who believed almost literally in the ideals learned in church, in college, in political meetings. But these well-established men and women had seen enough to realize the gap between the practices of American industrial life and the principles of morality, honesty, and open opportunity they had been taught. They also saw the comfortable little communities of their childhood, identified with every social virtue, losing their influence and independence to an increasingly national, industrial, and urban-based economic system. Yet they did not reject this new America. The more sophisticated progressives saw in the emerging social sciences and the new social and industrial organizations possible ways to marry the new technology to old moral standards. Few, however, saw any mass audience for reform until the turn of the century, when new conditions suddenly offered them an opportunity.

PROSPERITY AND A NEW
SOCIAL CLASS

McKinley, billed in 1896 as the "advance agent of prosperity," proved as good as his slogan. Returning affluence was an indispensible ingredient in progressivism, a comfortable cushion against the shock of new ideas and social experiments. It made people more tolerant and less defensive. They no longer grasped at the familiar to demonstrate their belief in the soundness of American institutions. Now they possessed the confidence to push toward careful changes. At last they felt ready to take control of the onrushing industrialism of the age.

Inflation, an untoward product of prosperity, helped progressives find an audience. People accustomed to a lifetime of sinking prices reacted with suspicion to the steady inflation which began late in the nineties and continued throughout the progressive era. Today's economists blame that inflation on fresh gold supplies and economic expansion, but contemporaries feared that trusts and labor organizations were ganging up on a helpless and disorganized public to raise prices. This conception of the public as "consumers" was new to the age. It reflected both the new stress in the economy on consumer goods—such as the new automobiles—and the rise of a new social group, the white-collar class of clerks, teachers, salespeople, technicians, and the like. An insignificant fraction of the population a generation before, these six million people, by the progressive era, formed about two-thirds of the urban middle class. Remaining close to their rural and small-town roots, they could still find the city's ways shocking. They lacked any economic organization and had to turn directly to politics for expression of their needs. With no traditional place in the political order, they naturally looked with some favor on insurgents. While few themselves became important in politics, they were the progressives' steady voting public.

A DISRUPTED SOCIETY

Americans saw a society that had always been open and individualistic turning into a world of large organizations. Members of some professions, even when they prospered, began to feel less important in the world or less independent in their lives. Clergymen saw their rich parishioners rise to dominance over them not just economically, but even as social and moral arbiters. Lawyers increasingly sold their services to corporations; earning more, they enjoyed less freedom and felt less important. Small businessmen who once lorded it over their suppliers now purchased their goods from the "barbed wire trust" or the "flour trust" at prices set in some big-city headquarters. If the goods came high, these merchants denounced "monopoly

Boys with high wheel bicycles.
Minnesota Historical Society

prices"; even if the price was attractive they felt a little smaller than before. They delighted when reformers promised to cut the trusts down to size.

Nor were men and women on the rise content to leave things as they were. College professors, for example, were growing in professional standing and income throughout the period, but as members of increasingly larger institutions, many dominated by wealthy benefactors, they too were ready to do battle. And besides, they dealt in ideas: if they could transform their new reform ideas into action, their status in society would rise with the reform movement. Men and women in the new urban professions such as social work, public administration, and city planning felt the same way. For them reform meant replacing amateur direction (or none at all) with their own expertise: they were reformers by profession.

445

24 GENUINE COLUMBIA P RECORDS AND THE OXFORD JR. TALKING MACHINE ALL COMPLETE

YOUR OWN SELECTION OF SUBJECTS

$8.75

THE NEW OXFORD JR. TALKING MACHINE IS A STRICTLY HIGH CLASS TALKING MACHINE FOR REPRODUCING STANDARD SIZE WAX CYLINDER RECORDS. IT IS A THOROUGHLY WELL MADE MACHINE AND NOT TO BE COMPARED IN ANY WAY WITH THE CHEAP MACHINES THAT HAVE BEEN SO EXTENSIVELY ADVERTISED RECENTLY.

IT IS A HIGH CLASS MACHINE, MADE IN AMERICA, made by expert and experienced workmen in one of the largest and most successful talking machine factories in the world. It is made of good materials throughout, fitted with a high class spring motor, with machine cut gears, everything about it strong and substantial. It is made with patent feed device which holds the reproducer firmly in place as it travels along over the surface of the record. There are cheap talking machines made without feed device, and with such machines the reproducer slips and slides off the surface of the record, but this trouble is entirely prevented in the Oxford Jr. Talking Machine, as the reproducer is held firmly and guided in its course over the surface of the record by the patent feed device, exactly the same as the highest priced machines. This machine is made with heavy, solid and substantial iron base, finished in black enamel, with gold stripe decorations. It is made with standard size tapered mandrel, and will use any standard size of wax cylinder record, Columbia, Edison or any other standard make.

THE REPRODUCTION of the human voice or of instrumental music, as rendered by the Oxford Jr. Talking Machine, is just exactly as good as with machines costing ten and fifteen times the price which we ask for this machine. It is made with a high grade, aluminum style D I reproducer, with mica diaphragm and Brazilian sapphire reproducing point. It is equipped with black and gold horn with large extra wide bell, the body of the horn made of the best sheet steel, with fine black enamel finish; the bell made of solid brass, highly polished, giving the machine a most handsome and ornamental appearance. The tone qualities of this large black and gold horn are unexcelled, adding greatly to the volume of sound and naturalness and sweetness of tone.

THE OXFORD JR. TALKING MACHINE is not a toy. It is a high class machine, a machine that cannot be purchased in the ordinary market at less than double our price. Made of good materials all the way through, strong and substantial, easy to operate, made with fine clock work motor, automatic feed device and extra large black and gold horn.

FIFTY THOUSAND RECORDS PER MONTH. Under our new contracts with the largest manufacturer of records in the world they are to furnish us for these outfits 50,000 high class standard size wax cylinder records per month, genuine Columbia P Records, the exact same records that have for years been sold at 50 cents, and today cannot be purchased in any other market for less than 25 cents each. By contracting for this enormous quantity of one million records (more than fifty car loads), the largest order ever placed for talking machine records by any dealer anywhere in the world, we have succeeded in reducing the cost to us just the merest fraction over the actual cost of labor and materials, the lowest cost at which high class graphophone records have ever been purchased by any dealer, and in making up these outfits, consisting of the OXFORD JR. TALKING MACHINE AND TWENTY-FOUR OF

THESE HIGH CLASS STANDARD SIZE RECORDS AT $8.75, we are giving you the benefit of the saving which we effect by means of our tremendous purchasing power. **UNDERSTAND, OUR SPECIAL PRICE $8.75** includes the 24 Columbia P Records, the Oxford Jr. Talking Machine complete with clock work motor, style D I aluminum reproducer, large black and gold horn, an outfit that a few months ago could not have been purchased for less than $15.00.

No. 20K5010 Oxford Jr. Talking Machine and 24 Columbia P Records, complete outfit, just as illustrated and described above. Shipping weight, 20 pounds. Price..... **$8.75**

No. 20K5011 Oxford Jr. Talking Machine Outfit, consisting of Oxford Jr. machine as illustrated and described above and 48 Genuine Columbia P Records. Price...... **12.95** Shipping weight, 30 pounds. Make your selection of Records from the list on pages 199 and 200, the list of genuine Columbia P Records.

THE TYPE F H HARVARD DISC TALKING MACHINE

$15.90

The Large Flower Horn with which this machine is equipped, possesses, to an unusual degree, the magnificent acoustic or tone qualities which are peculiar to the latest type of flower horns. The unusual musical qualities of the flower horn, its ability to reproduce sound more absolutely true to the original music, is due to the peculiar curves and the extra wide flaring bell, which avoids the usual retardation of the sound waves, thereby giving a deep, clear and natural tone to every note.

THIS HORN is made with fine baked on enamel finish, ornamented with gold stripes, and besides the great improvement which it makes in the musical quality of the machine, also contributes greatly to the beautiful appearance of the outfit.

THE MELLOWNESS OF TONE AND REAL MUSICAL QUALITY of the reproduction, as rendered by the Type F H Harvard Talking Machine, is due partly to the new sound analyzing reproducer with which it is equipped and partly to the special acoustic properties of the flower horn, or rather to the combination of these two features. This reproducer is the latest product of the largest talking machine manufacturer in the world and represents the result of years of constant experiment and improvement. It is called the "sound analyzing" reproducer because of its ability to bring out every tone clearly and with the exact tone quality of the original music. It not only increases the volume of sound, but enriches the quality and reveals tones which with the earlier and less perfect types of reproducers were lost entirely. It is equipped with the automatic needle holder by which the needle is clamped into place and held securely by a spring lever; a slight pressure upon this lever instantly releases the needle, thus avoiding the use of the annoying set screw arrangement used in other reproducers.

GENERAL CONSTRUCTION. The Type F H Harvard Disc Talking Machine is made with golden oak cabinet of plain but elegant design, substantially made, all corners dovetailed and with removable top to afford access to the motor for oiling or occasional cleaning. The swinging arm and bracket, supporting the horn and reproducer, are beautifully designed and made from aluminum, highly ornamental and non-tarnishable. The turntable, of a special composition metal, is 10 inches in diameter, the cabinet measures 11¼ inches square by 5¼ inches high, the horn is 19 inches long with bell 17 inches in diameter. This machine is equipped with a powerful spring clockwork motor, made throughout from brass and the best quality of steel, all gears and pinions machine cut to insure absolutely even and smooth running qualities. Perfectly uniform speed, essential to perfect reproduction, is obtained by the improved automatic governor and worm gear, perfect control of the speed is obtained by the new tension screw speed regulator, and the motor is stopped or started simply by pressing in or pulling out a small knobbed rod.

USES ANY KIND OF DISC RECORD. This machine is adapted to any style, any size or any make of flat disc record. Just think of the great variety of selections available for use with this machine and the wonderful possibilities for entertainment which it affords.

No. 20K5048 The Type F H Harvard Disc Talking Machine, with golden oak cabinet, large flower horn, sound analyzing reproducer, exactly as illustrated and described above. Shipping weight, 35 pounds. Price.. **$15.90**

Sears, Roebuck catalog (1903).

PROGRESSIVE WOMEN

The progressive movement, like the reform movements that had dotted American life before the Civil War, offered some new opportunities for American women. Social work especially attracted daughters of the middle class seeking meaningful lives in a world outside the home. Many broke with the constricted Victorian role of household goddess and found careers in the burgeoning settlement houses or in the public schools.

Yet most of the new professional outlets for women conformed to old stereotypes of the woman's "proper" role. Women found most of their opportunities in the "angel of mercy" professions: teaching school, nursing, and social work. These were the areas supposed to require a female's tender touch. They were not the highest-paying posts in the white-collar world.

Women's political activity increased markedly. The National Federation of Women's Clubs, a preserve of genteel culture and dabbling in the arts, turned to serious political and philanthropic activity. The new president of the federation informed its members in 1904 that "Dante is dead. He has been dead for several centuries, and I think it is time we dropped the study of his *Inferno* and turned our attention to our own." The president of the National Association of Manufacturers warned businessmen to watch out what reform ideas their wives absorbed at the club meetings. Yet his worries may have been unnecessary. The clubwomen pursued stoutly middle-class reform goals, while the more radical women exhausted their energies in the fight for women's suffrage rather than in broader feminist or social crusades.

The progressive mind

A half-century of rapid industrialization and urban growth had produced a special new generation of men and women ready to grab for control of their onrushing society. Delicately poised between the private, individual virtues of an agrarian order and new demands for efficiency and collective efforts, they reflected their dual heritage in their often-conflicting ideas. They determined to uphold pure and absolute moral standards which they feared would otherwise perish on the battlefield of the economy. Yet their greater sophistication in economics, psychology, jurisprudence, and sociology was teaching them to distrust large abstractions and to devise flexible techniques that could monitor progress while insuring social justice. Similarly, they longed to keep open the hallowed avenues of individual opportunity while they recognized the need for organization in every part of the common life and were themselves prolific organizers. Caught between old dreams and new insights, these energetic men and women struggled with evangelical zeal and deep sincerity to achieve what were, in fact, conservative changes in the social order.

A NEW ENLIGHTENMENT

Few men and women active in the progressive movement were original or consistent thinkers—people in the midst of furious activity rarely are—but they gained strength and inspiration from a new "enlightenment" that, like its eighteenth-century predecessor, worshipped at the shrine of science. Men had longed dreamed of a "science of society." By the dawn of this century, thinkers in almost every field thought they saw this dream coming true. The pragmatists—Charles Sanders Peirce, William James, and John Dewey—announced an end to sterile wrangling over ultimate truths. Philosophers needed only to study the way scientists and technicians used concepts in their work. Finding truth in the laboratory, they maintained, was simply a matter of determining what an idea *did*, what difference it made, what effect it had. Physicists did not argue about what "force" really was; they simply traced its effect. The social sciences could do the same. Social engineers could empirically study how things worked—an electoral system or a court or a factory—without worrying whether they had properly defined words like *democracy* or *justice* or *equity*. Political scientists asked what interest groups wanted rather than what principles ought to govern political choices. Sociologists examined where prostitution flourished, what its social costs were, and how it could be controlled rather than simply arguing the morality of "tolerating" the social evil.

This pragmatic approach struck sympathetic chords throughout intellectual life. Only recently having achieved separate identity as academic disciplines, the new social sciences rapidly moved on to find roles in the bureaucratic organizations arising about them. Political scientists and economists at institutions like the University of Wisconsin operated as a research bureau for progressive reformers, studying railroad economics, analyzing taxation levels, investigating working conditions, and the like. Sociologists and philosophers became innovators in education and social work. John Dewey developed a laboratory school at the University of Chicago which allowed him to observe empirically what did and what did not succeed in the classroom. This stress on practical application tempered grand theorizing and introduced a refreshing empiricism which both shattered old beliefs within the learned professions and informed Americans about their country. This "revolt against formalism," as it has been called, reached everywhere. The great architectural innovators of the day, for example, liberated themselves from outmoded traditions of design, allowing the functions their buildings would serve to determine the form of their architecture. Louis Sullivan and Frank Lloyd Wright saw a lightness and simplicity in the clean lines of the new bridges and machinery that the heavy masonry edifices about them lacked. In keeping with a practical, scientific age, their work—which they identified with democratic values—replaced forbidding imitations of aristocratic rockpiles with easier, more open buildings.

A NEW LITERATURE

Literature as well felt the influence of science. Writers struggled to accommodate the new realistic mentality to their traditions of idealism and romance. Adopting "naturalistic" techniques of piling detail on detail, Frank Norris presented a vast social panorama in *The Octopus* (1901) and *The Pit* (1903), novels dealing with the excesses of big business. Theodore Dreiser in *Sister Carrie* (1900), *The Financier* (1912), and *The Titan* (1914) portrayed in graceless yet effective prose a distinctly modern world. His unsentimental treatment of sexual experience caused a publisher to suppress *Sister Carrie* for a decade. Dreiser's huge, gloomy novels, with their rich and accurate detail, seemed to penetrate as none had done before the mysteries of the urban scene.

Urban progressivism

Progressivism found its first target in the cities. The urban middle class had long been offended at the notion that rich men in baronial mansions made common political cause with the urban poor, whose tenements made their cities unhealthy and unsafe. Mismanaged and corrupt government that granted large favors to the rich and small favors to the poor, they argued, prevented anyone from controlling the direction of urban growth. Sporadic revolts of the middle class had occasionally brought in temporary reform administrations, but until late in the nineteenth century their achievements were slight. Then in the nineties, reformers, with European models of municipal government before them, experience in managing large business enterprises behind them, and the new social sciences for guidance, boldly attacked the job of reorganizing the cities.

NEW HEROES

The first of these urban reformers was Hazen S. Pingree, a wealthy manufacturer who became mayor of Detroit in 1890. Sobered by the depression of the nineties, Pingree moved beyond the old-fashioned reformism of "good government" and "driving the rascals out" to become a champion of social justice and to set a standard of positive municipal achievement. His program included lowering the cost of public utilities, fairer taxation, public ownership of some utilities, improvements in lighting, sewers, transit, roads, schools, and parks, and even relief for the poor during depression.

Pingree was the first of a series of reform mayors, often flamboyant men, who spread progressivism to a national audience. These included the colorful Samuel M. ("Golden Rule") Jones of Toledo and his successor Brand Whitlock, James D. Phelan of San Francisco, Seth Low of New York, Tom

Johnson of Cleveland, and Mark M. Fagan of Jersey City. Amid exciting controversy and with considerable fanfare in the press, these men, aided by various reform groups, dispelled the fatalism that had long surrounded the subject of city government. Not only did they bring some serious reform, they also educated a new generation of urban-minded reformers, men who overcame the typical American bias in favor of rural and small-town life to become the first important group of public figures to embrace the city as (in the words of one of them) the "hope of democracy."

Yet democracy seemed strangely served in many of the municipal reforms. Progressives preferred organizing governments which limited rather than extended the people's control over their officials. In response to a tragic tidal wave, Galveston, Texas, replaced its ineffectual government with a commission of five men who served together as their local legislature and separately as the government's administration. In 1908 the town of Staunton, Virginia, hired a manager, a trained expert, to run their city. Hundreds of smaller cities adopted these commission and city-manager plans. Other cities acted to strengthen their mayors against the city councils and aldermen. Everywhere corrupt political parties were the enemy. The main thrust of urban reform was to give power to more expert, more businesslike, and better-educated people. It was, in part, a revolt of the suburbs (then still within city limits in most cases) against the center cities. It improved the tone and the performance of government, and in the process helped many of the poor. It brought efficiency and sometimes social justice. But democracy—if by that we mean popular participation in politics, including by the poor—was more the urban progressives' slogan than their achievement.

IMMIGRANTS

Part of this distrust of the urban masses stemmed from widespread fears of an "undesirable" foreign element, immigrants from southern and eastern Europe, whom the federal commissioner of immigration officially labeled as "indigestible." The years between 1903 and the outbreak of the European war in 1914 saw an average annual migration of just under a million people. About two-thirds came from Russia, Poland, Austria-Hungary, the Balkans, and Italy. To most Americans these were disconcerting people, speaking strange tongues, practicing alien religions, possessing little of what passed for American manners or civic ideals. Many settled in the cities, another cause for suspicion among pastoral-minded Americans. Here the immigrants, observers claimed, formed the voting fodder for political machines, the labor force to undercut domestic workingmen, and the potential public for agitators.

Elaborate but faulty government studies indicated that this "new immigration" was different in motive and in effect from the past waves of new-

Mulberry Street, Lower East Side, New York City.
Library of Congress

comers: men outnumbered women or children in the new migration by about two to one, and many of these men were so-called birds of passage, planning to earn a nestegg and then return to their native lands rather than becoming citizens. Actually, large numbers of men had always been a characteristic of earlier stages of immigrations—women and children often came later—and the birds of passage were evidence not of changed motives behind these movements of people, but of improved transportation across the oceans which made it possible for some workers to move back and forth in response to changing employment possibilities.

Progressives had no single response to the new immigrants. Some supported restriction, and federal regulation of immigration, which began in 1890, introduced some "reforms" which in fact shut out a small percentage of newcomers. Ellis Island in New York Harbor, opened in 1892 as the main receiving station, became known among immigrants as "Heartbreak Island," since about one in five migrants would be detained there while officials determined their eligibility to enter the country. (Nine out of ten of these unfortunates were eventually admitted.) People might be excluded for any of a long list of reasons: paupers, lunatics, criminals, the diseased, laborers being brought to this country by an American employer, polygamists, prostitutes, anarchists, and people likely to become public charges were all forbidden entry.

Once immigrants reached their new country, they often profited from the services progressive agencies offered. School reformers struggled with some success to accommodate the city schools to this new public. Settlement house workers and other welfare reformers frequently sympathized with their plight, identified with their aspirations, and eventually learned to appreciate some parts of their cultures. Despite racist ideas and a constant movement in favor of laws sharply restricting entry, most progressives remained optimistic and wanted only the most inconsequential restrictions on immigration. That generation belonged to the pioneers in social work, education, and city government who continued to work for the eventual "Americanization" of these new members of the nation. The restrictionists' turn would come soon enough.

THE MUCKRAKERS

Americans everywhere suddenly became aware of this municipal reform movement in October 1902 when *McClure's Magazine* published Lincoln Steffens's "Tweed Days in St. Louis." The battle of idealistic reformers against municipal corruption was a highly dramatic, highly moralistic story. Steffens's series of articles on urban problems covering many cities set the theme: the common guilt for corruption, the common responsibility to eradicate it. Journalists themselves could be the heroes of the piece: Ida Tarbell disclosing the crimes of Standard Oil, Upton Sinclair exposing the meatpacking industry, Ray Stannard Baker teaching the public about labor racketeering. Theodore Roosevelt, one of the great phrase makers of American history, came up with the derisive name that stuck to this school of writers: muckrakers.

Muckraking dominated American journalism between about 1902 and 1906. About ten mass-circulation magazines and many newspapers featured exposés touching on almost every part of American society, and a number of widely sold books, such as Upton Sinclair's *The Jungle* (1906), spread the curiously optimistic message that, although American institutions had massive faults, Americans were fighting to correct them. This trend reflected the growth of a literate audience convinced that it could understand the world around it. The literature of exposé was not new to America—*Harper's* had

Public comfort stations, Indianapolis—a progressive era reform.
Bass

Immigration to the United States, 1900-1920

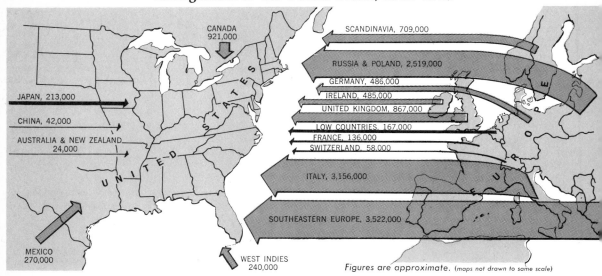

CANADA 921,000

SCANDINAVIA, 709,000

RUSSIA & POLAND, 2,519,000

GERMANY, 486,000

IRELAND, 485,000

UNITED KINGDOM, 867,000

LOW COUNTRIES, 167,000

FRANCE, 136,000

SWITZERLAND, 58,000

JAPAN, 213,000

CHINA, 42,000

AUSTRALIA & NEW ZEALAND 24,000

ITALY, 3,156,000

SOUTHEASTERN EUROPE, 3,522,000

MEXICO 270,000

WEST INDIES 240,000

Figures are approximate. *(maps not drawn to same scale)*

"muckraked" the Tweed Ring in the 1870s—but the style and scope of this journalism in the progressive era was novel. Nobody had expected so large an audience for reform, and there had never been such a corps of bright, young journalists with time, enthusiasm, and financial backing to look into the dirty corners of American life. The size and enthusiasm of the audience (people read Steffens and then joined municipal reform movements) convinced many of the people uncovering societies' problems that this exposure was itself curing the nation's ills. In fact, people detected progress so quickly that the craze for exposure soon faded. And as the public lost some of its enthusiasm, magazines, now caving in before pressure from their advertisers, switched to less controversial topics.

Progressive legislation

STATE PROGRESSIVISM

Urban reformers characteristically pursued a trail of corruption from city hall to the state legislature. Moreover, the limitations of most city charters narrowed the possibility for local reform. State legislatures controlled most taxes, often the local police, sometimes municipal franchises. And they could be bought: the street car magnate refused a hearing in Chicago might still win his battle by bribing legislators downstate in Springfield. Urban progressives beginning with Pingree, who became governor of Michigan in 1897, found the trek to the statehouse as natural a part of their ideals as it was of their ambitions.

State progressivism had clearer claim to the title of democratic reform. Efficiency-minded reformers found agrarian interests dominating many state legislatures; to get a hearing for their programs, the progressives worked to open the political system; in coalition with rural and small-town reformers, they displayed greater concern for economic legislation. Their chief instrument for political reform was institution of the direct primary, in which parties selected their candidates for major offices through elections instead of conventions. Another weapon in the progressive arsenal was the initiative and referendum, which allowed citizens to bypass an unresponsive legislature by petitioning for propositions to be included on the ballot. A more extreme method was the recall, by which citizens could get rid of an official who displeased them before his term of office ended.

In states where progressivism went farthest, such as Wisconsin under Governor Robert La Follette, progressives not only made changes in the structure of government, but also passed positive social legislation. These measures included railroad and grain-elevator rate commissions, higher taxes on corporations, improved banking laws, factory-inspection acts, workmen's compensation, limitations in the hours that women and children could work, and improvements in school and park systems.

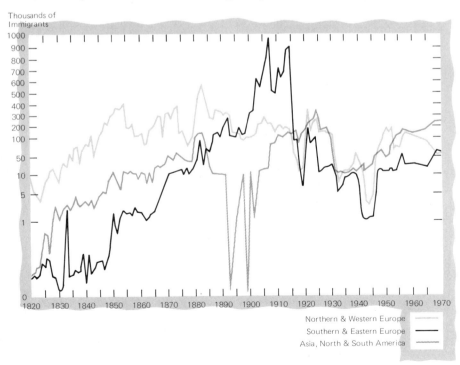

Immigration

NATIONAL NEEDS

Even statewide progressivism was not enough to meet the many problems transcending state boundaries. For one thing, federal courts could review state social legislation, and in this era courts often struck down reform efforts. In *Muller* v. *Oregon* (1908), however, the Supreme Court accepted a state law limiting women's working hours to ten a day. Louis D. Brandeis presented the Court with 102 pages of sociological data on the effect of work upon women and the state's need to protect their health and welfare, and he then limited himself to only two pages of legal precedent. This "Brandeis brief" became a model for the new school of "sociological jurisprudence," popular in law schools but far less so among older judges. Courts still invoked the rights of property and the sanctity of private contract to restrict the states' power to police their citizens in the interest of the general welfare.

Congress, too, had a role to play. Areas that had voted for prohibition of alcoholic beverages wanted federal laws to prevent shipments entering from other states. Cities that had launched crusades against prostitution wanted an end to "white slavers" bringing in girls from across the river. Nor could states adequately protect the purity of their meats or drugs. And progressives winced each time a United States senator had to be elected. States sought means to make this a direct popular election rather that a decision of purchasable state legislatures. The Seventeenth Amendment, ratified in 1913, at last achieved this goal. Finally, there were inherently national issues which deeply concerned the progressives: tariff schedules, banking policy, conservation, nationwide railroad regulation, and the control of interstate corporations. Here were areas for Congress to act and for a president to lead. Fate gave the progressives a president they could follow.

Theodore Roosevelt

On September 6, 1901, Leon Czolgosz, a poor, demented misfit with vague notions of anarchism, fired two shots at President McKinley, whose death a week later brought into the White House the youngest and most unusual president America had so far known. Hero of San Juan Hill, rancher and author of books about the West, Theodore Roosevelt had also prowled the streets of New York at night in a long cape to sweep down dramatically on corrupt policemen. A governor of New York whose progressive record had induced Republican bosses to exile him to the ceremonial boredom of the vice-presidency, he was not one of those faceless "available men" who had made careers of not giving offense to people. He was a leader for the new generation of self-righteous young crusaders. An aggressive moralist, he turned the White House into a "bully pulpit." An activist, he used his office to shape opinion and influence legislation. And in some areas, such as foreign policy and conservation, he seized upon long-dormant executive powers to mold the presidency into something like the mighty office it has since become.

Sensing the uncertainty and potential hostility of party leaders, Roosevelt quickly promised to continue McKinley's policies and retained almost all of his cabinet. Throughout his tenure, he struggled to keep good relations with the powers in Congress, especially the leading Republican senators, Nelson Aldrich, John C. Spooner, Orville H. Platt, and William B. Allison. These four men in their almost nightly gatherings over cards and billiards determined the course of the Senate. Along with Mark Hanna and, after 1903, the iron-handed Speaker of the House Joseph Cannon, these conservatives kept a tight rein on the national government. Roosevelt never fought them directly, but he found new resources in the presidency that eroded their position and prepared the way for a more liberal Congress which would enable his rival Woodrow Wilson a decade later to rush into legislation much of the progressive program.

TRUSTBUSTER

Roosevelt moved cautiously, especially in his first term. Yet he made even his caution seem dramatic. His action against the "trusts" especially created the image of the beloved "Teddy," the most admired American since Abraham Lincoln. Old fears of monopoly had gained fresh impetus from developments late in the nineties. In 1897, at the depression's end, eighty-six large corporations were capitalized at about $1½ billion. By 1904, 318 were worth $7½ billion, and they included the gargantuan United States Steel Corporation, the first billion-dollar company. Trusts were so huge that the public feared that they could force up prices in order to realize their exaggerated expectations of profit. Consumers, helpless in the marketplace and baffled by inflation, soon looked to government for aid.

Roosevelt began by pressing for new laws to require national licensing of corporations and to increase the power of the Interstate Commerce Commission (ICC) over the railroads. He got laws from Congress—creating a Bureau of Corporations and limiting railroad rebates—which were clearly too weak to affect the large corporations. He then turned to executive action, making use of the Sherman Antitrust Act to prosecute the Northern Securities Company, a new, overgrown, and unpopular railroad holding company.

With the stock market reeling at the news, J. P. Morgan offered to have underlings get together to "fix it up." Roosevelt noted that the financier regarded him "as a big rival operator." The president would have none of it:

Roosevelt with Booker T. Washington at National Negro Business League.
Culver Pictures

the whole point was to demonstrate the superior power of government over any private concern. And Roosevelt gained his point: the courts eventually dissolved Northern Securities. Occurring at the same time as Roosevelt's equally vigorous action in the anthracite coal strike of 1902, this landmark prosecution convinced the public that they could turn to government as an arbiter above the conflicts of private interests, however huge. Roosevelt considered this an important lesson, which he drove home in a series of speeches preaching his "Square Deal."

Roosevelt could now use the threat of antitrust prosecution to demand cooperation from big business, and he believed in such cooperation far more than he did in conflict. In 1905 he and United States Steel struck a "gentlemen's agreement" which set a pattern for government–industry relations. Steel agreed to cooperate with the Bureau of Corporations, and in return the government would allow the corporation to correct any breaches of federal law without recourse to litigation. Historians still argue over whether this was a triumph for the forces of reform seeking to check the trusts or a victory for big business in search of a painless buffer against public anger.

WORKERS

While perhaps less upsetting than the specter of rapacious trusts, the new strength of labor unions represented another threat to the middle class to which Roosevelt responded. William Dean Howells had expressed a popular sentiment: "The struggle for life," he wrote, "has changed from a free fight to an encounter of disciplined forces, and the free fighters that are left get ground to pieces between organized labor and organized capital." Unions, weak since the debacle of 1886, began a steady and this time more permanent rise in membership and power during the same period trusts were forming. Inflation drove skilled workers into unions as it ate away at the gains they had made in the long era of sinking prices. Businessmen, fearful of halting the advance of prosperity and in a position to pass along labor gains as price increases, offered a less desperate resistance than in the past. The American Federation of Labor gained most, growing over 700 percent in the twenty years after 1897, with the sharpest growth in 1897–1904, the years of industrial concentration. AFL leader Samuel Gompers tirelessly announced the conservative goals of labor; but with prices rising, 2½ million workers organized, and various socialist and anarchist movements active outside Gompers's control, middle-class Americans worried that they were caught between two great organized interests, above and below them. "The unorganized public," lamented a leading progressive, "where will *it* come in?"

COAL STRIKE

Roosevelt found his opportunity to define the kind of labor activity of which he approved and to establish the presidential role in labor disputes during the anthracite coal strike of 1902.

The miners, seeking higher wages and a union contract, held out for five months, maintained their discipline, and kept the strike from spilling over into the soft-coal fields (whose workers steadily contributed funds to the striking hard-coal miners). This excellent strike management by the twenty-nine-year-old United Mine Workers leader John Mitchell paid off. Roosevelt dramatically summoned the owners and Mitchell to the White House in an attempt to settle the strike. The owners came, but refused to speak to Mitchell. Infuriated, TR regretted that the dignity of his office precluded his taking the owners' spokesman, George F. Baer, "by the seat of the breeches and the nape of the neck" and defenestrating him. Roosevelt did the next best thing. He pressured Wall Street to push the unwilling owners into mediation and to get the willing workers back into the mines. While the public rejoiced over household furnaces again stoked with hard coal, the carefully selected board of arbiters gave the union a 10 percent pay raise and management a similar price hike. Although the miners had actually lost their prime demand—union recognition—the labor movement had scored a triumph in showing the nation that workers could strike without disorder or threats of revolution. And the president, of course, had demonstrated his authority.

LEADER OF THE PROGRESSIVES

Roosevelt was in a strong position going into the election year of 1904. Progressives, perhaps making comparisons with his predecessor, accepted the limited reforms of his first term. Conservatives, certain that he was no radical and pleased at his deference toward leaders like Aldrich and Cannon, offered their cautious backing as well. The Democrats, not wanting a third straight Bryan campaign, turned to a conservative, Judge Alton B. Parker of New York. This did not prevent business from heavily financing Roosevelt's campaign. With the Republicans a clear majority nationally, Roosevelt swept to an enormous victory—as did numerous progressives in state contests.

Intoxicated by the breadth of his victory, Roosevelt became bolder. He proposed that Congress make the District of Columbia a model community, clearing slums, inspecting factories, banning child labor. He called for stricter regulation of the railroads and a minimum wage for trainmen. But Congress remained nearly as conservative as before, and few of Roosevelt's programs made any headway. The president responded by picking a single objective, railroad regulation, and sticking to it. Here he showed great political skill. Threatening the party's leadership with a divisive fight on the tariff, he forced action on a bill that allowed the ICC to fix railroad rates. He had to accept several conservative amendments allowing judicial review of the commission's findings, but the resulting Hepburn Act (1906) was the first effective law regulating the railroads. The following year Roosevelt skillfully piloted through Congress the Pure Food and Drug Act and the Meat Inspection Act, which gave the federal government some power to protect the health of consumers. Americans had taken a tentative step toward a welfare state.

CONSERVATIONIST

Conservation was another open field for a determined president, and was one of Roosevelt's passions. He had written feelingly of the West and of the wilderness and sincerely desired their preservation. Still, this romantic mentality never dominated his conservation activities. He stood for the efficient administration and rational use of the nation's resources. Roosevelt set aside nearly 150 million acres of public lands as national forests and removed over 80 million acres of mineral land as well as 1½ million acres of water-power sites from public sale. Those resources, when leased to private interests, could then be used for long-range economic goals set and regulated by conservation-minded national administrators. The Newlands Reclamation Act, which Roosevelt helped push through Congress in 1902, established a revolving fund from land sales to finance irrigation projects in arid western states. Roosevelt also created five national parks, sixteen national monuments, and fifty-one wildlife refuges. His activities made conservation a national enthusiasm. Most states launched conservation commissions, and many private organizations formed to advance the cause. Nowhere else was the progressive mentality, mixing standards of rational efficiency with romantic sensibility and moral crusading, so evident as in the conservation movement. And nowhere else were Roosevelt's achievements so large, so permanent, and so unquestionably helpful.

Theodore Roosevelt's foreign policy

In foreign policy, Roosevelt enjoyed great freedom. Few Americans believed that they had any significant stake beyond the nation's borders. Roosevelt had only to avoid offending the public's vague preconceptions about our role in the world. Otherwise, he could do pretty much as he pleased.

Roosevelt and his circle set directions in American foreign policy for decades to come. Elihu Root reorganized the army during his stint as secretary of war. Alfred Thayer Mahan effectively argued for a strong navy to maintain and extend national power, influencing an entire generation of leaders who moved the nation from a weak naval power to one of the world's leading forces at sea. Henry Cabot Lodge supported an active diplomacy from his post as chairman of the Senate Foreign Relations Committee. John Hay, who remained as secretary of state until 1905, left the legacy upon which Roosevelt built. And all were his close personal friends.

THE FAR EAST

Like Hay, Roosevelt worked to maintain America's commercial position in China. This required a constant fine tuning of the balance of power in Asia, no mean feat in the fact of growing Japanese naval power and the uncertain strength of tsarist Russia. This delicate balance collapsed in 1904 when Japan launched a surprise naval attack and proceeded to crush the Russians by land and by sea. However, the Japanese lacked the resources for a long war and welcomed Roosevelt's mediation. With considerable tact, Roosevelt succeeded in convening a conference at Portsmouth, New Hampshire, in 1905, and then persuaded the Japanese to accept a compromise peace settlement in which they waived the large indemnity they had demanded but gained considerable territory, including control of the Korean peninsula.

Roosevelt's triumph at Portsmouth—he won a Nobel Peace Prize for his efforts—created problems with Japan. The Japanese blamed Roosevelt for their postwar financial difficulties. The president found further need to placate Japan when the San Francisco school board ordered all its Oriental students into a segregated school. It took a White House conference to change the school board's policy and a "gentlemen's agreement" with Japan to halt the flow of Japanese laborers into the West Coast. Then Teddy, fearing he had made too many concessions, tried a threatening gesture by sending the American fleet—second largest in the world—on a visit to Japan. This tour of the "Great White Fleet" was another Rooseveltian production: failing to intimidate anyone, it was nonetheless wildly popular, a masterpiece of grandstand diplomacy.

LATIN AMERICA

Closer to home, Roosevelt was more aggressive. He hoped to end European interventions in Latin America, even if the United States had to become the hemisphere's bill collector to do it. In 1903 when the Dominican Republic defaulted on $40 million in bonds held by European investors, Roosevelt took over the Dominican customs service to pay off the debts and to control the Dominican government. This policy soon achieved the status of a "corollary" to the Monroe Doctrine: in the face of "chronic wrongdoing" or "impotence," the president announced to Congress in 1904, we would exercise "an international police power." Under the terms of the Roosevelt Corollary, American interventions in Latin America became more frequent, and American economic penetration, especially in the countries washed by the Caribbean, increased substantially in the first two decades of the twentieth century.

The most spectacular feat of Roosevelt's diplomacy was the beginning of construction on the interoceanic canal across the isthmus of Panama. Here he was not playing to the grandstand but pursuing an obvious national interest. The growth of our naval power had revitalized the long-standing desire for a closer water link between the two American shores. In 1901 the Hay-Pauncefote Treaty cleared the way for an American canal by ending an old obligation to share control of such a canal with England. Then the battle was on to select a route: partisans of the water-level route through Nicaragua lost out to skillful lobbyists for a French-owned canal company that possessed legal rights and a few excavations through the rough fifty miles between the oceans in Panama—then still a province of Colombia. Hay proceeded to negotiate a treaty with Colombia providing for a ninety-nine-year lease for a six-mile-wide strip across the isthmus. The Colombian Senate unanimously decided that the treaty offered insufficient compensation and rejected it.

Roosevelt was furious. Dealing with those "dagoes," he bellowed, was like trying to "nail currant jelly to a wall." The canal company then took a hand, persuading the Panamanians to revolt against Colombia. They had tried before, but this time, with an American cruiser quickly sent to the area, their former rulers were helpless. The United States instantly recognized the new republic and rapidly signed a treaty for a permanent lease on a ten-mile-wide zone for the same terms rejected by Colombia—$10 million outright and a quarter-million-dollar annual rental. Through it all, Roosevelt never lost his self-righteous aplomb. Many Latin Americans refused to forget his arrogance and disdain. Few incidents generated such long-term hostility. Eventually the United States, in 1921, gave Colombia $25 million—a monetary apology for Roosevelt's behavior. Colombia then recognized the Panamanian Republic. Meanwhile, the canal opened to traffic in 1914 and the United States dominated the Caribbean.

William Howard Taft

Roosevelt ended his administration in a posture of futile crusading against a conservative Congress. Nonetheless, he retained so much popularity that he was the first president since Andrew Jackson able to name his successor. William Howard Taft was the man, all three hundred and more pounds of him. Taft had been a good federal judge, a competent governor of the Philippines, an effective secretary of war, and, most important, a loyal Roosevelt man. A distinguished legal thinker and an excellent administrator, his chief liability was a distaste for politics: he lacked the necessary energy, joy of combat, and ability as a campaigner. His election, however, was a foregone conclusion. Taft ran as a careful progressive against William Jennings Bryan, and his administration was supposed to be a workmanlike orchestration of Rooseveltian themes. It did not work out that way.

FOREIGN AFFAIRS

In foreign policy, Taft tried to follow Roosevelt and yet make his own mark. Taft gave his tactics a new and unfortunate name: "dollar diplomacy." He meant this in a positive sense: an alternative to diplomacy by bullets and a boost for underdeveloped economies. But history has taken the phrase as a blunt rationale for an informal American empire. In a few areas Taft went beyond his predecessor: he sent marines into Nicaragua in 1912, a small contingent of them remaining until 1933. He tried without success to put American bankers in charge of the finances of Haiti, Honduras, Costa Rica, and Guatemala. And he was equally interested, but unsuccessful, in creating a substantial American economic presence in Manchuria.

TAFT AND THE PROGRESSIVES

Domestic policy proved even more difficult for Taft. TR's last programs had enhanced the expectations of the progressives and sharpened the caution of the Old Guard. Taft lacked the smoothness to run with both forces the way Roosevelt had. And he lacked the progressive style Roosevelt had flourished even at his most cautious. Taft, for instance, initiated far more antitrust prosecutions in his four years than Roosevelt had in seven, yet Taft remained in the public eye the friend of the corporations. So too, Taft's reform accomplishments far exceeded Roosevelt's: further railroad-rate regulation in the Mann-Elkins Act of 1910, a postal savings plan, industrial safety measures, the establishment of a Children's Bureau, and an eight-hour day for federal employees. He also had a hand in the passage of the Sixteenth Amendment, allowing a federal income tax—a necessity for later social legislation. Yet he goes down in history, as he went down with his contemporaries, an opponent of progressivism.

Much of this rests on Taft's political ineptitude. He could not sell himself or his policies to the public. Somehow he always managed to alienate even the progressives, who gave the strongest support to the reforms he achieved. He never learned TR's trick of holding them back to get a passable bill without earning their enmity. And they could sense that he never liked them: the conservative leaders, especially Aldrich, simply appealed more to him as people. They weren't so evangelical, so pushy, so insistent; they were more his kind, appreciating good food and leisure and a friendly round of golf.

Several incidents divided Taft from the progressives. He failed to support George Norris's successful attempt to break "Boss" Cannon's hold on the House of Representatives. Then Taft botched the Payne-Aldrich Tariff of 1909. He had pushed for sharp reductions to benefit consumers, but when Aldrich's Senate committee tacked on 847 amendments, most of them raising rates, Taft failed to aid the progressive senators who resisted. When the crippled bill went through, he not only signed it, but told a tariff-conscious Minnesota audience that it was "on the whole . . . the best bill that the Republican party ever passed."

Then in one final disaster Taft fell into a position which appeared to be flatly anticonservationist and anti-Roosevelt. This was the dizzily complex Ballinger-Pinchot affair. Roosevelt and his chief forester, Gifford Pinchot, Taft believed, did not always use "the legal way" of reaching their conservationist goals. Taft had appointed as secretary of the interior, Richard A.

*A man of great girth, President Taft, it was said,
rose from his seat in a street car and offered it to three ladies.*

National Portrait Gallery, Smithsonian Institution

Ballinger, a western lawyer who would follow the law strictly. Eventually conflict had to come, and when it did Taft let it grow from an intramural argument between Ballinger and the chief forester into a public scandal resulting in Taft's firing of Pinchot—the symbol of conservation and one of TR's intimate friends.

REENTER THEODORE ROOSEVELT

Roosevelt returned in 1910 from a long hunting trip to Africa laden with big-game trophies and a trunkful of mail from unhappy progressives. Once home, he found Taft cool and the party hot with discontent. After a brief period of uncharacteristic silence, TR boomed out a new progressive platform in a speech at Osawatomie, Kansas, in August. Calling for a "New Nationalism," Roosevelt coupled the "Square Deal" program left over from the end of his presidency with a general call for an extension of federal power. The executive branch in particular, he argued, must become "the advocate of human welfare." Once again the progressives had their familiar hero.

By 1911 Roosevelt had leapt into the electoral ring, smashing Taft in primary after primary. Nevertheless, Taft kept a thin margin of control over the Republican convention, beating back a number of credentials challenges and securing renomination on the first ballot. Roosevelt, claiming that he felt as fit as a bull moose, then accepted the nomination of the new Progressive party of 1912, which quickly became popularly known as the "Bull Moose" party. Their convention in August was more like a religious revival than a traditional political meeting. Adopting a platform that became a major text for twentieth-century reform, the "New Nationalist" Progressives called for strict regulation of large corporations rather than continuing the effort at breaking them up. It supported progressive changes in the mechanics of government such as a nationwide presidential primary, campaign contribution disclosure laws, and the initiative, referendum, and recall. And it restated virtually all the economic and social legislation that had been suggested by progressives in the previous decade, such as workmen's compensation, the prohibition of child labor, unemployment insurance, and social security (then called social insurance).

ENTER WOODROW WILSON

With the Republicans divided, the Democrats saw their first real opportunity in twenty years; as much by luck as by design, they finally took it. After forty-six ballots they nominated Woodrow Wilson, by any test their ideal candidate. Born in Virginia and raised in the South, Wilson had landed on the national scene like some meteor from another world. Two years before he was known principally among educators for his role as the dynamic president of Princeton University and among political scientists and a small segment of the literate public as an author of several books on political theory and history. Then he had been elected governor of New Jersey in 1910. An instant success, he pushed through a full progressive program and impressed a large public with his high-minded oratory. His call in 1912 for a "New Freedom" for individuals to compete with large organizations spoke directly to the hopes and fears that industrial America had stirred.

THE ELECTION OF 1912

The high point of progressive sentiment came in 1912. Even Taft, the most conservative of the three candidates, stood for many reforms. But Roosevelt and Taft had made each other's cause hopeless. The Republican majority divided, and Wilson won easily with only a little more than 6 million out of nearly 15 million votes cast. Roosevelt's new party actually outpolled the Republicans, with the Socialist party candidate, Eugene V. Debs, also receiving almost a million votes. If many Americans wanted no more changes, they were profoundly silent about it. The mandate seemed all for progress. Few noticed that this had been the smallest voter turnout (in proportion to population) since the rise of the modern two-party system in Jackson's time.

The Wilson administration

Woodrow Wilson presided over the flowering of national progressivism and oversaw its demise. But in the first years everything, or at least everything domestic, rolled on in splendor. The Democrats, controlling both houses of Congress, were prepared to follow their president. Wilson instantly seized the initiative. His inaugural address set the tone of high idealism that was to characterize his presidency and established areas for legislation: tariff reform, a new banking and currency system, industrial regulation, and conservation of natural and human resources.

A NEW FINANCIAL SYSTEM

Congress, prodded by an aggressive president, made good on most of these promises. Wilson called them into special session to reform the tariff and broke precedent by appearing in person to present his program—a daring act Theodore Roosevelt must have envied. The speedily passed Underwood Tariff not only cut rates, it also enacted a federal income tax. The president then held Congress in session throughout the summer—a cruel undertaking before the days of air-conditioned chambers—to enact currency and banking reform. The movement for a new financial system had recently gained impetus from a congressional committee's sensational reports of the power and extent of the "money trust." The investigation, conducted by Representative Arsène Pujo, showed that the interconnected interests of J. P. Morgan and John D. Rockefeller controlled over $22 billion of the nation's wealth. Riding this current, Wilson pushed through the Federal Reserve Act, unquestionably the domestic triumph of his administration.

The Federal Reserve Act created a national banking and currency system to replace the largely private system that had endured since Jackson's time. The Federal Reserve system consisted of twelve Federal Reserve banks—essentially banks for bankers that could issue currency in exchange for secured notes which banks received from their borrowers. A Federal Reserve Board, appointed by the president, exercised control over the amount of commission—called the rediscount rate—that banks paid for the privilege of chang-

Orpen's portrait of Thomas Woodrow Wilson.
Library of Congress

ing their notes into Federal Reserve bills. The result was a somewhat more decentralized currency system (no longer were all assets tied to Wall Street), a more flexible currency—no longer directly fluctuating with the price of gold—and a banking system under some measure of public control through the Federal Reserve Board.

It was hardly a radical measure. Bankers named a large minority of directors of district banks, and Wilson put conservative bankers on the Reserve Board. The act substantially removed the currency and banking issue from the national arena and offered at least the start of a reliable banking system. Whether the system took public control of banking or simply lent the power of government to the bankers themselves remained to be seen.

PROGRESSIVISM AT ITS HEIGHT

Wilson continued to press important reforms. The Smith-Lever Act of 1914 financed the valuable work being done by the agricultural extension services to improve farming methods. It also, inadvertently, paved the way for an organization of American farmers much like comparable groups in American industry and labor: the American Farm Bureau Federation, an organization of, by, and for the most prosperous farmers. The Federal Trade Commission Act replaced Roosevelt's Bureau of Corporations with an independent regulatory agency with far more power than any agency had had before. Wilson staffed it with men reluctant to interfere with the needs of business as businessmen saw them. Then the Clayton Antitrust Act strengthened and made more definite the provisions of the old Sherman Antitrust Act as well as vaguely promising labor some protection from antitrust actions and injunctions. Even so, as congressional progressives had predicted, many of the law's restraints on big business eroded under court decisions. And what Samuel Gompers had hailed as labor's "Magna Carta" quickly proved but another weapon in the arsenal of the corporations battling the unions when judges found it no bar against issuing injunctions to prevent strikes and boycotts. As Mr. Dooley, fictional creation of the era's favorite political satirist, said, "What looks like a brick wall to a layman is a triumphal arch for a corporation lawyer."

Essentially the American system had become one of voluntary cooperation between business and government punctuated by occasional bouts of open conflict. Perhaps the goal, which Wilson and Roosevelt each in his own way stated, of making business behave should be taken quite literally: businessmen were learning caution and a small measure of social responsibility. This rather small price was all the progressives asked of them, despite their rhetoric of being at Armageddon battling for the Lord.

A BALANCE SHEET

National progressivism had largely run its course before the nation turned its attention to foreign affairs in 1914, when war broke out in Europe. Here and there later laws extended some of its directions: in 1915 the humanitarian La Follette Seaman's Act improved conditions in the merchant marine; the Federal Farm Loan Act (1916) and the Warehouse Act (1916) brought some relief to the eternal problem of farm credit; the Keating-Owen Act outlawed child labor—until the Supreme Court voided it in 1918; the Adamson Act raised railroad workers' salaries. Nonetheless, the Wilson administration, by bringing the progressive movement to fruition, also pointed sharply to its limitations. It had been a movement for and by the middle classes. Quite aware of the existence of poverty, in general progressives were nevertheless rarely more than cautiously paternalistic toward the poor. In some areas, as in agriculture, by improving the conditions of those on top, they deflected concern for those in more serious need. And their definition of the public was sharply limited. Many immigrants did not fit the progres-

Keystone capers gently satirized authority on the silent screen.
Culver Pictures

sive model of a good citizen. Worse yet, except for a few noble exceptions, the progressives were no more responsive than their less moralistic compeers to the needs of Afro-Americans. In fact, their era coincides with the very lowest point in black people's search for a place in modern American life.

Black Americans during the progressive era

Progressivism was for whites only. Southern progressives were in the fore-front of the movement to disfranchise blacks as a means of purifying the bal-lot in their states. Nationally, the Republican party offered little to their loyal black constituents. Theodore Roosevelt pleased blacks by allowing Booker T. Washington to dine at the White House, but when this raised a storm of protests he never repeated the invitation. Roosevelt distributed some patronage to loyal blacks—but only if they had Washington's approval, meaning that they were not loudly calling for either social or political rights. And Roosevelt scandalized blacks by dishonorably discharging three com-panies from a highly decorated Afro-American battalion on the basis of un-proven charges against them—a miscarriage of justice that remained uncor-rected for sixty-six years before the army changed the discharges to honorable in 1972. Taft's policies offered blacks no more, and black politi-cians supported him largely because they had no place else to turn: Roose-velt's Progressive party of 1912 was lily white, and the Democrats were even worse on racial issues.

The return of the white South to the seat of national government during the Wilson years spelled disaster for blacks. Wilson himself was a bigot, pleased to support his cabinet's rigid segregation of the federal civil service. During his tenure in the White House, more militant black leaders came to the fore, and their clashes with Wilson were particularly violent. In one cele-brated incident involving William Monroe Trotter, the aggressive editor of the black newspaper the *Boston Guardian*, Wilson ordered Trotter out of his presence for using "insulting" language in protesting segregation in the civil service.

Such limited political prospects for blacks help explain Booker T. Wash-ington's success. His disillusionment with the possibilities of political achievement for blacks extended to most of his community. Poor blacks had little faith in their political leaders. In so far as historians can determine what they felt, their hearts seemed to be with the prophets of black nation-alism or a return to Africa, men like the rough-hewn Bishop Henry M. Turner, who called for a black exodus from the United States. And even middle-class blacks, especially in the South, saw their future principally in education and economic advancement, judging that political assertion would only increase the violence and hostility directed against them. The best policy seemed to be Washington's: to keep the white oppressors off their backs while developing community strength and economic power.

A NEW ACTIVISM

One of Washington's opponents, Adam Clayton Powell, Sr., asked in 1906: "What are the results of Washington's leadership?" He answered:

> Lynchings are increasing and riots are more numerous. The race is humiliated by Jim Crow laws, and woefully handicapped in its intellectual and moral development by inferior schools. In a word, under Dr. Washington's policy the two races in the South are a thousand times further apart than they were fifteen years ago and the breach is widening every day.

While it was unfair to blame Washington's policy for this state of affairs, Powell's description of the situation was undeniably accurate. A prominent New York minister and community leader, Powell was typical of the new men coming to oppose Washington for both his submissive style and his policy. Powell's son, Adam Clayton Powell, Jr., would have an extraordinary and controversial career dedicated almost wholly to eradicating from both black and white minds the Booker T. Washington image of the black leader.

W. E. B. DU BOIS AND THE "COLOR LINE"

The greatest of Washington's opponents in every respect was William Edward Burghardt Du Bois. As a publicist, scholar, author, and one of the founders of the modern civil rights movement, Du Bois left a large imprint on American life and thought. Massachusetts-born, educated at Fisk and Harvard, arrogant and brilliant, he rapidly emerged as the great interpreter of Afro-American life. In 1900 he issued the warning that continues to echo:

> The problem of the Twentieth Century is the problem of the color line, the question as to how far differences of race, which show themselves chiefly in the color of the skin and the texture of the hair, are going to be made, hereafter, the basis of denying to over half the world the right of sharing in their utmost ability the opportunities and the privileges of modern civilization.

Du Bois argued that black Americans had to build their own enterprises to achieve racial pride (he was also one of the first theorists of pan-Africanism). Yet blacks could not achieve this manhood without an assertion of their rights, without striving for and achieving full equality in American life. Du Bois saw the need for both the self-help tradition of Washington and

In this photograph W. E. B. DuBois is second from the right in the second row. DuBois (1868–1963) spoke for militant blacks who challenged Booker T. Washington's leadership. Their meeting near Niagara Falls in 1905 contributed to the founding of the National Association for the Advancement of Colored People.
New York Public Library.

the integrationist philosophy of Frederick Douglass. Everything had to be done at once: to wait for political rights as Washington counseled was to risk losing self-respect; to reach for them without economic and moral force behind them—as in Reconstruction—would be to court disaster. And Du Bois, who had thoroughly studied his people's past and their present circumstances, knew that life behind the veil of segregation had denied them most of the resources they required for the gargantuan task.

473

FOUNDING THE NAACP

Du Bois's answer was sharply elitist: men like Du Bois himself—what he called the "talented tenth" of the black population—would have to save the race. There was a harsh realism to Du Bois's views. He helped to build a generation of black leaders. This meant attacking Washington for his industrial-education theories: the community's limited resources had to go into educating the talented tenth, not raising "the man farthest down." It meant insisting on political rights and social privileges. Under Du Bois's inspiration a group of men disenchanted with Washington's leadership gathered at Niagara Falls in 1905. The Niagara Movement formulated demands which set the tone for a half-century and more of protest: an end to racial discrimination in employment, in the courts, in business, and in labor unions; universal suffrage; the demolition of the Jim Crow system; and higher education for the able. The movement attracted no mass following, but it did stir some white liberals such as John Dewey and Jane Addams to join with Du Bois in founding the National Association for the Advancement of Colored People, an interracial organization dedicated to ending legal and political discrimination. Du Bois became editor of its journal, *The Crisis,* and before leaving to seek more radical alternatives he had made of it the first permanent and effective lobby for black rights.

BLACK RENAISSANCE

Du Bois's efforts were part of a renaissance in Afro-American life. As if in challenge to the rising white racism, black leaders and artists showed a new militancy and a fresh pride in their common experience. Around the turn of the century a number of important works by black authors and artists suddenly began to appear: the sculpture of Meta Warwick Fuller, the poetry of Paul Lawrence Dunbar, Charles W. Chesnutt's novels, Du Bois's writings. One of the greatest works of black literature in this period, James Weldon Johnson's *Autobiography of an Ex-Colored Man,* was published anonymously in 1912. It showed an acceptance of black folkways and especially black music—ragtime and jazz—that earlier black writers had avoided in deference to white critics. Other signs of growing racial pride were the rising popularity of black dolls around 1910, calendars with black themes, and—in a rather different area—the founding in 1915 of the *Journal of Negro History,* which joined Du Bois's Atlanta University publications as a vehicle for the investigation of the black experience in America.

A NEW AGE

Booker T. Washington died in 1915. His power had been steadily waning in the black world for several years, and his passing marked the end of an era. In fact, the symbolism was peculiarly apt. Washington's world was passing

Marcus Garvey led a massive black nationalist movement after the war.

in the most fundamental sense. The Great War had broken out in Europe, and it affected blacks even more than other American citizens. With war production opening new opportunities in the factories and cities, the steady trickle of black families northward suddenly turned into a flood. From 1915 onward increasing numbers of blacks moved into northern cities, creating urban ghettos and spawning a new culture and politics. A "new Negro movement" among black intellectuals sparked a Harlem literary renaissance which became a rage in New York literary circles during the 1920s. A new prophet, Marcus Garvey, a Jamaican who came to the United States in 1916, led a massive but short-lived nationalist movement, the Universal Negro Improvement Association. At its height, during 1920 and 1921, some 4 to 6 million Afro-Americans supported his attempt to form a beachhead for black Americans in Africa. Garvey extolled everything black and rejected the white world and any attempt to become assimilated by it. His message found audiences not only among American blacks, but throughout the world, influencing nationalists in Africa and the Caribbean. His uniforms and parades and his swagger filled emotional needs among lower-class blacks that the interracial civil rights groups could not. When his plans for an African kingdom went awry and the federal government sent him to prison for some of his dealings in connection with this project, the movement collapsed. He remains, however, a hero of black nationalists.

Beyond progressivism

RADICAL MOVEMENTS

Blacks were not the only Americans to find their needs taking them beyond the remedies that progressivism could provide. The progressive era marked as well the high point of American socialism and anarchism. Many progressives, in fact, saw their activities as a response to these radical threats. The Socialist party reached its greatest electoral strength in the 1912 presidential election when it gained nearly a million votes—about 6 percent of the total. A more radical group, the Industrial Workers of the World (IWW or Wobblies), appealed to rootless and exploited western workers such as lumberjacks and miners. None of these movements, however, grew into major socialist parties such as mark the political history of other industrial nations, and historians continue to argue the reason why. All assign varying degrees of significance to the social mobility of American workers, the cultural divisions among racial and immigrant groups within the working class, the success of progressive and liberal political reforms in the twentieth century, and the divisions within and suppression of radical movements during and immediately after World War I. One thing is certain: after wartime and immediate postwar repression, American radicalism fell into a disarray from which it never emerged.

AMERICA GOES MODERN

"The fiddles are tuning . . . all over America," said a visitor in 1912. Indeed they were, and making strange sounds. Charles Ives, the first important American composer, experimented with tonalities similar to those Stravinsky and Schönberg were using in Europe. Scott Joplin created ragtime, which quickly passed into popular music. W. C. Handy elaborated black American blues into a complex idiom. White Americans discovered Dixieland jazz.

A number of American painters tried to transfer progressive ideals onto canvas. Called the "ashcan school" because they insisted on depicting the grimier sides of modern life, their great contribution to a new style was the art show they organized in 1913 at the Sixty-ninth Regiment Armory in New York City. Here Americans—some quarter-million of them—met modern art. The show was large and conservative overall, but it contained a sampling of the works of Cézanne, van Gogh, Matisse, Rouault, and Picasso. These artists, whose classic works now hang in even the most staid museums, then seemed shocking. They were nonrepresentative, or sensual, or distorted—strange mirrors reflecting an even stranger world that most Americans hesitated to see as their own. Critics had a field day: Theodore Roosevelt preferred the Navaho rug hanging in his bathroom (a derogatory judgment in 1913) to the cubist art he saw in the armory. Yet he found the show a relief from the dullness of most works of art, a sign that the American public might soon see things the same way.

"THE VILLAGE"

Poets, artists, novelists, and critics gathered in little knots, experimenting with new forms of art and new ways of life. A vigorous bohemian culture flourished in New York City's Greenwich Village. For six or seven years before the war "the Village" was what it has since been reputed to be: the home of social experimentation, serious writing, and men in flannel shirts living in what was then called "sin" with cigarette-smoking women with short hair. People discussed the new ideas of Sigmund Freud in apartments painted orange and black, they attended plays, parties, and impromptu events.

It was not an idle game: Floyd Dell, Max Eastman, and John Reed published *The Masses*, the best radical journal in American history. The Provincetown Theater produced Eugene O'Neill's remarkable dramas with their naturalistic dialogue and heavy symbolism. Isadora Duncan danced, and Edna St. Vincent Millay acted and wrote poetry. Many progressives hung around, enjoying the scene. The Village offered a good and richly productive life. And a very short one. By 1917 everything about the Village was in decline except the rents, the prices in the restaurants, and the tourists.

This bohemia was America's first try at being "modern." These practitioners of "liberation" sought changes more radical than the progressives. They questioned the possibility of an adequate moral code to guide the world. They expressed skepticism about man's progress. They wondered if they were in fact superior to the non–Anglo-Saxons living around them. Most Americans did not entertain such doubts. To the progressives in particular, these attractive new voices could only be nagging irritants, suggesting that perhaps all might not be well even after they had fought their good fight.

NEW LIFE STYLES

Yet these vivid splotches of experimentation fitted closely into the rest of American life. Almost every magazine contained articles worrying about the rising divorce rate, the sinking birth rate, and the restless "new woman." Profound changes were, in fact, taking place in these sensitive areas of marriage, family, and sex. The divorce rate jumped dramatically: from one divorce for every twenty-one marriages in 1880 to one in nine by 1916. The birth rate among native-born Americans, in decline since colonial days, suddenly became a cause for alarm as the public began comparing it to immigrant fertility. Teddy Roosevelt with characteristic verve championed the "full baby carriage" to avoid "race suicide" among Anglo-Saxons. Reformers like Margaret Sanger risked arrest by publicizing birth control techniques for the poor. And, as the Kinsey Reports documented decades later, the sharpest changes in sexual behavior—the sexual revolution that every generation considers its own contribution to American culture—occurred in the generation coming of age in these years. While others worried, the Village experimented. America quickly discovered its bohemia: fashionable urban Americans worked hard in the 1920s to copy its style.

Wilson and the world

MISSIONARY AMERICA

Wilson, although he expected to make his mark in domestic affairs, never doubted that he had lessons to teach the rest of the world as well. He was determined to raise the moral tone of American diplomacy by turning from cynical professional diplomats to idealistic amateurs. In meeting party obligations by naming William Jennings Bryan secretary of state, he made a good start in this direction: wholly without experience in diplomacy, Bryan retained the high moral tone of his great crusading days, and he planned to fill critical places in the State Department with "deserving Democrats."

Wilson's foreign policy generally continued that of Roosevelt and Taft under a different name and rhetoric. Intent on achieving American-style democracy in the rest of the world, he intervened as freely as his predecessor in the Caribbean: the United States stayed in Nicaragua, reentered Santo Domingo, and virtually took over Haiti. Wilson continued to defend the Open Door in China, and policy there still fluctuated with the perceived threat that Japan posed to our interests. Wilson began his administration intent on maintaining a balance of power in Asia. He concluded the Lansing-Ishii Agreement in 1917 by which we vaguely condoned Japanese penetration into China, and Japan just as vaguely promised to abide by the Open Door.

WILSON AND REVOLUTION

Wilson's first dilemma in foreign affairs came in Mexico. The revolution there, which began in 1910, was no minor coup or change in dictators. A whole generation struggled for and against social and economic change and constitutional democracy. Here was a serious test of Wilson's idealism.

American investors had long prospered in Mexico under the dictatorship of Porfirio Díaz, who encouraged foreign investment and kept the lid on popular discontent. The democratic reformers who took power in 1910 were less accommodating, and when their leader, Francisco Madero, was murdered in 1913 by Victoriano Huerta, foreign investors and European governments scarcely shed a tear. But Wilson refused to follow the path of the other powers and the unbroken American tradition of recognizing whichever government was in power. He would not recognize Huerta's "government of butchers."

Wilson hoped this new policy of nonrecognition would bring down the Huerta government, which in any case controlled only part of Mexico. When Huerta survived, Wilson found himself without a policy. Those he had hoped to help rebuffed offers to mediate and even to intervene. Wilson was troubled by the contradiction of trying to settle a nationalist uprising from outside: opposing factions became friends facing this clumsy embrace from the north. Meanwhile, the American fleet ominously patrolled the Mexican coast in watchful wait for their orders or an incident.

In April 1914 a minor Mexican official arrested some American sailors who had gone ashore in Tampico. His superior promptly released them and offered apologies. The United States admiral demanded a twenty-one gun salute to the American flag, and Huerta refused. Wilson thought he had to back his admiral and sent more naval force to the area. Hearing of a German ship on its way with munitions for the Mexican government, Wilson ordered his fleet to seize its port of destination, Veracruz. Gunboat diplomacy, so often a farce, suddenly turned to tragedy. To Wilson's horror, the Mexicans dared to resist. Casualties for both sides ran into the hundreds: Wilson had blundered to the brink of a senseless war with our southern neighbor. Only an offer to mediate by Argentina, Brazil, and Chile allowed Wilson a last-minute escape hatch. As negotiations dragged on, tempers cooled. Then in July, democratic forces under Venustiano Carranza finally succeeded in driving Huerta out of Mexico City.

This was America's first experience of responding to a modern national revolution. Wilson's effort was long on ambition but short on achievement. In fact, even Carranza's victory did not end Wilson's Mexican embroglio. He foolishly mistook the swashbuckling bandit Pancho Villa for a Wilsonian progressive, realized his error, and then had General John J. Pershing chase Villa's army three hundred miles into Mexico. His mistake here typified the rest of his Mexican policy: he grasped at whatever in the uncertain course of revolution looked familiar, progressive, and American, then discovered that it was none of these things. That was not how the rest of the world behaved, a lesson Wilson learned later and to his sorrow.

War in Europe

In late summer 1914 a Serbian nationalist assassinated Austrian Archduke Franz Ferdinand. This seemingly minor incident of isolated violence provoked a chain reaction through the complex system of European alliances and led Britain, France, and Russia into war against Germany and Austria-Hungary. The resulting conflict, the climax of decades of increasingly serious confrontations around the globe, would weaken Europe and touch off at least half a century of worldwide turbulence and instability.

Like Germany, the United States was a relative newcomer in the club of world powers. But unlike its Central European counterpart, America was not surrounded by established powers and felt few constraints upon its expansionist muscles. Isolated by two oceans, Americans initially saw little reason for the European war to affect them directly. When brutal military stalemate shattered the widespread expectation of rapid victory and a speedy peace, Americans began more thoughtfully to assess their own position and the fate of the corrupt and greedy Old World states. Americans understood that the only victor from a struggle between equals was the outsider, the noncombatant. And during the early years of the war Americans reveled in their neutrality, cherished their isolation, and watched themselves grow stronger as Europe exhausted itself. The refrain of a popular song expressed a common attitude:

> *I didn't raise my boy to be a soldier,*
> *I brought him up to be my pride and joy,*
> *To live to place a musket on his shoulder,*
> *To shoot some other mother's darling boy. . . .*
> *There'd be no war today*
> *If mothers all would say*
> *I didn't raise my boy to be a soldier.*

The barbarism and lawlessness of the war shocked Americans. The horrors of trench warfare and the deadly new gases revealed rationality and civilization as only thin veneers, the gilt on modern man rather than his substance. And, almost unconsciously, Americans began assigning responsibility for the awful events. Feeling more comfortable if they could distinguish between outlaw and victim, evil and righteousness, they gradually dropped their impartiality. Although Americans never doubted the moral superiority of their nation to either side, between the combatants Germany emerged the greater villain. The United States had fewer economic and cultural ties with Germany than with England, and Germans seemed more clearly to have violated international law. They followed the invasion of neutral Belgium with the introduction to warfare of the submarine, a weapon which ignored traditional rules requiring ships to warn and search enemy vessels before sinking them. With some exceptions—such as socialists and German-Americans—most people in the United States sympathized with Great Britain. But beyond this vague pro-British leaning and a general belief in America's higher morality, there was little consensus on how Americans should respond to the war.

PACIFIST AND INTERVENTIONISTS

The large prewar pacifist movement viewed the conflict as a ghastly mistake to be avoided even at the cost of abandoning certain traditional neutral rights. Secretary of State Bryan, for example, privately favored Great Britain but valiantly strove for absolute impartiality. He sponsored the Wilson administration's early ban on loans to belligerents and urged the president to forbid American citizens from traveling on the ships of warring nations. He warned that extending credit—which as a practical matter would go mostly to Britain and France—and allowing Americans on British ships would inevitably lead to conflict with Germany. But Wilson moved away from Bryan's position of careful noninvolvement and insisted on observing only theoretical neutrality. When the president lifted the ban on loans and de-

West Point Museum Collections, United States Military Academy.

manded that Germany safeguard the lives of Americans on British ships, Bryan resigned from the cabinet. He and many pacifists charged the president with abandoning neutrality in practice on the pretext of upholding it in principle.

A more vocal and colorful coalition argued that Wilson's policies were not strong enough and advocated increased military "preparedness." Labeling Germany as the troublemaker and Britain as a guardian of civilization, interventionists felt that America's national honor would eventually require entry into the war. The most bombastic and influential spokesman for preparedness was America's beloved ex-President Theodore Roosevelt; even more colorful was Buffalo Bill, lending the glamour and symbolism of his Wild West show to preparedness parades. Trumpeting the conviction that Americans were becoming "soft" and deriding pacifism as unmanly, Roosevelt and others believed that a firm stand and a righteous war would strengthen America's moral fiber and earn the nation new respect around the globe. The advocates of preparedness lobbied for military appropriations and for a harder line against German submarine warfare.

WILSON'S NEUTRALITY

Steering a middle course, Wilson sought to uphold traditional neutral rights yet avoid war. The two goals proved irreconcilable. Freedom of the seas was a neutral right, but with the British navy enforcing a tight blockade of Germany, America's "neutral" trade benefited only Britain and its allies. When shortage of capital threatened to limit British and French purchases in the United States, Wilson permitted Americans to extend credit to these belligerents and loftily justified growing Anglo-American economic ties as perfectly consistent with neutrality. Moreover, America's rigid insistence on neutral rights threatened the effectiveness of Germany's new weapon, the submarine. Wilson demanded that Germany abandon surprise attacks and follow the traditional procedure of first warning and then removing passengers from a besieged ship. He announced that Germany would be held to "strict accountability" for any loss of American life on the high seas.

But the German government depended upon its submarines to cut off supplies to Great Britain. It could only warn Americans that they traveled on English vessels at their own risk. When in May 1915 a torpedo sank the *Lusitania,* a British passenger liner which also carried munitions, hundreds of innocent people died, among them many Americans. The deed outraged the country and strengthened the forces favoring preparedness, but the president maintained that there was an admirable quality of being "too proud to fight" and continued trying to negotiate neutral guarantees. After the sinking of the French passenger ship *Sussex* in March 1916, Wilson finally

Eugene Debs, a Christian Socialist, said to the jury that sent him to prison:
"Gentlemen, I abhor war. I would oppose it if I stood alone."
Brown Brothers

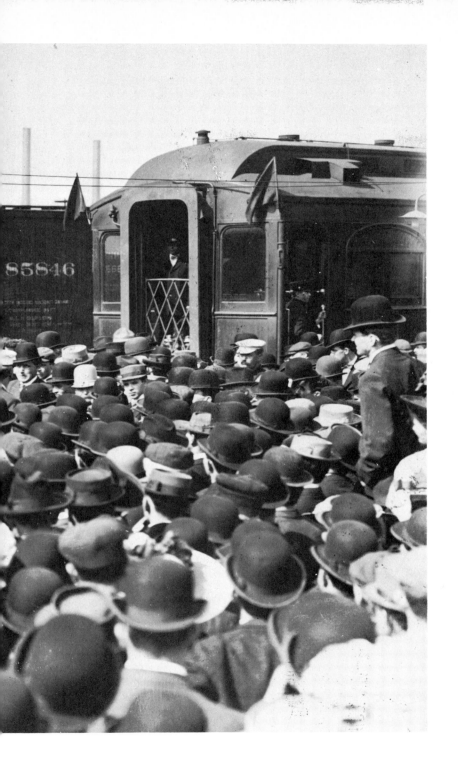

delivered an ultimatum: the United States would sever relations unless Germany ceased its methods of submarine warfare. Reluctant to bring America into the war, Germany acceded to the demand, promising to uphold the rules of visit and search. Wilson's supporters in the election of 1916 could claim that he had "kept us out of war."

The *Sussex* pledge was not a workable formula for peace. Wilson's ultimatum made the issue of war or peace dependent upon decisions in Berlin, and German military officials ultimately considered the submarine campaign more important than the risk of American involvement. In January 1917 Germany announced the resumption of unrestricted submarine warfare. Wilson had warned in an earlier address that a moment might come when the United States could not preserve both honor and peace and asked Americans not to "exact of me an impossible and contradictory thing." Now the country knew that war lay only one torpedo away.

WILSON'S HOPES

The issue of neutral rights did not alone bring America into the war. Wilson nurtured a growing desire to have a hand in shaping the postwar peace. Like most Americans, the president believed deeply in the superiority of the American way and in the corruption of the Old World. The war revealed the disastrous consequences of the old diplomacy of secret treaties, diplomatic intrigue, and spheres of influence. Wilson shared the progressives' faith that the world was marching upward on an evolutionary path toward democracy, liberalism, and open diplomacy. A devout Presbyterian, he believed that the years of horror and devastation should be put to a higher end and become a transitional phase to this new and better order. As war weakened the European powers and America emerged stronger, Wilson began to believe he could act as a peacemaker—not just as an ordinary mediator but as an impartial architect with power to construct the new world on the ruins of the old. The president at first attempted to use America's neutral position to bring the warring nations to the conference table. He sent his close personal friend and special emissary, Colonel Edward House, to meet with European leaders, but neither side was seriously interested in genuine compromise.

Wilson realized that he could play a major role in a postwar peace conference only if America joined the war as a belligerent, and his own personal sympathy for England together with the submarine issue made this alternative more and more likely. Then, in March 1917, shortly after Germany's declaration of unrestricted submarine warfare, Great Britain turned over to the State Department a telegram from German foreign minister Alfred Zimmermann inviting Mexico, which produced much of the allies' oil, to declare war against the United States in the event of hostilities. This revelation of

German designs, threatening our southern border and petroleum interests, outraged Americans; anti-German sentiment flooded the country, and in April 1917 Wilson went before a special session of Congress to ask for a declaration of war.

Wilson had already articulated the purposes for which he believed America should fight: not for victory, but for a "peace without victory." Through war, Americans would bring to the world "American principles, American policies," which "are also the principles and policies of forward-looking men and women everywhere. . . . They are the principles of mankind and must prevail." The sense of mission and the desire to spread the American way worldwide stretches from the first colonists to the present, but these goals had no more eloquent or dedicated champion than Woodrow Wilson.

America at war

In 1917 and 1918 Americans no longer hummed "I didn't raise my boy to be a soldier." They sang "It's a long way to Berlin, but we'll get there" or the famous patriotic bombasts of George M. Cohan, such as "Johnny get your gun, . . . take it on the run, . . . hear them calling you and me, every son of liberty. Hurry right away, no delay, go today . . . over there!"

Americans made a small but significant contribution to military victory. The American Expeditionary Force in France, commanded by General John J. Pershing, relieved some of the pressure on British and French forces and helped launch a series of counteroffensives which eventually led to an armistice. On the sea, where German submarines threatened British supply lines, America's small navy and large shipbuilding capacity helped maintain Allied control of the Atlantic. America's economic potential and financial power were its most important wartime assets, and their employment in the Allied cause had lasting consequences. Private financiers granted millions of dollars of credit to England and France before America joined the war, and after American entry Congress authorized the federal government to extend financing directly. In 1914 British investors had a huge investment stake in America: by 1919 the United States had liquidated this indebtedness and reversed the tables, becoming a great creditor to Britain. By the end of the war, various nations of the world owed America over $10 billion. This loaned money was a stimulant, not a drain on the American economy, for most of it went into the purchase of products made in the United States. Industry boomed and huge commercial farms expanded agricultural production. World War I made America the richest and most productive country in the world, a transformation which led directly to the consumer society of the twenties, to farm overproduction, and to the complex war-debt problem which plagued future diplomacy.

WILSON'S PEACE PLANS

Wilson participated in the war effort wholeheartedly, but he believed America's goals differed significantly from those of its allies and took care not to identify their cause with his own. Insisting that the United States was an "associate," not an "ally," the president operated American troops as a separate entity and refused to merge them into a unified command. When the Bolsheviks overthrew the tsarist government in Russia and published the secret agreements among Allied governments, Wilson had even more reason to dissociate America from Allied war aims. He promulgated his own peace program, the famous Fourteen Points. This articulation of traditional American principles called for open diplomacy, freedom of the seas, armament reductions, free trade, an adjustment of colonial claims, self-determination, and a League of Nations to guarantee independence and territorial integrity. It was Wilson's vision of a purified, harmonious, and liberal world.

But Wilson did not expect a just and peaceful world to appear automatically out of his good intentions. Like others of his generation, he believed that fact gathering, detailed study, and scientific problem solving provided the means to reorder the world. Early in the war he created The Inquiry, a commission charged with drawing together information and plans to bring to the peace conference. It attracted some of the foremost experts and intellectuals of the day, all rallying to help the former president of Princeton construct a new world. Today, when governmental reports and investigatory commissions are commonplace, The Inquiry hardly seems a unique undertaking. In the early twentieth century, it was an exciting new experiment in governmental activity. Financing studies of incredible detail, The Inquiry compiled information on such subjects as boundary disputes, ethnic distribution and relations, land tenure patterns, and rainfall and topography. Although created to provide advice for the peace conference, it went far beyond European affairs (many of its reports, for example, dealt with Latin America), and no subject or part of the world was beyond its scrutiny. The Inquiry symbolized the progressive era: its bureaucratic attention to detail; its energy and optimism; its conviction that the world's problems could be cataloged, understood, and solved; its belief that the war would usher in a new era of American leadership in a more moral and rational world.

THE HOME FRONT

The Inquiry was not the only new governmental bureaucracy. The War Industries Board nationalized raw materials and production; the War Trade Board controlled imports and exports; the Food Administration monitored farm production and urged Americans to observe "wheatless" and "meatless" days. The government regulated prices, supervised fuel supplies, and ran the railroads. The war brought America's first major experiment with a government-directed economy, and many of the experts who manned the wartime emergency boards would later use the experience to fight the economic depression under the next Democratic president, Franklin Roosevelt. One of the small group of radical intellectuals who opposed the war, Randolph Bourne, characterized the men who staffed the wartime bureaucracies:

> The war has revealed a younger intelligentsia, trained up in the pragmatic dispensation, immensely ready for the executive ordering of events, pitifully unprepared for the intellectual interpretation of the idealistic focusing of ends. . . . They are a wholly new force in American life, the product of the swing in the colleges from a training that emphasized classical studies to one that emphasized political and economic values. . . . There seems to have been a peculiar congeniality between the war and these men. It is as if the war and they had been waiting for each other.

ONE HUNDRED PERCENT AMERICANISM

The most controversial of the new agencies was the Committee on Public Information, headed by journalist George Creel. In preceding decades, journalism, like everything else in American life, had undergone extensive centralization. National news services, the Associated Press and the United Press, provided the national and international stories for local papers throughout the country, making news dissemination more efficient, more accurate, and less costly, but also rendering it easier to control from above. Working through the AP and UP, which agreed to voluntary censorship, Creel found wartime news management a less difficult task than it had been during the Civil War or than it might have been in the previous decade of fiercely independent, sensationalist newspapers. And just as The Inquiry attracted many scholars and intellectuals, George Creel also hired hundreds of artists and writers willing to turn their talents to wartime propaganda. The Creel committee's "informational" pamphlets flooded the country and advertised the Allied cause throughout the world. In fact, many critics charged that it oversold the war, creating a spirit of intolerant "100 percent Americanism."

German-American citizens were the most obvious target for the patriotic frenzy. Comprising the country's largest single group of foreign born, German immigrants numbered more than 2.3 million. Many schools banned German language from the curriculum; sauerkraut became known as "liberty cabbage"; and people of German origin felt the suspicion, scorn, and hatred of their neighbors. The president himself capitulated to the "anti-hyphenate" hysteria, striking out against those aliens who "poured the poison of disloyalty" into America and proclaiming that "such creatures of passion, disloyalty, and anarchy must be crushed." Thousands of German aliens were arrested and placed in internment camps.

The pressure for total conformity also bore down upon pacifists and radicals, whose opposition to the war was quickly branded as unpatriotic. Local vigilante groups sprang up to safeguard American life against "aliens" and "radicals." The American Protective Association, a private group which persecuted dissenters of any sort, enjoyed semiofficial governmental sanction. And the government itself led the crusade. The attorney general organized raids against the Industrial Workers of the World and arrested many members of this radical labor union; the postmaster general banned socialist publications from the mails; and the government prosecuted and imprisoned Eugene Debs, the aged socialist leader, for a relatively innocuous statement questioning the goals of the war.

This widespread violation of traditional civil liberties raised concern among some libertarians. They organized the American Civil Liberties Union, a private pressure group which has continued to champion the rights of the individual, including that of dissent, to the present day. There were others, too, who had reservations about the ethical consequences of the war. Franklin K. Lane, Wilson's secretary of the interior, refused to give the *New York World* an interview on the "moral benefits of the war." He wrote:

> This would be sheer camouflage. Of course, we will get some good out of it, and we will learn some efficiency—if that is a moral benefit—and a purer sense of nationalism. But the war will degrade us. That is the plain fact, make sheer brutes out of us, because we will have to descend to the methods that the Germans employ.

But such expressions were rare and seldom made publicly. To most Americans, the war provided an opportunity to Americanize America completely and bring the same values to the rest of the world. It was a chance for achieving purification, patriotism, and peace, even if these goals had to be reached through intolerance, oppression, and war. The repression of the postwar Red Scare and the disillusionment of the twenties were legacies of the crusade "to save the world for democracy."

Who were the progressives? George F. Mowry, in *The California Progressives* (1951) and *The Era of Theodore Roosevelt* (1958), describes the typical "progressive profile." Richard Hofstadter, *The Age of Reform* (1955), suggests some sources of progressivism. Robert H. Wiebe, *Businessmen and Reform* (1962), describes a different group of progressives. Russell B. Nye, *Midwestern Progressive Politics* (1951), deals with an important tradition. William L. O'Neill, *Everybody Was Brave* (1969), is the most detailed account of women in the movement. Michael P. Rogin and John L. Shover, *Political Change in California: Critical Elections and Social Movements, 1890–1966* (1970), contains an important analysis of electoral support for progressive candidates. On the muckrakers, see David M. Chalmers, *The Social and Political Ideas of the Muckrakers* (1964). Best of all, read the progressives' own writings. Lincoln Steffens, *The Autobiography of Lincoln Steffens* (1931), and Jane Addams, *Twenty Years at Hull House* (1910), are both splendid.

How did the progressives deal with the problems of the cities? Were they democratic or elitist? Samuel P. Hays, "The Politics of Reform in Municipal Government in the Progressive Era," *Pacific Northwest Quarterly* 55 (1964): 157–69, and J. Joseph Huthmacher, "Urban Liberalism and the Age of Reform," *Mississippi Valley Historical Review* 49 (1962): 231–41, take diverging viewpoints. Both articles have been widely anthologized. On particular cities see Melvin G. Holli, *Reform in Detroit* (1969), and William D. Miller, *Memphis During the Progressive Era* (1957). Maldwyn A. Jones, *Destination America* (1976), offers a well-balanced look at the role of immigrants and at moves to restrict their entry into the United States.

Did the progressives succeed in revitalizing state government? There are studies of many states. Among the best are Richard M. Abrams, *Conservatism in a Progressive Era: Massachusetts* (1964); Mowry on California, cited above; and Sheldon Hackney, *From Populism to Progressivism in Alabama* (1969). David P. Thelen, *The New Citizenship: Origins of Progressivism in Wisconsin, 1885–1900* (1972), offers perspectives which extend beyond that important progressive state.

Was national government conservative or progressive in the era? Roosevelt, always fascinating, has attracted many biographers. Henry Pringle, *Theodore Roosevelt* (1931); John M. Blum, *The Republican Roosevelt* (1954); and William H. Harbaugh, *Power and Responsibility* (1961), are all excellent. William Manner, *TR and Will* (1969), studies his relationship with William Howard Taft. Henry Pringle, *The Life and Times of William Howard Taft* (1935), is a fine large-as-life portrait. Richard Lowitt, *George W. Norris: The Making of a Progressive* (1963), presents a leading national progressive. Gabriel Kolko, *The Triumph of Conservatism . . . , 1900–1916* (1963), offers harsh judgments on national progressivism, as does from an entirely different perspective Martin Albro, *Enterprise Denied: Origins of the Decline of American Railroads, 1897–1917* (1971). For important groups outside the mainstream see David A. Shannon, *The Socialist Party of America: A History* (1967); James Weinstein, *The Decline of Socialism in America, 1912–1925* (1967); and Melvyn Dubofsky, *We Shall Be All: A History of the Industrial Workers of the World* (1969).

Woodrow Wilson in war and peace: Was the New Freedom a policy both for the nation and the world? Arthur S. Link, *Woodrow Wilson and the Progressive Era* (1954), is a fine introduction; Arthur S. Link, *Woodrow Wilson* (5 vols. to date, 1947–), is magisterial; Alexander L. and Juliette L. George, *Woodrow Wilson and Colonel House: A Personality Study* (1956), is psychoanalytical and fascinating; John M. Blum, *Woodrow Wilson and the Politics of Morality* (1956), is elegant and thoughtful. On Mexico see Robert F. Smith, *The United States and Revolutionary Nationalism in Mexico, 1916–1932* (1972). The best introductions to Wilson's diplomacy are Arthur S. Link, *Wilson the Diplomatist* (1957), and N. Gordon Levin, *Woodrow Wilson and World Politics* (1968). For material on the home front consult Frederick L. Paxson, *American Democracy and the World War* (3 vols., 1936–48). For a fascinating picture of the effect of the war on American culture see Henry F. May, *The End of American Innocence . . . , 1912–1917* (1959).

11

THE BUOYANT TWENTIES

1918-1932

AL CAPONE

Among the great celebrities of the 1920s was the gangster Al Capone. He received fan mail from all over the world, including requests to "rub out" irritating neighbors. The lucky visitor to Chicago might catch a glimpse of the "big fellow" lolling in his seven-ton, silk-upholstered limousine complete with bodyguard in the front seat nursing a machine gun on his lap. The extravagant Capone customarily wore a fifty-thousand-dollar diamond ring and carried fifty thousand in cash in his wallet. Meticulous and fond of personal luxury, Al slept between monogramed silk sheets; his solid silver toilet seat also bore his initials.

Born in 1899 in Brooklyn, Capone learned about life from the city streets. No boy would linger an instant longer than necessary in the fetid tenements, and the schools and churches gave scant attention to poor Italian immigrant children. The street gangs offered escape, adventure, and violence. In his teens Capone joined the notorious Five Pointers of Manhattan's lower East Side. The police arrested him three times in New York, once for disorderly conduct, twice on suspi-

cion of homicide. Capone became a protégé there of the gangster Johnny Torrio, who summoned him to Chicago after the World War.

Under the benevolent eye of Chicago's antiprohibition Mayor "Big Bill" Thompson ("I'm wetter than the middle of the Atlantic Ocean"), Capone engineered perhaps fifty of the city's five hundred gangland slayings in the course of the twenties. Best known for bootlegging liquor, he also dabbled in the protection and prostitution rackets. The brutal slaying of seven North Side gang members on Saint Valentine's Day, 1929, Capone dismissed with characteristic brio as "bad public relations." "A real goddam crazy place," remarked his Five Pointers pal Lucky Luciano after a visit to Chicago: "Nobody's safe in the streets."

Capone always lived with danger. He acquired a country estate in Wisconsin and added machine gun emplacements to a lookout tower near the main house. Later he built a shorefront home near Miami, Florida, and offered to join the local Rotary Club—but time was running out. In 1929 President Herbert Hoover, between *thwunks* of early-morning exercise with a medicine ball, ordered Secretary of the Treasury Andrew Mellon to "get" Capone. The ensuing battle sounded more exciting than it was. A melodramatic government agent named Eliot Ness grabbed the headlines, and Capone, to the dismay of his associates, planned wholesale murder of the Chicago branch of the Internal Revenue Department. Meanwhile, quiet work by Internal Revenue agents bore results. Capone drew an eleven-year prison sentence for tax evasion and eventually went to Alcatraz. Afterward he survived with his family in rural Pennsylvania until 1947, when syphilis conquered his brain. The writer Rafael Sabatini conceded Capone to have been "a center of that atmosphere of treachery, intrigue, shots in the dark, and raw power in which historical romance best grows," but disqualified him as a hero because "he really seems to have no ideals."

Capone once described his career as "heroic." Theodore Roosevelt's heroic Americans were hunters, cowboys, frontiersmen, soldiers, naval heroes; but in the crowded slums gangsters were heroes. Capone rivaled New York's Governor Al Smith as the first successful public figure of recent immigrant stock. Purveying liquor and women was a career open to talent: Capone was only twenty-nine at the height of his power.

Crime offered the immigrant American denied other opportunities a risky but enriching path of advancement. Organized crime also fed on the cleavage between the big city and the small town. In making unlawful certain elements of urban night life such as drinking, gambling, and prostitution, rural legislatures opened the way for a new kind of

American entrepreneur. Then, as always, Americans loved a man who got ahead. Not only did newspaper headlines and crime stories bespeak America's fascination with these new celebrities: one of the finest novels of the age, F. Scott Fitzgerald's *The Great Gatsby*, reached into this lurid world of bootlegging and racketeering to find a hero about whom some spoke in whispers "who had found little that it was necessary to whisper about in this world."

Jack Levine, *Gangster Funeral*
Collection of Whitney Museum of American Art, New York

1918–1932

The red scare

America's brief participation in World War I had lasting effects. In the disturbing times just afterward—the era known as the "Red Scare"—shocking events moved hard upon one another, and groups of people reacted almost primitively in fear or hatred or simple ignorance. The war passion, so well orchestrated by the Committee on Public Information, endured longer than the fighting, releasing emotions which sought out fresh enemies.

In a rapid demobilization the government released half a million soldiers at once and over the course of the year 4 million more. The economy fluttered and prices rose. In the labor market uncertainty came to seem almost normal: some 9 million men moved from wartime jobs to work in a peace-

496

time economy, and strikes hit industries no longer under federal constraints. Across the Atlantic a new specter rose to replace the defeated Hun—Russian communism (then called Bolshevism). A few thousand American soldiers actually engaged Russian troops in Siberia early in 1919.

1919: WINTER AND SPRING

Viewed as a band of nihilistic fanatics, American Bolsheviks were accused of influencing the first great domestic drama of 1919, the general strike in Seattle, Washington. The very idea of a "general" strike, when all workers would rally in defense of a few, had almost no precedent in the United States. A "Committee of Fifteen" set up to supervise the operation, even when it conscientiously attended to problems of public safety and health, sounded vaguely foreign and sinister. The strike crippled Seattle: its "pulse . . . had ceased to beat," wrote one journalist after seeing the deserted downtown streets. Yet the shipyard owners, the target of the strike, suffered no special deprivation. Mayor Ole Hanson portrayed the strike leaders as Bolsheviks, and gradually public opinion came to support his employment of private police to ensure public order. Lacking a well-defined goal and the means to accomplish it, the strike dissolved in early February after just two weeks.

During that episode Mayor Hanson's actions had earned for him the reputation of a vigorous anti-Communist. In late April, while he was away on a Victory Bond tour, his office received a package wrapped in brown paper. Some liquid leaking from the box burned a table. The liquid proved to be acid, the package a bomb. In Georgia Senator Thomas Hardwick's maid picked up a similar parcel which exploded in her hands and face. These events, trumpeted in newspaper headlines, caught the eye of a clerk from the New York City central post office as he rode the West Side subway home. After reading the description of the packages, he dashed from the train at the next station and caught the downtown express. Back at the post office he found more than a dozen similar packages he had set aside for insufficient postage three days earlier. All contained homemade bombs. Additional explosives were discovered in transit. The press compiled a "bomb honor list" of famous citizens, including Supreme Court justices and John D. Rockefeller, Jr. In June bombs went off in eight major cities, and an Italian anarchist blew himself to bits with his own device when he stumbled on the stone steps of Attorney General A. Mitchell Palmer's house in Washington, D.C.

These bomb-throwers gave the American Left a reputation for vitality far out of proportion to its actual strength. The number of Communist party members in America during 1919 was relatively small—something like fifty thousand. The larger Socialist party's idea of revolution was one of gradual, democratic ascendance through the electoral system. Its eloquent leader, Eugene V. Debs, languished in the Atlanta federal penitentiary for actively opposing the war. Yet this shrinking Left became the principal object of popular fears.

1919: SUMMER AND FALL

Further events contributed to social tensions during 1919. On a hot August day, a black teenager in Chicago accidentally floated over an invisible line and into a bathing area reserved for whites. Greeted by a barrage of stones, in confusion he abandoned a floating railroad tie, swam a few strokes, sank, and drowned. The episode, seen by hundreds of bathers, sparked full-scale rioting in Chicago that ended with thirty-eight dead—twenty-three blacks and fifteen whites. Another race riot erupted in July in Washington, D.C.; later disturbances came in Knoxville and Omaha. All were related to the vast migrations of blacks to cities and to the North for jobs during World War I, to new militancy as a result of military service, and to the resistance of all-white neighborhoods to black encroachments.

In early September the Boston police, infuriated by an autocratic chief, walked off their jobs, leaving the city defenseless. As in Seattle, the Bolsheviks were blamed. President Wilson called it a "crime against civilization." The chief simply hired a largely new force to maintain public order. A few weeks later labor strikes paralyzed the steel and coal industries. Many steel workers still put in a twelve-hour day and a six-day week, while in the coal mines conditions were unsafe and unhealthy. These strikes, like thirty-six hundred others that broke out in 1919, aimed primarily at preserving collective bargaining or the simple economic gains of the war. The corporations, aggressively resisting unionism, promoted the "American plan" or nonunion open shop. Like most of the other walkouts, those in steel and coal ultimately failed; the steel companies refused even to discuss terms with the striking workers and resisted unionization in their industry until the 1930s. Throughout the twenties labor unions never regained the influence and membership they had achieved under a friendly wartime administration. An Industrial Conference held in Washington in November 1919 dramatized the stubbornness of the big corporations; they flatly rejected the principle of unrestricted collective bargaining. Many insisted that laborers choose their spokesmen from within the factory, seeking to avoid all but company-oriented unions.

THE PALMER RAIDS

Many of the charges linking labor strikes with Bolshevism, Attorney General A. Mitchell Palmer knew to be wild exaggerations. But Palmer soon joined the popular clamor. In September the Justice Department deported to Finland and Russia some two thousand "undesirable" aliens, mostly Russian Jews, on the *S.S. Buford.* One newspaper reported the hysterical entreaties of wives and children as "Reds Try to Free Commie Pals." The evangelist Billy Sunday wanted more Bolsheviks sent to sea in "ships of stone with masts of lead." Another 249 aliens embarked to Finland in November.

On the night of January 2, 1920, acting almost simultaneously in thirty-two major cities, agents from the Justice Department and local police rounded up thousands of alleged Communists. Often held in violation of constitutional rights, sometimes denied food, water, heat, or sanitary facilities, a few of the prisoners succumbed to serious disease or death. A Detroit paper photographed a man kept in filthy surroundings for some days, without water to wash or shave, and labeled the picture "Unkempt Bolshevist."

The Palmer raids were the high point of the Red Scare. A few days later the New York State Assembly refused to seat five duly elected Socialist members, but former Supreme Court Chief Justice Charles Evans Hughes and other prominent Americans protested vigorously. In Washington acting Secretary of Labor Louis F. Post refused to deport many of the aliens Palmer had rounded up. As depression approached, people turned from dramatic public events to the pressing need of making a living. Suppression, too, had its effects in bringing agitation to an end. Those wanting social change were dispirited; reformers retreated into private worlds of business, writing, and the arts.

The league of nations

The postwar period was a time of innocence assaulted by experience. Having finished a war it thought it could handle on the simplest and purest moral terms, the nation discovered that these terms meant little to Europe, a continent it thought oddly ungrateful to the United States and unresponsive to an eminently reasonable and virtuous American guidance.

President Wilson himself had cast the national interest into a perfectly honest, if self-deceptive, rhetoric of liberal internationalism. He envisioned a world peace-keeping organization hospitable to capitalism and free trade, with the United States occupying the leadership. This League of Nations would control both old-fashioned imperialism and new threats of social revolution.

Even though cheering throngs greeted him in London, Paris, and Rome, Wilson soon discovered that promising a lasting peace was easier than creating one. In Paris he met with representatives of Great Britain, France, and Italy to draft the Treaty of Versailles and construct "a just and lasting peace." Wilson was most effective in scaling down Allied territorial demands and in setting boundaries that conformed in the main to lines of nationality. He himself desired punishment for Germany, but opposed the

DRINK
Coca-Cola
DELICIOUS · REFRESHING

5¢

In the course
of time there is occa-
sionally developed an article so singular in its superiority
as to be absolutely peerless in
its class. That is the rank
assumed by COCA-COLA among
the world's harmless, delicious,
temperance beverages.
On sale at all founts and car-
bonated in bottles

5¢

Yesterday

exorbitant reparations the Allies successfully demanded. On this and other matters, he believed that an American presence in a League of Nations, which he fused with the Versailles treaty, would remove persisting inequities.

AMERICA STAYS OUT

Yet Wilson did little to prepare the Senate or the American people for acceptance of the League; initial support disintegrated in a year of controversy. On his mission to Paris he failed to take along Senate Republicans —now the majority party following the 1918 congressional elections—and showed open contempt for the new chairman of the Senate Foreign Relations Committee, Henry Cabot Lodge of Massachusetts. Anti-League senators he called "bungalow-minds," their heads "knots tied to keep their bodies from unraveling." Besides Wilson's slights, the Republicans also had selfish reasons to suspect the League. If the Wilson cause triumphed here as it had in war, they would have less hope for success in the next elections. Senator Lodge, who had endorsed limited American participation in some kind of international group as early as 1915, proposed a series of reservations that would have exempted the Monroe Doctrine and other traditional American policies from League jurisdiction. The central point of controversy between Lodge and Wilson was Article X of the League Covenant, which seemed to compel America into a collective-security arrangement. The president's partisan attitude, his insistence on making it a "Wilson" League, and his refusal to accept any reservation coming from Lodge forced the Republicans into various forms of opposition, and ultimately doomed the chances for Senate ratification of the Versailles treaty.

Republicans were not the only group estranged from the League. Young men and women active in the Progressive Era had wanted the League to spread the moralism of Wilson's Fourteen Points throughout the world. But the compromises forced on him at Paris discouraged these idealists and led them away from political involvement. Some concluded that the Fourteen Points were merely propaganda to counter Russian Bolshevik allegations about secret Allied agreements concerning the postwar division of spoils. Even in setting eastern European boundaries along ethnic and national lines, the president was suspected of creating buffers against Russia.

Wilson also lost the support of several traditionally Democratic immigrant groups who violently rejected the Versailles treaty. Irish Americans joined their homeland in fearing the large number of votes the English controlled in the League Assembly, which they supposed would slow the movement for Irish independence. Italian Americans resented giving Fiume to the new state of Yugoslavia. Versailles ignored the Jewish campaign for a new national homeland. German Americans saw the reparations as punitive. All these ethnic groups would vote Republican in 1920.

Although weakened by influenza, Wilson attempted to revive flagging support for the League by a direct appeal to the people. He went west on a speaking tour. Admitting that the treaty was flawed but claiming that the League would correct inequities, Wilson, after some thirty speeches, felt the tide running in his direction. But on September 25, 1919, he suffered a breakdown in Colorado and, a few days after returning by darkened train to the White House, a paralyzing stroke. Had he died then, the Treaty of Versailles with the League built into it would have sailed through the Senate. As it was, he lived and people gossiped; it was whispered that the barred windows of the White House held a demented man within. (They had been put there to prevent Teddy Roosevelt's boys from breaking windows with wayward baseballs.) Although Wilson earlier had drafted acceptable amendments to the League Covenant, now he stood fixed against compromise. When in November the Senate voted on the treaty with the Lodge reservations, administration Democrats joined the League's opponents to defeat it. Again, in March 1920, southern Democrats combined with outright adversaries rather than accept the taint of Lodge's hand.

Was our failure to join the League a tragedy? No one can say with certainty. League membership might have quickened our will to act against fascist aggression in the 1930s. On the other hand, America played a vigorous international role in the 1920s and could move swiftly and more freely outside the League in the thirties. It cannot automatically be assumed that staying independent was either a disaster or a boon to world peace. The uncertainty of the debate over collective security in 1919 remains an uncertainty now.

Economic internationalism

The Senate's refusal to ratify the League of Nations represented not so much a victory for isolationism as the work of a successful coalition ranging from the antiimperialist Senator William E. Borah to the expansionist Henry Cabot Lodge. Even those Republicans who opposed the League often shared the central vision of Wilsonian internationalism: a free-trading world with equality of competition and respect for property rights. Wilson's Republican successors agreed on the importance of keeping the world safe for America's peaceful economic expansion, and they pursued a vigorous involvement in world affairs.

World War I began a decade of rapid economic growth. During the war young, highly trained professionals found a niche for their talents within the bureaucracy of government. They worked with businessmen to heighten production and, after the war, to promote prosperity and industrial investment abroad. Postwar fears of widespread economic disruption and unemployment made business expansion an imperative means of warding off social revolution. Herbert Hoover, infatuated with the guiding power of government which the war revealed, constructed during the twenties an active Department of Commerce, whose job was "to inspire and assist in cooperative action" the growth of American business.

During the 1920s Americans generally believed, somewhat mistakenly, that their own consumptive capacity could not absorb the high production that their factories now maintained. Businessmen joined with government in directing concerted drives to expand exports and to encourage investment of capital in foreign lands. Investment served two purposes: foreigners would inevitably use a portion of the borrowed capital to purchase American products, and investments, by helping the debtor country build up its economy, served as a bulwark against social revolution and the spread of Bolshevism. Economic expansion, not political instruments such as the League of Nations, came to be seen as the best road to world stability.

ECONOMIC EXPANSION ABROAD

Before World War I the United States had little capital invested abroad and presented only a distant competitive threat to the major exporting countries of the world. After the war, European nations which had contracted vast debts in the United States undertook agonizing programs of economic reconstruction. The United States, physically untouched by combat and greatly enriched by wartime profits, became an important industrial exporter and a powerful creditor for the first time in its history. Industrial products, rather than agricultural goods, now constituted the bulk of American sales abroad. Just as the age of the automobile characterized life at home, so the expansion of America's foreign trade depended to a large degree upon the export of automobiles, automotive accessories, and petroleum for the relatively new internal-combustion engine. By 1928 these products made up over 20 percent of American exports, although before the war they had constituted a bare 7 percent.

In the realm of finance, New York began to replace London as the hub of the world's credit market. Americans loaned billions of dollars abroad, particularly in Germany, to assist foreign governments and industry. In Latin America, a new form of investment was perfected—the branch business. Rather than loaning capital to Latin Americans to build their own factories, mines, or agricultural enterprises, Americans simply established branches of industries whose home offices lay within the United States. This mode of business organization—the multinational corporation—permitted American businessmen to take advantage of cheap foreign labor supplies and to avoid tariff barriers in the host country. The long-term consequence of the establishment of branch businesses in Latin America, a trend which would extend worldwide after World War II, was the development of a particularly viru-lent strain of "Yankeephobia." Companies such as Standard Oil, RCA, United States Steel, Anaconda Copper, Swift and Company, and United Fruit became synonymous with "Yankee imperialism" to many Latin Americans.

America's new technology brought in its wake a new cultural influence abroad. Motion pictures were surely among the most popular export prod-ucts, and the entire globe joined in idolizing the great screen stars of the twenties. The way in which movies spread, popularized, and distorted the image of America in foreign lands has had a lasting, if difficult-to-define, im-pact upon the United States' relations with other peoples.

DISARMAMENT

In 1921 Secretary of State Charles Evans Hughes invited Britain, France, Italy, the Netherlands, Belgium, Portugal, China, and Japan to a conference on naval disarmament and Far Eastern questions. Another sign of America's new prominence, it was the first major international conference ever held in Washington. Before a startled audience at the opening session, the imposing and dignified secretary of state wasted few words on the formalities of wel-come and, quickly abandoning platitudes, offered specific proposals for the suspension of naval construction and the scrapping of existing ships. Hughes in thirty-five minutes sank "more ships than all the admirals of the world have sunk in a cycle of centuries." The time did seem propitious for naval disarmament. Each country felt pressure for economy in government and feared an arms race similar to the one which preceded World War I. The naval agreement reached in Washington was remarkable in its scope. The nations agreed to scrap over 2 million tons of vessels and to limit their ton-nage to precise ratios: 5 for the United States, 5 for Great Britain, 3 for Japan, and 1.67 each for France and Italy.

The initial foreign policy interest of Warren G. Harding's new Republi-can administration was in naval matters, but the Washington Conference also tried to deal with the uncertain balance of power in the Far East. In a four-power treaty the United States, Britain, France, and Japan agreed col-lectively to guarantee the status quo in Asia. A nine-power treaty provided a pledge to maintain the Open Door in China and outlawed spheres of in-fluence. These agreements, never supported by Japanese militarists, would be violated by them within less than a decade.

The Washington treaties (nine in all) represented a major contribution to disarmament, and they spurred a peace movement which reached fruition in the Kellogg-Briand Pact of 1928. France originally proposed a binational re-nunciation of war to the United States, and Coolidge's secretary of state, Frank B. Kellogg, expanded upon the idea. He suggested that all nations of the world sign a declaration outlawing war as an instrument of national policy. With no enforcement procedures, the pact reflected the well-intentioned hopes of the period. Together with the League of Nations and the Washington treaties, it created an international structure which most Americans hoped would keep the peace. But these arrangements of trust proved inadequate in the 1930s to deal with international disruptions growing out of worldwide economic depression and resurgent nationalism.

Republican policy

Even before his illness President Wilson seemed to fade from public view. Between December 1918 and July 1919 he stayed abroad at the Paris Peace Conference, returning home once for a brief ten-day trip in March. After his cerebral hemorrhage in the fall, he remained secluded in the White House. He could no longer provide the domestic leadership the nation and his party sorely needed.

Wilson retained, however, a jealous interest in the selection of his successor, asking that the coming election be a "great and solemn referendum" on the League of Nations. Then he cavalierly dismissed the other likely Democratic candidates as they acquired prominence and finally decided he would have to run again. But his party would not consider a third term, and although he lived on until 1924—outlasting his replacement Warren Harding—his influence was at an end.

The strongest Democratic presidential candidate was Wilson's own son-in-law William Gibbs McAdoo, secretary of the treasury until he resigned late in 1918. Ambitious to a fault, McAdoo stood high in public opinion polls; but Wilson would not support him, and the canny McAdoo divined that 1920 would be an inauspicious year for the Democratic party. Another Wilsonian, Attorney General Palmer, hoped to use the Red Scare as a means to the presidency. But as the hysteria subsided, so did Palmer's presidential prospects. The candidate actually chosen at the Democratic convention was Governor James Cox of Ohio. Although the favorite of anti-Wilsonian machine bosses in New York, Chicago, and Indiana, the moderately progressive Cox adopted an administration position in his lackluster campaign. The vice-presidential candidate, Franklin D. Roosevelt, a relatively obscure New Yorker but for his surname, proved a more attractive campaigner than Cox.

The Republican nomination was sought eagerly. By 1920 the Democrats were receiving blame for everything from the war settlement to the high cost of living, from worsening unemployment to declining farm prices. General Leonard Wood was a popular candidate who had been favored by the late Teddy Roosevelt, and Governor Frank Lowden of Illinois had important agrarian support. But the two men, especially Wood, indulged in an orgy of campaign spending that received bad publicity and deadlocked the convention voting. The handsome Ohio Senator Warren G. Harding stood waiting in the wings. With the help of prominent senators and party bosses, Harding won the nomination. Governor Calvin Coolidge of Massachusetts was a natural choice for vice-president; he had become famous during the Boston police strike for his injunction, "There is no right to strike against the public safety by anybody, anywhere, anytime."

Cox was no match for Harding in 1920. The expansive newspaper publisher from Marion—dubbed the "Ohio Marionette" by opponents—obfuscated the issues, talking around them. He even tried to take both sides on the question of United States membership in the League of Nations, but gradually adopted a clearly negative position. While Cox and Roosevelt hustled around the country pumping for the League, Harding stayed near the front porch of his Marion home. The strategy worked for Harding, as it had for William McKinley, and the votes came pouring in on election day; Harding won by nearly a two-to-one margin.

President Harding—a much loved man—and Mrs. Harding in Ohio.
Photoworld

HARDING

Presidents Harding and Coolidge were ill equipped to understand the economic and industrial complexities of the 1920s. The task was too much for the affable Harding, but he worked hard and showed himself capable of some remarkably good judgments, particularly in selecting a few members of his cabinet. Charles Evans Hughes, formerly governor of New York and Supreme Court justice, became secretary of state; Herbert Hoover took the post of Commerce, Henry C. Wallace that of Agriculture. Andrew Mellon, head of the Treasury Department, was an able spokesman for business.

But the presidency never went well for Harding. During his first two years in office the economy was in severe depression following its deflation by the Federal Reserve Board. Because of the hard times, voters almost gave the Democrats control of Congress in the off-year elections of 1922. Worse still for Harding, it gradually became apparent that a number of his appointees were crooks. Trouble came first in the Veterans' Bureau under Charles R. Forbes, who later spent a term in prison for embezzling a quarter-million dollars of public funds. The corruption under Harding reached up to the cabinet. Secretary of the Interior Albert Fall had managed to make improvements on his New Mexico ranch at a cost of a hundred and seventy thousand dollars even though his annual salary was only twelve thousand dollars. Fall had persuaded the naive Navy Secretary Edwin Denby to transfer out of the public domain oil reserves at Elk Hills, California, and Teapot Dome, Wyoming. For this service the grateful oil magnates who leased the properties, Edwin L. Doheny and Harry F. Sinclair, had "loaned" Fall considerable sums. The trail of corruption even skirted the offices of the president's confidante Attorney General Harry Daugherty, when Jesse Smith, a notorious "fixer" with an office in the Justice Department, committed suicide in Daugherty's apartment and left a fifty-thousand-dollar joint bank account he maintained with Daugherty. The extent of the Harding scandals may have been exaggerated, but they were dramatic.

President Harding learned something of the scandals before he started out on a trip to Alaska in the summer of 1923. During the long train ride west he played bridge incessantly and seemed deeply troubled in mind and body. After a speech in Seattle, he became sick while en route to San Francisco. There, confined to his hotel bed, he died on August 2 when a blood clot reached his brain.

COOLIDGE

The new president, Calvin Coolidge, was a flinty little man of straitlaced habits and overpowering rectitude; he would not be betrayed by his intimate friends, for he had none. Famous as a public man of few words and frigid disposition—when told that Coolidge died, someone asked, "How can they tell?"—his exterior was misleading. Almost affable in reality and possessed of a calculating political sense bred by years of experience in Massachusetts politics, Coolidge gradually eased Daugherty out of the cabinet and appointed a bipartisan committee to investigate the "Harding scandals."

The deceased president served as scapegoat for the scandals, and the Democrats, with the 1924 election approaching, ran into a scandal of their own. William Gibbs McAdoo, the candidate of western and southern Democrats, had received considerable sums in legal fees from oil financier Doheny and was promised far more. McAdoo's opponent at the Democratic convention in New York City in June 1924 was the state's reform governor, Alfred E. Smith, a spokesman for the new urban constituency of ethnic Democrats. The candidates, representing rural and urban America, battled to a hundred-ballot stalemate, appalling the country and wrecking their party's hopes. The compromise nominee, lawyer John W. Davis, lost badly to Coolidge. A third-party candidate, Senator Robert La Follette of Wisconsin, earned 5 million votes for his reformist and foreign policy views.

Andrew Mellon was known to many contemporaries as the greatest Treasury secretary since Alexander Hamilton
Culver Pictures

By and large, the Harding and Coolidge programs were of a piece. Both men opposed reforms that might dampen the business climate. The progressive impulse, vibrantly alive as late as 1916 with the passage of the Adamson Act prescribing an eight-hour day for railroad workers, now lay dormant. Late in 1919 the journalist Walter Lippmann asked: "Can anyone name a single reform initiated or carried through since the Armistice?" Basically, progressivism had depended on presidential leadership, and although a reform impulse survived in Congress as well as in some local and state governments, it served mainly to restrain business-oriented national administrations rather than to initiate programs of its own.

CONGRESS

Congressional opposition, for example, thwarted the plans of Treasury Secretary Andrew Mellon for years. A Pittsburgh industrialist and one of the world's richest men, Mellon sought to lower federal taxes on the wealthy. This would free capital, he reasoned, for industrial investment here and abroad. But only after seven years in the cabinet did he accomplish the chief goals he had set forth in 1921. Opposition from progressive midwestern Republicans stymied Mellon until the Democrats, sensing the popularity of his efforts, supported him in 1927 and 1928.

Congress also resisted the White House in other areas. It had cooperated in the early twenties on some important legislation to help the farmers: the Capper-Volstead Law of 1922 exempted farmers' cooperatives from prosecution under the antitrust laws; the Fordney-McCumber Tariff passed in the same year protected agricultural produce; and the Agricultural Marketing Act of 1923 offered intermediate term credits. Actually, many if not most farmers fared reasonably well during the twenties. But the major farm issue of the decade sharply divided the two branches of government. Proponents of the McNary-Haugen Bill wanted the Agriculture Department to assure a minimum price for produce. To control foreign marketing, a government-owned corporation would purchase surplus agricultural crops at a good price and then sell them abroad. As a result of artificially created scarcity, domestic prices would rise; farmers would pay the government an equalization fee to offset its expenses. Twice the bill passed Congress; twice President Coolidge vetoed it.

A similar stalemate developed over proposed construction of an electric power and nitrate plant at Muscle Shoals on the Tennessee River in northern Alabama. During World War I the federal government had produced nitrates there, and the question was how to dispose of uncompleted government facilities on the river. Henry Ford offered to lease the plants and construct "a great new Detroit" in the Tennessee Valley—a mixed blessing, some said. He withdrew his offer, however, when congressional opponents called his demand for a ninety-nine-year lease a "giveaway" of public lands and water power. Then Senator George Norris of Nebraska helped expose a gambit by General Electric, under the guise of private power companies, to take over the region. Finally, Congress passed Norris's own bill for government operation, which Coolidge angrily vetoed in 1928.

Harding and Coolidge fared better in their attempts to aid business through appointments to the federal regulatory agencies. By the end of the decade, the Federal Reserve Board, the Federal Trade Commission, and the Interstate Commerce Commission had majorities who generally subverted the regulatory functions for which the agencies had been presumably created. They conceived of their powers as designed to aid business and promote prosperity. The Supreme Court, changed considerably after four new appointments by Harding alone, usually adopted a "hands-off" attitude toward business. One reason unions fared so miserably in the twenties was unsympathetic treatment by the courts. In *Bailey* v. *Drexel Furniture* (1922) the Supreme Court even rejected a law regulating child labor. In *Adkins* v. *Children's Hospital* (1923) the Court declared invalid a District of Columbia minimum-wage law for women on grounds that it interfered with liberty of contract.

The economy

The economy of the 1920s had its soft spots—notably the textile industry in New England, coal mining in Pennsylvania and West Virginia, and wheat farming in the western Middle West—but in general it was vibrant and strong. Great productivity brought automobiles, radios, household appliances, and even houses within reach of most American families. The number of automobiles in the course of the decade tripled, from 9 to 27 million, and led to a boom in highway building and real estate. Electricity and interior plumbing became customary items rather than luxuries in all except rural homes. Productivity and economic growth were hallmarks of the decade.

The coming of plenty owed a great deal to the war itself. The invention of new machines and concepts of engineering management go back to the last century, but their use became essential in 1917–18. Mass production proved itself in building ships and airplane motors. The plants themselves, as well as standardized production along the assembly line, lasted into peacetime. Electricity also speeded the revolution in production: in 1914 some 30 percent of manufacturing was electrified; in 1929 seventy percent of all factories benefited from the ease and versatility of the new power source. Everything became mechanized: loading devices, highway pavers, an important new warp-tying machine in textiles. Higher wages were a cause as well as a result of technical advance, making the introduction of still more labor-saving machinery desirable. And the government helped. High tariffs aided the young chemical industry; subsidies sustained the airlines. The Department of Commerce worked to extend American markets abroad and at home it provided businessmen with all varieties of useful statistical data. Trade associations, encouraged by the Republican administrations, helped to control the domestic market and maintain prices through the use of shared cost-accounting procedures; efforts to simplify sizes and designs helped eliminate waste in industry.

THE CONSUMER

The film and radio played a principal part in the formation of the postwar mass-consumer society. They wore down old ideals of thrift and self-denial and suggested hedonistic roles to replace them. The life style of the movies was open to all through consumer credit—"a dollar down and a dollar forever." While in 1920 only 5 percent of the twenty largest corporations directly served the consumer public, by 1929 the figure had risen to 45 percent, headed by the automobile industry. All this meant that the average American was the best-fed and best-clothed person in history. Ordinarily, he owned both an automobile and a radio, both of which increased his mobility and, along with the movies, destroyed the isolation of village and farm. Sports heroes and movie stars became national heroes. Some women entered business and the professions. Modern America was being born.

The economy of the twenties also posed the question of the relationship of industrialism to the environment. Economic growth was an ambiguous blessing. With it came a level of consumption that tore the tops off the nation's forests and despoiled many natural resources. I'll Take My Stand (1930), a protest by southern writers against mass-consumption values and material progress, expressed the feelings of those who preferred the land, perhaps a farm or a village community, to the intangible world of credit. The brutal tempo of the assembly line destroyed the amenities of daily life, and the illusion of power over nature forced an abandonment of the religious sense—of a mysterious nature and its awesome strength. For the most part, however, Americans did not foresee what would happen to the air and water and forests of the land, nor did they notice the subtle changes wrought by servitude to the machine.

WELFARE CAPITALISM

The prestige of businessmen has never been higher than it was in the twenties. Once considered inferior to those in the medical and legal professions, they now took on an aura of professionalism: even Harvard University had founded a School of Business. A managerial revolution stemming from

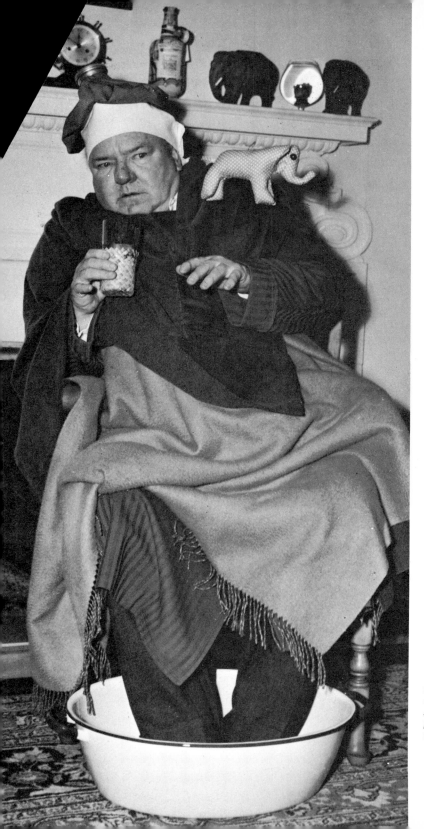

W. C. Fields remarked that his
father, one of the "Great
Immorals," held the Chair of
Applied Electricity at state
prison
Culver Pictures

widespread distribution of corporate stock placed the direction of giant industries in the hands of executives (not owners) with larger interests than immediate profit. The first sustained corporate attempt to treat human problems resulting from industrialization, the movement known as welfare capitalism, had origins in the nineteenth-century paternalistic strain of men like Andrew Carnegie and George Pullman (who built a model town—Pullman, Illinois—for his railroad works' employees). It also drew strength from the progressive era (by which time most of the business leaders of the twenties had come to maturity) and from the war with its spirit of sacrifice for the general good. Especially after the deadly combat with labor in 1919 and the depression of 1920–22, some businessmen saw the importance of avoiding strikes in order to maintain high levels of purchasing power and demand for consumer goods.

Welfare capitalism took varied forms in the 1920s. Accident, illness, and death benefits became quite common, along with provision for plant safety and on-the-job medical services. Several hundred companies offered pension plans; a few even tried profit sharing, relief payments to laid-off employees, or a guaranteed annual wage.

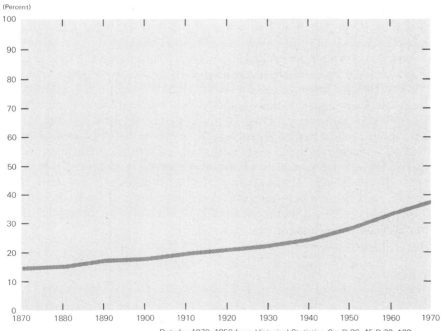

(Percent)

Data for 1870–1950 from Historical Statistics, Ser.D 36–45, D 72–122;
Data for 1960 and 1970 from Statistical Abstract of the United States 1971,
No. 347. Alaska and Hawaii are included in 1960 and 1970 Figures.

Women as percentage of labor force

For all the promise of welfare capitalism, it was regarded suspiciously by unions. What would happen in hard times? Under the weight of the Great Depression the various plans in fact collapsed. Moreover, the movement promoted company unions with leaders chosen from among the workers; the 1.5 million members (in 1929) of these unions had little bargaining power, for they could not strike. Nor had the laboring man made enormous strides in the twenties. Although real wages rose about 15 percent, the wealthy were taking a proportionately much greater share of the increased profits. The average work week declined from six to five-and-a-half days, while the rapid growth in technological efficiency led to a substantial rate of unemployment. Had prosperity continued, labor might perhaps have received a more equitable share of profits; the Depression prevented a completely fair test of corporate welfarism.

LABOR IN RETREAT

Organized labor had great difficulties in the face of mass-produced consumer goods, rising wages, and welfare capitalism. Membership fell from over 5 million in 1920 to less than 3.5 million in 1929. Defeat in the strikes of 1919 had depleted union treasuries and discouraged militant action throughout the decade. The American Federation of Labor looked after skilled workers in elite unions rather than organizing the new mass-production industries. Even the successful drive to abolish the twelve-hour day in the steel industry owed far more to Secretary of Commerce Hoover than to union agitation. Toward the end of the decade, however, the AFL supported efforts to organize southern textile workers. Conditions in the South were deplorable: in Elizabethton, Tennessee, young girls worked fifty-six hours a week for sixteen to eighteen cents an hour. In Marion, North Carolina, textile owners evicted strikers from their homes and prevailed on state troops and county sheriffs' deputies to guard the mills. Statistics tell a story at Marion: one outbreak of violence left six strikers killed and twenty-five wounded; in an ensuing trial, the law-enforcement officers involved won acquittal, while the local union leader was sentenced to prison. Much of the southern textile industry eluded unionism for many years.

Social themes

Social history is at the core of the 1920s. Even some of the dominant political issues—immigration restriction, the Ku Klux Klan, Prohibition, the presidential hopes of New York's Roman Catholic Governor Al Smith, the Sacco-Vanzetti case—were at heart questions not of the political or economic process but of what kind of country America should be. Different seg-

John Steuart Curry, Baptism in Kansas
Collection of Whitney Museum of American Art

ments of the electorate took varied positions on these issues. But the main camps were of city against country, foreign-born against native-born, "wet" against "dry," Catholic against Protestant.

Rural areas, especially the South and its heartland in the fundamentalist "Bible Belt," had long resented the economic advantages of the cities. Now, in the 1920s, as the radio and automobile spread the urban culture and prosperity and sophistication bred urban condescension, the ruralists felt themselves a beleaguered minority in a hostile nation that had once held their values. They fought back on a variety of social issues.

PROHIBITION

The Prohibition Amendment, added to the Constitution in 1919, had passed quickly in state legislatures because drinking "German" beer or diverting money from the war effort for liquor seemed unpatriotic. But Prohibition was above all an inheritance from the Progressive Era and a movement that inspired great hope. Social workers promised that asylums and jails would be emptied. In a time when people and notably intellectuals believed naively in "science," the eugenicists announced that banning alcohol would improve the race. Doctors no longer raised the specter—seriously advanced in the nineteenth century—of spontaneous combustion, but they did confuse morals and medicine in their professional opinions. In addition, taxes would fall, husbands would leave the dirty saloons and return to their families. Prohibitionists promised a "sort of millenial Kansas afloat on a nirvana of pure water."

Instead America got poisoned whiskey and a growing problem of organized crime. But the prohibitionists had perhaps gotten what they wanted: first, a way of exercising control over the immigrant by closing his saloons, and second, the kind of gratification a deeply felt cause can give—a sense of personal purification and moral glory. Many of the less fanatical "drys" eventually admitted that the "noble experiment" had failed, and when the Depression brought a compelling need for liquor tax revenues, Prohibition was repealed in 1933.

THE KU KLUX KLAN

The white-sheeted fraternal order of the Ku Klux Klan flourished and then disintegrated during the course of the decade. Founded in 1915 in Georgia as an imitation of the Reconstruction Klan, the new organization gathered its 2 million members chiefly during the early twenties. It was anti-Negro in the South but mainly anti-Catholic both there and in the rest of the country. The Klan's popularity came from the lure of secrecy and from association with religious and patriotic institutions. One of the Klan's most popular songs, sung to the tune of "The Battle Hymn of the Republic," combined symbols of both:

> *We rally round Old Glory in our robes of spotless white,*
> *While the Fiery Cross is burning in the silent, silv'ry night,*
> *Come join our glorious army in the cause of God and Right,*
> *The Klan is marching on.*

The Klan lost face when financial and sexual scandals struck some of its leaders in the mid-twenties. Decline also resulted from success. One of the

Klan's triumphs came in helping to ensure that Governor Al Smith of New York would not win the Democratic presidential nomination in 1924. The Klan did its part to spread anti-Catholic rumors that the pope, crowded in the Vatican, aspired to new headquarters in the Mississippi Valley and that his minions were tunneling their way under the Atlantic Ocean to give orders to Smith in New York. Wily Jesuits had killed President Harding with "hypnotic-telepathic thought waves," and even the dollar bill bore a rosary cleverly inscribed in the background.

The Klan—which could with some justification claim to have "elected" a number of congressmen and senators in the South and West—also contributed some small part, along with organized labor and most social workers, to ending the decades of immigration that had given so much to variety and mobility in American life. In 1921 Congress passed a law setting immigration quotas based on the proportion of each ethnic group to the general population in 1920. When the formula proved too generous to southern and eastern Europeans, the Johnson Act of 1924 reduced quotas and set back the date of computation to the census of 1890, when fewer aliens had infected the "pure" American culture. In the following quarter-century fewer European immigrants came to the United States than in the single year of 1907.

RURAL-URBAN TENSIONS

The antiforeign and antiradical sentiments of the postwar years found near-perfect expression in the Sacco-Vanzetti case. Nicola Sacco and Bartolomeo Vanzetti had been found guilty in 1921 of murdering a factory paymaster and a guard during a robbery in South Braintree, Massachusetts. Recent evidence suggests that Sacco alone was guilty of the crime, but it is plain from the court transcript that Judge Webster Thayer permitted the prosecuting attorney to exploit the defendants' draft evasion and anarchist beliefs in order to secure a conviction. Numerous appeals and finally a special investigatory commission headed by the president of Harvard University merely postponed their execution until 1927. In the meantime, Vanzetti's touching letters from prison, along with publicity given the case by radicals, made it a *cause célèbre* throughout Europe as well as among American intellectuals.

The Scopes trial in Dayton, Tennessee, became a symbol for the decline of the old ways. In 1925 John T. Scopes, a high school biology teacher, challenged the Tennessee law that forbade the teaching of Darwinian evolution in public schools as contrary to biblical literalism. When Scopes was indicted, the ruralists' great champion William Jennings Bryan volunteered to help the prosecution. Now increasingly given to the defense of Prohibition

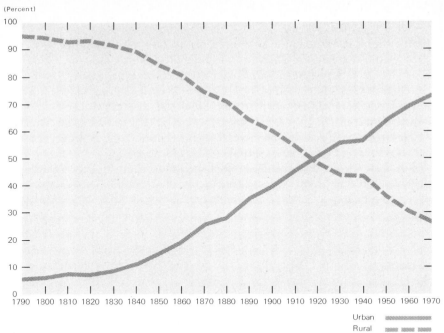

(Percent)

1790 1800 1810 1820 1830 1840 1850 1860 1870 1880 1890 1900 1910 1920 1930 1940 1950 1960 1970

Urban ▨▨▨▨▨
Rural ▭ ▭ ▭

Alaska and Hawaii are included in the 1960 and 1970 figures.
Data from Statistical Abstract of the United States, 1971

Urban and rural populations

and to religious fundamentalism, Bryan was confronted in Dayton by the famous criminal lawyer and agnostic Clarence Darrow. During one sultry day Judge Raulston of Gizzard's Cove moved the proceedings out onto the courthouse lawn, and there Darrow exposed Bryan's simplistic religious beliefs. Actually, Darrow displayed an equally childlike faith in science, and Bryan's rural provincialism had its counterpart in the lawyer's urban narrowness. Bryan died ten days after the trial, and with his passing much of the heart went out of the rural crusades.

In the long view, the new urban culture was winning out. The census of 1920 was premature in declaring that more people lived in the cities than in the country; it took as its definition of "urban" a population of twenty-five hundred or more, which included many a hinterland village. By 1930, however, metropolitan areas had increased greatly in size at the expense of rural America. Young people left the farms to seek excitement and their fortunes in the city, and economic needs drove whole families to a city factory life. The cities' victory over the countryside went deeper even than population figures suggest. The countryside's moral victories in passing antievolution laws and Prohibition were short-lived. Urban culture had all the big weapons: advertising, the new mass media of radio and the movies, and the products—such as the automobile—that forced the countryside to urban styles, markets, and values. *Variety*, a show business newspaper, conducted a survey of popular taste in motion pictures and discovered that even country people did not want movies on country subjects: "Stix Nix Hix Pix" read the famous headline.

Above all, the needs of a mass-production economy forced the ruralists aside. Their values of thrift and restraint fell before the need for consumer credit to extend consumption. The film, broadcasting, and advertising industries increased the expectations of the masses and turned them toward the leisure and pleasure patterns of citydwellers. With the values of rural America increasingly fading and its economic health in jeopardy, bigotry and intolerance against the Catholic, Jew, and Negro resulted. Ironically, these groups had less to do with destroying the old values than the mass-production and mass-consumption needs of the new corporations.

City Voices over the radio
Minnesota Historical Society

WOMEN AND THE FAMILY

By the 1920s many of the institutional functions of the family had declined. Recreation moved outside the home to the movie house and the automobile. Family size was becoming smaller—particularly in urban areas, where an increase in apartment living also substantially reduced the time traditionally used in maintaining a home. Concurrent with smaller families came a more subtle but equally important change: the family was beginning to turn inward toward a greater preoccupation with the proper upbringing of children, the growth of their personalities, and their education. Such a concern brought with it a new emphasis on the role of the woman, her place as mother, household manager, and consumer tending to supersede that of household worker.

At the same time, while young unmarried women predominated in the female work force, the percentage of working married women increased steadily, as did the number endeavoring to remain at their jobs after marriage. Between 1900 and 1930 the total number of employed women doubled, but the number of employed married women increased fourfold. In these years their work shifted away from traditional domestic services and manufacturing toward clerical, professional, and trade-oriented work. Some clerical occupations have ever since been considered "women's work."

The early twenties appear to have been a peak period for professional gains among women, many of which had been achieved before World War I. While there has been an absolute gain in the number of professional women since that time, women's position relative to men has steadily declined since the twenties. One Ph.D. in seven went to a woman in 1920; this dropped to one in ten by 1956. The percentage of women on college faculties fell from 30 percent in the mid-twenties to 24 percent in the mid-sixties.

With increased employment came an increasing variety in female dress and a greater sexual freedom. Robert and Helen Lynd's *Middletown* (1925), a pioneer sociological study of Muncie, Indiana, reported changes in the lives of women. The growing use of contraception introduced more freedom into their personal lives and made it possible to control the size of their families. Even in the city's high school over half of the junior and senior girls agreed that "petting" was nearly universal at teenage parties. And while the traditional roles of men and women remained almost as separate subcultures, divorce was on the rise as well.

Yet in today's view the short-skirted "flapper" was not really free but a frivolous object in a masculine world. Nor did the vogue of Freudian psychology contribute to the liberation of women. Freud and other psychoanalysts, each in his own way, stressed the uniqueness of feminine sexuality and inadvertently made women seem relatively out of place as professional and social beings.

Even granting women the vote was really not such a great stride forward. For after the Nineteenth Amendment took effect in 1920 the threat of a women's political coalition dissolved: women simply voted as their husbands did, and even the League of Women Voters took a position of political neutrality.

The women's rights movement, so prominent in the activity of suffragettes fighting for their vote during the progressive era, became split in the twenties. After gaining the vote their first goal was to fight against discriminatory practices and legislation; a state and national campaign began for the passage of equal-employment laws. But to those women who had fought desperately for social welfare legislation to protect their hours and conditions of labor, the new campaign threatened to jeopardize hard-won victories. In short, by the twenties the accomplishments of women were paradoxical: they went to work but did "women's work"; they consolidated some of their sexual freedom, but a new view of women emphasizing their feminine roles seriously minimized chances for fruitful social careers.

LITERARY ACHIEVEMENT

The 1920s was no aesthetic wasteland. America's most culturally productive period since the 1850s, the decade produced a great number of fine writers and artists. The novels of Sinclair Lewis, F. Scott Fitzgerald, and Ernest Hemingway are of particular importance. Lewis's characters are sometimes burlesques, but he is often brilliant in observing the small things that contain the culture of a people. Lewis possessed a phonographic, as well as a photographic, memory. In *Main Street* (1920), which satirized the dullness of a small midwestern town, and in *Babbitt* (1922), which parodied the materialistic businessman, he studied the surfaces of life and mined the native American vein of self-criticism. Both best sellers, their success illustrates our profound liking for didactic literature. Lewis's popularity suggests that many Americans stirred restlessly in the twenties.

F. Scott Fitzgerald portrayed the wealthy, whose glamor and vitality tantalized and disturbed him. *The Great Gatsby* (1925) studies the powerful and vulnerable Jay Gatsby—authentic American, self-made man 1920s style—a bootlegger who aspired to success and love through sheer will. In Gatsby the American genius attempted to force reality itself to bend and be shaped anew. This arrogance was a deep-seated trait in the American psyche and a powerful force in a nation that so far had conquered all before it.

Ernest Hemingway, the master of short, crisp dialogue, revealed in *The Sun Also Rises* (1926) and *A Farewell to Arms* (1929) the capacity for both heroism and disillusionment that war could produce. Hemingway wrote about a generation of American young men and women born around the turn of the century and brought to maturity during the war. The phrase

A first step: women win vote
Brown Brothers

"lost generation" was usually applied to the American writers who lived in Paris after the war. They had lost not only their own sense of country but also the restricting past; found was the revelation through art of a new style of stoical, almost indifferent courage, concepts that the older generation could not accept.

Intellectuals generally were critical of American life in the twenties. H. L. Mencken attracted many with snide remarks about the "puritanism" of the American "booboisie." Asked why he stayed in a country he despised so much, he replied: "Why do people go to the zoo?" Some writers cited the newly popular cult of Freudian psychoanalysis in attacking what they saw as America's repressive small-town morality. Protesting America's hostility to new ideas and its smug materialism, they turned to European culture and the worship of art. A few, such as Joseph Wood Krutch in *The Modern Temper* (1929), went beyond criticisms of American culture to a bleak view of all industrial society, civilized out of all belief and in need of some rejuvenating force.

A number of intellectuals saw this hoped-for rebirth in the very social changes that frightened other Americans. The city with its strange new peoples could offer the diversity writers found lacking in the villages. Some, like Randolph Bourne, envisioned America as a salad bowl of races and groups rather than a melting pot, a variegated world in which each exotic group preserved its own life and culture for the enrichment of all. This cultural pluralism would become increasingly important in the twentieth century.

The first cover of Sinclair Lewis's Main Street, a feminist novel about life in a small western town.

BEHAVIOR

The twenties digested startling changes in American manners and morals, as standard notions of propriety disintegrated. The World War in particular disrupted social patterns which had been based on Victorian ideals, but it did not create the ideas and movements of the twenties. The new thought and behavior blossomed from prewar seedlings and often employed or reflected the advancing technology of the period.

In the cultural development of the twenties, few events loomed more significant than the arrival of the "new psychology." This movement received impetus as early as 1909 from the American tour of its greatest prophet, Sigmund Freud, but came to fruition in the professional and popular mind only during the postwar decade. In its variously distorted forms, Freudianism quickly became an apparent influence in most literature and entertainment, affecting thousands who had never heard of Freud.

The dual influence of sex and repression in human behavior dominated the national understanding of the new psychology. Sexual restraint preached

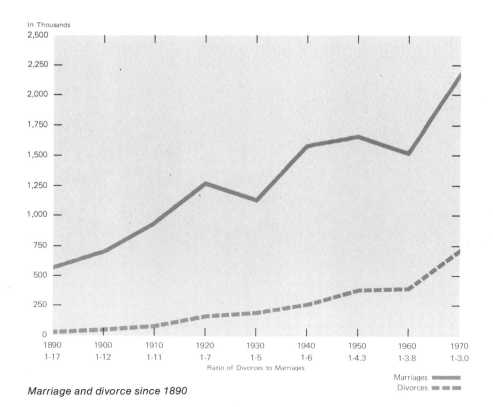

Marriage and divorce since 1890

by late-nineteenth-century social guardians seemed now positively counter-productive; social problems stemmed from an unhealthy containment of sexual urges. To be unrestrained, to release inner desires and tensions, became a worthy goal. Such conclusions in general psychological theory provided a ready rationalization for ignoring custom and violating taboos.

The general currency of Freud's ideas and his intellectual respectability were important in making sex a fit subject for mixed-group discussion among the sophisticated. At the modish cocktail parties of the twenties men and women talked about sex under the guise of science, spicing their remarks with choice selections from tempting psychoanalytic vocabulary. The desire to be shocking encouraged daring rather than caution; with this accelerator, sex, as a topic of conversation, moved in a few years from nonentity to notoriety. The new psychology was not alone in its support of the revolution in manners and morals. Other, more tangible influences, affecting the young in particular, shaped innovative social patterns.

Automobile ownership spread rapidly in the twenties and provided a mobility previously unknown. Yet the family car could be used for more than commuting to work or driving about on a Sunday. As closed cars increasingly dominated the market, the automobile became in effect a room on wheels which could be moved and stopped beyond prying eyes and interruptions. Soon automobiles were being held directly responsible for a portion of the birth statistics. Sexual experimentation was not, of course, limited to parked cars. Petting parties were in vogue before the war, and magazines discussed the "petting question" throughout the twenties. Yet the automobile remained uniquely available for the passionate and the curious.

Wary guardians of morality were shocked to discover sex barely disguised in brazen forms of popular culture, such as jazz—immediately suspect for its Negro origins. Beyond that, defenders of hymnal and hearth quickly saw insidious sensuality within the music itself. Jazz often featured the "passionate crooning and wailing" of the saxophone—a far cry from the parlor piano—and no one could doubt the corruption and disarray evidenced in the threatening evil of syncopation. Dancing in the twenties passed from fad to fad in a fury of exuberant creativity, including early dances like the Horse Trot, the Grizzly Bear, and the often berated Bunny Hug, while the famous Charleston came later in the decade. One religious newspaper tied together sex, the new dances, and music in one broad condemnation: "The music is sensuous, the embracing of partners—the female only half dressed—is absolutely indecent; and the motions—they are such as may not be described, with any respect for propriety, in a family newspaper."

The growing mass-culture industries of the twenties may have heard the critics, but they catered to the demands of their audience. During the day radio stations broadcast a variety of programs including inspirational and educational material; but in the evenings, during "prime time," most stations concentrated on popular music, especially jazz. Similarly, the motion picture industry churned out a mixed product, but the movies which drew the largest audiences relied heavily on sex as a theme, some of the earliest pictures being the most explicit. Yet even after luring Postmaster General Will Hays from the Harding cabinet to maintain moral standards within the industry, many pictures, conforming on the surface to the old morality and the happy ending, nevertheless depended for their appeal on plots permeated with sexual innuendo.

On the newsstands the evidence of a new kind of popular literature glared: the confession and sex magazines. *True Story*, founded in 1919, achieved the most spectacular success in the genre, by 1926 reaching a circulation of nearly 2 million on the strength of such stories as "What I Told My Daughter the Night Before Her Marriage" and "The Primitive Lover." Frequently, as in the movies, these provided a moral ending or gratuitous preaching of trite homilies, but the subject was clearly the same. Interestingly, remarkable similarities appeared between the "confessions" in pulp magazines and the case studies of popular psychoanalysts, revealing perhaps one more unintended influence of Freudian theory.

Many of the cultural clashes of the twenties stood clearly revealed on the battlefield of women's fashion. Social conservatives idealized the nineteenth-century woman, her skirts reaching the ground, a face plain and scrubbed, with her long hair in a bun. Nonetheless, fashion trends in the twenties embraced the same freedom from old forms implied by the changes in music, dancing, and entertainment; and in doing so, they came into direct conflict with the older image of woman. Skirts rose from ankle to knee in the first half of the decade; bobbed hair became stylish, first among the young but soon for women of all ages; cosmetics came to be not only permissible but also essential—the beauty industry expanded astonishingly during the twenties.

With increasing leisure and prosperity, Americans gave far greater attention than ever before to sports. Some encouraged participation; golf, for instance, aided by the developing role of the country club as a social center, became especially popular. But the public showed a tendency to watch professional athletes rather than participate. Golf itself boasted Bobby Jones and Walter Hagen; tennis proclaimed Bill Tilden; in football Red Grange should perhaps top any list; Babe Ruth gave a lift to baseball; boxing fans thrilled to two Dempsey-Tunney fights. Huge crowds attended college football games and millions heard the first professional sportscasters on their radios. Spectatorship emerged as an art.

The cultural turmoil of the twenties was inescapable. By the end of the decade, even a religiously and socially conservative family in some obscure hamlet might have owned or listened to a radio. Such slight exposure still changed their world. No earlier decade had so stirred American society.

RECAPTURING THE TWENTIES

Before leaving the 1920s, we might take some account of why the decade lives so vividly in the popular historical imagination. The first generation to make celebrities a major attraction, it saw itself as heroic, risque, extravagant. It lived in the newspapers. In the southern Indiana town of Kokomo in 1923, one famous celebrity, the Ku Klux Klan's Grand Dragon of the Realm, descended by plane to join a gathering of some two hundred thousand devoted followers. Although he wore white robes to symbolize moral purity, this Grand Dragon was to serve a score of years in prison for assaulting his secretary and driving her to suicide by poison. Four years later, in New York City, swirling crowds enveloped the shy Charles Lindbergh, who had just completed the first solo flight from New York to Paris. Lindbergh's flight was a triumph of the machine age; yet it occasioned a feeling of regeneration, a momentary rebirth of the American pioneer spirit. Abroad, on the French coast of the Mediterranean at Cap d'Antibes, the American novelist F. Scott Fitzgerald and his wife Zelda danced late at night on a moonlit patio strewn with broken champagne glasses. Such moments beg to be relived and felt anew in more complex and less romantic times. The twenties have become one of our enduring legends. Yet to leave it as legend is to fail to understand that era as well as the decades following it.

Because the 1920s are seen through the decade's own flashing images, its real self is hard to recapture. Each age has had its own vision of the twenties. Contemporaries viewed the period as one of cultural conflict: countryside versus city, Anglo-Saxon versus immigrant, tradition versus modernity. During the Great Depression, many writers who believed in the public drama of the twenties saw it as a hedonistic "jazz age," a national sin of frivolity for which the hunger and unemployment of the thirties were retribution. The decade was a youthful fling, an aberration in the serious march of American history. By the 1950s this garish portrait had been softened by nostalgia: the escapades had been fun. Besides, not all Americans had spent their time in seven-day bicycle races or ninety-day flagpole sits. Some had found the years after World War I rewarding because—like the years after World War II— they had been just that: a spreading economic plenty, marked by a million homes electrified, a million cars to drive over mile upon mile of new highway. Everywhere there were more and better houses, appliances, movies. Essentially, what was good about the twenties was what was also good about the fifties, and if a few intellectuals wanted to complain, let them.

Viewing the twenties from the seventies, we can see clearly yet another aspect—the beginning of the age in which we live, the age of mass consumption, spreading cities, national media and markets, standardized products available to the millions, and a sometimes equally standardized culture just as available. Very much in the American mainstream, the twenties

posed all the modern hopes and problems—of the city, of intergroup relations, of the relationship of industrialism to the environment—with which
we have striven to live since.

Hoover and the depression

For inscrutable reasons President Coolidge declared in 1927: "I do not
choose to run again." His successor would be Secretary of Commerce Herbert Hoover, who had won enormous fame as an engineer and humanitarian. Against Hoover the Democrats ran Alfred E. Smith, the able governor of New York. Hoover probably would have won the 1928 presidential
election because of "Republican" prosperity no matter whom the Democrats nominated, but his opponent had special liabilities. A Roman Catholic
and antiprohibitionist, Smith drew solid support from the "ethnics" in the
big cities, but bigotry lost him normally Democratic votes in the South and
elsewhere. Moreover, Smith had a strain of urban provincialism that prevented him from reaching out to decent Americans of the West and South
in gestures of compromise and friendship. A reporter asked him about the
needs of the states west of the Mississippi. "What are the states west of the
Mississippi?" Smith, half-jokingly, replied. Smith polled an impressive vote
in the big cities, but Hoover became president.

Herbert Hoover, who perfectly catches the twenties' image of restless pro-
ductivity, is an ideal American success story—it is a supreme irony that the
Depression overtook his presidency. Born in the Quaker hamlet of West
Branch, Iowa, in 1874, Hoover lost his mother and father while yet a child.
He grew up with the country in Iowa, Oregon, and California. At Stanford
University he studied geology and two years after graduating embarked on
ship to work as a mining engineer on the goldfields of Western Australia.
From 1897 to 1914 Hoover circled the globe no less than eight times, main-
tained offices in London, New York, San Francisco, Shanghai, Mandalay,
and Saint Petersburg, and accumulated a modest fortune.

The new president dreamed of abolishing poverty in America. Like Fred-
eric Winslow Taylor and other great technicians of his day, Hoover practiced industrial rationalization—the complete ordering and standardizing of
production. He set out to rationalize the operations not of a single plant but
of an entire technological economy. In his little book *American Individualism* (1922) he sometimes sounds like a reformer out of the progressive
era: he wanted "pioneers" to invade "continents of human welfare of which
we have penetrated only the coastal plain." He believed in an activist government, helping business and controlling its worst excesses.

Hoover and his predecessor Coolidge presented a striking contrast. Coolidge would not have a telephone in his office; Hoover had several. Coolidge

never smoked; Hoover smoked incessantly. Coolidge slept almost twelve hours a night, took a long nap in the afternoon, and still complained of being tired. Hoover got up at six-thirty, played with a medicine ball for exercise, and often worked eighteen hours.

While Hoover opposed having the government dictate solutions to social problems, he did not object to extensive government activities; his use of the Commerce Department was an advance in governmental involvement. His concept of organization blended a taste for voluntarism and individual decision with a commitment to collective effort. He believed that rational and decent people would freely cooperate if shown the necessity of doing so; the large units essential to an industrial society would receive their energies from the bottom up and their efficiency from the top down. The ends in view were always the potentially contradictory ones of productivity and freedom. Hoover worked toward a justification for American business and took credit for the great material advances made in the twenties.

THE GREAT CRASH

For some time Hoover had been warning against a day of reckoning in the economy. Signs of impending collapse multiplied. Speculative excesses in real estate and the stock market created a dangerous probability of rapid deflation. In 1928 consumer spending fell off, housing construction declined, and inventories increased. These trends led to a cutback in production—the clearest warning of all.

The Federal Reserve Board did little to discipline the stock market speculation of the late twenties. Open market operations (the selling of government securities to decrease the amount of money in circulation) began in earnest in 1928; but the inventory of these debts was too slight to deflate the boom. Raising the rediscount rate (the interest charged member banks for loans) came too late to have much effect. By 1929 loans from non-banking sources eclipsed those from banks. Money from all over the world came to Wall Street, where brokers were willing to pay a whopping 12 percent interest for short-term financing. Raising the government interest rates penalized small businessmen and farmers and scarcely deterred speculators accustomed to borrowing at any rates. The crash came suddenly on Thursday, October 24, 1929.

The stock market revived a bit during the winter of 1930, but once spring came it dropped precipitously again and continued to drop, month by month, until it reached bottom in 1932. The *New York Times* index average of stocks sank from around 300 at its height in 1929 to 38 by July 1932. Some individual stocks did far worse; Montgomery Ward plummeted from 138 to 4. Many corporations went bankrupt. A few tycoons committed suicide—the head of Rochester Gas and Electric took gas. Samuel Insull, whose

Hoover got all the blame. A "Hooverville" in Seattle
Wide World

jerry-built structure of holding companies had collapsed like a deck of cards, fled to Europe.

The stock market crash alone does not explain the Great Depression. John Kenneth Galbraith in his study of the crash lists five fundamental weaknesses in the economy. (1) *The unequal distribution of income:* In 1929, five percent of the population with highest incomes received about one-third of all personal earnings. Because their spending could be reduced more abruptly than that of ordinary people, the rich, once the market crashed, contributed to quick and decisive deflation. (2) *The bad corporate structure:* Holding companies and investment trusts could not have been better designed to fall into a deflationary spiral once a weakening of dividends curtailed operating investments. (3) *The weak banking structure:* Too many independent banks meant that when one failed and its assets were frozen, others felt the repercussions; once several failed, a domino effect ensued. (4) *The foreign balance.* (5) *The miserable state of economic knowl-*

530

edge: Both political parties endorsed the gold standard and also the balanced budget. The kind of public spending that we now suppose helps to alleviate bad times was forbidden by economic authorities who exerted great influence. Worst of all, the money supply itself virtually dried up.

Willing and anxious to use the government within certain limits to cushion the Depression, the activist Hoover abandoned laissez-faire (which never really existed in pure form in America) and tried to avert the impending disaster. He persuaded a conference of governors and mayors to speed up their own works projects. A group of leading businessmen agreed not to reduce wages. Hoover made reassuring public statements and asked Congress for legislation to regulate the banking system. He gave promise of doing whatever was necessary to end the hard times.

THE HOOVER PROGRAM

conservative little gov intervention

Before the Great Crash the president had signed into law the Agricultural Marketing Act of 1929, which embodied his favorite notion of cooperative marketing. If farmers could control their production and marketing, they could obtain higher prices. To assist them, the new law set aside a half-million dollars to finance large marketing cooperatives. Unfortunately, the scheme never received a fair chance. The Depression affected farmers so ruinously that the government money simply was a relief fund. The act was not equipped to deal with the major problem of continuing surplus. Popular among congressional progressives was a domestic allotment program that would restrict the amount of a crop sold on the domestic market. Some features of this plan, along with some from McNary-Haugen, came into practice during Franklin Roosevelt's New Deal. The Smoot-Hawley Tariff of 1930 also aimed to help farmers by raising import duties on foreign agricultural products.

Roosevelt had more gov. spending ↓ cut down unemployment

Hoover believed that if businessmen would have faith and cooperate for the social good, then public confidence would be restored. To encourage business he at first lowered taxes and reduced government spending, but these formulas proved inadequate. Early in 1932, after some hesitation, Hoover signed into law the Reconstruction Finance Corporation, which he later termed his most important antidepression measure.

The RFC could loan money to financial institutions in industry, commerce, and agriculture. Since nearly twenty-three hundred banks had gone under during 1931, the RFC loaned over $1 billion to banks and trust companies and brought renewed stability to the financial system. When unemployment continued to rise, the RFC was empowered to make loans to states for relief and public works projects. Hoover himself appointed to its board cautious men who did not spend the vast sums available to them. As a result, these activities of the RFC created few jobs and seemed a failure. Yet many of its institutional divisions were direct precursors of various New Deal agencies.

Lack of jobs had caused three thousand workers to march from downtown Detroit in March 1932 to the Ford plant in Dearborn. When they reached the township line and refused to turn back, the police opened fire with revolvers and then a machine gun. Four marchers died and scores lay injured. In the spring veterans began to march on Washington to demand early payment of their soldiers' bonus, due in 1945. When the Senate defeated the bill in June, as many as fifteen thousand men stayed on, camping just outside Washington on Anacostia Flats. After an incident General Douglas MacArthur, disobeying Hoover's explicit order, moved on the veterans' shacks, which were set afire. The veterans dispersed, a baby died from other causes shortly afterward, and Hoover took all the blame.

Depression diplomacy

Americans hummed throughout the twenties an optimistic refrain of rising production figures, growing consumption, and economic expansion abroad. But just as government leaders failed to see the warning signs of impending

Shanties in flame, 1932
National Archives

economic collapse at home, the frailty of international prosperity likewise escaped them.

The Great Depression, in its international dimension, had roots reaching back to the war debt and reparations settlements of the Treaty of Versailles. The United States had loaned various Allied governments over $10 billion, and even though most of this money had been used to purchase products in this country, the Republican administrations insisted that the debt be repaid. Allied governments and a few sympathetic Americans argued that repayment was both impossible and unfair. The Allies were burdened with vast, expensive programs to reconstruct their devastated countries and economies. If Europeans were required to send tax money to the United States, which had already reaped tremendous profits from the war, the recovery of world commerce would be slowed and everyone would suffer. Moreover, the borrowed money had been expended in a common effort, and Europeans pointed out that they had made a much costlier sacrifice in terms of human lives than had the United States. Finally, the United States' high tariff barriers hampered the Allies' ability to sell their exports in the United States. With their taxpayers already overburdened and the large American market virtually closed, the Allies could raise the revenue needed to pay the United States only through high reparations—the payments exacted from Germany for wartime damages.

Americans opposed high reparations that would cripple the German economy for years to come, but presidents from Wilson to Hoover all refused to relate the obviously interdependent questions of war debts and reparations. Rather than substantially scaling down war debts, which would have permitted a realistic reduction of Germany's reparations, the United States helped Germany meet its payments by privately investing in German bonds. Until the late 1920s this arrangement worked: the United States loaned money to Germany; Germany had enough capital to pay the European Allies; the Allies could meet their war debts to the United States. The great weakness of the arrangement was that Germany's economic well-being and all of Europe's ability to meet financial obligations depended, to a great degree, upon a continued outward flow of private American investment capital.

INTERNATIONAL DEPRESSION

The collapse of the New York Stock Exchange in 1929 signaled an abrupt end to the expansive American economy and the beginning of grave problems for international finance. As credit dried up, American businessmen began to recall capital invested abroad, particularly in Germany. Plagued by financial difficulties ever since the war, the German government now faced total bankruptcy. Without new funds from the United States, Germany suspended its reparations payments and threatened default on the huge volume of bonds which American investors and bankers had bought throughout the twenties. And the European Allies could not hope to meet war debt obligations without reparations. The structure of world prosperity was crashing down. President Hoover bowed to reality and announced in June of 1931 a one-year moratorium on all intergovernmental debts. But just as Hoover's measures to cope with the domestic economic crisis seemed too late and too limited, so this eleventh-hour gesture, delayed even longer by French opposition, did little to halt the worldwide financial contraction from plunging into deep depression. Suspension of debt payments, in fact, augmented the alarm among international financiers, who rushed to convert their assets into gold. Unable to maintain liquidity, England was forced to abandon the gold standard.

International depression initiated a decade of global instability and threats to peace, ultimately culminating in World War II. Although the League of Nations, the Washington treaties, and the Kellogg-Briand Pact contributed little to the maintenance of peace in the thirties, these instruments were not wholly to blame for the crises which led to World War II. The most basic cause of international problems was economic disruption. Hard times led to a worldwide upsurge of nationalism, and in Italy, Japan, and Germany this trend took the form of territorial expansionism. Elsewhere, including the United States, economic problems created a desire to avoid foreign involvement in order to concentrate on difficulties at home.

THE FAR EAST

The first major diplomatic crisis following the onset of the Depression occurred in the Far East. Japan's economy, in difficulty even before 1929, deteriorated further from the effects of worldwide depression. The consequent social and economic unrest strengthened militant nationalists, who charged that civilian government had compromised Japanese security in the naval disarmament agreements of the Washington treaties. In the Mukden Incident of September 18, 1931, a few staff officers of the Japanese Kwantung army in Manchuria blew up a Japanese-owned railway and falsely proclaimed that the Chinese had committed the deed. In "retaliation," the commander of the Kwantung army quickly defeated the local warlord and conquered Manchuria without the knowledge or approval of the civilian government in Tokyo. At first, the Hoover administration seemed not to notice this violation of the Washington treaties and the Kellogg-Briand Pact. Secretary of State Henry Stimson hoped that the civilian administration in Tokyo, which was friendly to the United States, could resume control over the Kwantung army and order its withdrawal. When this leadership was replaced with one that gave belated approval to the military's conquests, the situation took on a more somber tone.

The international responses to the Mukden Incident and Japanese aggression revealed the extent to which world economic crisis debilitated the collective security arrangements constructed during the twenties. Although the League of Nations dispatched the Lytton Commission to investigate events in Manchuria and subsequently condemned the Japanese action, no government would willingly employ force against the Japanese. The League of Nations charter, the Washington treaties, and the Kellogg-Briand Pact—all had been violated, but collective security apparently worked only if it reflected the national interests of the states involved. By 1931 European and American leaders believed that their countries' paramount interests lay in avoiding foreign difficulties and concentrating on domestic ills.

Washington's ultimate response to Japan's occupation of Manchuria took the form of nonrecognition, a concept later affirmed by the League of Nations. This Hoover-Stimson Doctrine professed refusal to recognize the legality of any move violating treaty agreements concerning the sovereignty of China and the maintenance of the Open Door. Non-recognition permitted the United States to make clear its moral opposition to Japanese actions while, at the same time, making no commitment to back up its opposition with force.

Because Japan and Germany continued their expansionism throughout the thirties, it has been easy to condemn the United States and other major powers for not taking a stronger stand against Japanese activities in 1931. Yet if nonrecognition seems an unrealistic method of halting aggression, how much more unrealistic was a policy of military force against the Japanese? How would an American president, least of all one as unpopular as Herbert Hoover, have convinced Congress and the American people that, despite the daily closing of banks and the rising rate of unemployment, the national interest required a costly war in China? Even the frequently suggested alternative of establishing economic sanctions against Japan takes on an air of unreality when considered in the context of the Depression. With the United States and European countries all trying to boost exports, the governments could not seriously entertain the idea of voluntarily suspending sales in a lucrative market. In fact, many American businessmen believed, in view of continued instability in China, that a strong Japanese dominance on the mainland might be beneficial to United States trade and investment. Theodore Roosevelt had pursued such a pro-Japanese policy some twenty years earlier when he had acquiesced to Japan's occupation of Korea. The United States had always had far more important economic ties with Japan than with China.

While the Japanese action offended Americans and violated the cherished Open Door principle, it did not represent a serious challenge to American economic or strategic interests. On the whole, the Hoover-Stimson policy seemed well tailored to America's needs: it expressed disapproval

Lucky Lindy represented the new technology and the old individualism, 1927
Brown Brothers

without committing the United States to any course which would have proved militarily and economically unwise.

By the time Hoover left office, the role of the United States in the world had changed greatly. No longer the expansive, self-assured power of the twenties, the country drew inward, politically and economically. The issue of war debts and reparations remained unsettled; the status of the Japanese in Manchuria and the future of China remained cloudy; and the growth in many countries of nationalist parties of the extreme Right and Left threatened to transform the relatively calm political world of the 1920s.

HOOVER AND ROOSEVELT

Bad luck and poor political judgment plagued Hoover. His socially conscious efforts in some areas went unnoticed under the burden of the Depression. He so lacked political sensitivity that he allowed photographers to snap him feeding meat to his dog on the White House lawn while people neared starvation throughout the country. Before a large audience Hoover was uninspiring. He read his speeches in a low, rapid, monotonous, nearly inaudible tone, standing stiffly with one hand in the pocket of his blue serge suit and making no gestures. The nation needed someone with the more informal gifts of political statesmanship. Franklin Roosevelt, who could say "My old friend" in a dozen languages, provided the presence and the skill. Nourished by much the same economic and social philosophies, the different personalities of these two men largely determined their differing responses to the economic crisis.

Things to think about: 1918–1932

Was the United States better off for not entering the League of Nations? For two viewpoints see Arthur Link, *Wilson the Diplomatist* (rev. ed., 1963), and Arno J. Mayer, *Politics and the Diplomacy of Peacemaking* (1968).

How can one account for the severity of the "Red Scare" of 1919? Stanley Coben's *A. Mitchell Palmer* (1963) and his article "The American Red Scare of 1919-1920," *Political Science Quarterly* (1964), are keys to understanding this phenomenon.

How did the thinking of Harding and Coolidge differ from that of Herbert Hoover? The best book on Harding is Robert K. Murray, *The Harding Era* (1969); the best on Coolidge is Donald McCoy, *Calvin Coolidge* (1967). Perhaps Hoover's own *Memoirs* (1952) give the best introduction to his thinking, but see the sophisticated interpretation in William Appleman Williams, *The Contours of American History* (1962), Joan Hoff Wilson's *Herbert*

Hoover (1974), and Martin Fausold and George Mazusan, eds., *The Hoover Presidency* (1974).

How did prohibition help to promote social change during the 1920s? An entertaining and often insightful account is Andrew Sinclair, *Era of Excess* (1962).

What role did the automobile play in the decade's economic and social history? See Allan Nevins and Frank E. Hill, *Ford: Expansion and Challenge, 1915-1933* (1957).

What was the role of the stock market crash in the Great Depression? John Kenneth Galbraith has written a fascinating account, *The Great Crash* (1955), but also consult George Soule, *Prosperity Decade* (1947).

What forms did economic diplomacy take in the twenties and what was its role in bringing on the Depression? See Joan Hoff Wilson, *American Business and Foreign Policy, 1920-1933* (1971), and Herbert Feis, *Diplomacy of the Dollar* (1973).

12

A NEW DEAL, NOT A NEW DECK

1932-1940

unemployment
big problem

WOODY GUTHRIE

Today Woody Guthrie remains one of America's larger-than-life heroes, a folk balladeer who inspired several generations of singer-activists. Woodrow Wilson Guthrie was an authentic voice of the troubles, and the hopes, of the Great Depression. Growing up in rural Oklahoma, he developed his unique guitar style listening to his relatives and to radio broadcasts of the famous Carter family singers. In the early thirties he watched the Great Plains turn into a giant Dust Bowl and experienced first-hand the descent into poverty. Like the fictional Joads of John Steinbeck's *Grapes of Wrath,* Woody hit the road to California. His encounters with other people undergoing "hard travelin' " (as he put it) sharpened his social consciousness and shaped the lyrics of a flood of songs, over a thousand by some people's count. With his folksinging sidekick Cisco Houston and actor Will Geer, Woody rambled around migrant labor camps, singing and raising the spirits of the impoverished workers. If the "Okies' " potato stew "had been just a little bit thinner," he wryly observed, "some of our senators could have seen through it."

bank holiday

538

Robin Carson, photographer. Used by permission of Woody Guthrie Publications, Inc.

As his radicalism deepened, Guthrie began writing for the left-wing *People's Daily World,* but music remained his true medium. During the thirties he wrote a set of songs for the Oregon Department of Interior, including "Grand Coulee Dam" and "Roll on, Columbia," extolling public power projects. Later in the decade New York City intellectuals "discovered" Woody as a true proletarian minstrel, and he joined the left-wing urban folk revival. But unlike some other artists, such as Burl Ives and Josh White, Woody generally shunned commercial performances. He preferred the freedom of the open road and working-class audiences. With Pete Seeger and several other politically radical musicians, he formed the Almanac Singers who toured the country singing to farm and factory laborers and participating in unionization campaigns.

Increasingly Woody became concerned with the spread of fascism, and songs such as "The Sinking of the Reuben James" expressed his fervent desire for American intervention in the European war. In 1943 he joined the Merchant Marine. Still, he considered song his most potent weapon, and his battered guitar carried the slogan, "This Machine Kills Fascists."

A wiry little man with bushy dark hair, Woody Guthrie, like Franklin Roosevelt, never lost faith in the country during the Depression. "I hate a song that makes you think that you're not any good," he once said. "I'm out to fight those kinds of songs." But unlike Roosevelt, Woody embraced socialism as the solution to the nation's plight. His radicalism sprang from the American heartland and, in many ways, looked backward. Woody believed that the dry, blistered prairie could be revived and that the weather-beaten people could recapture the pioneer spirit and regain the seats of power. Ballads such as "The Oregon Trail" and "Oklahoma Hills" reflected his pride in America's rural heritage. His hope lay in a people's socialist revolution. Commonly viewed as a lyrical description of America's natural beauties, his most famous song, "This Land Is Your Land," had a final, little-known verse calling for an end to private property and capitalism.

1932–1940

1932   *Roosevelt defeats Hoover*
1933   *"Hundred Days" session of Congress; beginning of New Deal*
            Agricultural Adjustment Act
            Tennessee Valley Authority
            National Industrial Recovery Act
            Twenty-first Amendment ratified, repealing Prohibition
1934   *Indian Reorganization Act*
            Tydings-McDuffie Act
            Nye Committee begins its investigation
1935   *Social Security Act*
            Supreme Court declares NIRA unconstitutional in Schecter v. U.S.
1936   *Roosevelt elected to second term*
            Germany occupies Rhineland
            Civil war begins in Spain
1937   *Fight over Roosevelt's "court-packing" plan*
            Marco Polo Bridge incident begins Japanese invasion of China
1938   *Munich Conference*
1939   *Germany invades Poland; war begins in Europe*
            John Steinbeck, The Grapes of Wrath
1940   *Roosevelt elected to third term*
            United States adopts preparedness and defense measures

FDR

During the 1928 presidential campaign Herbert Hoover had taken credit for the decade of Republican prosperity; when the economy collapsed, he got the blame. By early 1932 Hoover's chances for reelection appeared dismal. The dispersal of the Bonus Marchers—which seemed to reflect an indifference to human misery—made his chances hopeless.

Among the Democrats Franklin Delano Roosevelt was the front-runner, but the popular New York governor could not trace an unobstructed path to the nomination. Al Smith, by 1932 Roosevelt's confirmed enemy, retained significant support, especially in the Northeast. John Nance Garner of Texas, Speaker of the House, commanded strength in the South and also enjoyed the backing of the powerful newspaper publisher William Randolph Hearst. Roosevelt entered the Chicago nominating convention burdened by a three-to-one defeat to Smith in the Massachusetts primary and a loss to Garner in California. Through the first three ballots, Roosevelt failed to achieve the necessary two-thirds, but then William Gibbs McAdoo

F.D.R.: In fine spirits
Wide World

FDR and Herbert Hoover, 1933
UPI

switched the California delegation from Garner to FDR, who won on the fourth ballot and chose the outspoken Garner as his running mate.

The campaign sharpened the great contrast between the buoyant Roosevelt and the dour Hoover. The president campaigned with energy and determination but unlike Roosevelt failed to project any sense of optimism or confidence. Immediately after the fourth ballot, the new Democratic nominee, breaking with tradition, boarded a plane for Chicago to accept the nomination in person. "Let it be now the task of our party to break foolish traditions," he proclaimed to the cheering delegates. Running against the unpopular incumbent, Roosevelt could be dynamic and vague at the same time—a technique making some fear that he lacked the requisite intellectual depth to be president. Yet in the atmosphere of crisis this superficiality appealed to the voters. Roosevelt overwhelmed Hoover on election day, the Republican president winning only six of the forty states he had carried four years before.

FDR AND THE DEPRESSION

During the four months between the voters' repudiation of Hoover and the swearing-in of the new president, the Depression exacted its cruelest toll upon a leaderless nation. By 1933 more than 25 percent of the civilian labor force lacked jobs, but economic statistics cannot adequately convey the gloom and despair. To people who thought economic progress inevitable, the hard times threw into question traditional American values. The collapse of thousands of banks—by Roosevelt's inauguration forty states had closed all banks—revealed how quickly savings acquired through hard work and sacrifice could vanish. But the nation's mood was one of resignation; the economic calamity seemed to defy human powers. A popular country-music song reflected the general spirit of hopelessness: "For fear the hearts of men are failing. . . . The Great Depression now is spreading, God's will declared it would be so." Meanwhile, Roosevelt and Hoover circled each other like wary gladiators, coming together only in two brief and unproductive meetings. The president-elect refused to accept Hoover's proposals and remained vague about his own solutions.

The pampered son of an aristocratic New York family, FDR grew up in a handsome white house at Hyde Park on the Hudson River. Supremely confident of the country's future, young Franklin learned to be a fierce competitor, not in the harsh business world but on the playing fields of Groton Academy and later at Harvard. FDR's school days, especially at the Reverend Endicott Peabody's Groton, ingrained the notion that members of his social class should offer their talents in service to those less fortunate. Roosevelt, however, was no student. Fraternities and athletics seemed more important to the editor of the *Harvard Crimson*, and he left college unencumbered by fundamental doubts. His uncomplicated creed consisted of love of

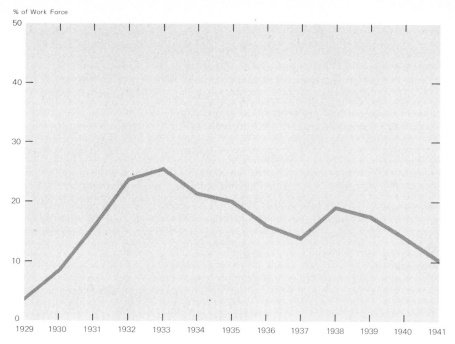

% of Work Force

Out of work in the Great Depression

school, God, and country. Such an upbringing and privileged position had never brought him to question traditional American pieties. His later life did little to shake his self-assurance. The young country squire passed the New York bar exams without graduating from Columbia Law School; won his first contest for public office in his Dutchess County home territory; married a distant cousin, a niece of President Theodore Roosevelt; survived revelation of an affair with his secretary; and took over TR's old job as assistant secretary of the navy after supporting Woodrow Wilson for the presidency. In 1920 the Democratic party nominated Roosevelt for vice-president. He met his only serious setback, a severe attack of polio which left his legs paralyzed for life, with characteristic courage and even turned the handicap into a political asset. Cheated by wealth out of birth in a log cabin or even above the family drugstore, FDR's crippled legs gave the Hudson River aristocrat the underdog's image. For a nation requiring reaffirmation of basic values as much as sophisticated analyses of economic problems, FDR was the perfect evangelist for the fundamental soundness of the American system.

ROOSEVELT TAKES CONTROL

Immediately after taking the oath of office, Roosevelt sounded the dominant themes of the first years of his presidency. He rallied the nation to a war against depression, comparing the battle to the one it had successfully fought against the Kaiser's Germany little more than a decade earlier. Americans had to act "as a trained and loyal army"; he himself would ask Congress for "broad Executive power to wage war against the emergency, as great as the power that would be given to me if we were in fact invaded by a foreign foe."

FDR freely invoked his persuasive talents to cheer a discouraged people and to rally them with the combative spirit he had always displayed. The first president to make effective use of radio, Roosevelt, an affable and winning conversationalist, delivered "fireside chats" from the White House to advise listeners of new programs and to assure them that government was taking bold action. No longer an abstraction hidden away in Washington, the president sent soothing messages and inspirational little pep talks into homes throughout the nation.

All the president's vibrant tones, however, would soon have sounded flat had he not been able to offer some concrete successes. Roosevelt's campaign and early presidential speeches predicted swift and decisive action against depression. After the November election a variety of advisers—the "Brains Trust"—went to work on myriad programs. FDR and his staff labeled their actions the "New Deal," a phrase designed to emphasize FDR's departure from the ways of the past.

The unemployed sit before their shack on New York City's waterfront
Russell Lee, Library of Congress

The New Deal was primarily a product of the personality, style, and values of the president. Unencumbered by grand theories or philosophical subtleties, FDR saw his job as achieving rapid economic recovery. Rather than probing alternative means of organizing and ordering a complex industrial society, Roosevelt vigorously employed the power of the executive in a not-always successful or coherent search for prosperity. The result of his efforts was a chaotic and sometimes contradictory set of programs. The New Deal ultimately erected institutional barriers against further economic collapse and protected the upper two-thirds of society against economic disaster. It brought the welfare state to America while preserving the traditional values of a capitalist economy and a democratic political system. At a time when economic disaster forced some nations of the world to abandon one or both of these latter institutions, FDR's achievement was not small.

The hundred days

Moving on a broad front during the first one hundred days of FDR's administration, the New Dealers attempted to revive the confidence of both businessmen and consumers and to stimulate economic growth. They hoped to restore the cycle of mass production and mass consumption, the basis of prosperity during the twenties.

The chaotic banking system demanded immediate attention. State decrees had already closed banks in most areas, and Roosevelt quickly dramatized his leadership by declaring a national bank "holiday," a move affecting only eight additional states. The holiday, together with a banking bill rushed through Congress in emergency session, set the style for the early New Deal. FDR's inaugural address had contained tough talk about driving money changers from the temples, but the suspicion that he meant nationalization of banks, a step some advisers urged, proved illusory. Large banking interests and former advisers to Hoover drafted much of the Emergency Banking Relief Act, which employed the power of the national government to prop up the existing banking structure rather than to change it in any fundamental way. Following the lead of the White House, congressmen shouted approval of the measure even before receiving copies of the final bill. Thus, the familiar Roosevelt pattern emerged: extravagant rhetoric followed by much less radical action. And it all worked. The bank holiday, the Emergency Banking Relief Act, and FDR's soothing assurances that the peoples' savings were now secure helped restore faith in the banking system, an essential ingredient in recovery.

During the rest of the "Hundred Days," FDR offered a bewildering array of programs. The Civilian Conservation Corps (CCC), a personal favorite of the president, paid young men to work on forest and other reclamation projects. The Public Works Administration (PWA), administered by Secretary of Interior Harold Ickes, financed a variety of programs to create fresh job

opportunities across the country. And more grants went to the states for relief programs.

FDR also launched a broad experiment in regional planning in the six-
hundred-mile-long Tennessee Valley. During the 1920s Senator George Norris of Nebraska had attempted to introduce direct governmental development of the area, but not until the early New Deal did such a project
come to fruition. The Tennessee Valley Authority (TVA) built fifteen
dams, providing government-owned electric power plants and flood control.
Although it also produced phosphate fertilizers, sponsored innovative farming techniques, and encouraged new business enterprises, low-cost power remained TVA's best-known function. Serving as a yardstick by which the government could measure private utility rates, TVA drove down the price of
electricity throughout the area.

The New Deal also tried to eliminate or at least minimize some economic
risks for the average citizen. The Federal Deposit Insurance Corporation
(FDIC) made the federal government ultimate insurer of deposits (up to

*Civilian Conservation Corps
(CCC) men unload to begin on a
new public works project in the
midwest*
Nebraska State Historical Society

FDR appointed Frances Perkins as Secretary of Labor. She was the first woman to hold a Cabinet position.
Wide World

five thousand dollars) in savings institutions. The Securities Exchange Act required companies to disclose information about all stocks and bonds sold on the market and created the Securities and Exchange Commission (SEC) to protect investors from fraudulent practices. The Home Owners Loan Act authorized a federal agency to rescue property owners from foreclosure, and farmers received similar assistance from the Farm Credit Administration. In less than two years the government refinanced about one-fifth of home and farm mortgages. Measures such as these offered immediate relief and some promise of future security; but the New Deal's main hopes for lasting recovery rested upon its agricultural program and its most sweeping measure, the National Industrial Recovery Act.

THE AAA AND NRA

New Dealers tried to solve the perennial agricultural dilemma of surpluses and low prices. After resorting to the unpopular expedients of destroying corps and slaughtering baby pigs in order to boost farm prices, they turned to the less controversial method of reducing overproduction through acreage reduction. Under the first Agricultural Adjustment Act the government, through the Agricultural Adjustment Administration (AAA), paid producers

548

Total crop from eighty acres near Aurora, Nebraska—all tumbleweeds
Nebraska State Historical Society

Dust storms on the Great Plains darkened the sky as though it were night,
Alma, Nebraska
Nebraska Historical Society

Big Business
" Labor
" Govt.

of several basic commodities to limit the number of acres under cultivation. A "processing tax," levied on processors of farm products such as cotton ginners and millers, provided the revenue for the program.

The National Industrial Recovery Act (NIRA), the New Dealers' trump card in their showdown with the Great Depression, was the most comprehensive program enacted during the Hundred Days. Section 7a of this act guaranteed labor union members the right to collective bargaining and took a tentative step toward making the federal government a referee in labor-management disputes. The act authorized industrywide boards to draft "codes of fair competition" establishing fair wages, working conditions, and prices. The National Recovery Administration (NRA) undertook the unenviable task of securing compliance with the codes and encouraging consumers to support only participating businesses. The NRA adopted the American eagle (colored blue) as its symbol, and employed a former army officer, General Hugh Johnson, as its administrator. General Johnson organized a massive NRA parade down New York's Fifth Avenue and continually urged consumers to "buy under the Blue Eagle." "It is the women in the home—and not soldiers in uniform—who will this time save the country," he proclaimed. "Housewives will go over the top to as great a victory as the Argonne." Behind the patriotic trappings, the measure represented a hardheaded attempt to achieve recovery through a working partnership between large corporate interests and the federal government. Suspending antitrust laws and shelving hallowed pieties about free competition, Roosevelt and his Brains Trust moved toward a planned economy—the type of system adopted during World War I.

RESULTS OF THE HUNDRED DAYS

Architects of the Hundred Days declared total war against the Depression, but Roosevelt and his lieutenants gained only nominal victories. The economy did pick up during early 1934; yet by the spring of 1935 all the indicators revealed only minimal improvements. Unemployment remained high (nearly one-fifth of the labor force), and national income still totaled less than in 1931. Many things explained the disappointing results. Too many programs worked at cross purposes or were simply ineffective. The effort to stimulate buying power through public works projects conflicted with FDR's early commitment to a balanced budget. Acreage reduction failed to decrease crops because farmers simply retired their least productive fields and applied more intensive methods to the remaining land. Farm income rose, but the rest of society, including the unemployed and the hard-hit urban laborers, bore the cost in higher food prices.

The failure of government–business cooperation under the NRA was the Roosevelt administration's gravest disappointment. Large corporations dominated formulation of the "codes of fair competition," and the interests of labor, small businessmen, and consumers received too little attention. Some of the codes seemed little more than carbon copies of large industries' informal trade agreements drafted during the 1920s. Section 7a of the NIRA proved of limited use to organized labor; businessmen could evade the wage and hour provisions and continued to promote company-dominated unions in violation of the act. Hugh Johnson's blustering façade failed to disguise his incompetence as an administrator. An official investigation, headed by the reformist lawyer Clarence Darrow in 1934, revealed a number of irregularities in the NRA, and Roosevelt secured Johnson's resignation in September. By the time the Supreme Court declared the NIRA unconstitutional in *Schecter* v. *U.S.* (1935), the decision seemed merciful.

Immediate recovery required mutual confidence between Roosevelt and corporate interests, but many big businessmen never fully trusted FDR and remained suspicious of governmental meddling in their affairs. The president sometimes gave businessmen reason to doubt his sincerity about cooperation by adopting a self-righteous tone and assailing them for greed and selfishness. The NRA, like other early New Deal programs, neither brought together all groups in the country nor stimulated the economic energy needed to lift the nation out of depression.

The diplomacy of economic recovery

Roosevelt believed that foreign policy could contribute to domestic recovery, but like the array of programs initiated during the Hundred Days, the jerry-built diplomacy of the early New Deal lacked coherence. Seeking advice from both economic nationalists like Rexford Tugwell and liberal internationalists like Secretary of State Cordell Hull, Roosevelt adopted conflicting means to promote the general goal of prosperity at home.

THE LONDON ECONOMIC CONFERENCE

Before leaving office Hoover had promised United States participation in a world economic conference, and Roosevelt initially seemed willing to cooperate. Proclaiming the importance of stabilizing currencies and trade, FDR appointed Secretary of State Hull head of the United States delegation to the London meeting in 1933. In order to help revive world commerce, Hull planned to commit the new administration to lower tariffs. But he was astonished to discover, upon reaching London, that the president had decided not to submit a new tariff bill to Congress. The embarrassed secretary thus "arrived with empty hands," as he phrased it. Although undercutting tariff reform, Roosevelt still appeared to favor stabilizing world currencies in relation to gold. But as the conference progressed, more nationalistic advisers finally convinced Roosevelt that any agreement in London might hamper New Dealers' efforts to manipulate the value of the dollar upward and to stimulate recovery at home. When Raymond Moley, who had superseded the disgruntled Hull in London, agreed to an innocuous joint statement approving currency stabilization, FDR abruptly and testily repudiated the action.

Roosevelt's tactless conduct toward the other participants in the London Economic Conference provoked controversy. His defenders claimed that the nations could never have reached meaningful agreement and that Roosevelt's actions simply provided a convenient scapegoat for failure. They also pointed to the importance of currency flexibility in combating domestic depression and the need for raising, rather than stabilizing, the general level of prices. But critics of Roosevelt viewed the conference as a lost opportunity. America's unilateral approach, they believed, prevented solving worldwide problems through international action, and the new president's reversal strengthened the position of European nationalists who argued that cooperation was futile. On balance, Roosevelt did sacrifice the appearance, if not the reality, of international cooperation for measures he thought would assist economic recovery at home. In the retrospective light of World War II, his course may seem misguided; considering his own preoccupation with domestic depression, the action appears understandable.

EFFORTS TO ENCOURAGE EXPORTS

Although America's conduct at the London Economic Conference struck a blow at free trade and internationalism, Cordell Hull continued to work for the lowering of tariffs. In a manner of speech which turned r's into w's, the handsome Tennessean repeatedly stressed that a "reciprocal trade agreement program to reduce tariffs" was the only path to lasting world peace. By 1934 he convinced the president that his plan would stimulate domestic recovery by keeping the world open to American exports. In the spring, over the protests of businessmen in protected industries, Roosevelt swung the Democratic Congress behind the Trade Agreements Act of 1934, which allowed him to manipulate tariff duties in exchange for concessions to American exports abroad. Like other New Deal measures, this bill gave the executive branch unprecedented control in an area previously reserved to Congress. Hull busily negotiated tariff agreements with many countries, but the reciprocal trade act proved no recipe for recovery or harbinger of world peace.

The desire to stimulate exports likewise influenced Roosevelt's decision to extend recognition to the Soviet Union. The lure of a potentially vast Soviet market, from which nonrecognition had largely excluded the United States, combined with more favorable attitudes toward the Soviet Union to permit a change in policy. The Depression had called into question America's traditional bias against governmental planning; and businessmen, intellectuals, and policymakers increasingly became intrigued with the efficiency of centralized direction. The purge of Leon Trotsky, who had advocated international revolution, and the triumph of Joseph Stalin, who concentrated primarily on building socialism at home, eroded the USSR's image as an international troublemaker. In fact, American policymakers hoped that accommodation with the Soviet Union might serve world peace by countering Japanese expansion in the Far East. In addition, the widespread default on World War I debts made Russia's refusal to pay, which had been a crucial stumbling block to recognition in the twenties, seem less onerous. In 1933, more than fifteen years after the start of the Russian Revolution, the United States finally extended recognition to the USSR.

Labor unions and businessmen joined antiimperialist congressmen and editors in urging yet another new direction in our foreign relations. Charging that cheap labor, sugar, cotton, and other products from the Philippines hurt the United States economy, they demanded that immigration and tariff barriers be applied to the islands. The cry to free the Philippines, which American marines had brutally taken over a generation earlier, now echoed throughout the United States. In the Tydings-McDuffie Act of 1934, Congress made the islands a semisovereign commonwealth and promised full independence in ten years.

THE GOOD NEIGHBOR POLICY

Roosevelt's policy toward Latin America, touted as a new departure termed the "Good Neighbor" policy, actually originated in the Hoover administration. Government officials under Hoover and many businessmen had concluded that military intervention in Latin America brought more ill will than advantages. A leading investment banker, Thomas P. Lamont, remarked that "the theory of collecting debts by gunboats is unrighteous, unworkable, and obsolete." An ounce of goodwill was worth a pound of gunpowder, and the Depression highlighted the expense of armed occupation. The State Department also felt some embarrassment at strongly denouncing Japanese troops in Manchuria while the United States Marines marched around sovereign states of the Caribbean. Shortly before Hoover left office, a memorandum by Undersecretary of State J. Reuben Clark officially repudiated the (Theodore) Roosevelt corollary, which had justified military interventions.

The principles of the Clark memorandum met a challenge in the new Democratic administration when political turmoil in Cuba threatened United States strategic and economic interests. In 1933 Hull dispatched Sumner Welles, an austere New England aristocrat who reportedly once laughed at a joke and then, catching himself, murmured: "Pardon me. You amused me." Confident of his judgment and ability, Welles sailed into Havana intending to mediate among the various factions and to set up a new government. But his plan did not go smoothly. When Ramón Grau San

Martín gained the presidency and threatened measures which sounded radical to United States sugar interests, Welles urgently requested American military intervention. Roosevelt, however, refused to permit any landing of troops and, as an alternative to occupation, employed the more subtle weapons of nonrecognition and denial of economic assistance. Before Welles returned to Washington, he fanned the ambitions of Colonel Fulgencio Batista, who subsequently overthrew Grau and instituted a conservative regime which lasted until Fidel Castro's revolution in 1959. The United States quickly recognized Batista and solidified his military regime by lowering the sugar duty and abrogating the unpopular Platt Amendment.

The Cuban incident illustrated the nature of the Good Neighbor policy. Roosevelt sincerely wished to avoid further military incursions, and the days of American occupation of Caribbean countries were numbered. At the Montevideo conference of 1933 and again at Buenos Aires in 1936, Hull signed pledges formalizing the United States' commitment to nonintervention. Roosevelt dutifully liquidated all American protectorates in the Caribbean. But his actions toward Cuba also indicated that the United States had other, more subtle, means of getting its way. The president's new authority to lower the tariff barriers, combined with creation of the Export-Import Bank—which could extend loans to countries wishing to purchase American products—provided considerable leverage over impoverished Latin American governments. In addition, departing American troops were replaced by local militias trained and equipped by the United States. In every ex-protectorate, an oppressive military dictatorship ultimately sprang up to maintain the order previously guaranteed by the United States Marines. Critics throughout the hemisphere began to suspect that a more accurate catchphrase for Roosevelt's policy was "Good Neighbor of Dictators."

Despite its limitations, the Good Neighbor policy did make some friends in Latin America. When relations with Mexico's President Lazaro Cardenas deteriorated, Roosevelt sent a veteran of the Wilson administration, Josephus Daniels, as ambassador to Mexico. Daniels's conciliatory attitude often bordered upon insubordination toward his less flexible superiors in the State Department, but he successfully worked for an accommodation which allowed Mexico to nationalize American oil interests. Like other New Deal policies, the Good Neighbor policy was a mixture of expediency and idealism. It represented less a shift in objectives than a tactical change in the traditional policy of increasing American political and economic influence in the Western Hemisphere.

Radical alternatives

In retrospect, Franklin Roosevelt towers over the politics of the thirties. But in those days other voices with more sweeping programs challenged FDR. From the avowedly fascist Silver Shirts of William Dudley Pelly to the

Communist followers of Earl Browder and William Z. Foster, numerous political radicals vied for public attention.

One of the earliest and most interesting challenges came out of the past in the person of Upton Sinclair, the muckraking author of *The Jungle* (1906). In 1934 Sinclair deserted the Socialist party and, with the support of unemployed laborers and farmers in southern California, captured the Democratic nomination for governor. Sinclair's program called for converting California's idle factories and untilled farmlands into nonprofit cooperatives. He hoped that state-sponsored enterprises, operating alongside the capitalist system, would not only solve the immediate problem of relief but also demonstrate the superiority of socialism. Calling his program End Poverty in California (EPIC), Sinclair predicted that within a few years the only poor person in the state would be a hermit who voluntarily exiled himself from the cooperative commonwealth. The Roosevelt administration initially gave tacit support to its party's nominee but began to back away when established interests in California, including many party leaders, came out strongly against Sinclair. His gubernatorial chances evaporated in the face of a full-scale media campaign which attacked EPIC as communistic, atheistic, and un-American. Small-time Hollywood actors who could put on an accent or play a "radical foreigner" suddenly found employment posing as Sinclair's "supporters" in campaign "documentaries." By election day the movement had collapsed. The Republican nominee swept to victory and put an end to Sinclair's dream.

Twentieth-century populists from the Great Plains demanded increased attention to farm problems. Congressman William Lemke of North Dakota sponsored a bill calling for the national government to supply farmers with all the cash needed to repay their mortgages and to buy back and refinance every farm foreclosed after 1928. When the House, with strong White House urging, rejected Lemke's plan, he became an implacable foe of Roosevelt, eventually leading a third-party movement in 1936. Milo Reno, another veteran of farm radicalism, urged currency inflation, a traditional populist cure-all. By the mid-1930s, Reno's Farm Holiday movement demanded that the government guarantee farmers their cost of production and provide greater mortgage relief. In spectacular displays, his followers blocked highways, dumped milk cans along roadways, and forcibly stopped eviction sales. Reno also called for a "farm holiday," a kind of rural general strike, and in 1935 seemed to be contemplating an alliance with Huey Long, the hero of small southern farmers.

HUEY LONG

Huey Pierce Long was the most enigmatic and certainly the most threatening of FDR's challengers. Raised in the impoverished hill country of northern Louisiana, a breeding ground for populist and socialist ideas, Long

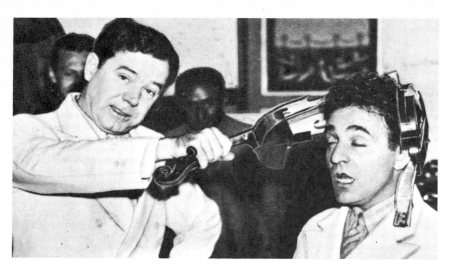

Huey Long at play

turned keen intelligence and utter ruthlessness into a mercurial political career. Elected governor at the age of thirty-five, he taxed oil companies' profits and used these revenues (or at least that portion not ending up in his own coffers) to upgrade the life of Louisianans. Even as he provided better schools, free textbooks, and more roads, Long consolidated his political control and ran the state with an iron hand.

In 1930 Long brought his considerable oratorical skills and flashy clothes to Washington and from the floor of the United States Senate began to build a national reputation. An early supporter of Roosevelt, Long quickly broke with the president and, with a slogan borrowed from William Jennings Bryan—"Everyman a King"—championed his "Share-Our-Wealth" program. Long advocated not only a radical redistribution of wealth but a reconstruction of American society. He proposed liquidating large fortunes, allowing no one to hold "more than a few millions of dollars," and redistributing wealth so that every family would have "a home and the comforts needed for a home, including such things as a radio and an automobile." In addition to this "homestead" idea, Long's most famous proposal, the plan included several other features. The federal government would guarantee everyone as much education, including college and professional training, as his capabilities allowed. Work hours would be regulated in accordance with consumption needs, providing every worker a minimum annual income of between two thousand and twenty-five hundred dollars. The state would handle farm production much as Joseph managed the agricultural system of ancient Egypt, stockpiling grain during the years of plenty to provide for years of famine. When farm warehouses contained enough for current demands and the needs of the near future, farmers could work on public improvement projects or even return to school for a time.

Part buffoon, part demagogue, but at least one part democratic leader, Long attracted a great deal of support. While his associate Gerald L. K. Smith, a spellbinding evangelist, preached the gospel across the South (a famous journalist called Smith "the gutsiest and goriest, loudest and lustiest, and deadliest and damnedest orator ever heard on this or any other earth"), Huey the "Kingfish" attracted a national following. More than twenty thousand Share-Our-Wealth clubs sprang up and the organization claimed over 7 million members. Some believed that Long was preparing for a full-scale presidential bid in 1936, but he probably aimed at the 1940 balloting. Roosevelt's political advisers considered Long a dangerous adversary. Then one day after leaving Governor O. K. Allen's office in the skyscraper capital at Baton Rouge (a journalist's observation of Allen: "A leaf blew in his window, he signed it"), as Long strode down the marble corridors an assassin's shot rang out, and Long fell fatally wounded. Gerald L. K. Smith tried to keep the movement alive, but without Long's unifying presence, "Share Our Wealth" quickly fizzled.

FATHER COUGHLIN AND DR. TOWNSEND

FDR's other chief rival was the Roman Catholic priest Father Charles Coughlin. Employing a melodic Irish brogue, Father Coughlin broadcast weekly his increasingly political radio messages. Challenging FDR at his own game, the radio preacher became one of the most popular figures on the airwaves. When CBS, alarmed at his growing militancy, dropped his show, Father Coughlin broadcast independently the "Golden Hour of the Little Flower" from the Shrine of the Little Flower in Royal Oak, Michigan. In 1934 his volume of mail exceeded that of the president and Amos 'n' Andy. Forming a movement called the National Union for Social Justice, Father Coughlin advanced vague, often contradictory programs which emphasized inflating the currency with silver and nationalizing the banking system. His popularity, especially among low-income Catholics in middle western cities, led to more and more extravagant rhetoric. His sermons increasingly touched anti-Semitic as well as anti–New Deal themes. Finally, Coughlin openly entered politics as one of the organizers of the ill-fated Union party of 1936.

Another founder of the Union party, Dr. Francis E. Townsend, was the most unlikely looking radical of all. This white-haired country doctor, then living in California, spearheaded a sweeping recovery-retirement scheme. The Townsend plan provided that the government give everyone over the age of sixty a monthly pension, the only conditions being that the recipient quit work and spend the entire sum within the month. The program promised to provide relief and security for the elderly, to create jobs for younger workers, and to stimulate general economic recovery through its forced-spending provisions. Many people over sixty embraced the plan with almost religious fervor, and Townsend clubs sprang up throughout the nation singing "Onward Townsend Soldiers." The good doctor's followers formed an important political constituency that not even passage of the Social Security Act could eliminate. Few people questioned the dire need of the nation's elderly, but the program's detractors correctly pointed out that the monthly payments would have eaten up over half the federal government's income and supported only about ten percent of the population. Even Dr. Townsend's best economic minds stumbled over the problem of financing his plan.

FDR AND THE RADICAL CHALLENGE

None of these figures achieved his hopes for personal power, and their movements ultimately faltered. Some peddled inflated oratory rather than serious programs; others sounded ugly strains of racism. Dr. Townsend's right-hand man viewed the old people's campaign as an opportunity to turn a quick buck, and Milo Reno referred to the New Deal as the Jew Deal. But all of the agitation should not be dismissed as the work of demagogues or cranks. Despite his great appeal, Franklin Roosevelt had failed to win his war against the Depression, and the despair of 1933 became anger and frustration by 1935. The proposals of Long, Coughlin, and others indicated deepseated discontent and growing pressure for more radical measures. The popularity of unusual programs which seemed to promise social justice for the common person also clearly reflected a wisespread antibusiness sentiment.

Carefully gauging the political winds, Roosevelt after 1935 abandoned phrases about cooperation with the business community. The president's harsh campaign attacks on "economic royalists" signaled no movement toward a government takeover of the economy or toward any significant redistribution of the nation's wealth, but they did help blunt the radical challenge. Rather than destroying or revolutionizing the old order, Roosevelt offered a new series of measures designed, through greater government intervention, to remedy gross inequities. The New Deal's legacy proved not to be socialism or fascism but an Americanized version of the capitalist welfare state.

The welfare state

By the spring of 1935 Roosevelt confronted a number of difficulties. The economic picture appeared brighter than two years earlier, but New Deal programs had not stimulated enough recovery to forestall attacks from both the Left and the Right. While the mixed group of radical spokesmen demanded that FDR translate his tough talk into positive action against giant businessmen, corporate interests were disillusioned and not a little frightened by the Roosevelt administration. In August 1934, the American Liberty League, a pressure group dominated by leading industrialists, launched a full-scale assault against almost every New Deal measure.

Rising discontent, failure of the NRA, and the elusiveness of economic recovery might have deterred and embittered a person of less confidence and optimism, but Roosevelt began searching for other ways to meet the challenge. In June 1935, as congressmen prepared to escape the humid Washington summer, the president demanded that the lawmakers act on a series of brand-new measures, including greater relief expenditures, labor legislation, a tax bill, and Social Security. His message to Congress sounded what some historians call the "Second New Deal," signifying a fundamental philosophical shift toward smashing large economic units, and what others term the "Second Hundred Days," indicating another sudden rush of legislative ac-

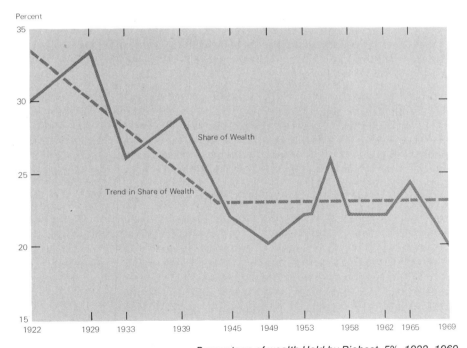

Percentage of wealth Held by Richest .5%, 1922–1969

Source: From James D. Smith and Stephen D. Franklin, "Economic Inequality The Concentration of Personal Wealth, 1922–1969," 64, American Economic Review (May 1974), p. 165

tion. The second phrase seems more accurate. Roosevelt never established clear-cut ideological guidelines, and the bills coming out of Congress and the White House lacked any unifying concept. If a pattern emerged from the new acts, it was that of a welfare state: a series of government programs designed to protect some of the groups and individuals who could not adequately fend for themselves.

The idea was not new. Bismark's Germany began such a program in the late nineteenth century, and the British Liberal party of Lloyd George implemented a similar policy between 1906 and 1914. Few Americans maintained that the national government bore no responsibility for its citizens' well-being, but reasonable people could differ over how far its jurisdiction extended. Conservatives maintained that greater *federal* charity and protection would destroy individual initiative, sap moral vitality, and destroy the political independence necessary for democratic government. But recovery from the Depression (and the political fortunes of Roosevelt and his party) seemed to require a greater extension of national power, and after 1935 FDR began to graft a welfare state onto a market economy.

WELFARE MEASURES

To aid unemployed workers and to boost the economy in general, Congress granted Roosevelt's request for much larger relief expenditures. Almost $5 billion, a sum totaling over half the 1936 federal budget, went mostly to Harry Hopkins's Works Progress Administration (WPA), which financed a variety of conservation and public works programs. In addition to the much-caricatured leaf-raking and ditch-digging jobs, Hopkins's agency employed millions of workers building bridges, post offices, city halls, and local recreation centers. The vast infusion of national revenues, in the absence of large business investments or a high level of consumer spending, effectively stimulated the economy.

The Social Security Act of 1935 created a complex system of income maintenance for people facing financial disaster. In addition to the well-known retirement benefits, the law extended aid to dependent children, assistance to the blind, and money for unemployment payments by state and local governments. Social Security, a major pillar of the welfare state, suffered from significant limitations. Financed largely through payroll taxes, it reduced already slim take-home salaries and exempted many workers, including agricultural laborers and most public employees. Nevertheless, it did place an economic floor under a sizeable portion of the population and proved the most popular of all New Deal programs.

Another New Deal measure of 1935, the so-called Wealth Tax, attempted to shift the federal tax burden to persons whose income and accumulated wealth enabled them to pay most easily. Roosevelt proposed increased inheritance taxes, gift taxes, and steeply graduated levies on corporations and large individual incomes. The program raised a tempest among the wealthy, and Congress pared down some of the bill's features, rendering it ineffective in significantly redistributing wealth or in tapping many new sources of revenue. Despite its limitations, the act did establish a precedent for government action affecting income redistribution.

Several other significant pieces of legislation came during the Second Hundred Days. The Public Utilities Holding Company Act authorized the Securities and Exchange Commission to break up monopolistic utility companies. The Banking Act of 1935 strengthened the Federal Reserve System, giving a central Board of Governors greater control over regional banks, and increased federal authority over currency matters. Establishment of the Rural Electrification Administration (REA) created a government agency offering low-interest loans to nonprofit power cooperatives in farm areas. Since private electrical lines then reached only one out of every ten farms, the REA brought rural life into the twentieth century. Electricity and running water, amenities taken for granted in urban America, finally became realities on the farm.

Later New Deal measures expanded the welfare programs. Housing legislation of the early thirties had simply guaranteed residential mortgages, but in 1937 Roosevelt finally supported creation of the United States Housing Authority (USHA), a federal corporation authorized to construct low-cost units. The USHA completed only a few complexes before 1941, and, like other well-intentioned New Deal ventures, it promised considerably more than it delivered. The Fair Employment Standards Act of 1938 established minimum wages and maximum hours for employees in interstate businesses. The law contained numerous exemptions and provided a minimum rate of only forty cents per hour, but it did attempt to fulfill the New Deal's commitment to its blue-collar constituency. Finally, the Agricultural Adjustment Act of 1938 brought together and updated a number of farm programs. This second AAA relied upon broader controls over production and higher price supports for basic commodities. Although often revised and augmented in the direction of greater reliance upon acreage retirement (the soil bank program of the 1950s), the second AAA remained the heart of the government's farm program into the 1970s.

THE NEW DEAL AND LABOR

The New Deal came out fully behind organized labor in 1935. For several years Senator Robert F. Wagner of New York had campaigned, without White House support, for a new federal act protecting labor unions, and in the spring of 1935 FDR finally endorsed the crusade. Signed into law in July, the National Labor Relations Act (the Wagner Act) guaranteed workers in interstate businesses the right to unionize and to bargain collectively through their own representatives. A National Labor Relations Board (NLRB) was created to enforce the act's provisions and to prevent management from engaging in a number of "unfair" labor practices, such as establishing their own company-dominated unions.

Enactment of the NLRA coincided with a great expansion of labor unions. The American Federation of Labor's long-standing commitment to trade unionism grew increasingly less tenable in an advanced industrial economy. Dissidents within the AFL urged formation of unions encompassing all laborers, regardless of trade, in a specific industry. By 1935 the Committee for Industrial Organization (which later became the Congress of Industrial Organizations, or CIO), led by unionists such as crusty John L. Lewis of the United Mine Workers and David Dubinsky of the International Ladies Garment Workers, split off from the parent AFL. The CIO chose the auto industry as one of its first targets. Section 7a of the NRA had already stimulated some unionization there, and CIO organizers, building upon this foundation, employed the new tactic of the sit-down strike to win significant victories against General Motors and Chrysler in 1937. Rather than walking picket lines, striking automotive workers remained in their plants and frustrated attempts to bring in replacements. Shortly after GM came to terms, another industrial giant, United States Steel, capitulated without a fight. Several "Little Steel" companies refused to settle, provoking a violent Memorial Day confrontation at Republic Steel's Chicago plant. But by the outbreak of World War II, organized labor's new militancy, together with the Wagner Act, resulted in unionization of most major industries.

ELECTION OF 1936

The welfare state proved an immediate political success in the presidential election of 1936. The Republican candidate, Governor Alfred M. Landon of Kansas, offered solid progressive credentials extending back to the Bull Moose days of Teddy Roosevelt. Hesitant to attack New Deal measures too vehemently, the colorless Landon did little more than promise to administer them more efficiently. The rag-tag Union party headed by William Lemke brought together most of the remnants of FDR's radical opposition, including Father Coughlin, Dr. Townsend, and Gerald L. K. Smith. But without the magnetism of the fallen Huey Long and undercut by New Deal welfare measures, the party drew less than a million votes. Roosevelt won a smashing victory, driving the Republican party back to the two bastions of Maine and Vermont, the only states Landon carried against the president. Roosevelt's Democratic bandwagon also rolled successfully through congressional districts. When the new Congress convened, only nineteen members of the GOP sat in the Senate and 197 in the House of Representatives.

WPA

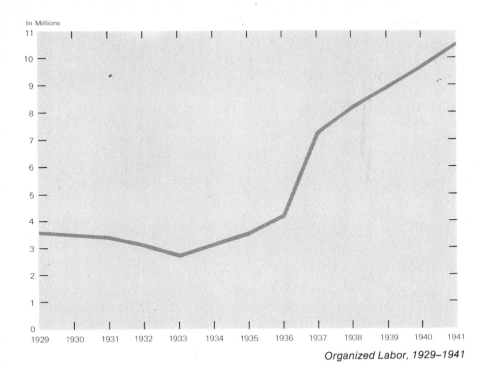

Organized Labor, 1929–1941

The waning of the new deal

The electoral landslide of 1936 gave FDR an overwhelming popular mandate and a solid working majority in both houses of Congress. The November victory marked the height of his political strength, but events soon conspired against the president. A head-on collision with the Supreme Court in early 1937 put the first major dent in the New Deal steamroller.

THE COURT FIGHT

From the beginning, traditionalists on the Supreme Court obstructed Roosevelt's efforts to meet the Depression. A bloc of four justices—Willis Van Devanter, James McReynolds, Pierce Butler, and George Sutherland—interjected their nineteenth-century judicial and social philosophies into the debate over twentieth-century problems. These aged judges, all in their late seventies, viewed with suspicion any program—state or national—which extended governmental power into areas traditionally reserved for private business decisions. The Four Horsemen, as their critics labeled them, were op-

"Nine Old Men"—The Supreme Court of 1935
Underwood and Underwood

posed by anoher bloc of three justices who generally approved governmental measures to deal with the economic crisis. In the middle sat Chief Justice Charles Evans Hughes, a skilled judicial politician whose views sometimes seemed to fluctuate according to the way the majority of associate justices leaned, and the enigmatic Owen J. Roberts. When Roberts lined up with the traditionalists in 1935 and 1936, a number of key New Deal programs, including the NRA and the AAA, were declared unconstitutional by the Supreme Court. In the NIRA case, *Schecter* v. *U.S.*, Chief Justice Hughes appeared to lay down an exceedingly narrow view of the national government's authority over economic affairs, causing FDR to fume about the justices' "horse and buggy" interpretation of the Constitution.

The gravest constitutional crisis came over the Court's position toward the New Deal measures enacted in 1935. Justice Roberts's earlier decision invalidating the processing tax of the first AAA and Justice Sutherland's vitriolic opinion striking down an act regulating the coal industry suggested

564

that few pieces of legislation would survive the Court's scrutiny. Needing only to attract the vote of Roberts, the Four Horsemen seemed to constitute a formidable barrier against the popular sentiment expressed in Roosevelt's 1936 landslide.

Buoyed by victory and anxious over the future of his programs, Roosevelt moved against the Court in February 1937. Initially, he avoided a frontal assault in favor of an all-too-transparent ploy. In a message asking Congress to reorganize the entire federal judiciary, the president argued that a bench staffed by aged justices contributed to a serious backlog of undecided cases. He proposed that Congress allow the executive to appoint new justices to the Supreme Court if judges over the age of seventy failed to retire. Under the guise of assisting the Court, Roosevelt's plan would have allowed him to add up to six new justices to the Supreme Court and to override the anti–New Deal bloc then threatening such legislation as the Social Security Act.

The "court-packing" scheme raised an immediate furor. The president's opponents—and even some of his Democratic supporters—saw it as a naked political assault upon the Constitution. During congressional hearings on the bill, a string of distinguished witnesses spoke out against the plan and urged representatives to reject any change in the number of Court members. Chief Justice Hughes, whose carefully manicured goatee enhanced his magisterial image, proved to be as resourceful an infighter off the bench as on it. In a letter replying to a query from Senator Burton K. Wheeler, Hughes threw the Court's prestige against Roosevelt without openly entering the fray. Citing the justices' record of speedy decision making, Hughes demolished FDR's claim of a backlog of cases.

Forced to retract earlier justifications, by the spring of 1937 FDR openly admitted that his plan aimed at obtaining a majority of justices favorable to his programs and at reversing the political decisions of the five obstructionists. Stripped of rhetoric about crowded dockets and superannuated justices, the court-packing plan appeared as a means of enforcing a popular dictum that the Court should follow election returns, in this case the referendum of 1936. FDR was insisting that the Supreme Court accept his and the Democratic Congress's view of constitutional interpretation and not make their own independent judgment on social and economic questions. In effect, Roosevelt challenged the old constitutional principle that the American polity consisted of carefully balanced institutions, the Supreme Court operating as a check against a popular majority.

In late March 1937 the court-packing plan suffered a serious setback when the Supreme Court upheld a Washington state minimum-wage law almost identical to one it had invalidated only a year before. Owen Roberts, the Court's swing man, sailed back into the pro–New Deal camp, reversing his earlier position. The reasons for Roberts's quick shift are unclear. Apparently he changed his mind sometime after the 1936 elections but before

FDR announced his court-packing scheme. Quickly labeled as "the switch in time to save nine," Roberts's flip-flop in *West Coast Hotel* v. *Parrish* (1937) undercut much of the necessity for Roosevelt's radical assault upon the Court. The *Parrish* decision suggested that the new five-to-four majority might look more favorably upon government regulation of the economy.

Roosevelt continued to push his measure but only met further rebuffs. In May, Justice Van Devanter's long-expected retirement gave the president an opportunity to make his first appointment. Following Van Devanter's resignation, Senate support for the court-packing plan nearly vanished, but Roosevelt still persisted. He had firmly committed his prestige to the fight and had no assurance that Justice Roberts would stay with the New Deal. In addition, the president had long ago promised the first vacancy to Senate Majority Leader Joseph Robinson, a sixty- five-year-old southern conservative whose enthusiasm for innovative programs was less than overwhelming. Assured of his long-coveted judgeship, Robinson kept the Senate in session through the hot summer months, hoping to ram through at least a compromise measure. Suddenly, in mid- July, overworked from leading the floor fight on the bill, Robinson suffered a heart attack and died. And the Court bill died with him.

THE "DEPRESSION" OF 1937

The Court fight had scarcely ended when FDR was faced with another challenge—renewed economic depression. In late 1936 and during the first half of the following year, conditions had gradually improved, but in August of 1937 the economy suddenly nose-dived. Business indices plummeted even faster than under Hoover, and Republicans gleefully labeled it "Roosevelt's depression." By New Year's, the stock market showed a decline of over 40 percent, industrial production slipped by almost one-third, and unemployment rolls increased by four million workers. As prosperity vanished, America's poor once again faced hunger.

What caused the economic downturn? The brief post-1935 prosperity had lacked a solid base. Unemployment stayed high and the important construction industry remained weak. The volume of long-term investment lagged behind short-term commitments because many businessmen questioned Roosevelt's ability to manage the economy. Several government actions which contributed to the downturn indicated that the New Dealers had not yet solved the mysteries of the economic cycle. FDR's attachment to a balanced budget forced a sharp cut in relief expenditures, including termination of the PWA. The resultant contraction of consumer spending coincided with the beginning of Social Security taxes, which further diminished purchasing power. The administration succeeded in simultaneously shaking businessmen's confidence and reducing buyers' ability to purchase goods.

Beset by conflicting advice, FDR vainly searched for a quick solution. Initially blaming the problem on business's reluctance to invest —a "strike of capital," as he called it—the president considered more vigorous antimonopoly actions. But eventually he returned to the path of greater government expenditures, a course which forced him to abandon his predilection for a balanced budget. In 1938 Roosevelt successfully asked Congress for slightly under $4 billion in relief funds, and he revived the PWA and refilled the WPA's job-creating pipeline. This strategy of "priming the pump," which paralleled the theories of the English economist John Maynard Keynes, substituted federal government expenditures for private investment and purchases. By midyear the economy began to catch hold again, and conditions steadily improved through 1939 and 1940, when international dangers produced substantial increases in military spending. Ultimately, the huge governmental outlays during World War II pushed the economy above pre-1930 levels.

THE CONSERVATIVE COALITION

Following close upon the Court fight, the depression of 1937 marked another setback for the New Deal. It indicated the essential failure of Roosevelt's programs to restore prosperity and strengthened the hand of the president's critics in government and business. Although voters still supported FDR, they also opposed any fundamental extensions of New Deal measures, and the rise of a more substantial congressional opposition soon demonstrated the limits of Roosevelt's power.

The president considered some Democratic congressmen, especially a number of southerners, more troublesome than some Republicans. FDR sought revenge against these Democrats who accepted the New Deal's standard in election years but deserted it during congressional rollcalls. In one of his "fireside chats," he compared his Democratic opponents to the "copperheads" of the Civil War era and threatened to purge the worst traitors in the 1938 off-year elections. Picking several senators, mostly southerners, as his main targets, Roosevelt supported rival Democratic nominees in the state primaries. The move backfired. The president's intrusion into local politics gave incumbents a good issue; they simultaneously asserted their support for most New Deal measures and their independence from presidential dictation.

Following the attempted "purge" of 1938, the president confronted an opposition force composed of anti-Roosevelt Democrats and an augmented GOP. This so-called conservative coalition never amounted to a solid bloc—

its composition shifted with specific issues—but Roosevelt found it increasingly difficult to push bills through Congress. During the 1939 session, for example, Congress stopped relief appropriations, voted to investigate charges of corruption in several New Deal agencies, and narrowly failed to add crippling amendments to the National Labor Relations Act.

In one sense, emergence of a more effective congressional opposition marked a return to normality. Later relations between the executive and legislative branches rarely went as smoothly as during Roosevelt's early years. With the passing of economic crisis, congressmen became less willing to give the president the latitude he enjoyed during his first years in office.

THE END OF REFORM

By 1939 the era of reform had ended. The New Deal's piecemeal approach, held together primarily by Roosevelt's commanding presence and personality, required broad-based support from normally conflicting interests. Once initial recovery began, groups whose stake in the existing order once again seemed secure proved reluctant to sanction new measures or to extend existing programs. Although total economic recovery remained elusive, the New Deal became, in effect, the victim of its own partial success. Farm interests, for example, that had received large subsidies from the national government, generally opposed programs designed to aid the urban poor. White southerners remained wary of any proposals which threatened racial control in their region, coming out particularly strong against an antilynching bill.

The New Deal also confronted a pervasive resistance to change. The desperate conditions of 1933–34 supplied the primary impetus for the furious pace of legislative action. The New Deal did not erase old ideas about balanced national budgets, limited federal action, and individual initiative; it proceeded despite them. By the late thirties the economic situation no longer seemed as grave, and businessmen's claims that excessive New Deal interference blocked final recovery seemed more reasonable than they had several years earlier. Even during the 1937 recession, demands for decisive governmental action remained muted. Only in times of great crisis—war, economic disaster, or domestic upheaval—do the majority of Americans demand that their representatives seek bold solutions to basic problems. By 1938 such a time had passed.

The culture of depression

The Depression confirmed many intellectuals' and writers' estrangement from America's predominantly middle-class society. During the 1920s many had become critics of American life; the Sacco-Vanzetti affair of the 1920s especially seemed to symbolize the injustice in the American system. The Depression crystallized this disillusionment. The collapsing economy indiscriminantly dragged people under and trampled them without regard to their own will. Individual action, it seemed, counted for nothing, and the plight of the faceless people brought to life in John Steinbeck's *Grapes of Wrath* (1939) seemed to demand collective action. Searching for a solution, many writers shed their "virus of liberalism" and embraced socialism or communism. In 1932 when Communist William Z. Foster ran for president, his endorsements included fifty-three writers and artists, among them Sherwood Anderson, John Dos Passos, Lincoln Steffens, Edmund Wilson, Granville Hicks, Sidney Hook, Langston Hughes, and Matthew Josephson.

For many writers, the infatuation with communism was short-lived. John Dos Passos quarreled with the party in 1934, beginning his swing to the right, and T. S. Eliot, Joseph Wood Krutch, Edmund Wilson, and Sherwood Anderson all became critics by the mid-thirties. Their dissatisfaction stemmed, in part, from a distaste for the new form of "proletarian" literature, which seemed to demand that art be the servant of social change and the instrument of massive class upheaval. They found it difficult to reconcile the roles of a serious writer and a social agitator. Choosing the former, they abandoned politics and the ideologies of collectivism in favor of individual expression and the pursuit of artistic excellence.

PROLETARIAN LITERATURE

Yet proletarian literature set the distinctive tone of the decade. Granville Hicks, dean of the new style, suggested that anything which deserved the name "art" should contain elements of class struggle and impel the reader to identify with the oppressed, but ultimately victorious, hero. Authors, Hicks proposed, should consider themselves members of the proletariat. The plots of proletarian novels and plays were often as stereotyped as the Horatio Alger fantasies of a previous generation. Heroic workers called a strike against villainous employers; brutal repression illuminated the class struggle; in a glorious moment of conversion, workers perceived the benefits of a collectivist state and triumphantly joined the worldwide working-class upheaval. The basic plot could be spiced with special effects. In a proletarian stage adaptation of Theodore Dreiser's *American Tragedy*, for example, a loudspeaker periodically droned, "We have given a name to Fate. It is the Economic System."

Playwright Clifford Odets and novelist John Steinbeck were the best practitioners of this style. Odets wrote *Waiting for Lefty* in response to a request for a simple play workers could stage at any meeting place. But his popularity went beyond the union halls, reaching to successful Broadway productions. Steinbeck generally avoided crude stereotypes and single-minded eco-

Proletarian Art: The Thomas Hart Benton mural section entitled "The Changing West"
The New School for Social Research

nomic motivation but still basically adhered to the new art form which emphasized class struggle. The Joad family of *The Grapes of Wrath*, driven from the misery of dusty Oklahoma to a nightmare of unemployment and oppression in California, remains a popular symbol of dispossessed people.

Left-wing musicians made a similar effort to blend their art form into the working-class struggle. During the early thirties a group called the Composers Collective tried to create a new proletarian music in which both words and melody would express militancy. "Music is propaganda—always propaganda—and of the most powerful sort," wrote a member of the Collective. Several years later other radical intellectuals began discovering working-class militancy in native American folk music. Activists found new songs among folk artists such as Aunt Molly Jackson, an organizer for the National Miners Union, and Jim Garland, a miner in the Kentucky coal fields. These agitator-performers sang about America's "common folk" and added their own radical themes to traditional tunes. Jim Garland used the music of "Greenback Dollar" for his attack upon the capitalist system:

570

We worked to build this country, mister,
While you enjoyed a life of ease;
You've stolen all that we built, mister;
Now our children starve and freeze.

By the end of the decade, the American Left fully embraced the folk music of proletarian minstrels such as Garland, Aunt Molly, and Woody Guthrie.

MOVIES

While some literary figures and musicians puzzled over the relationship between art and social action, motion picture makers catered to the desires of millions. Few people ever read the proletarian novelists, but movie stars who dazzled two earlier generations still awe and entertain audiences today. W. C. Fields, the Marx brothers, and even John Wayne's early westerns, still enjoy both critical and popular acclaim. More than the faded memories of FDR, the now slightly-blurred images of the great figures of the silver screen provide a link with the past, a reminder of the contrasting moods of the decade of the Depression.

One popular type of movie—gangster films—reflected the hard-boiled exterior of the thirties. James Cagney and Edward G. Robinson often portrayed gangsters, and toward the end of the decade Humphrey Bogart made the role his own. Exuding a tough-minded attitude toward life's problems and opportunities, Bogart and Cagney represented the survival of the self-made man who, without moralizing or equivocating, lifted himself out of poverty. They portrayed both the cynical opportunist and the eternal humanist. Cagney could push a grapefruit into a troublesome girlfriend's face yet weep over his kindly old mother; and Bogart, as a small-time crook on the lam, could furnish the money to straighten a crippled girl's foot. Although the analogy should not be pushed too far, such movies paralleled the New Deal's often opportunistic yet basically humanitarian reaction to the problems of the Depression.

If some movies reflected the hard-boiled tone of the thirties, others offered escape from the problems of the day. The intricately staged musicals of Busby Berkeley, with hundreds of chorus girls dancing in perfect harmony, provided hours of beauty and symmetry for people whose lives contained too little of either. The enormously popular *Flash Gordon* serials carried viewers into futuristic struggles between forces of light and darkness for control of sophisticated technology. As the comic strip hero, bleached-blond former swimming star Buster Crabbe typified the all-American boy, while Charles Middleton as "Ming the Merciless," who ruled twenty-first-century Mongo, personified the yellow, red, and almost every other menace. The action-filled "B" Western entranced would-be cowboys all across the country.

*Count Dracula (Bela Lugosi)
rivaled King Kong and
Frankenstein's monster for
stardom in the horror movies of
the 1930's*
Culver Pictures

By the opening reel every Saturday matinee-goer could spot his white-hatted, two-gunned hero, be he Ken Maynard, Hopalong Cassidy, or a more obscure wrangler such as "Crash" Corrigan. And no one could miss the outlaw gang—generally led by smartly dressed lawyers, bankers, or railroad men who threatened the decent people of the community. Whether repeatedly riding past the same clump of trees, leaping off the same cliff, or firing scores of shots without reloading, the good guy invariably survived the most bloodless violence ever put on film.

Radio

The decade of the Depression marked radio's emergence as a truly mass medium. During the twenties many people considered radio a novelty: they tinkered with primitive crystal sets, searching for distant stations through a bewildering maze of signals. Just before the Depression the national govern-

Young John Kennedy, London
Magnum Photo Inc.

ment regulated wireless transmissions—assigning wavelengths and setting power levels for individual stations—and manufacturers reduced the size, complexity, and cost of radio receivers. Between 1930 and 1940 the number of homes with sets more than doubled, and business found the medium an effective means of reaching large numbers of people. Advertisers, euphemistically known as "sponsors," began presenting a wide variety of programs, many of them beamed nationwide over the two major networks, NBC and CBS. Mass audiences meant higher-priced entertainers. Bob Hope, Bing Crosby, and Jack Benny replaced such lesser-known radio acts as the "Cliquot Club Eskimos."

Radio offered a wide range of attractions, but market demands dominated programming tastes. Most sponsors measured artistic value by ability to attract listeners and sell products. Certain subjects, particularly sex, were taboo. A mildly suggestive sketch involving Mae West and a wooden dummy, Charley McCarthy, outraged enough people so that Miss West's voice was subsequently banned from the airwaves. Some series attracted millions of loyal fans. Two white vaudevillians created a show based upon black characters; "Amos 'n' Andy" remained on the air for more than thirty years, burlesquing black lives for largely white audiences. "Soap operas," involving the exciting careers and carefully sanitized loves of larger-than-life heroines, spiced housewives' daily routines. A Detroit entrepreneur, George Trendle, invented "The Lone Ranger," a nondrinking, noncursing, nonkilling hero who quickly rivaled Saturday matinee cowboys for juvenile acclaim. Following this success, Trendle introduced "The Green Hornet" and "Sergeant Preston of the Yukon" (and his lead dog "Yukon King"), two other nightly favorites that ran for almost twenty years.

Radio also offered a limited amount of more serious entertainment. CBS carried the New York Philharmonic, and NBC the Metropolitan Opera on Saturday afternoon. Later in the decade NBC formed its own symphony orchestra, a distinguished ensemble under the direction of Arturo Toscanini. Several theater-radio programs offered top-name talent—such as Charles Laughton, Clark Gable, and Cary Grant—in first-rate productions. Other projects concentrated upon developing material uniquely suited to radio; Orson Welles's "Mercury Theater of the Air" provided a number of aural innovations, some of which he adapted for the screen in his classic motion picture *Citizen Kane*.

Perhaps radio's greatest impact came through its ability to bring far-off events into people's homes. On-the-spot newscasts dramatized spectacular events of the thirties—the Munich Conference, the explosion of the dirigible *Hindenburg* over a New Jersey airport, and Joe Louis's rise to the heavyweight championship. Some skillful broadcasters even improved upon reality. When Bill Stern, breathlessly describing a thrilling, zigzag run by "Crazylegs" Brown, discovered that "Breakaway" Smith was actually carrying the ball, the fast-talking sportscaster simply invented a last-second lateral pass, and the proper ballcarrier skipped across the goal line. Imaginative baseball announcers such as the semiliterate ex-fireballer Dizzy Dean routinely turned easy outs into spectacular catches and lazy fly balls into booming drives. When Orson Welles presented his realistic radio adaptation of *War of the Worlds*, an H. G. Wells story of a Martian invasion, he created pockets of hysteria across the nation. Frantic callers jammed CBS's phone lines, and Welles had to go back on the air to assure people that his production was pure fiction.

Assessing the new deal

The New Deal offered the most to Americans whose income and accumulated wealth placed them in the upper two-thirds to three-fourths of the economic structure. It eventually revived business prosperity without radical redistribution of wealth or serious interference with the economy. Through more vigorous governmental intervention, the national administration became the promoter of economic growth and the agency charged with preventing any repetition of the Great Depression. For middle- and lower-income groups, the New Deal offered a variety of programs which, in addition to promoting general prosperity, guaranteed minimum wages, encouraged unionization, financed home construction, underwrote farm income, and provided support for the aged and temporarily unemployed. Roosevelt thus extended concrete assistance to meet the exigencies of the thirties and established some degree of insurance against future disasters.

Yet the decade was also a time of unfullfilled hopes and all-too-limited advances. One of the New Deal's most obvious shortcomings was the failure to deal with the hard-core poverty infecting many areas of the country. In his 1937 inaugural FDR himself promised to meet the needs of the one-third of Americans who remained ill-clothed, ill-housed, and ill-fed. All too often, though, opposition from more powerful and better-organized political and economic interests frustrated efforts to aid the very poor. As the nation would discover during the early 1960s, three decades of federal welfare programs still left millions of needy poeple largely unassisted. Appalachia, the black belts in the south, and urban ghettoes serve as reminders of the limits of the new welfare state.

BLACKS IN THE GREAT DEPRESSION

The New Deal's relationship to black people illustrated both the positive impact and the shortcomings of reform measures. Already on the bottom of the socioeconomic ladder, black workers were hit particularly hard by the Depression. Roosevelt himself developed a strong appeal to black voters, reversing traditional voting patterns. Eleanor Roosevelt served as the presi-

Eleanor Roosevelt and singer Marian Anderson, 1939
Acme

dent's unofficial emissary to blacks, and she displayed a genuine desire to deal with America's long-standing racial dilemma. But the New Deal had no consistent policy to meet the special problems of black Americans. Each bureau followed its own approach, and assistance varied according to the interest and concern of the persons in charge. Harold Ickes's PWA and Harry Hopkins's WPA supplied badly needed jobs and showed sensitivity to the plight of black workers. After some hesitation, Hopkins issued a general ban against discriminatory hiring practices, and during the late thirties and early forties blacks comprised a sizeable percentage of the WPA work rosters. But some recovery programs actually worked against the interest of blacks. Payments in exchange for restriction of cotton acreage reduced the number of black laborers and sharecroppers required on southern plantations, and AAA officials failed to prevent white landlords from retaining funds intended for black tenants. As long as many unions maintained segregation, federal legislation advancing the rights of organized labor rebounded against black workers. In fact, growing unionization and minimum-wage laws often resulted in layoffs of blacks. And always mindful of southern Democratic support, many New Dealers proved reluctant to overturn Jim Crow practices on federal projects. On some WPA sites black and white laborers drank from segregated buckets with separate dippers.

The New Deal's ambivalent record divided the leadership of the black movement. Old-line NAACP leaders, especially Secretary Walter White, faced challenges from younger and more militant spokesmen. The "young Turks," who included Ralph Bunche and sociologist E. Franklin Frazier, wanted the NAACP to modify its traditional preoccupation with civil and political rights and exert greater pressure for basic economic assistance to blacks. Being able to sit front and center in a desegregated theater, dissidents reasoned, meant little to a black family lacking money for a decent meal. Some militant NAACP members encouraged black-white cooperation through the more egalitarian CIO unions and advocated a class-based drive for a greater share in the economy. Breaking completely from the organization he had helped to create, the historian and writer W. E. B. Du Bois urged blacks to avoid white-owned businesses and to establish nonprofit cooperatives within their own communities. Dominated by the black elite and closely tied to white philanthropists, the NAACP rejected such new directions and maintained its traditional crusade against legal discrimination, placing renewed emphasis upon a national antilynching law. Without a Marcus Garvey to ignite the masses, most blacks remained unorganized and received limited benefits from the New Deal.

THE INDIAN NEW DEAL

The Roosevelt administration also dealt with the plight of native Americans. In reality, however, the origins of the "Indian New Deal" lay in the 1920s. Throughout the twenties, reformers discussed Indian affairs, and the Meriam Report of 1928, initiated by Herbert Hoover and financed by John D. Rockefeller, Jr., called for a radical overhaul of federal Indian policies. Better medical services, reform of educational institutions, and restructuring of the Indian Service headed the list of suggested changes. In addition, the Meriam Report proposed careful reevaluation of the policy, set forth in the

Dawes Act of 1887, of "allotting" tribal lands to individual Indians. The Meriam Report encouraged reformers, particularly those who favored strengthening tribal institutions and halting the transfer of Indian lands to whites which was occurring as a result of the allotment program.

The impact of the Depression on native Americans forced the issue of reform, and several members of the Roosevelt administration displayed strong interest in Indian affairs. In particular, John Collier, FDR's choice as commissioner of Indian Affairs, played a key role in pushing the Indian Reorganization Act— sometimes called the Wheeler-Howard Act or simply the IRA— through Congress in 1934. Incorporating Collier's conviction that further erosion of tribal customs and legal rights would be disastrous for Indians, the IRA sought to strengthen tribal units and to revive the communal heritage of native Americans. The law prohibited further allotment of tribal lands, authorized annual appropriations to acquire additional acreage, and, if members of a tribe desired, permitted organization of stronger tribal governments. Using the authority of his office to promote what he called "Indianhood," Collier supported publication of new texts on Indian history, revamped educational institutions, encouraged revival of native handicrafts, and inaugurated a new policy of toleration for Indian religions.

Just as the Indian New Deal was not totally new, it was not completely successful. Collier's policies failed to satisfy many groups. Christian missionaries, for example, bitterly protested Collier's decision to tolerate "pagan" native American religions. More important, many native Americans and non-Indian reformers believed that Collier's ideas reflected a romantic attachment to an outmoded way of life and that the strengthening of tribal ties only delayed Indian people's inevitable rendezvous with twentieth-century society. As a result of such opposition, a number of tribes, including the Navajo and several in Oklahoma, rejected reorganization under the IRA. And if Collier failed to rally all native Americans to a revival of tribalism, he also could not convince the national government to support a full-scale assault on the Indians' economic and social problems. The government provided better medical services, more money for public works on reservations, and funds to increase cattle and crop production. But federal money never matched the needs of native Americans, and debates continued to rage over the practical effectiveness of the renewed emphasis on tribalism.

THE LIMITS OF PLANNING

Perhaps the greatest failure of the New Deal was its lack of coherent planning and organization. Some members of the administration—particularly Rexford Guy Tugwell, who served in a number of capacities—urged more attention to planned development, but such efforts ran into numerous constitutional, political, and fiscal difficulties. Several outstanding examples of frustrated programs—such as the broad regional aims of the Tennessee Valley Authority and the Resettlement Administration's "greenbelt" towns for low-income families—illustrate the opportunities lost.

TVA's dams reduced the danger of floods, and its generators brought billions of kilowatts to the valley's residents. But the broader hopes of TVA's major architect, Arthur Morgan, became subordinated to the fight to extend public power. Morgan hoped that TVA would provide the basis for a general rehabilitation of the region—planned communities, folk-art programs, and new industries. Morgan's vision, however, simply cost too much money and confronted too many vested political interests. Cheaper electrical rates offered a less ambitious yet politically attainable goal.

The history of the Resettlement Administration offers another example of lofty ideals and less grandiose accomplishments. Established in 1935 and headed by the controversial Tugwell, the agency provided loans and assistance to poor farmers untouched by other programs. The RA also ran a number of camps for migrant workers in California. Tugwell's most ambitious endeavor called for governmental construction of planned communities to resettle poor families near metropolitan areas but outside the teeming slums. Suburban projects, it was believed, would provide both low-cost housing and grassy spaces generally available only to the more affluent. The back-to-nature bias of the program raised hopes that the towns' residents would develop a type of participatory democracy and a vigorous communitarian spirit. With his own agrarian preferences, Roosevelt showed a great interest in the greenbelt towns, but the planners' dreams soon ran into hard political and economic realities. Local politicians, land developers, and wealthy suburbanites comprised a complicated pattern of vested interests which blocked land acquisition. The extensive federal direction associated with the communities allowed critics to label them as communistic and un-American. Tugwell's radical image lent credence to such charges, and the program never proceeded beyond one town each in Maryland, Wisconsin, and Ohio. This attempt to reverse the influx of the poor into decaying central cities and to establish a more decentralized pattern of settlement thus ended in failure.

Tugwell's failure with his greenbelt towns reflected a more general problem—how could New Dealers extend their favorite programs beyond the borders of Washington, D.C.? Some states, particularly urbanized ones such as New York and Pennsylvania, and a few cities did embark on "little New Deals," adopting new programs and expanding their social welfare budgets. Taken as a group, states did increase expenditures for public service, especially where New Deal measures such as unemployment compensation were linked to state participation. But the "little New Deals" generally played out long before Roosevelt's bigger deal, and most states and cities never even joined the game. Many powerful state leaders worked to keep federal officials out of their territories, and some state actions, such as passage of an-tilabor laws and increases in highly regressive sales taxes, actually conflicted with national policies. Although Roosevelt's conservative opponents constantly complained about Washington usurping too much power, many new studies of the New Deal's actual impact stress how limited it was on the local level. In most cases New Dealers found themselves simply unable to impose national policy on forty-eight different states.

Recognizing the complex subjectivity of many judgments, several general conclusions still emerge. Most obviously, FDR and his aides, although averting total collapse and providing the beginnings of economic revival and a welfare state, never achieved full recovery until the massive government spending during World War II underwrote greater production and fuller employment. The New Deal provided security for a majority of Americans, but it also missed opportunities to do more and preserved far more of the economic system than it transformed. The 1930s represented a new deal, not a new deck, for the American people.

A resurgent nationalism

The worldwide economic crisis of the thirties destroyed the internationalist spirit of the twenties. Attempts to cope with domestic problems encouraged expansionist adventures in Germany, Italy, and Japan and withdrawal from world concerns in England, France, and the United States. The resurgent nationalism of the Depression decade washed away collective security arrangements and crested in another world war.

In the United States, economic stringency led to a retreat from formal empire, a concentration upon trade expansion, and a sentiment favoring political isolationism and nonentanglement. The desire to remain aloof from foreign wars had existed throughout the twenties, but the outbreak of fighting in Manchuria and Italy's bellicose gestures toward Ethiopia deepened American determination to avoid distant conflicts. Reflecting the growing isolationist mood, Congress in early 1935 soundly defeated Roosevelt's proposal to join the World Court. During the debate, a Minnesota senator who feared that membership in the international body would impair American sovereignty shouted, "To hell with Europe and the rest of those nations." As a means of deterring invasions and preserving world peace, Roosevelt requested congressional authority to institute an arms embargo against aggressors. Instead, isolationist senators passed a bill requiring that any embargo apply equally to all belligerents. They hoped that this Neutrality Act of 1935 would preserve impartiality and preclude involvement in foreign disputes.

As Americans turned inward, the Italian dictator Benito Mussolini sought to alleviate his country's domestic ills by enlarging its African empire. In October 1935 his armies marched into Ethiopia, a proud kingdom which had never succumbed to colonialist rule. Isolationists praised Roosevelt for quickly invoking the Neutrality Act, but the president intended that the "impartial" arms embargo would work primarily against Italy, a country with which the United States normally traded. Roosevelt next called for a "moral embargo" on strategic commodities. In this way, United States policy paralleled the League of Nations's recommendation of economic sanctions against the aggressor. But the height of the Depression proved a poor time to expect voluntary curtailment of exports. In the end, neither the United States nor members of the League enforced an effective boycott, and each lamely blamed the other for failure to halt aggression. Italy's invasion, like Japan's incursion a few years earlier, met nothing more than worldwide moral outrage.

A reappraisal of America's role in World War I provided support for the policy of insularity. The revisionist historians of the 1930s contended that Americans in 1917 had been tricked into a war in which they had little national interest. According to this interpretation, Wilson and his advisers were never neutral and steered the United States into belligerency because of their own sympathy for England. Moreover, by permitting American bankers and munition makers to incur heavy debts to Allied nations, the government had encouraged an economic tie that made neutrality virtually impossible. Walter Millis's influential *Road to War* (1935), a Book-of-the-Month Club selection, was perhaps the most scholarly of the revisionist works, but more sensationalist treatments bore such titles as *Blood and Profits* and *Merchants of Death*. In a decade of high unemployment and business collapse, Americans readily accepted the proposition that an unholy alliance between bankers and businessmen had plunged the nation into World War I. Between 1934 and 1936, a Senate investigating committee headed by Republican Gerald Nye of North Dakota publicized sensational exposés of businessmen who profited from arms races and war. The Nye committee's reports transformed the image of the crusade to save the world for democracy into an ignominious intrigue to fill the coffers of unscrupulous businessmen. The "munition makers' conspiracy" became an easy explanation for world turmoil, and decent Americans resolved never again to be maneuvered into foreign quarrels or to sacrifice their sons for profiteers.

The revisionist interpretation of World War I and the Nye committee's findings briefly redeemed Germany. The picture of the hated Hun softened into one of an unfortunate victim of an unjust peace. If Adolf Hitler's anti-Semitism and militarism alarmed Americans, his desire to reunite German-speaking peoples and his repudiation of the Versailles settlement seemed understandable. Late in 1933, following the virtual collapse of a World Disarmament Conference in Geneva, Hitler terminated Germany's eight-year participation in the League of Nations and began to rearm in contravention of the Versailles treaty. Quickly boosting military expenditures by 90 percent, he restored compulsory military service, built an air force, and planned an army that would outnumber France's. In March 1936 Nazi troops reoccupied the strategic Rhineland, in further violation of the Versailles agreement. Fascist armies were on the move, but their threat seemed distant to most Americans and did not yet impair vital economic or strategic interests.

THE SPANISH CIVIL WAR

A few months after Hitler's legions goosestepped into the Rhineland, civil war broke out in Spain, providing further experience for the military machines of Hitler and Mussolini. Lending sophisticated weaponry and thousands of soldiers, the two fascist leaders supported the uprising of General Francisco Franco, who promised to institute a fascist state and restore traditionalism on the Iberian penninsula. Loyalist (republican) forces appealed to the world for assistance in crushing the rebellion, but only the Soviet Union sent aid. Britain, France, and the United States, fearful that the conflict might spread if more foreign powers took sides, adopted policies of nonintervention. The United States Congress extended the arms embargo to cover civil wars, an act which departed from traditional practice by denying weapons to legitimate goverments as well as to rebels. Gradually Franco's superior firepower wore down the Loyalists, and the ultranationalist, conservative regime which would govern Spain until the 1970s assumed power.

The Spanish Civil War provoked some Americans to revaluate the policy of nonentanglement. Catholic groups passionately backed Franco, whom they viewed as a strong anti-Communist fighting to maintain religion and order. Many left-wing American intellectuals took up the Loyalists as a cause célèbre. Disillusioned with the depression-riddled capitalist system and fearful of the repressive and demagogic fascist regimes, young writers and artists fervently supported the Soviet-organized international brigades which assisted the republicans in Spain. Caught up in the romanticism of the crusade, cadres of Americans such as the "Abraham Lincoln Battalion" crossed the Atlantic. Many of these men died cursing their country for its indifference to the plight of free Spain.

AGGRESSION IN THE FAR EAST AND EUROPE

As Germany and Italy carved out spheres of influence, Japan continued its expansion. In the summer of 1937, following an exchange of shots between Chinese and Japanese troops stationed near the Marco Polo Bridge southwest of Peking, Japanese columns swooped southward through Peking, Shanghai, Nanking, and Shantung. The weak Nationalist government led by Chiang Kai-shek failed to halt the invaders and retreated to the interior city of Chungking, leaving the important seaports to the enemy. Japan, confronted with population pressures and a shortage of raw materials, announced a plan for an East Asian Co-Prosperity Sphere and demanded that China accept a position of political and economic subserviency.

The attack against China, a violation of the Washington Treaty agreements, stunned many Americans, but events in Europe distracted them from Far Eastern problems. Hitler and Mussolini formalized their friendship into an Axis; Italy withdrew from the League; and in mid-1938 Hitler proclaimed Austria as part of the Third Reich. While Franco triumphed in Spain, Hitler announced his intention to annex the Sudetenland, a portion of Czechoslovakia which contained 3.5 million Germans. Hitler's new move threatened a direct confrontation with France and Britain. But these countries, beset by political instability, economic trouble, and military inadequacies, were unprepared for a showdown. Desperately wanting peace, British and French leaders hoped that Hitler's desire for *Lebenstraum* (living space) would be appeased once he gained the Sudenten territory. Meeting Hitler at Munich in September 1938, they agreed to German occupation of the Sudentenland, and Hitler assured them he would seek no more territory.

The Munich settlement, like the collective security structure of the twenties, did not bring peace. Within the next year, Germany annexed the rest of Czechoslovakia, made demands on Poland and Lithuania, formed a military alliance with Italy, and secured its eastern flank by signing a non-aggression pact with the Soviet Union. On September 1, 1939, German troops stormed into Poland. England and France drew the line at further appeasement, and the world plunged into the second major war of the century.

AMERICA'S RESPONSE

The American response to the kaleidoscopic events preceding the invasion of Poland had been ambiguous and ineffectual. A gap of perception widened between the White House and Congress. In a 1937 speech Roosevelt had murmured some cautious phases about "quarantining" aggressors, but Congress just passed another Neutrality Act aimed at preserving non-involvement. When the president asked for funds to develop naval bases in the Pacific, the House recoiled for fear of provoking Japan. Roosevelt desperately pressed for modification of the Neutrality Act, but many congressmen became convinced that he, like Wilson, was contriving with Britain and France to drag the country into a remote war. Official reports from Europe to the State Department urged that America take a stronger stand and predicted war was imminent; yet William Borah, chairman of the Senate Foreign Relations Committee, roared that he possessed even better sources of information and believed the crisis was overblown.

The economic depression and rising nationalism of the thirties resulted in cycles of aggression and appeasement which would haunt postwar diplomats and fascinate historians. Searching for an explanation of appeasement, analysts have flung indictments in all directions. Some assign almost total responsibility to Britain and France, portraying the United States as an innocent bystander. Others blame America's isolationism, pointing out that Britain and France lacked the military and economic might to make a strong stand without American cooperation. Most would probably agree that the American desire for nonentanglement was, if not the direct cause of appeasement, certainly its handmaiden.

Looking back on what now seems a clear course of open-ended aggression, postwar historians and policymakers have generally viewed negotiations such as the Munich Conference as foolish agreements which whetted expansionists' appetites rather than satisfying them. And just as the misapplied historical lesson of World War I guided an unfortunate course of noninvolvement during the thirties, the disastrous consequences of appeasement later justified inflexible diplomacy. After Munich, compromise became associated with appeasement and war; hard-line stands became identified with preserving the peace. Perhaps the real significance of the thirties lies not in determining who was responsible for appeasement or why, but in the revelation that Americans in the twentieth century have persistently tried to relive and redeem past mistakes in present situations. Ghosts of previous failures— a "munitions makers' conspiracy" or a "Munich"—have substituted for policies based upon contemporary realities.

Things to think about: 1932–1940

How did the Depression affect the nation? In addition to the more scholarly works listed below, two journalistic accounts provide readable surveys: Frederick Lewis Allen, *Since Yesterday: The Nineteen-Thirties in America* (1939), and Edward R. Ellis, *A Nation in Turmoil: The Great American Depression, 1929-1939* (1970). Studs Turkel, *Hard Times: An Oral History of the Depression* (1970) contains reminiscences as well as other perspectives on the difficulties of the 1930s. Compare Hoover's presidential leadership with FDR's leadership and style. Joan Hoff Wilson, *Herbert Hoover* (1975), and Hoover's own works, *The Memoirs of Herbert Hoover: The Cabinet and the Presidency 1920-1933* (1952), and *The Great Depression, 1929-1941* (1952), provide insights into this often-misunderstood man. Albert U. Romasco, *The Poverty of Abundance* (1965), is a good study of Hoover's response to the Depression. Two leading historians, Arthur Schlesinger, Jr., and Frank Freidel, are writing multivolume studies of Roosevelt, and each has published several volumes. Perceptive accounts of Roosevelt are James M. Burns, *Roosevelt: The Lion and the Fox* (1956), and Rexford G. Tugwell, *The Democratic Roosevelt* (1957).

How did the New Dealers try to solve the nation's social and economic problems? How successful were their efforts? William E. Leuchtenburg, *Franklin D. Roosevelt and the New Deal, 1932–1940* (1963), offers a generally positive assessment and remains the best one-volume treatment of the New Deal. Edgar E. Robinson, *The Roosevelt Leadership, 1933–1945* (1955), criticizes the New Deal for going too far; and Paul K. Conkin's influential survey, *The New Deal* (2nd ed., 1975), criticizes reformers for not doing enough. Ellis Hawley, *The New Deal and the Problem of Monopoly: A Study in Economic Ambivalence* (1965), provides numerous insights into the New Deal. James T. Patterson, *Congressional Conservatism and the New Deal* (1967) discusses Roosevelt's growing opposition in Congress. Raymond Wolters, *Negroes and the Great Depression: The Problem of Economic Recovery* (1970), and David Conrad, *The Forgotten Farmer: The Story of the Sharecroppers and the New Deal* (1965), are basic works. Donald McCoy, *Angry Voices: Left-of-Center Politics in the New Deal Era* (1958); David H. Bennett, *Demagogues in the Depression* (1969); and T. Harry Williams, *Huey Long* (1969), treat FDR's rivals on the Left. John Braeman et al., eds., *The New Deal* (2 vols., 1975), contains some sparkling recent essays on the New Deal at the state and local as well as the national level. Valuable specialized studies include Bernard Bellush, *The Failure of the NRA* (1975), Donald Parman, *The Navájos and the New Deal* (1976), and Otis Graham, *Toward a Planned Society* (1976).

What happened to American culture and society during the 1930s? Daniel Aaron and Robert Bendiner, eds., *The Strenuous Decade: A Social and Intellectual Record of the 1930's* (1970), is a valuable collection of primary materials. Charles C. Alexander, *Nationalism in American Thought, 1930–1945* (1968) offers a concise interpretation of many social and cultural developments, while Richard Pells, *Radical Visions and American Dreams* (1973), is more difficult but also more insightful. Daniel Aaron, *Writers on the Left* (1961) discusses literature, and Andrew Bergman, *We're in the Money: Depression America and Its Films* (1971) and Robert Sklar, *Movie-made America* (1975), treat motion pictures. One can gain an appreciation of Woody Guthrie through his books *Bound for Glory* (1964) and *Seeds of Man* (1976), as well as through his many songs. *Dust Bowl Ballads* (1964), a one-record album, and the three-record Library of Congress recordings (1964) are valuable social documents from the 1930s.

How did FDR's foreign policy from 1937 to 1939 reflect domestic as well as global pressures? John E. Wiltz, *From Isolation to War, 1931–1941* (1968) and Robert A. Divine, *The Illusion of Neutrality* (1962) are convenient summaries. Arnold Offner, *American Appeasement: United States Foreign Policy and Germany, 1933–1938* (1969), Dorothy Borg, *The United States and the Far Eastern Crisis of 1933–1938* (1964), and Lloyd Gardner, *Economic Aspects of New Deal Diplomacy* (1964), are more specialized studies. Manfred Jonas, *Isolationism in America, 1935–1941* (1966), is an interpretation of isolationist sentiment, Wayne S. Cole, *Charles A. Lindbergh and the Battle against American Intervention in World War II* (1974), is more specialized.

13

COLOSSUS OF THE WEST

1940-1953

DOUGLAS MACARTHUR

"To join the Long Gray Line had been the lodestar of all my hopes since the sound of the bugles ushered me into the world," Douglas MacArthur once reminisced. Born at a western frontier garrison in 1880, MacArthur literally grew up along with the modern army, spending all but the last thirteen of his eighty-four years actively associated with the military. His father rose through the ranks to major general, winning the Medal of Honor during the Civil War, fighting Indians on the Great Plains, and serving in the Philippines during the Spanish American War. "Always before me was the vision of West Point, that greatest military institution in the world," MacArthur later wrote. Also encouraged by his mother "Pinky," an aggressive army wife, young Douglas entered West Point in 1899. While his mother lived nearby during his four years at the Academy, MacArthur compiled an outstanding scholastic and athletic record. Upon graduation, he astutely chose the Engineer Corps, a branch offering the best chance for rapid advancement.

586

U.S. Army Photo

As President Hoover's army chief of staff, MacArthur achieved national attention when he directed the dispersal of the Bonus Marchers in 1932. He considered the demonstration a Communist plot and feared that "an incipient revolution [was] in the air." Attired in his heavily decorated uniform, the general watched the action personally. "It was a good job, quickly done, with no one injured," he told a reporter during a lull in the operation. But before the day ended, scores of persons lay injured. Still, MacArthur declared, his vigorous campaign was a great success and was welcomed by the "distressed populace." Many other observers, however, did not share his enthusiasm. Democratic presidential aspirant Franklin Roosevelt linked MacArthur with Huey Long, privately warning that they were the two most dangerous men in the country. People wanted strong direction, FDR claimed, and MacArthur provided "the famous symbolic figure—the man on horseback." But Roosevelt's own kind of leadership obviated the need and the desire—if any such mood really did exist in the thirties—for MacArthur's style of command. FDR retained MacArthur as chief of staff until 1935, when the general became military advisor to America's new commonwealth, the Philippines.

From 1935 until 1951 MacArthur's career was linked to the Far East and to war; he finally assumed the Napoleonic role denied him at home. In 1937 he even resigned from his beloved army, preferring the Philippines to another stateside assignment, and became field marshall for the Philippine government. The only American ever to hold such a rank, MacArthur designed his own gold leaf-encrusted garrison cap, later adding the sunglasses and corncob pipe which became his trademarks during World War II. Shortly before Pearl Harbor he returned to active duty and directed the unsuccessful defense of the Philippines. In 1942, officials ordered him to evacuate his underground headquarters on Corregidor, and with his dramatic farewell, "I shall return," he regretfully left for Australia. He continually urged an American war effort centered on recapture of the islands, and in 1944 he finally waded ashore at Leyte, announcing: "By the grace of Almighty God, our forces stand again on the Philippines." And a year later MacArthur presided over the Japanese surrender ceremonies aboard the battleship *Missouri*. "Show him where to sign," he snapped to his chief of staff when the Japanese representative stopped to read the surrender document.

Sent to Tokyo as supreme commander of the occupation of Japan, he took complete charge of the radical reconstruction of Japan's society, government, and economy. He later said that he wished history to remember him as "one whose sacred duty it became once the guns were silenced, to carry to the land of our vanquished foe the solace and hope and faith of Christian morals."

The general was in Tokyo when the Korean conflict broke out in 1950. His brilliant marine invasion behind North Korean lines at Inchon showed that he had lost none of his military daring, but his arrogant attitude toward President Truman as well as his cavalier disregard for Chinese intervention indicated a growing sense of omnipotence. Openly criticizing the Truman administration's policy of "limited warfare," he pushed for an all-out effort, telling sympathetic Republican supporters that there was "no substitute for victory." Meanwhile, other military experts questioned MacArthur's own tactical and strategic decisions, and even foreign observers commented upon his open disregard of the military's traditional deference to civilian control. When President Truman flew all the way to Wake Island (five thousand miles) to meet with the general, who had traveled nineteen hundred miles, British Prime Minister Clement Atlee remarked, "I thought it a curious relationship between a government and a general." MacArthur continued to challenge the president, his commander-in-chief, until Truman finally recalled him in 1951.

Amid great popular acclaim and sympathy, MacArthur returned to the United States, but unlike Generals De Gaulle and Eisenhower he never could grasp the elusive ring of political power. A candidate for the 1952 Republican nomination, he gave the keynote address to the delegates who selected Eisenhower. Touring the nation with his wife and young son, MacArthur tried to summon support for the old virtues—what he called "the simple, eternal truths of the 'American way'"—but the aristocratic MacArthur lacked Ike's common touch. Reflecting upon his career, MacArthur once concluded, "I believe it was destiny."

1940 Roosevelt elected, defeating Wendell Willkie
Selective Service Act
Destroyers-for-bases deal
1941 Battle of the Atlantic
Lend-Lease Act
Atlantic Charter
Japanese attack Pearl Harbor, December 7; America
    declares war
1942 Domestic war mobilization
Fair Employment Practices Commission
Allied campaign in North Africa
1943 Detroit race riots
1944 Invasion of Europe; landing at Normandy, June 6
Roosevelt elected to fourth term
Gunnar Myrdal, An American Dilemma
Bretton Woods Conference
Dumbarton Oaks Conference
1945 Yalta Conference
Atomic bomb dropped on Hiroshima, August 6
Vice-President Truman becomes president on Roosevelt's
    death
United Nations formed
1946 Republicans take control of both Houses of Congress
1947 Taft-Hartley Act
Truman Doctrine announced
Marshall Plan proposed
1948 Truman elected in his own right
1949 North Atlantic Treaty Organization formed
Communists come to power in China
USSR explodes atomic device
1947–51 Loyalty campaign and spy trials
1950 Outbreak of Korean conflict
Rise of Senator Joseph McCarthy as popular anti-
    Communist
1951 Twenty-second Amendment
1952 Eisenhower elected president

From September 1939, when Britain and France came to Poland's defense, until April 1940, when the German *Blitzkrieg* (lightning war) swept westward, an eerie quiet settled over Europe. The nations watched each other warily, preparing their defenses and perfecting their war machines, but there was no sign of battle. "There is something phony about this war," Senator William Borah remarked. In the United States, the Roosevelt administration and much of the public began hastily to discard the isolationism that had enshrouded their foreign policy for at least a decade.

Roosevelt quickly asked Congress to replace the Neutrality Act's arms embargo with a "cash and carry" provision requiring belligerents to pay cash for American products and to transport them in non-American ships. The Neutrality Act actually imperiled neutrality, the president argued, because American merchantmen could still enter hostile waters with nonmilitary goods and get involved in some "incident" leading to war. Despite such assertions, most congressmen realized that, since Britain and France controlled the Atlantic, they were the only countries that could possibly benefit from "cash and carry." When Congress passed the new Neutrality Act, spurred by the invasion of Poland, America took a giant step away from nonalignment.

On April 9, 1940, the derisively termed *Sitzkrieg* (sitting war) exploded into action. Within two months, German troops overran Denmark, Norway, Holland, Belgium, and Luxembourg and thundered into Paris. Italy joined the attack, hurling armies into France from the south. Three weeks before Bastille Day, in the same railway car in which the Germans had capitulated over twenty years earlier, French leaders signed an armistice. The rapid fall of France created a myth of Nazi invincibility and raised the possibility of England's early defeat; it shattered American illusions about noninvolvement. Congress quickly passed rearmament appropriations and a Selective Service Act. The executive branch, given a bipartisan flavor by the appointment of Republicans Henry Stimson as secretary of war and Frank Knox as secretary of the navy, abandoned all pretense of neutrality by supplying war materiel directly to Great Britain. After the German *Luftwaffe* began to bomb English cities in the Battle of Britain, the new prime minister, Winston Churchill, appealed for even more aid. With scarcely a glance at the Constitution, FDR transferred fifty World War I destroyers to England in return for British naval bases in the Western Hemisphere.

DOMESTIC DEBATE OVER FOREIGN POLICY

The election of 1940 showed broad support for the president's policy. Bypassing several stalwart isolationists, the Republicans nominated Wendell Willkie, an internationalist who strongly favored the Allied cause. Willkie campaigned primarily against a third term for Roosevelt and the weak economy. "Twice is enough for any man," read one Republican campaign button. As election day approached, however, Willkie grew more desperate: he charged that a vote for Roosevelt was a vote for war, and the president countered with the extravagant promise that "your boys are not going to be sent into any foreign wars." But the election was neither fought nor won primarily on issues of foreign policy. The nation seemed content assisting England with measures short of war.

Yet opposition to any foreign involvement persisted. Some senators warned against a replay of the presidential maneuvering which they believed had led the nation into World War I. During debate over repeal of the arms embargo, men as diverse as the aviator-hero Charles A. Lindbergh, the socialist Norman Thomas, and former President Herbert Hoover conducted radio appeals against revision of the Neutrality Act. After the controversial destroyers-for-bases deal, General Robert E. Wood of Sears Roebuck organized the America First Committee. This isolationist group contended that Hitler did not menace United States security and that all-out aid to Britain would make intervention a certainty.

Pro-Allied spokesmen countered America First and isolationist sentiment with jeers and organizations of their own. During the 1940 campaign, FDR spiced his speeches with rhythmical barbs against "Martin, Barton, and Fish," three prominent Republican isolationists. The folk singer Woody Guthrie set his political criticism to a catchy tune ending "they say 'America First,' but they mean America next."

On a more practical level, Kansas newspaper editor William Allen White organized the Committee to Defend America by Aiding the Allies. Expanding to three hundred local chapters within a few weeks, its contributors included the wealthy banker J. P. Morgan and the militant labor leader David Dubinsky. Members of White's group had originated the destroyers-for-bases idea, and some urged the president to take even more decisive action against fascism.

AMERICA AS AN ARSENAL OF DEMOCRACY

Germany's aerial assault did not crack England's will but did severely strain its economy. In December 1940 Churchill warned Roosevelt that Britain's ability to purchase goods in the United States would soon be exhausted. In response, Roosevelt set forth a new plan to "lend-lease" munitions to the Allies. Drawing a homey analogy, Roosevelt reminded Americans that if a neighbor's house catches fire, "I don't say . . . 'Neighbor, my garden hose cost me fifteen dollars; you have to pay me fifteen dollars for it.' No, I don't want fifteen dollars—I want my garden hose after the fire is over." In a fireside chat a few days after Christmas, he further justified his program, explaining that the only way to avoid "the agony and suffering of war which others have to endure," was to become "the great arsenal of democracy." The Lend-Lease Bill, cleverly numbered H.R. 1776, passed Congress overwhelmingly, though isolationists grumbled that lending war supplies was similar to lending chewing gum.

As isolationists charged, it was unrealistic to suppose that the United States could support the British cause without eventually becoming a belligerent, and FDR was less than candid about the obvious dangers of all-out American aid. While he assured Americans that assistance to Britain would keep the country out of war, military officials recognized the risks and made preparations. In the early months of 1941 British and American military strategists secretly coordinated plans to concentrate upon Europe first in the event the United States entered a two-front war against both Germany and Japan.

Hitler's relentless pressure on Great Britain suddenly subsided after he made his fateful decision to invade the Soviet Union. Most isolationists believed the Bolshevik regime represented a greater threat than the Nazis and hoped the two countries would destroy each other in a protracted struggle. But Soviet Russia's entry into the war did not reduce Roosevelt's determination to aid the Allies; rather, it strengthened his hope that Hitler could be defeated without America entering the struggle. To the horror of most conservatives, FDR stretched the concept of an "arsenal of democracy" and extended Lend-Lease to Joseph Stalin.

The crowning point of Anglo-American cooperation came in the Atlantic Conference of August 1941, when Roosevelt and Churchill met on a destroyer off the coast of Labrador. Roosevelt and Churchill issued an eight-point declaration of principles, the Atlantic Charter. Like Wilson's Fourteen Points, the charter disavowed territorial expansion, upheld self-determination and free trade, and proclaimed the need for "a wider and permanent system of general security." American leaders exacted a price for this alliance. During the Depression, England had moved toward a system of imperial preference, preserving markets and raw materials within the empire from outside competitors. The United States, anxious about its own international economic position, vigorously opposed carving the world into restricted economic spheres. With England's survival now dependent upon United States cooperation, the Roosevelt administration succeeded in gaining assurances that Britain would keep trade and access to raw materials open equally to all nations.

In an effort to ensure the arrival of Lend-Lease supplies, Roosevelt next ordered the navy to convoy American goods as far as Iceland. When German submarines sank several American vessels in the Atlantic, the president condemned these "outrages," sometimes distorting events by claiming that German attacks were unprovoked (in at least one incident, the reverse was true). As isolationists predicted, Lend-Lease and close cooperation with Great Britain finally led to an undeclared naval war with Germany.

AMERICA GOES TO WAR

American military participation in World War II came about not through a spectacular collision with Germany but via the "back door" in Asia. Historically committed to the "Open Door" and to the territorial integrity of China, the United States had opposed Japanese expansion throughout the thirties. But it refused to back up its objectives with force. Even Japan's sinking of an American gunboat *Panay* in December 1937 provoked little public clamor for retaliation. When pressure finally mounted for some action to halt Japan's advances in China, Roosevelt threatened economic boycott. In mid-1939 he terminated the Treaty of Commerce and Navigation with Japan, leaving the United States free to curtail or prohibit exports.

When German victories left the French, Dutch, and British colonies in Southeast Asia vulnerable to Japanese pressure, Roosevelt made good his threats. Claiming that America's own security required the stockpiling of strategic materials, the president banned the American sale of aviation fuel and high-grade scrap iron to Japan. After Japan firmed up its alliance with Germany and Italy, Roosevelt expanded the embargo to include other strategic products, promised loans and military assistance to China, and bolstered America's Pacific defenses. But Japan still pushed into Indochina in search of iron ore and coal. As Japanese transports steamed toward Saigon in July 1941, the president "froze" Japanese funds in the United States, placing trade between the two countries under complete presidential control. Products from the United States, particularly petroleum, remained vital to the Japanese economy, and this new step in what Secretary of State Hull called the "general tightening up" directly challenged Japan's Far Eastern policies.

The Japanese government insisted that the United States recognize Japan's special position in China and help Japan gain access to raw material in Southeast Asia. Prime Minister Fumimaro Konoye, a moderate, believed that the United States would negotiate rather than risk a two-front war. But Japan's impatient militarists wanted to fight. Konoye appealed for a summit conference to break the deadlocked negotiations. Although Konoye and Roosevelt both knew that prolonging the diplomatic impasse would give the Japanese militants their war, neither leader could sacrifice what he considered vital national interests in Asia. Roosevelt refused the Japanese invitation; Konoye resigned; and War Minister Hideki Tojo took power.

American officials expected a Japanese attack in Indochina or possibly in the Philippines. Confused by the welter of intelligence data and radio signals, they missed Japan's real objective. On December 7 Japanese pilots, soaring across the clear Hawaiian skies, found America's Pacific fleet neatly arranged and unprotected in Pearl Harbor. The bombs fell, and stunned Americans turned on their radios to discover that their country was at war.

repair facility
would ot
been the
place to hit.
Oil storage
reserves

The war in Europe

After Pearl Harbor, Germany quickly fulfilled its alliance with Japan by declaring war on the United States. Great distances, the location of allies, and the terrain made warfare in the Pacific far more expensive and difficult than war against Germany, and so Anglo-American strategists decided to concentrate on the Atlantic theater. The defeat of Japan meant little if Germany rolled to victory in Europe, but the newly created Joint Chiefs of Staff realized that if they stopped Hitler, Japan was finished as well.

midway
Japanese
lost
manpower

Roosevelt rejected Woodrow Wilson's example of insisting that the United States remain an "associate" rather than a full "ally." Instead, FDR merged the Joint Chiefs with a similar body in Britain to create a unified strategy. A single high command, however, did not eliminate fundamental disagreements. British planners favored nibbling at the edge of German power, expecting the Soviet Union to hold off the Nazi's main thrust in eastern Europe. Churchill advocated first an invasion of French North Africa and a gradual "closing in" until the Allies could stab successfully into the German heartland. A more direct confrontation, he argued, risked a demoralizing and disastrous battlefield defeat. Americans strenuously objected, believing that the British strategy would drain energy and resources into marginal campaigns having little effect on the war's ultimate outcome. Less confident that the Soviet Union could withstand the German assault alone, General George C. Marshall argued that Anglo-American armies should relieve pressure in the east by opening a second front in France.

Roosevelt initially supported his general's recommendations, even promising Soviet leader V. M. Molotov in May of 1942 that the United States would seek a cross-channel invasion of France. But an assault could not be prepared before the spring of 1943, and Roosevelt felt that such a long delay would hurt morale at home and increase demands for an Asia-first strategy. He needed some rapid victories, and a landing in France ran a large risk of failure. Opting for quick if small successes, FDR swung his support behind Operation Torch, the code name for an invasion of French North Africa.

Once the campaign began in the fall of 1942, another basic disagreement arose. Whichever political faction the Allies backed in French Africa would

Attack on Pearl Harbor, December 7, 1941
Wide World

A 1st country was Russia, next was Italy, the Nasi Germany, then Spain.

TOTALITARIAN STATE?

Total gov. control.

probably become the government of France following an Allied victory. Britain supported Charles de Gaulle, a relatively unknown leader of the Free French movement who denounced as traitors the Vichy regime currently governing France in collaboration with the Nazis. Roosevelt intensely disliked the egotistical and authoritarian de Gaulle. Instead, he supported Vichyite army officers in North Africa who, in return, broke with their pro-

German government and convinced the French army in Africa not to oppose the American advance. Making a deal with ex-collaborationists may have been militarily sound, but liberals in the United States warned against helping fascist-leaning elements gain control of the future French government. The assassination of the American-backed leader ultimately opened the way for de Gaulle's rise, but America's wartime opposition to the man who would lead France during much of the next generation hurt United States–French relations long after the war.

While Anglo-American forces advanced through North Africa during the winter of 1942, Soviet troops finally halted Hitler's offensive at Stalingrad. By the end of 1942, these victories augered well for the Allies, but the So-

He seemed to always make the right decisions @ first (handwritten)

World War II, European Theater

Allied Offensives

Father land (handwritten)

USSR

FINLAND

Farthest German Penetration stopped at Stalingrad, Nov., 1942

Atlantic Ocean

NORWAY

SWEDEN

Leningrad

Moscow

North Sea

DEN.

Baltic Sea

Stalingrad

IRELAND

GREAT BRITAIN   NETH.

Berlin   Warsaw

Soviet Offensive June 1944

London

Brussels

GERMANY

POLAND

"Overlord" begins June 1944

Normandy

BELG.

CZECH.

Paris

Vienna

Budapest

FRANCE

SWITZ.   AUSTRIA   HUNGARY   RUMANIA

Bucharest   Black Sea

YUGOSLAVIA

BULGARIA

ITALY

PORTUGAL   SPAIN

Rome   Anzio   Naples   ALB.

GREECE

TURKEY

Sicilian and Italian campaign begins July 1943

SICILY

Oran   Algiers   Tunis

Mediterranean   Sea

Casablanca

"Torch" begins October 1942

TUNISIA

Tripoli

Alexandria   Cairo

El Alamein

MOROCCO

ALGERIA   LIBYA   EGYPT

F D R liked to pilot large ships
Wide World

[handwritten margin notes: U.S. were giving philipeans for dependen in 1945 anyway? / dutch east Indies → & philipeans / Japan & Pearl / to put American fleet out o t commission temporarialy.]

viets, who had felt the brunt of German power alone, suffered staggering casualties. Again Stalin demanded a second front; and once more Britain pressed for delay, this time in favor of a campaign into Sicily and Italy. The United States reluctantly accepted the British plan, and the Soviets became increasingly suspicious of their allies' good faith.

THE ITALIAN CAMPAIGN

Allied armies landed in Sicily during the summer of 1943 and invaded Italy in the fall. Meeting heavier resistance than expected, they took great losses, and the prolonged fighting further delayed the second front. But the operation did give the United States and Great Britain a strong position in determining postwar Italian politics. The new government of Marshal Pietro Badoglio, which took power from Benito Mussolini, represented little change in Italian ruling circles and contained no leftist or Soviet-supported elements. British and American governments supported the conservative regime without even consulting Stalin about the future of this defeated enemy.

The Italian offensive aggravated an atmosphere of distrust among the Allies which lasted long after the guns ceased firing. To allay Soviet suspicions that Britain and the United States might make a separate peace with Germany, leaving Russia to fight alone, Roosevelt had announced at the Casablanca Conference in January 1943 that the United States would remain in the war until the Axis surrendered unconditionally. Britain also agreed eventually to open a front in France. But these moves hardly soothed Stalin's bitterness when he compared casualty lists and wondered if his allies purposely delayed relieving pressure on the Soviet Union. While Russian troops exhausted themselves against Germany, Anglo-American armies were pecking off a sphere of influence around the Mediterranean. Stalin carefully derived a precedent from the Italian campaign: those armies which liberated an area would decide the type of government established there. It was a lesson he would employ later in Eastern Europe, where Soviet armies would have a free hand.

OVERLORD

Toward the end of 1943 British strategists proposed to follow up the Italian campaign with forays into Greece, Turkey, and the Balkans. But Americans preferred invading France to hasten the defeat of Germany and to avoid further delay in the Pacific theater. The proponents of a second front finally prevailed, and General Dwight D. Eisenhower, commanding the Allied Expeditionary Force in Great Britain, received orders to begin Operation Overlord, code name for the cross-channel assault. In a daring maneuver, with success dependent largely upon the unpredictable weather in the English channel, Allied troops landed on the beaches of Normandy on June 6, 1944. Confused by diversionary strategems, the Germans failed to organize a successful defense, and Allied forces pushed eastward throughout the summer. Within three months, American troops liberated Paris and entered Germany; and Soviet armies swept across Poland, closing in from the east. A last-ditch German counteroffensive which temporarily crashed through Allied lines was halted in the Battle of the Bulge in December. In the spring of 1945, Allied armies crossed the Rhine and headed toward Berlin as Soviet troops raced toward the German capital from the other direction. The war in Europe was swiftly drawing to a close.

The war in the Pacific

Americans still faced a lengthy and perplexing fight in the Far East. Immediately following the attack on Pearl Harbor, Japan quickly enlarged its "Co-Prosperity Sphere": Guam, Wake, Hong Kong, Singapore, Java, and the Philippines all fell within a few months. But a decisive American naval victory at Midway in June 1942 forced Japan on the defensive. American forces sunk four aircraft carriers and shot down 275 planes. For the next three years American forces chipped away at the Japanese Empire, slowly closing in on the home islands.

The American military establishment was divided over Far Eastern strategy. General Douglas MacArthur, commander of the army in the South Pacific, urged an offensive launched from his headquarters in Australia and proceeding up through New Guinea and the Philippines to Japan. When Japanese troops had driven him from the Philippines in May of 1942, he promised to return as a liberator; his critics charged that his enormous vanity

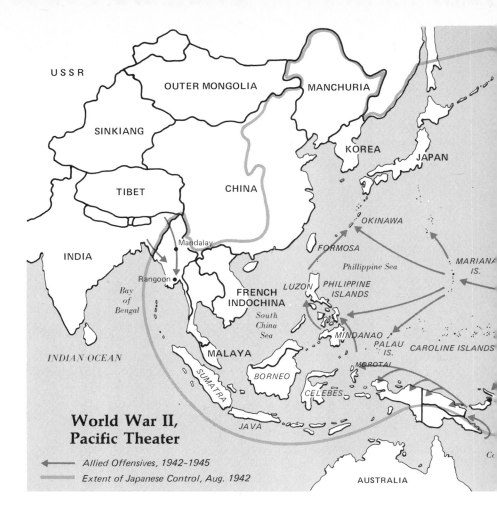

World War II, Pacific Theater

← — Allied Offensives, 1942–1945
— Extent of Japanese Control, Aug. 1942

and personal pride colored his assessment of strategy. But MacArthur and his supporters within the army argued that the plan was both militarily sound and politically imperative. If the United States did not control the Philippines when the war ended, the radical, anti-American Huks might gain power and undercut America's future position in the Pacific. Admiral Chester Nimitz and the navy dissented from MacArthur's view, advocating an advance through the smaller islands of the central Pacific as the most direct route to Japan. Beseiged by conflicting advice, the Joint Chiefs permitted simultaneous offensives along both the southern and central routes, thereby splitting Japanese defenses.

In June 1943 the two-pronged offensive began, gradually "leapfrogging" toward Japan, and in late 1944, while Nimitz's forces closed in from the center, MacArthur returned to the Philippines, attributing his success to "bomb, torpedo and strafing air attacks, timely maneuvers, and the definite partiality of Almighty God." Success in island hopping assured the United States of naval bases scattered throughout the Pacific.

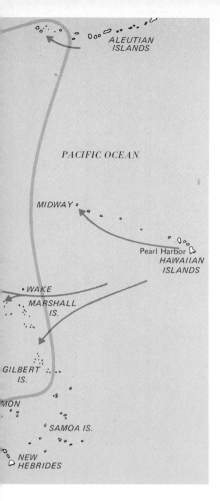

PACIFIC OCEAN

ALEUTIAN ISLANDS

MIDWAY

Pearl Harbor
HAWAIIAN ISLANDS

WAKE
MARSHALL IS.

GILBERT IS.

MON

SAMOA IS.

NEW HEBRIDES

Kamakasi means devine (wind.) It had saved them before. + drivers didn't care whether they lived on died

THE CHINA TANGLE

A strong and independent China, capable of resisting Japan on the Asian mainland as Americans moved in from the sea, would have reduced American casualties and hastened victory. But chances for stability in China looked dismal. The growing Communist movement—popular with the peasants, relatively free from corruption, and militarily effective against the Japanese—frightened American policymakers with its radical economic program. Yet the American-backed Nationalist government of Chiang Kai-shek remained as incompetent, corrupt, and unpopular as it had been for decades. One American official aptly described the basis of Chiang's regime as "one-party government, a reactionary policy, and the suppression of democratic ideas with the active aid of his gestapo." While Americans urged a vigorous offensive against Japanese troops, Nationalist officials preferred to rake off profits from American aid and to oppose Mao Tse-tung's Chinese Communists. Civil war seemed as grave a threat to China as foreign invasion.

Despite the chaos in China, the United States persistently pretended that Chiang was a strong ruler and world leader. Chiang participated in Allied conferences dealing with the Far East, and Roosevelt insisted that China sit alongside the major victorious powers on the United Nations Security Council. Even Stalin promised to support Chiang rather than Mao in return for some concessions to the Soviet Union in Outer Mongolia. In early 1942, after proceeding to China to organize a military effort against the Japanese, General Joseph W. Stilwell discovered that Chiang's Kuomintang armies were hopelessly inadequate; he vainly tried to promote internal reforms and cooperation with Mao's forces. Eventually, Roosevelt had to choose between backing Stilwell, who viewed Chiang as China's major problem, and Chiang, who demanded Stilwell's dismissal. Roosevelt recalled his general and continued to pour assistance into the Nationalist cause. But all of America's moral and material support could not make Chiang effective, and Mao's forces increased their popularity by leading the Chinese military effort against the Japanese invaders. The ultimate Communist takeover of China in 1949 shocked the American public, imbued with the wartime myth of Nationalist strength. But Chiang's fall was a fairly predictable result of the tangle of wartime events in China.

Wartime diplomacy

DOMESTIC POLITICS

At least two things did not change drastically during the war—the conduct of partisan politics and the popular appeal of Franklin Roosevelt. Early military reverses and more extensive federal controls provided the Republicans with potent issues during the 1942 congressional elections. And after picking up forty-six House and nine Senate seats, some GOP strategists anticipated capturing the White House in 1944. But always the canny politician, Roosevelt generally struck the image of a wartime statesman above petty politicking. At a 1943 press conference he announced that he would shelve domestic reforms and concentrate upon winning the war—"Dr. Win-the-War," he said, had succeeded "Dr. New Deal." Accepting his party's nomination for a fourth term in 1944, FDR abandoned his role as the Great Commander long enough to crush his much younger Republican opponent, Governor Thomas E. Dewey of New York. Just before the November balloting, the president squelched rumors of ill health with a vigorous and highly successful campaign tour. Roosevelt and his running mate, Senator Harry S. Truman of Missouri, defeated the GOP ticket by 432 to 99 electoral votes and by over 3½ million popular votes. By late 1944 Roosevelt and his supporters confidently looked forward to reviving the New Deal at home, ending the war, and establishing a peaceful world order.

IMF AND UN

"We are going to win the war, and we are going to win the peace that follows," Roosevelt said a few days after the attack on Pearl Harbor. But what had the long and bloody battles of World War II accomplished; how did Americans envision the postwar world? Dean Acheson, an important policymaker of the postwar period, entitled his memoirs of these years *Present at the Creation.* Indeed, the task of rebuilding the world must have seemed as vast and complex as that undertaken in those initial "seven days."

The economic nationalism arising out of the Depression had undermined international free trade and disrupted rates of exchange among the world's currencies. The Roosevelt administration hoped, after the war, to restore a favorable, predictable climate for trade and investment. On the battlefield, the United States challenged German, Italian, and Japanese attempts to create exclusive spheres of influence, and also made its ally, Great Britain, promise to move away from its imperial preference system as a price of American aid. In the Bretton Woods Conference of July 1944, the Roosevelt administration revealed its blueprint for a postwar international economic system which was designed to prevent a relapse into depression. The president opened the conference by stressing the connection between the economic order and the spread of freedom: "Commerce is the life blood of a free society. We must see to it that the arteries which carry that blood stream are not clogged again, as they have been in the past, by artificial barriers created through senseless economic rivalries." The subsequent Bretton Woods Agreements established the International Monetary Fund (IMF) to fix rates at which different countries' currencies could be exchanged and pledged participating nations (which did not include the Soviet Union) to move their currencies rapidly back onto an international gold standard. The conference also created the International Bank for Reconstruction and Development (latter called the World Bank), an agency which would help insure world stability by making capital—largely American—available for recovery and development. Taken as a whole, the Bretton Woods Agreements promised stable currencies and an international economic environment favorable to trade and investment.

Shortly afterward at Dumbarton Oaks in August 1944 and later at San Francisco in April 1945 American policymakers helped create an international body which could settle disputes collectively—a United Nations (UN). In the UN's General Assembly, every member nation received one vote, but real power lay with the Security Council, a body dominated by the five victors (U.S., USSR, Britain, France, and Chiang's China) which had to agree unanimously to any UN action. The UN was to help maintain a stable, peaceful world order. Together with the IMF, the UN was to help safeguard a world open to American financial resources, political influence, and democratic ideas. Both institutions embodied American liberal values: they were to work against economic or political spheres of influence (except in Latin America, where the United States jealously guarded its own). Though considered steps toward a new internationalism, the IMF and UN were also expected to serve specifically national objectives. America's political, humanitarian, economic, and strategic motives in the postwar period, Dean Acheson observed, could not "be separated in the intellectual equivalent of a cream separator."

YALTA AND INTERNATIONAL TENSIONS

Divisions within the Grand Alliance between Great Britain, the Soviet Union, and the United States threatened America's postwar plans. Churchill sought to protect Britain's far-flung empire, particularly the Indian subcontinent and the rich oil fields of the Middle East, and his wartime strategy had reflected this goal. Stalin envisioned elimination of any future German threat and creation of a series of friendly pro-Soviet governments in Eastern Europe. These two leaders, both at home with the idea of swapping and balancing spheres of influence, reached an informal agreement in 1944 permitting Soviet predominance in Rumania and Bulgaria in return for British preeminence in Greece. But American policymakers feared that American influence would be shut out and hesitated to endorse such backroom diplomacy. As the war drew to a close, discrepancies in postwar political and economic aims surfaced, widening schisms among the Allies.

At the Yalta Conference of early 1945, Churchill, Stalin, and Roosevelt reached vague agreements to divide occupied Germany and to hold free elections in Eastern Europe. But the course of battle and the destruction of old power arrangements, rather than formal wartime agreements, shaped the course of events. Stalin's forces drove into Berlin about the same time as the American army advanced through Germany from the west, and Germany was eventually divided into four zones of occupation. Anglo-American troops occupied zones of influence around the periphery of Europe, supporting friendly governments in France, Italy, and Greece. Red armies swept the Nazis out of Eastern Europe, becoming predominant in that sphere. Pro-Soviet groups came to power in Rumania, Hungary, Bulgaria, Albania, and Poland. In Poland Communist-led resistance forces took total control despite Stalin's promise to hold elections and to include an Anglo-American–backed group which had sat in London as a government-in-exile during the war. Stalin believed his military victories and his country's particular vulnerability from the west justified creation of friendly regimes in Eastern Europe. Always fearful of "capitalist encirclement," he sought to create a buffer zone of Communist states with which the Soviet Union could trade. Republican critics at home soon would denounce the Yalta Conference as a

Churchill, Roosevelt, Stalin at Yalta
Wide World

betrayal of democracy in Eastern Europe and a gift of territory to Russia, but free governments had not existed there before nor did the Western Allies ever have a military presence in those lands.

TRUMAN AND ATOMIC DIPLOMACY

Stalin's creation of a sphere of influence in Eastern Europe may have seemed essentially defensive to him, but it appeared aggressive to Britain and the United States. The Soviet threat to an open world challenged the very principles for which Americans had fought the war. In this clash between what the United States and the USSR each defined as vital strategic and economic interests, both began to view the other as a direct threat to its own well-being. When Roosevelt unexpectedly succumbed to a massive stroke and Vice-President Harry S. Truman assumed diplomatic leadership, relations deteriorated further. Roosevelt had tried to get along with Stalin, but the new president, who met the Soviet leader for the first time at Potsdam in July 1945, quickly sided with those who urged a harder line.

While a "cold war" began to develop between the United States and the Soviet Union over the nature of postwar Europe, the situation in the Far East remained fluid. Japan could not win the war, but its tenacious resistance at Iwo Jima and Okinawa in early 1945 seemed to indicate that years of hard fighting and possibly a million more American casualties lay ahead. At Yalta, Stalin had agreed to enter the war against Japan, but experience in Eastern Europe made American officials increasingly less eager to draw Soviet troops into Asia. They searched for a way to save American lives without relying upon full Soviet participation. Atomic power provided the answer.

In 1940 President Roosevelt had established a special committee to coordinate military research, and a year later he created the more extensive Office of Scientific Research and Development (OSRD). In addition, the president, unknown to Congress, spent over $2 billion for research on and development of an atomic bomb. Under the direction of J. Robert Oppenheimer, the collaborators on the "Manhattan Project" finally broke through the complexity of scientific problems, and in July 1945 the United States exploded a primitive atomic device in New Mexico. At Potsdam, Truman learned of his country's new weapon and sent an ultimatum to Japan demanding unconditional surrender.

Development of this new and frightful weapon presented America's political and scientific leaders with a grave choice. Some urged Truman not to employ the bomb against Japan. "If the United States were to be the first to release this new means of indiscriminate destruction upon mankind, we would sacrifice public support throughout the world, precipitate the race for armaments, and prejudice the possibility of reaching international agree-

The atomic bomb, dropped on two civilian population centers
Wide World

ment on the future control of such weapons." But in a decision which still nags the conscience of many Americans, Truman and his principal advisers decided to drop the bomb, first on Hiroshima and three days later on Nagasaki, two major Japanese population centers. The president rejected the alternatives of warning Japan about the new weapon, demonstrating its power on a barren island, or dropping it on less populated areas. He opted for maximum surprise and devastation "in order to shorten the agony of war," as he put it. The bombs did bring Japan's surrender on August 14, 1945. But America's victory had a bitter taste and left lingering doubts about our self-proclaimed benevolence.

The awesome power of the new bomb also contributed to a general hardening of America's attitudes toward the Soviet Union. Wearing "this weapon rather ostentatiously on our hip," as one official put it, the United States felt it could make stronger demands regarding Soviet conduct in Eastern Europe. Americans believed their economic power could also be used as diplomatic leverage. The Soviet Union badly needed assistance for postwar reconstruction, and when Stalin requested aid following the end of Lend-Lease the Truman administration again made it clear that he would have to keep Eastern Europe open to American trade and ideas.

Truman's tough, anti-Soviet tone found encouragement from many sources: respected statesmen such as Churchill, top advisers such as Averell Harriman, Americans of Eastern European descent who were an important part of the Democratic coalition. To these people, the USSR's denial of democratic freedoms, its new power position in Europe, and its support of leftist movements around the globe made it a dangerous threat. Many Americans came to believe that Stalin, like Hitler, had to be stopped, and with their overwhelming nuclear and economic power they were in no mood to compromise.

As Truman's attitude grew more inflexible, Stalin's mirrored it by degrees. Russians never understood America's outrage at the Eastern European situation. They had not protested Anglo-American hegemony in Italy or Greece, and America alone occupied Japan. Surely, Stalin argued, his nation, which had suffered the greatest casualties and property damage during the war, deserved minimal guarantees for its own future security. Truman's uncompromising stance did not force Stalin to change but only strengthened his desire for security. Stalin badly needed loans, but not at the price of what he believed was his country's most basic strategic interest—keeping a tight hold over Eastern Europe. He turned instead to other solutions, announcing a new Five-Year Plan to rebuild Soviet industry. To help his reconstruction effort, Stalin expropriated what he could from the occupied European territories and closed off the area from almost all Western influence.

There were some Americans who decried the deterioration in Soviet-American relations and condemned the Truman administration's hard line.

Many had no sympathy for communism but perceived that the bomb offered no realistic way to rid Eastern Europe of pro-Soviet regimes. Believing that a militant attitude would only further close trade and communication links, liberals such as Henry Wallace advocated accommodation rather than saber rattling. In 1946 Wallace left Truman's cabinet and two years later ran for president on a third-party platform which advocated defrosting the cold war.

The cycle of distrust between the United States and the Soviet Union became self-perpetuating, as a new cold war rhetoric changed the way in which each country viewed the world. Soviet charges of "imperialist warmongering" met American cries against an "international Communist conspiracy." Fear of "capitalist encirclement" matched apprehension about "Soviet aggression" which had to be "contained." America's allies were called "running dogs" or "lackeys of Wall Street"; Russia's were "satellites" or "enslaved peoples." Which side of the "Iron Curtain" was truly "liberated" depended upon whether one looked from the East or from the West. More than a cycle of events, the cold war became a battle of rhetoric and images, filtering down from the diplomats to people on the street. The cold war was a mentality, pervasive and convincing, which took its initial shape from events and then assumed a life of its own. The very words and expressions used in postwar years became increasingly less a description of reality and ever more a determinant of it.

The war at home

For Americans, World War II was more than a global military conflict. The stresses of war forced significant internal changes, even though the United States was the only major belligerent whose own territory escaped the ravages of combat.

Most obviously, the conflict revived the American economy and extended the role of the national government. The war, not New Deal measures, finally restored prosperity. Between 1939 and 1945 the country's total economic output almost doubled, and the massive unemployment of the 1930s became a bad dream. War-related industries not only hired all able-bodied men, but eagerly sought women ("Rosie the Riveter"), teenagers, and retired people. The fight against the Axis helped to heal old antagonisms between big business and the Roosevelt administration; "dollar-a-year" men from large corporations assumed key positions within wartime governmental bureaucracies. The close relationship between big business and military contractors formed the basis of a powerful, if hard-to-define, pressure group which President Dwight Eisenhower later termed the "military-industrial complex," people who profited from continuing a high level of military spending.

"Rosie the Riveter" symbolized the new job opportunities for women during the war
National Archives

The enormous increase in production raised the specter of runaway inflation, and Roosevelt responded with a series of economic measures designed to control prices and allocate resources more efficiently. Barely familiar with the myriad New Deal agencies, people suddenly discovered a whole new series of "alphabet agencies" regulating the wartime economy. The Office of Price Administration (OPA) established price ceilings on goods, services, and rents. The government entirely prohibited manufacture of some products, such as automobiles and the OPA rationed a variety of items, including sugar, meat, and canned goods. Price controls and rationing, following upon the lean years of the Depression, produced some discontent. Families had to pool or trade ration coupons (for items such as baby shoes, cigarettes, tires) and to find substitutes for scarcities such as gasoline (although an automobile powered with kerosene hardly made for a pleasant Sunday afternoon's drive). Under-the-counter transactions in rationed products became frequent: some women were able to find nylon hose on the black market and avoid the unpopular substitutes of silk stockings or leg makeup. Despite the hardship, governmental regulations did prevent a dramatic inflationary spiral, and price increases remained under those of World War I.

Selling the war

As in the First World War, the government established a propaganda bureau, the Office of War Information (OWI). In time, people with backgrounds in advertising assumed day-to-day control of the OWI, and to the displeasure of those who favored a less manipulative approach the OWI borrowed more and more techniques from the advertising world. But remembering how passions raised during World War I contributed to the postwar Red Scare, the Roosevelt administration generally avoided attempts to create a blind, chauvinistic spirit of "one hundred percent Americanism." The government kept a generally restrained tone, preferring, for example, the folksy patriotism of Norman Rockwell paintings to more inflammatory anti-Axis materials.

Neither did the government inflame fighting men with the superpatriotic idealism of our first Great Crusade. Few soldiers set out singing patriotic ditties such as "Over There." Instead, the hard-bitten, matter-of-fact attitude of Bill Mauldin's cartoon characters, Joe and Willie, reflected the less emotional tone of the GIs of World War II. Defeating the Axis was something that had to be done, but few soldiers sloshing through Europe considered it a glorious undertaking.

Despite the low-key approach of most OWI efforts, the war inevitably affected most areas of American life. Popular culture, for example, bolstered the Allied cause. Comic book heroes—Superman, Dick Tracy, and even

Norman Rockwell's "Freedom From Want."
Reprinted with permission from The Saturday Evening Post © 1945, Indianapolis, Indiana

Little Orphan Annie— battled against the Axis. Several famous Hollywood filmmakers produced classic war documentaries, and others turned out less artistic entertainment which glorified America's military exploits. Leading men such as John Wayne (who never actually served in the armed forces) fought up and down studio backlots liberating countless "Pacific" islands. Two popular movie serials featuring "Don Winslow of the Coast Guard" played up Japanese attempts to infiltrate the West Coast. Even cowboy stars, in addition to their normal quota of cattle rustlers and bank robbers, mixed it up with Nazi and Japanese agents. Noncombat movies also reflected the wartime atmosphere. James Cagney, who specialized in gangster heroes during the thirties, won an Academy Award for his portrayal of George M. Cohan, composer of "It's a Grand Old Flag." Backed by perhaps the greatest armada of American flags ever assembled in Hollywood, Cagney furiously danced and sang his way through "Yankee Doodle Dandy" and Cohan's other patriotic standards from the First World War. The film closed with a somber, no-nonsense meeting between a dying Cohan and President Roosevelt. *Wilson* (1944), another extravaganza, harkened back to the World War I experience and presented a none-too-subtle plea for the revival of Wilsonian internationalism following defeat of the Axis. Films such as *Mission to Moscow* portrayed the Soviet Union in a sympathetic light.

"Just gimme a coupla aspirin. I already got a Purple Heart."
Bill Mauldin

CIVIL LIBERTIES AND
CONCENTRATION CAMPS

The overwhelming popularity of the war limited dissent and helped prevent the widespread violations of civil liberties that had occurred during World War I. Although wars are rarely a time for vigilant protection of individual rights, members of the Roosevelt administration, particularly Attorney General Francis Biddle, remembered the governmental excesses of World War I and also the importance of ethnic voters to the Democratic coalition. Neither Italian Americans nor German Americans suffered active persecution. Unlike their position during the First World War, most socialist and Communist groups enthusiastically backed the antifascist crusade, and the government concentrated much of its attention upon the relatively small pockets of extreme right-wing, pro-Nazi sentiment, such as the German American Bund and Father Charles Coughlin's Crusade for Social Justice. Even here, the Roosevelt administration, limited by Biddle's constitutional scruples and several Supreme Court decisions, did not wage an all-out campaign against right-wing critics of the war.

Actually, pacifists and other conscientious objectors probably suffered as much from the government's coercive power as did pro-Axis groups. Nearly six thousand draft resisters, most of them Jehovah's Witnesses, failed to obtain status as conscientious objectors and went to prison. About twice this number performed all kinds of menial jobs, without pay, in public service camps. Many people complained about the regimentation and inadequate facilities in these installations, and even those objectors who were able to work outside the camps were required to return their wages to the government.

The notorious exception to the country's generally acceptable record on wartime civil liberties was the capitulation to racism and popular hysteria in the treatment of Japanese Americans. No anti-German literature approached the venom of anti-Japanese tracts or the crudity of songs such as "You're a Sap, Mr. Jap."

Immediately following the attack upon Pearl Harbor, Japan assumed the role of archvillain. Prowar spokesmen pictured Japanese as cunning, evil, almost subhuman little people, and this image of the Oriental enemy abroad dovetailed with long-standing racial antagonism on the West Coast. In California, Japanese Americans comprised a hard-working population whose thrift, success, and physical differences made them a frequent target for attack. The war intensified racial hatred, provoking calls for a crackdown on this potentially disloyal "fifth column." In northern California a guerrilla band of almost a thousand farmers (known as the "Bald Eagles") armed themselves to put down Japanese subversion. Congressman John Rankin of Mississippi proclaimed: "Once a Jap always a Jap. . . . This is a race war, as

far as the Pacific side of this conflict is concerned. . . . It is of vital importance to get rid of every Japanese whether in Hawaii or on the mainland." A
West Coast newspaperman called for the immediate removal of Japanese
Americans to the interior. "I don't mean a nice part . . . either. Herd 'em up,
pack 'em off, and give 'em the inside room in the badlands." Amid such a
climate of opinion, Americans may have accepted the moral burden of dropping atomic bombs on Hiroshima and Nagasaki with more ease than had
they been targeted for Munich or Milan.

Initially civilian and military leaders resisted West Coast pressure, but ultimately they capitulated. With the cooperation of the Roosevelt adminis-

Victory! V-J Day in Omaha
Nebraska State Historical Society

tration, officials (including California's Attorney General Earl Warren) first imposed a series of restrictions upon Japanese Americans and finally instituted a full-scale removal program. Claiming that military necessity dictated their decision, the government ordered citizens and resident aliens alike to sell their possessions and relocate in segregated areas away from the West Coast. After 1942, the army forcibly moved over a hundred thousand persons to various "resettlement centers." Even the libertarian members of the Supreme Court acquiesced in this concentration camp operation, holding in *Korematsu* v. *U.S.* (1944) that the judiciary could not interfere with the executive's wartime military decisions. Only many years later did the government agree to reimburse Japanese Americans for financial losses, but nothing could erase this flagrant violation of democratic principles.

WORLD WAR II AND BLACK AMERICANS

Antiwar sentiment found some support among black Americans. "What the hell do we want to fight the Japanese for anyhow?" asked one black GI. "They couldn't possibly treat us any worse than these 'crackers' right here at home." A slogan popular among draftees expressed a similar attitude: "Here lies a black man killed fighting a yellow man for the glory of a white man." Pacifist groups failed to gain many converts, but they did forge some important connections with black civil rights leaders during the war. In Chicago, pacifists and blacks established the Congress of Racial Equality (CORE), a militant but nonviolent direct action group. CORE, which became prominent during the civil rights movement of the 1960s, used the tactic of civil disobedience to desegregate public facilities in several northern cities.

CORE's activities during the war reflected a greater militancy, especially among lower-income blacks. Some leaders saw the war as an opportunity to force white America to live up to the democratic ideals it professed around the globe. The affinity of black voters for the Democratic party gave hope that FDR might lend support to their cause. When the president procrastinated—he basically considered blacks a group to be patronized rather than dealt with as equals—the black labor leader A. Philip Randolph planned a march on Washington in 1941 to protest job discrimination in the burgeoning prewar defense industry. The march's organizers enjoyed surprising success mobilizing ghetto blacks, a group generally untouched by older organizations such as the NAACP. In response to Randolph's constantly escalating estimates of the expected number of demonstrators (he ultimately predicted a hundred thousand), Roosevelt finally compromised. In return for cancellation of the march, he issued an executive order establishing a commission to deal with employment discrimination. Although the Fair Employment Practices Commission (FEPC) failed to live up to expectations, its establishment seemed to demonstrate the practical value of militant action.

Lunchtime
Library of Congress

The war years also brought more violent confrontations between blacks and whites. Rigid segregation in the military failed to prevent racial contact, and black-white tensions led to serious disturbances on bases at home and abroad. Black soldiers frequently complained that white officers ignored racist attacks upon them yet considered black protest a sign of disloyalty. Friction in the armed forces paralleled massive urban disorders. Southern blacks, migrating from rural areas, offered job competition for white workers, and the conflict sometimes spilled over into the streets. In several southern cities white laborers organized vigilante organizations to prevent the hiring of blacks, and a number of northern cities experienced full-scale race riots in 1943. Smoldering racial tensions in Detroit produced numerous predictions of trouble, but city officials seemed paralyzed. "I was taken by surprise only by the way it happened," confessed Detroit's mayor. After thirty-four deaths

617

and millions of dollars in property damage, federal troops finally restored order in the Motor City.

Despite encouragement from associates and especially from his wife Eleanor, FDR avoided any firm commitment to the civil rights cause. He offered several token appointments to blacks but never really understood the aspirations of black people. He did not wish to alienate the powerful bloc of southern Democrats in time of war and rejected suggestions that he devote a fireside chat to the riots or that Congress hold an investigation of racial tensions.

But fear of further violence led others to defuse the racial dynamite buried in urban ghettos. Apprehensive about controlling all their followers, most black leaders abandoned militant tactics such as marches and demonstrations after 1943. Black magazines and newspapers toned down their rhetoric, and the NAACP urged protestors to use legal and political means. Working with white liberals, black leaders sought to build a strong interracial and nonviolent movement. Publication of Gunnar Myrdal's *An American Dilemma* in 1944 symbolized the direction of the civil rights movement for the next several decades. Sponsored by the Carnegie Foundation, this study indicted the United States for its racial discrimination but optimistically concluded that Americans could eventually live up to their egalitarian ideals. *An American Dilemma* became the guidepost for a generation of liberals who struggled valiantly, if somewhat naively, to achieve racial justice through court tests, executive orders, and legislative actions.

Harry S. Truman

Succeeding a deceased president is always difficult, but Harry S. Truman found the ordeal of succession particularly cruel. Roosevelt, who guided the nation through depression and to final victory over the Axis, symbolized security at home and abroad to millions of Americans. Liberal Democrats considered FDR the heart of the New Deal tradition, and they eagerly awaited the end of the war when they could revive the battle against domestic problems. Even Roosevelt's detractors conceded his prestige and popularity both in the United States and around the world. Nothing in Harry Truman's background suggested the capacity either to match the fallen leader's personal appeal or to approach his presidential accomplishments.

Much in Truman's career invited comparison, rarely flattering, with his predecessor. A short, undistinguished-looking man who grew up in rural Missouri, Truman lacked Roosevelt's commanding presence or elite upbringing. During the First World War FDR served as undersecretary of the navy; Truman fought in the ranks. FDR prudently cooperated with the Democratic bosses but generally rose above the seamier side of political bargaining. Truman, although untouched by personal scandals, learned his trade

President Truman and actress Lauren Bacall
UPI

with the infamous Pendergast machine in Kansas City and always struggled to live down charges of bossism and cronyism. While FDR captured the spotlight during the days of the New Deal, Truman sat in the back of the Senate loyally supporting reform but never launching crusades. The 1944 Democratic convention selected Truman as vice-president primarily to replace Henry Wallace with a less controversial figure, and although Truman enjoyed his short time in that office, FDR rarely consulted him. "I don't think I saw Roosevelt but twice as Vice-President except at Cabinet meetings," Truman later confessed. When the squire from Hyde Park passed away, the man from Independence seemed all too small a successor.

AN UNCERTAIN MOOD

One historian has remarked that a sense of uncertainty—a "mood maybe"—characterized the immediate postwar period. Remembering the difficult transition in 1919–1920, many Americans feared the reappearance of economic problems once orders for military goods stopped and returning GIs glutted the job market. Both businessmen and workers eagerly anticipated the end of wage and price controls, and organized labor wanted to be released from its wartime pledge against striking. Republican leaders hoped that their party would regain some of the ground lost during almost twelve years of Roosevelt. And within Democratic ranks, many ardent New Dealers believed that Harry Truman could never offer the type of leadership which the reform cause needed to face mounting opposition.

Economic problems immediately tested the new president. Following the surrender of Japan, American consumers insisted on goods— nylon stockings, canned beer, electric toasters—which had been scarce or unavailable during the war. Demand for items such as cars and new homes quickly outstripped available supplies. At the same time, a number of labor unions struck for higher wages. The coal and auto industries shut down briefly, and only a presidential threat to draft workers into the army halted a nationwide rail walkout. Despite businessmen's calls for an end to governmental economic controls, commodity shortages and rising wages forced retention of price restraints until the middle of 1946. But the randomly enforced measures proved ineffective; prices skyrocketed and shortages increased. Wholesale meat prices in Chicago went up 22 percent in a single day—and even then customers kept buying. Large-city butchers often expected a tip for the laborious task of passing meat over the counter. Some car purchasers handed over several hundred extra dollars before a smiling auto dealer delivered one of the scarce Detroit specials. Such black market operations became a familiar part of life immediately after the war, and, as usual, people blamed the president.

THE EIGHTIETH CONGRESS

Wherever Truman turned, new difficulties appeared. Powerful members of the New Deal coalition, especially labor leaders, found the president a vacillating executive, unable to gloss over contradictory pressures with FDR's confident manner. Frustrated after so many years of launching futile attacks on Roosevelt, Republicans declared open season on Truman during the 1946 congressional election. "To err is Truman" and "Under Truman, Two Families in Every Garage," proclaimed Republican slogans, "Had Enough?" Millions of voters had. The GOP captured control of both houses of Congress and, outside the still solidly Democratic South, elected twenty-five governors. Republicans generally promised little; their bandwagon rolled along a trail of public frustration against an administration that seemed incapable of meeting postwar problems.

Truman gained strong bipartisan support for his anti-Soviet containment policy, but the president and the Eightieth Congress moved further and further apart on domestic issues. Adopting the advice of several liberal advisers,

Truman escalated his domestic promises as the 1948 presidential election neared. He asked Congress for a higher minimum wage, public housing construction, federal aid to education, a national health insurance plan, and farm legislation. Realizing that the Eightieth Congress would reject much of this legislation, he planned to align his administration with Roosevelt's New Deal and label GOP legislators as reactionaries.

The leader of congressional Republicans, Senator Robert A. Taft of Ohio, struggled to present an attractive alternative to Truman's aggressively liberal position. Known as "Mister Republican," Taft supported federal aid to education, some public housing, and a limited welfare program. To avoid charges that Republicans would dismantle the entire New Deal structure, he concentrated his attacks on the excessive cost of Democratic programs and their alleged threat to individual liberties. He suggested that Truman had gone beyond the course set by FDR, telling a nationwide radio audience that the president "has raised all the ghosts of the old New Deal with new trappings that Tugwell and Harry Hopkins never thought of." But Taft was no inflexible reactionary and labored to restrain ultraconservative Republicans in both houses of Congress.

Enactment in 1947 of the important Taft-Hartley Labor Act, which aimed at reducing the new power of unions, illustrated both the obstacles facing Truman and Taft's crucial position in the Eightieth Congress. While the president ineffectually opposed the Republican-sponsored measure, Taft skillfully maneuvered the bill through the Senate. He gained southern Democratic support and then helped soften the House's more extreme antilabor provisions in a conference committee. The Taft-Hartley Law outlawed the closed shop (which forbade the hiring of nonunion workers), prohibited political contributions out of union dues, and authorized injunctions against strikes which endangered national security. Truman immediately vetoed the bill, but Taft's fence mending paid off when Congress overrode the president's action. The law represented a victory for Taft's version of modern Republicanism, but it also handed the president a ready-made issue to attract union members in the 1948 elections.

REPUBLICANS, PROGRESSIVES, AND DIXIECRATS

Truman and his advisers made Congress the key issue in the 1948 campaign. The GOP convention bypassed Taft and selected their less controversial 1944 standard bearer, Thomas Dewey of New York. Dewey had won a landslide victory in the 1946 gubernatorial election, and teamed up with the popular California Governor Earl Warren for vice-president, the New Yorker seemed a sure winner in 1948. Unlike Taft, neither Dewey nor Warren could be linked directly to the Eightieth Congress. But Truman called

Congress back into special session and presented a long list of "must" legislation, much of it from the Republicans' own platform promises. "They can do this job in fifteen days, if they want to do it," Truman announced, but Republican leaders passed no new legislation and adjourned Congress after several weeks. Truman accomplished his purpose: identifying Dewey with the "do-nothing, good for nothing" Republican Congress.

Division within his own party made Truman's attacks on the Eightieth Congress a desperate necessity. Some Democratic professionals considered his chances for reelection so slim that they approached Dwight Eisenhower, unsuccessfully urging the popular general to accept the nomination. Former Vice-President and Secretary of Commerce Henry A. Wallace also led a revolt against Truman's leadership, mounting a bid for the White House under the banner of the Progressive party. The Progressive platform—which emphasized "Peace, Freedom, and Abundance"—included planks endorsing abandonment of America's containment policy, cooperation between the United States and the Soviet Union, an end to the draft, removal of racial barriers at home, and destruction of the stockpile of atomic bombs. Campaigning as the true heir to Roosevelt's foreign and domestic policies, Wallace's campaign resembled a curious mixture of urban radicalism and old-fashioned Bible Belt evangelism. Folksingers Woody Guthrie and Pete Seeger led voters in "Down by the riverside . . . we'll study war no more," and the Iowa-born Wallace contributed his rumpled midwestern presence. Wallace had no chance for the presidency, but his effort did threaten to undercut Truman's support among left-leaning Democrats, especially in the crucial state of New York.

An even more serious revolt occurred in the solidly Democratic South. When a coalition of liberals (led by Hubert Humphrey, then mayor of Minneapolis) and urban bosses pushed through a strong civil rights plank, some southerners walked out of the Democratic convention and launched a fourth political party. The States' Rights or "Dixiecrat" party offered Governor J. Strom Thurmond of South Carolina as its presidential candidate and pledged maintenance of racial segregation as the southern way of life. Much like Governor George Wallace's American party of 1968, the Dixiecrats of 1948 hoped to capture enough southern electoral votes to send the election to the House of Representatives.

THE ELECTION OF 1948

However limited their own chances for success, the candidacies of Wallace and Thurmond appeared to guarantee Truman's defeat. Dewey confidently held to his noncontroversial path, campaigning for fewer weeks, in fewer states, and with fewer personal appearances than the energetic Truman. He relied upon broad appeals to national and party unity. With "restoration of faith in ourselves, of competence in our Government, of unity of purpose among our people," he advised, "there is nothing, as a people, we cannot do." Such platitudes, the New Yorker hoped, would smooth over divisions within the GOP and, more important, contrast his sober positions with the "mudslinging," "cheap wisecracking," and "ranting, bombasting partisanship" of the Democratic president.

Facing predictions of disaster, Truman's attacks upon Dewey and the Eightieth Congress grew more strident. As approving Democrats yelled, "Give 'em hell, Harry," the president assaulted Republicans as "a bunch of old mossbacks, . . . gluttons of privilege, . . . all set to do a hatchet job on the New Deal." "If you let the Republicans get control of the government," he warned one audience, "you will be making America an economic colony of Wall Street." With his down-home, Missouri stump-speaking style, Truman reminded workers of the Taft-Hartley Act and told rural voters how Republicans "stuck a pitchfork in the backs of farmers by cutting down on funds for crop storage." He assailed the press as biased and claimed their polls predicting a Dewey victory were rigged to discourage Democrats from voting. Hoping to attract black voters in northern cities, Truman endorsed the civil rights cause more strongly than in the past. In July he issued an executive order desegregating the armed forces and the departments of the national government. Shortly before the end of his campaign, he became the first presidential candidate ever to make a personal appearance in New York's Harlem.

But despite Truman's efforts, almost all pollsters and political writers predicted a Dewey victory in November. Even as early returns showed Truman leading, most experts stuck by their forecasts. A famous extra edition of the staunchly Republican *Chicago Tribune*, which hit the streets with a banner headline proclaiming "Dewey Defeats Truman," became a collector's treasure when final returns showed a narrow Truman upset. Strom Thurmond's party failed to garner enough southern electoral votes to throw the contest into the House, and Henry Wallace ran a distant fourth.

The 1948 election revealed that the proliferation of candidates and issues either failed to arouse the voters' interest or confused them into staying home. Turnout across the country was light; only slightly more than 50 percent of the electorate cast ballots. In such a "decline election" of low vote totals, Truman and the Democrats could rely upon the Roosevelt–New Deal coalition to pull them through. But the president failed to gain any real mandate for new changes. The voters had rejected the dismantling of the New Deal, which the Eightieth Congress had threatened, but without calling for its further extension. The 1948 election would help define the shape of postwar politics, initiating a generation of stalemate.

Measured against the impressive record of his predecessor, Harry Truman's domestic accomplishments appeared meager, and his "Fair Deal," announced at the beginning of his second term, hardly made people forget Roosevelt's New Deal. Designed to adapt the basic domestic programs of the Depression decade to the new needs of the postwar period, the Fair Deal promised national health insurance, extension of Social Security, increases in the minimum wage, public power projects, public housing, federal aid to education, repeal of the Taft-Hartley Law, and civil rights legislation. This reform package, Truman's liberal advisers believed, would produce an ever-expanding economy and blaze a wider liberal path between socialism and fascism.

Truman's proposals initially cheered old New Dealers, but the little man from Missouri simply lacked the political muscle, and perhaps the desire, to push them through Congress. Congress did enact the National Housing Act of 1949 which provided money for slum clearance and authorized construction of almost a million low-income units (few were actually built). Legislators also granted Truman's request for an increase in the minimum wage (to seventy-five cents), for broader Social Security coverage, and for funds to carry on the work begun by Roosevelt's TVA and RA. But a coalition of conservative Republicans and southern Democrats blocked most of the president's requests and frustrated a number of his priority programs. Extensive lobbying by the American Medical Association helped bury his national health insurance plan under a barrage of propaganda labeling it as "socialized medicine." Southern committee chairmen and filibusters kept the president's civil rights promises effectively bottled up in Congress, and his hopes for federal aid to education foundered on the controversial issue of extending funds to parochial schools. In addition to legislative obstacles, Truman's domestic program suffered from controversy growing out of the developing cold war.

The cold war

TRUMAN DOCTRINE AND MARSHALL PLAN

American policymakers believed that communism flourished amid conditions of want and political disruption and withered in the face of prosperity and stability. "The only hope of stopping Soviet penetration is the development of sound economic conditions," Averell Harriman advised Truman. In early 1947 native Communist guerrillas threatened the British-backed regime in Greece, and Great Britain announced that it could no longer afford economic assistance. In response, Truman called for a massive aid program for Greece and neighboring Turkey as well. Overcoming resistance from congressmen who believed that replacing Britain as protector of the Greek monarchy would prove inordinately expensive and ill-advised, Truman finally received authorization for $400 million, primarily for arms. The Truman Doctrine heralded America's fight against left-wing revolutionary movements through foreign aid.

In the following year, the Truman administration sought to extend economic assistance to other European nations through the Marshall Plan, named after General George C. Marshall, the World War II commander who had become secretary of state. This new aid program was designed to revive the collapsing European economies, including Germany, as a means of warding off social disorder. At the same time, it would provide strong non-communist trading partners for American industries. Although the plan initially met strong domestic opposition, a Communist coup in neutralist Czechoslovakia convinced Congress to pass it by an overwhelming margin. In the next four years the United States distributed about $12 billion, primarily to Britain, France, and Germany.

Together, the Truman Doctrine and the Marshall Plan extended the fight against Communist movements throughout Europe and ultimately provided a pattern for foreign aid programs throughout the world. The money brought needed assistance to many nations and provided opportunities for American trade and investment abroad, but it also committed the United States to preserving the status quo in countries swept by change. The decline of the European colonial powers and Japan's bid for supremacy in the Far East had undermined old imperial structures and stirred nationalist movements. But the United States—once the champion of the right of revolution, social justice, and self-determination—increasingly supported colonialist nations (such as the French in Indochina) and corrupt elitist regimes (such as Chiang Kai-shek's in China). In its effort to "contain" totalitarianism, the United States often undertook the impossible task of "containing" social instability throughout the world.

In the vocabulary of the cold war, the terms *free peoples* and the *free world* came to be defined purely as anti-Communist, having little to do with respect for individual liberties or democratic values. One of the ironies of the cold war was that, in their determined effort to keep the world open to the spread of American ideals, Americans often allied themselves with violators of the very freedoms they sought to uphold.

COLD WAR SHOCKS

During Truman's second term (1949–1953) hostility between the United States and the Soviet Union deepened. No longer did the Red menace seem limited to Greece and Turkey: the entire globe became the arena for conflict between the "free" and "Communist" worlds, as Americans automatically considered revolutionary movements throughout the world part of a unified Communist conspiracy. Most policymakers opposed using America's military power to roll back the Communist threat and liberate "enslaved" peoples. But they also rejected the idea of negotiation—a term which implied concession and appeasement. Memories of the rapid spread of Nazism during the late 1930s remained vivid, and American leaders feared that a Communist success in one area would quickly snowball into a worldwide Red avalanche. As the strongest nation, the United States bore the heaviest responsibility for "containing" Communist expansion. Any Munich-like compromise could send outposts of the free world tumbling like a row of dominoes. "We cannot afford any more compromises," explained theologian Reinhold Neibuhr in a 1948 *Life* magazine article. "We will have to stand at every point in our far-flung lines."

Germany was the first battleground. American officials considered a strong, prosperous, and West-leaning Germany the key to political and economic stability in Europe. In 1948 Britain, France, and the United States agreed to merge the three non-Soviet zones of occupation into a single state of West Germany. The United States then undertook currency reform as a step toward reviving the German economy. When the American administrator, General Lucius D. Clay, introduced the revalued *Deutschmark* into West Berlin, a Western outpost inside the Communist zone, Stalin saw the action as a threat. The Soviet Union had suffered German invasions twice in the twentieth century, and Stalin believed that a weak, neutral Germany was essential to Russia's security. Viewing this as a capitalist conspiracy against Soviet interests, Stalin closed all surface access into West Berlin.

American officials reacted swiftly, interpreting Stalin's actions as a further step in an aggressive campaign to dominate Europe. "We have lost Czechoslovakia," explained General Clay. "Norway is threatened. We retreat from Berlin. When Berlin falls, Western Germany would be next." Some of Truman's military advisers wanted to blast their way into Berlin, but the president rejected this alternative. Instead, he authorized a massive airlift; planes began flying round the clock, bringing as much as thirteen thousand tons of supplies into the city in a single day. The president reinstituted the draft; began increasing the size of the army; and sent two squadrons of B-29s, the planes which carried atomic bombs, to Great Britain. His advisers hoped that this last action would signal how seriously they viewed the Berlin crisis (and secondarily that it would accustom Britons to having American warplanes on their soil).

The Truman administration also moved to safeguard America's long-range economic and political interests in Europe. Creation of the North Atlantic Treaty Organization (NATO) in early 1949 formalized the new strategy. Twelve nations, including the Big Three Allies—the United States, Great Britain, and France—signed this collective security arrangement which provided that an attack upon any member would be considered aggression against all. The treaty pledged members to develop "free institutions" and to encourage "economic collaboration between any or all" of the parties. As originally conceived, NATO lacked the ground forces to repel a nonnuclear invasion, and the United States refused to share its atomic weapons with other members. Rather than representing a spectacular strategic departure, NATO primarily offered the United States a new means for channeling aid and influence into Europe.

During 1949, a new series of events shook the United States. At home, exposure of alleged Communist spy rings raised fears about America's internal security. In addition, Mao Tse-tung's Communist forces finally drove Chiang Kai-shek off the Chinese mainland to the island of Formosa. The United States tried to support Chiang with military assistance, but what the chief American adviser called "the world's worst leadership" and "many other morale-destroying factors" doomed the Nationalist regime. Much of Chiang's army simply melted away, and 80 percent of the American-sent materiel fell into Communist hands. In an official "White Paper" Secretary of State Dean Acheson argued that Mao's victory was "the ominous result of the civil war in China" and "beyond the control of the government of the United States." But a number of Republicans charged the Truman administration with pursuing a "no-win" policy in Asia, and some Americans, nurtured on the wartime myth of Chiang's dominance, concluded that "Reds" in the State Department had "sold us out." Finally, only months after Chiang's collapse, President Truman made another startling announcement. At a late morning news conference, he informed White House reporters that the Soviets had exploded their first atomic weapon, a revelation which signaled the end of the United States' nuclear monopoly. As Republican Senator Arthur Vandenburg remarked, "This is now a different world."

Following the events of 1949, the "year of shocks," senior advisers in the State and Defense departments searchingly reviewed United States capabilities. By the spring of the following year, these officials and members of the National Security Council produced a comprehensive blueprint for future strategy. Labeled "N.S.C. paper number 68," the document reiterated assumptions which were already conventional cold war wisdom: the bipolarity of world affairs; the aggressive nature of international communism; and the validity of the "domino theory." The paper recommended that the United States radically increase both its own and its allies' military power. Americans had to stop "trying to distinguish between national and global security," and they could not worry about costs. Arguing that the country could afford, in fact prosper from, a massive military buildup (consuming as much as 20 percent of the gross national product), the framers of N.S.C. 68 concluded that the Communist threat required the United States to play the role of world policeman.

KOREA

N.S.C. 68 lay before President Truman in June 1950 when Communist North Korea attacked South Korea, an informal ally of the United States. Mystery still shrouds the origins of the Korean War. The Soviet Union equipped the North Koreans and possibly encouraged their invasion of the South. Yet the Soviet delegation was boycotting the United Nations at the crucial moment of attack, an absence which allowed the United States to circumvent a Soviet veto and gain United Nations support for the American-controlled defense of South Korea. Either the North Koreans invaded without consulting Stalin, or the Soviets never expected the United States to rush to South Korea's aid. No strong evidence supports persistent charges that America's unpopular South Korean ally, Syngman Rhee, actually provoked the North Koreans in order to save his tottering regime, but Truman's massive and immediate reaction does suggest that military operations in Korea came as no surprise to American officials.

Reacting swiftly and following the assumptions contained in N.S.C. 68, Truman implemented a worldwide containment policy. The situation in Korea made it "plain beyond all doubt," he argued, "that communism has passed beyond the use of subversion to conquer independent nations and will now use armed invasion and war." Two days after the outbreak of fighting in Korea, the president announced that our Seventh Fleet would protect Chiang Kai-shek's regime on Formosa from invasion by the mainland Chinese; that the United States would send arms and a "military mission" to support the French against the guerrilla forces of Ho Chi Minh in Indochina; that the government would give the Philippines additional assistance in their struggle against leftist Huk rebels; and that American naval and air forces would assist Syngman Rhee's government in repulsing the North Korean advance. Truman began augmenting American forces elsewhere, providing more troops for NATO in the early fall. And in a dramatic conference with British and French representatives, Secretary of State Acheson formally announced the United States' long-planned program for rearming West Germany and integrating it into the NATO system. The Korean conflict helped Truman convince congressmen to appropriate a much larger defense budget. In two years military expenditures more than tripled, making up nearly 70 percent of the 1951–52 federal budget.

The Korean War itself was a bloody, seesaw affair. Truman originally believed that air power could contain the North Koreans, but, as in Vietnam a decade later, strategists overestimated the military effectiveness of bombing. When the South Korean army rapidly disintegrated, the president sent in United States ground troops under the umbrella of a United Nations operation. North Korean armies still continued advancing south and sent Americans reeling back. Finally regrouping his troops, General Douglas Mac-

Arthur masterminded a brilliant marine landing behind enemy lines at Inchon in mid-September, 1950, and quickly reached the 38th parallel, the official boundary between the two Koreas. MacArthur then received presidential authority to move northward to take the Iron Curtain capital of Pyongyang, which he did in late October. As United States forces neared the North Korea–China border, Chinese Premier Chou En-lai condemned the "frenzied and violent acts of imperialist aggression" and warned that China could not tolerate such a threat. General MacArthur, however, downplayed the possibility, or the effectiveness, of Chinese intervention. Even after encountering Chinese "volunteers," the general confided to reporters in late November 1950 that the "war very definitely is coming to an end shortly." Two days after his prediction, Chinese troops stormed across the Yalu River, driving between MacArthur's widely scattered armies and forcing the United States to retreat south of the 38th parallel once again, this time with heavy casualties. When Americans, in yet another drive northward, pressed near the 38th parallel, Truman instructed MacArthur to seek negotiations rather than to mount another full-scale invasion into Communist territory. But the general, hoping to carry the war back into North Korea and ultimately to China, publicly opposed Truman's idea of "limited warfare" and attempted to subvert efforts to end the war at the 38th parallel. In a dramatic clash of wills, Truman "fired" the proud general on April 11, 1951.

Truman's decision reflected the administration's view that containment was a truly global strategy and that Korea was merely one part of a general struggle against Communist expansion. Policymakers had supported MacArthur's first drive into North Korea, expecting a relatively easy victory, but Chinese involvement threatened an interminable Asian land war which would weaken America's ability to defend its more vital European interests against a Soviet invasion. In the later words of General Omar Bradley, a protracted engagement in Korea would have been "the wrong war, at the wrong place, at the wrong time, and with the wrong enemy."

MacArthur and the "Asia-firsters"—a loosely organized group of some religious leaders, businessmen, and right-wing Republicans who urged all-out victory in Korea and "liberation" of Red China—made a fervent stand against the orthodoxy of containment. MacArthur triumphantly toured the country assailing the president, and his supporters called for greater efforts actually to roll back the "Red Menace." The general warned that "the insidious forces working from within" would lead America "directly to the path of Communist slavery." But the Truman administration rode out the storm. Senate hearings into MacArthur's dismissal revealed that most military strategists supported the president, and, after a wave of sentiment in favor of the World War II hero had subsided, most people rejected his scenario for a wider war in Asia. As Truman's presidency ended in January

Ike said, "I'll be darned" on hearing that President Truman had fired Douglas Mac Arthur
Wide World

1953, the war continued, but at a reduced level. In Korea, negotiators for both sides were sitting around a conference table which carefully straddled the 38th parallel.

Crusade for consensus

Events of the postwar years awakened fears that a foreign-directed Communist plot threatened to surround the nation abroad and to undermine it from within. Although generally associated with Senator Joseph R. McCarthy of Wisconsin and his followers, this second "Red Scare" was part of a much broader trend toward consensus and conformity. During the late forties and much of the fifties governmental officials and private watchdogs, seeking evidence of "un-American" ideas, looked into many Americans' activities and backgrounds. The national government established a loyalty program, marked by the absence of firm procedural safeguards, designed to unmask enemy sympathizers who were hiding in the sprawling bureaucracy. The House Un-American Activities Committee (HUAC), an important political stepping stone for an ambitious young Red baiter named Richard Nixon, devoted itself to uncovering evidence of internal subversion. Some state governments and private institutions, particularly the movie and broadcasting industries, also devised loyalty programs. In the entertainment industry, for example, people whose political ideas and organizational affiliations seemed too left-leaning found themselves on the unemployment rolls. They were on the infamous "blacklist," an ever-changing compendium of several hundred untouchables. Inquisitors examined people's associates, organizations, and even casual acquaintances for evidence of Communist or radical ties. When no direct link could be established to Communist organizations, investigators often labeled their prey as "fellow travelers," "pinkos," or "Fifth Amendment Communists." Employing the technique of guilt by association and sometimes grossly distorting facts, anti-Communist crusaders cast a shadow of fear over the lives of a number of innocent Americans and trampled upon basic constitutional liberties.

Doubts about the United States' position in a rapidly changing world helped to spread these exaggerated fears of a gigantic Red conspiracy. After four years of total war, Americans suddenly found themselves unable to "return to normalcy" as after World War I. Extension of Soviet control over Eastern Europe and spreading disorder elsewhere in the world appeared to demonstrate Stalin's aggressive designs. Leaders such as President Truman, by equating the Communist and Nazi threats, implied that a Communist form of totalitarianism had replaced the fascist version. Americans, it seemed, had to combat subversion everywhere, even perhaps in the most unlikely places. A Michigan congressman, for example, charged that modern artists, "soldier[s] of the Communist Revolution," sought to destroy people's attachment to logic and reality by saturating them with the "depraved" and "illogical" ideas of abstract expressionism.

POLITICS AND ANTI-COMMUNISM

Partisan politics also fueled the hysteria. Although Harry Truman enjoyed impeccable anti-Communist credentials, fears of Republican criticism impelled him to adopt an increasingly tough position against domestic subversion. During the 1948 elections Truman emphasized his anti- Communist actions, preventing Republicans from expropriating the issue for themselves. He established a tight internal-security program which failed to distinguish very clearly between persons accused of being Soviet agents and those merely suspected of holding unorthodox political ideas. Truman's attorney general warned that Communists were "everywhere—in factories, offices, butcher stores, on street corners, in private businesses." By 1950 the president himself proclaimed that the Soviet Union was a "modern tyranny led by a small group who have abandoned their faith in God. . . . We are on the right track and we will win—because God is with us in that Enterprise." Truman and his administration helped create a set of conspiratorial images and fears, elements which more extreme Republican Red baiters would carry even further when the opportunity presented itself.

The disturbing events after 1948, especially Mao's victory in China, Russia's acquisition of atomic weapons, and the Korean War, put the Truman administration on the defensive. Meanwhile, revelations of Soviet espionage activities within the United States gave immediacy to Republican charges of Communist penetration into sensitive government positions. Whitaker Chambers, a former associate editor of *Time* magazine, charged Alger Hiss, a Roosevelt aide who had been at Yalta, with being a member of the Communist party and passing classified material to the Soviets in the late 1930s. In a dramatic showdown, Chambers led congressional investigators to his Maryland farm and pulled microfilmed documents from a hollowed-out pumpkin. Alleged spies such as Ethel and Julius Rosenberg, who were executed in 1953 for espionage, and Hiss steadfastly proclaimed their innocence. Their denials of guilt—denials made more credible to some observers by the broad spirit of popular intolerance and by the tight control over access to the government's evidence—led those observers to claim that they had been framed by overzealous Red baiters. Until scholars enjoy easy and unrestricted access to old FBI intelligence records, the issue of particular people's guilt or innocence, let alone the question of the general extent of Soviet infiltration, must remain unanswered. But one thing seems certain: because of the multitude of wild accusations, the very real problem of Soviet espionage quickly became obscured by the multitude of wild political charges that came to have less and less to do with national security. "How much more are we going to have to take?" exploded Republican Senator Homer Capehart. "Fuchs and Acheson and Hiss and hydrogen bombs threatening outside and New Dealism eating away at the vitals of the nation. In the name of Heaven, is this the best America can do?"

ENTER McCARTHY

In the already frenzied atmosphere, a new anti-Communist spokesman made his belated debut. With a rasping voice and crude manners, Joseph McCarthy seemed a more likely candidate for the heavy in a B-movie than for a United States senator. But McCarthy capitalized on his image as a political primitive and followed a stormy career as a state judge with an upset victory in the Wisconsin senatorial race of 1946. The thick-set "Fighting Marine" proved a tough back-alley brawler, throwing political punches in all directions. Although fading pictures and old newsreels make him appear slightly comical—with his baggy suits and ill-matched ties—the Wisconsin senator became a powerful force in the early 1950s.

Facing reelection with an undistinguished record—the Washington press galley had voted him the worst of the ninety-six Senators—McCarthy seized the Communist issue as his return ticket to the Senate. He hurriedly assembled a patchwork of old material on Communist infiltration and, by adding his own embellishments, established himself as America's most feared Red baiter. In a 1950 speech before a Republican women's club in Wheeling, West Virginia, McCarthy waved a paper purporting to be a list of Communist party members and sympathizers employed in the State Department. His exact words and figures are forever lost—McCarthy had no finished text and a radio engineer innocently erased the only recording—but the Wisconsin senator charged somewhere between 57 and 279 employees with subversive connections. Although he never produced any such list and never proved any of his "documented cases," McCarthy continued to issue new and more sensational allegations. Claiming to name names and to present only the facts, he flung charges faster than his victims could refute them. Ironically, McCarthy uncovered no documented case of Communist subversion; in fact, he rarely even charged people with particular acts of espionage. Instead, he primarily concerned himself, in the words of social critic Dwight McDonald, with "dead souls," not with "actual, living breathing Communists but rather people who once were or may have been" members of the Communist party or other radical organizations.

McCarthy set the tone for much of the political debate of the next few years. A special Senate committee, chaired by the distinguished Democratic conservative Millard Tydings, tried to deflate McCarthy but only succeeded in giving him greater publicity. Other GOP members copied his rhetoric,

Joseph McCarthy

charging Democratic rivals with un-American sentiments and suspicious connections. Many Republicans who resisted such tactics stood by as less reticent colleagues freely used the Red brush against Democrats. In 1950 the defeat of Millard Tydings and the success of anti-Communist campaigns, such as those of senators Richard Nixon and Everett Dirkson, demonstrated the appeal of the Red issue and appeared to confirm the power of McCarthy and his followers.

The McCarran Internal Security Act of 1950 illustrated the caution with which politicians approached the anti-Communist issue. A hodgepodge of antisubversive legislation, the McCarran Act included sections requiring registration of Communist and Communist-front organizations and authorizing a number of detention camps to house internal enemies in times of crisis. Such provisions raised serious constitutional difficulties, but few congressmen wanted to provoke the McCarthyites' wrath by openly opposing the bill. Even Hubert Humphrey, normally a pillar of postwar liberalism, supported it on final passage. "I was very proud of you and your vote," he later wrote one of the seven senators who voted no. "I wish I could say the same for myself." Joined by Humphrey, a few libertarians urged President Truman to veto the measure. Truman prided himself on his desk plaque, "The Buck Stops Here," and he did reject the act, a veto which Congress quickly overrode.

As a coterie of right-wing Republicans and anti-Communist zealots attached themselves to McCarthy's coattails, even more sensational charges were flung. On the floor of the Senate, McCarthy strongly implied that General George Marshall, World War II hero and former secretary of state, had betrayed the American cause and sold out Chiang Kai-shek to the Communists. How else could anyone explain Communist successes, charged McCarthy, "unless we believe that men high in the Government are concentrating to deliver us to disaster? This must.be the product of a great conspiracy, . . . so immense as to dwarf any previous such venture in the history of man." Numerous other political and intellectual leaders felt the sting of "Senator Joe's" wild attacks, but fear of his supposed political invincibility and his unscrupulous methods silenced most potential critics. In a January 1953 editorial the *New York Post* asked plaintively, "Is McCarthy untouchable?"

McCarthy only appeared unassailable. The Wisconsin senator proved to be not the leader of a dangerous mass movement, as many intellectuals of the period feared, but the beneficiary of a peculiarly favorable set of political circumstances. Old-line conservative Republicans from the Midwest formed the foundation of McCarthy's power base, and he benefited from the support or acquiesence of other elites in postwar society. Seeing the anti-Communist issue as a potent weapon against the Democrats, most Republican leaders either encouraged or tolerated McCarthy's extreme attacks on the opposition. Leaders of the Senate hesitated to censure one of their own; prominent liberals kept quiet; and sensation-hunting newspapers gave McCarthy abundant coverage. And during the cold war's hottest days—the period of the Korean conflict—McCarthy's claims of Communist subversion carried considerable emotional appeal.

But following the 1952 election of the new Republican president, former General Dwight D. Eisenhower, and the cessation of hostilities in Korea, McCarthy gradually lost both his elite support and ultimately his popular credibility. To a Republican party out of power McCarthy was an asset; to a party in power, especially one which would end the Korean conflict, the raucous senator was an acute embarrassment. The Eisenhower administration initially tolerated McCarthy—Ike remarked that he would "not get down in the gutter with *that* guy"—but eventually the senator went too far.

Following his charges that the United States army contained Communist infiltrators, the various groups which had once sheltered him turned against the maverick senator. Eisenhower repudiated him; many (though by no means all) conservative Republicans deserted him; the army struck back at him; and a majority of senators officially ostracized him. During thirty-five days of nationally televised hearings, a special Senate committee investigated McCarthy's charges against the army. McCarthy, overconfident and pugnacious, came across on the TV screen as the town bully. The hearings, which became daily television spectaculars, helped break McCarthy's aura of political invincibility; six months later the Senate formally censured him for conduct unbecoming a member. His fragile power broken, McCarthy ended his days a pathetic figure, dying in 1957.

McCarthy's appeal proved shallow, but a spirit of consensus pervaded the nation. During the height of the cold war, radicalism in politics, social thought, or the arts became unfashionable. Legal prosecutions for unorthodox sentiments were less important than more subtle means of coercion, such as the blacklist. Left-wing sympathizers in the Hollywood film community discovered that producers suddenly closed doors to them; folksingers such as Pete Seeger and the Weavers found themselves barred from the airwaves; and the intellectual establishment, lined up behind militant anticommunism and containment, trumpeted the glories of the liberal, capitalist order. Writers such as I. F. Stone, who would become a "respectable" radical during the 1960s, stood out from the general consensus of the cold war period. A generation of liberals agreed with Arthur M. Schlesinger, Jr., that their proper position was in the "vital center" of the political spectrum.

Things to think about: 1940–1953

Why did the United States move from neutrality to belligerence between 1939 and 1941? In addition to the works cited in the previous chapter, the basic surveys are W. L. Langer and S. E. Gleason, *The Challenge to Isolation, 1937-1940* (1952), and *The Undeclared War, 1940-1941* (1953); Basil Rauch, *Roosevelt: Munich to Pearl Harbor* (1959); and Herbert Feis, *The Road to Pearl Harbor* (1950). Paul W. Schroeder, *The Axis Alliance and Japanese-American Relations, 1941* (1958), and Warren F. Kimball, *The Most Unsordid Act: Lend Lease, 1939-1941* (1969), are specialized studies. Bruce M. Russett's *No Clear and Present Dan-*ger (1972) is a brief interpretative essay in the "revisionist" tradition.

Assess the impact of total war upon the home front. What tensions did war produce? What changes did it bring? Chester Eisinger, ed., *The 1940's; Profile of a Nation in Crisis* (1969), is a valuable collection of source materials. Richard Polenberg, *War and Society, The United States, 1941-1945* (1971), and Geoffrey Perrett, *Days of Sadness, Years of Triumph* (1973), are good accounts of the war's impact at home. Jacobus ten Broek et al., *Prejudice, War, and the Constitution* (2nd ed., 1968), remains the best treatment of the internment of Japanese Americans. Lawrence S. Wittner, *Rebels Against War: The American Peace Movement, 1941-1960* (1969), and Richard M. Dalfiume, *Desegregation of the U.S. Armed Forces* (1969), relate their topics to broader social and political trends.

What was the relationship between wartime strategy and the Allies' postwar aims? Gaddis Smith, *American Diplomacy During the Second World War, 1941-1945* (1965), and Raymond G. O'Connor, *Diplomacy for Victory: FDR and Unconditional Surrender* (1971), are short summaries of wartime diplomacy. James M. Burns, *Roosevelt: The Soldier of Freedom* (1970), and Gabriel Kolko, *The Politics of War: The World and United States Foreign Policy, 1943-45* (1968), offer differing perspectives on the conduct of the war and postwar aims. Martin J. Sherwin, *A World Destroyed* (1975), analyzes the decision to drop the A-bomb.

How did both foreign and domestic considerations lead to the "cold war" between the Soviet Union and the United States? William L. Nuemann, *After Victory: Churchill, Roosevelt, Stalin, and the Making of the Peace* (1969), is one summary. Lloyd C. Gardner, Arthur M. Schlesinger, Jr., and Hans J. Morganthau, *The Origins of the Cold War* (1970), provides differing interpretations on this controversial topic. Recent works include Walter LaFeber, *America, Russia, and the Cold War, 1945-1971* (2nd ed., 1976); Richard J. Barnett, *Roots of War* (1972), Lloyd Gardner, *Architects of Illusion* (1970), Lisle Rose, *Dubious Victory* (1973), Joyce Kolko and Gabriel Kolko, *The Limits of Power* (1972), and David McLellan, *Dean Acheson* (1976).

Characterize the major developments in domestic politics between 1945 and 1953. Why did the Democrats face increasing challenges? Truman's own *Memoirs* (2 vols., 1955, 1956) are enlightening, and Bert Cochran, *Harry Truman and the Crisis Presidency* (1973), is a competent popular biography. See also Truman's salty reminiscences in Merle Miller, ed., *Plain Speaking* (1974). Eric F. Goldman's *The Crucial Decade— and After* (1960) offers some insights, and Richard Neustadt's *Presidential Power* (2nd ed., 1969) contains an analysis of Truman's leadership. The essays in Richard S. Kirkendall, ed., *The Truman Period as a Research Field* (1974), suggest the amount of scholarly conflict already raised by the Truman era. Alonso S. Hamby, *Beyond the New Deal* (1973), is thorough and generally pro-Truman.

Why must any explanation of McCarthyism consider a variety of political, social, cultural, and foreign policy developments? Richard Rovere, *Senator Joseph McCarthy* (1959), is a useful account. Michael P. Rogin, *The Intellectuals and McCarthy* (1967), summarizes previous scholarly interpretations of McCarthyism and offers a critique of these views. Recent studies include Robert Griffith, *The Politics of Fear* (1970), Richard M. Freeland, *The Truman Doctrine and the Origins of McCarthyism* (1972), and Robert Griffith and Athan Theoharis, eds., *The Specter* (1974). John Chabot Martin, *Alger Hiss* (1976), is a controversial biography of a controversial figure. Eric Bentley, ed., *Thirty Years of Treason* (1971), contains fascinating excerpts from the HUAC hearings.

14

RECENT AMERICA

1953-1977

MARTIN LUTHER KING, JR.

Few men have ever been so privileged as to hold an entire nation in their moral debt. A national commitment to end legal segregation made in the 1940s and '50s found no mechanism that could move at more than a glacial pace until the Reverend Martin Luther King's non-violent protest movement galvanized black and white Americans into effective action.

Born in Atlanta in 1929 to a family of middle-class black Americans, King chose his father's career, the Baptist ministry, rather than his mother's schoolteaching. King graduated from Morehouse College at the age of nineteen, earned a Bachelor of Divinity at the interracial Crozer Seminary in Pennsylvania, and in 1955 completed a Ph.D. in systematic theology at Boston University. While in Boston he met his future wife Coretta, an Antioch College graduate attending the New England Conservatory of Music. Returning to Montgomery, Alabama, King became pastor of the Dexter Avenue Baptist Church and led the successful city bus boycott of 1955–56. King's life was threatened and his home bombed as a result of his activities, but in 1957 he organized

638

what later became the Southern Christian Leadership Conference. Working after 1960 from Atlanta's Ebenezer Baptist Church, King became internationally famous for his nonviolent philosophy in seeking social change. He stood out as the main figure in confrontations at Birmingham and Selma, Alabama. As the principal speaker at the historic 1963 March on Washington, King delivered his famous "I have a dream" oration.

> I have a dream that one day on the red hills of Georgia the sons of former slaves and the sons of former slaveowners will be able to sit together at the table of brotherhood. . . . I have a dream that one day even the State of Mississippi, a desert state sweltering with the heat of injustice and oppression, will be transformed into an oasis of freedom and justice. . . . I have a dream that one day the State of Alabama . . . will be transformed into a situation where little black boys and black girls will be able to join hands with little white boys and girls and walk together as sisters and brothers.

In Stockholm the next year King received the Nobel Peace Prize—becoming the youngest peace laureate in history. But there were limits to King's movement and he found himself in deep trouble after 1965. In 1967 he spoke out against the Vietnam War. The next year he was assassinated, at the young age of thirty-nine, while in Memphis to encourage striking refuse workers.

Where King could go no farther, neither could the nation; the very successes of the civil rights movement revealed all that still remained to be done. It would be foolish either to discount the accomplishments of that movement or to be complacent with what it achieved. King himself understood this as well as any of his critics. The civil rights movement had achieved largely legal, not economic, gains and directly benefited middle-class blacks rather than the more desperate ghetto dwellers. Yet before King the streets of Watts and Harlem had had no effective voice and afterward a babel of voices sought to lead, direct, use, or uplift. These voices usually did not speak the idiom of Martin Luther King, but they might never have been heard in a community lacking the expectations and hope that black and white Americans had developed by the mid-sixties. King had a rare ability to articulate and dramatize ideas. He lived by the principles he had recommended to an audience at his church on the first night of the Montgomery bus boycott:

> If you will protest courageously, and yet with dignity and Christian love, when the history books are written in future generations, the historians will have to pause and say, "There lived a great people—a black people—who injected new meaning and dignity into the veins of civilization."

1953	*Stalin dies, March 5*
	Korean ceasefire, July 27
1954	*SEATO Pact, September 8*
	Senate censure of Joseph F. McCarthy
	Brown *vs.* Board of Education of Topeka
1955	*Geneva Summit Meeting, July 18–23*
	Montgomery Bus Boycott, December 1–January 1956
1956	*Eisenhower sends paratroopers to Little Rock, September 24*
	Eisenhower reelected president, defeating Adlai E. Stevenson
1957	*Soviet Union launches Sputnik*
1959	*Alaska, Hawaii admitted as new states*
	Fidel Castro takes control of Cuban government
1960	*John F. Kennedy (Democrat) elected president, defeating Richard M. Nixon*
	Sit-ins begin
1961	*Bay of Pigs invasion fails*
	Freedom rides
1962	Baker *vs.* Carr
	The Cuban Missile Crisis
1963	*Kennedy is assassinated, November 22; Lyndon B. Johnson becomes president*
1964	*Gulf of Tonkin Resolution passes Senate with two votes against it*
	Lyndon Johnson reelected president, defeating Barry Goldwater
1965	*Great Society legislation*
	Bombing of North Vietnam
	Race riots begin
1966	Miranda *vs.* Arizona
1968	*Tet Offensive in Vietnam, January–February*
	Martin Luther King is assassinated, April 4
	Robert F. Kennedy is assassinated, June 4
	Richard M. Nixon (Republican) elected president, defeating Hubert Humphrey
1969	*Moon landing, July 20*
1970	*Invasion of Cambodia*
1971	*Publication of Pentagon papers*
1972	*Richard M. Nixon is reelected, defeating George McGovern*
1973	*Vietnam ceasefire signed, January 15*
1974	*Richard Nixon resigns August 8, succeeded by Gerald Ford*
1976	*Jimmy Carter elected president, defeating Gerald Ford*
1977	*Panama Canal Controversy*

Eisenhower's foreign policy

President Dwight D. Eisenhower presided over something rare in recent American history: a brief era of peace. Behind his administration stretched the agonizing pasts of the cold war, the Second World War, and the Great Depression—itself a war against want. Ahead lay the heated debates of the

1960s and the debacle of Vietnam. The foreign policy tone of the fifties—after Korea virtually free of foreign conflict, real or impending—is nicely captured by the American general who wished above all, to be remembered as a man of peace.

A Kansan who enjoyed his undergraduate days at West Point, Eisenhower had achieved academic honors at Command and General Staff School. During World War II he demonstrated his military acumen commanding first the invasion of North Africa and later the second-front assault on Normandy; Montgomery of England and de Gaulle of France praised his skills at strategic maneuver. Concealing a determined will behind a self-effacing manner, General Eisenhower inspired confidence among his troops and with homefront Americans. Yet after the peace he showed no desire to impose his own military background on the demobilized nation. In Europe he had learned well the horrors of war. His *Crusade in Europe* recounts the entry into the Falaise Gap Zone in Normandy in 1944: "It was literally possible," he wrote, "to walk for hundreds of yards at a time, stepping on nothing but dead and decayed flesh."

After the war Eisenhower served briefly as president of Columbia University where he set up an academic "chair of peace" and inaugurated the American Assembly, a cold war "think tank" that would study international problems. President Truman appointed him commander of the new North Atlantic Treaty Organization in 1950. Then, a group of eastern Republicans led by Thomas E. Dewey and Senator Henry Cabot Lodge, Jr., persuaded him to run for president in 1952. Eisenhower later said that he ran to prevent the nomination of Ohio Senator Robert A. Taft who believed in less, rather than more, foreign involvement as the surest way to peace. Taft opposed the export of American institutions and believed the country should sustain itself on domestic markets protected by high tariffs—isolationist attitudes which Eisenhower thought selfish and immoral.

"Ike's" military glamour and easygoing personality made him an ideal presidential candidate in 1952. He handily defeated Adlai E. Stevenson, the Democratic governor of Illinois who had cracked down on gambling and modernized his state's government. The play of Stevenson's intellect failed to reach the voters; Eisenhower's simple approach—his promise, for instance, to "go to Korea"—did. And the Democratic candidate had to contend with corruption in the Truman administration and with Republican charges that the Democrats were "soft" on communism.

PRESIDENTIAL DIPLOMACY

President Eisenhower pursued a rather steady course of detente in foreign affairs. Perhaps the most important element in the so-called thaw was Eisenhower's dramatic reversal concerning the Korean imbroglio. The thorny prisoner-of-war issue had brought armistice negotiations to a stalemate. America maintained that some 132,000 captured soldiers did not want to return to North Korea and China; the Communists were understandably reluctant to leave South Korean president Syngman Rhee a highly trained army. Eisenhower and his Secretary of State, John Foster Dulles, decided on a daring tactic: the secretary informed neutralist Prime Minister Jawaharal Nehru of India that the United States might resort to atomic warfare in Korea and Manchuria if an agreement were not reached "very shortly." The Communists gave in on the POW issue but launched a major ground offensive only two weeks later. This heavy attack demonstrated the Communists' impressive military strength, but after a short time both sides avoided any further escalation. On July 27, 1953, American General Harrison and North Korean General Nan II initiated an armistice agreement which, for all practical purposes, restored the prewar status quo. Though the Korean War ended amid atomic threats and military clashes, the fact of peace overshadowed the sputtering cold war tactics.

Events in the Soviet Union aided Eisenhower in his apparent desire to resolve the victors' clash over the spoils of World War II. First the Soviets detonated a hydrogen bomb in 1953, which meant nuclear stand-off. Then on March 5, 1953, Stalin died; his nominal successor, Georgi Malenkov, acted to ease tensions. And by the later fifties, with First Secretary of the Communist Party Nikita Khruschev in control, the new doctrine of peaceful coexistence had replaced the older faith in Marxist militance. Discord did not suddenly melt away, but fresh conditions and leaders signaled an end to the most hostile phase of the cold war.

In Washington the Senate censure in 1954 of Joe McCarthy—for his unorthodox "hearings" accusing public figures of Communist affiliations—eased the public malaise and congressional carping that had plagued the Truman administration. At times Secretary Dulles seemed a throwback to an era of a fervent, crusading foreign policy. Eisenhower had to restrain his secretary from intervening in Vietnam and in the Formosa Straits. Dulles would go "to the brink" to contain communism, but he avoided the abyss—perhaps with more careful calculation than his critics acknowledged. Despite Republican rhetoric about freeing the "captive nations" behind the Iron Curtain, Dulles worked to stabilize the political situation in Europe. When West Germany entered NATO, the Soviets responded with the Warsaw Pact—a parallel agreement which linked together the Communist alliance in Eastern Europe. The treaty to reunite Austria also came under the secretary's tenure. The greater reliance of Eisenhower and Dulles on the threat of nuclear weaponry suggested that only a major world crisis would set off another war. This conservative intention, to achieve a holding action by gripping and controlling potentially dangerous forces, resulted in a peculiar anomaly: alongside the inflamed rhetoric of Secretary Dulles, Eisenhower exhibited in place of ideology a prudent attitude toward power. The United States sought to exercise intricate strategies in foreign relations, to deploy exact military force to balance that of the Soviet Union, and above all to live rationally with the fact of devastating power—in short, to regard the threat of apocalypse as a close intellectual problem.

Clear indication of a break with the earlier Truman-Acheson policy came when Eisenhower met Soviet leaders face-to-face at Geneva in 1955. There began an increased communication between East and West—the exchange of "people, ideas, and goods"—that has steadily grown since that time. There Eisenhower offered his "open skies" disarmament proposal: mutual aerial surveillance and an exchange of military data. The Soviets demurred (the American Senate, given the opportunity, might have done likewise). Nevertheless, Geneva produced a welcome change of mood. Tensions remained, but peace—meaning simply the absence of war—seemed possible.

PRESIDENTIAL DIPLOMACY: THE LATER YEARS

In the last part of the decade Eisenhower responded coolly and rationally to a series of potentially explosive events. After the Poles won greater autonomy from Moscow, the Hungarians demanded political independence as well as economic reform; in October 1956 a revolution broke out, which the Soviets put down with heavy military force. President Eisenhower never considered intervention. The West, in fact, soon divided over an Israeli-Anglo-French attack on Egypt in early November. This conflict had all the characteristics of a preventive war though with the stated aim of reopening the Suez Canal which Egyptian President Abdul Nasser had nationalized a few months earlier. Eisenhower condemned the colonialist attack and forced Prime Minister Anthony Eden to withdraw British troops. Then on October 4, 1957, the Soviet Union launched its first *Sputnik* earth satellite. A second, heavier instrument soon followed, and America suffered a major propaganda defeat. Instead of reacting belligerently, Eisenhower chose to "wage peace," as he phrased it in the sub-title to the second volume of his *Memoirs*. Dulles, now seriously ill with cancer, resigned in 1958, and the president increasingly employed his own favorite brand of diplomacy—personal meetings with foreign heads of state. Khrushchev's visit to America in 1959 had a relaxing effect, and another summit meeting was planned for the spring of 1960.

Yet Eisenhower disliked pacifism, believed in collective security, and never doubted that communism was a hostile force which threatened the nation's security. He shored up the European alliance and gave Germany a nonnuclear role in NATO. In the Middle East he even offered American soldiers, on request, to resist communism. During 1958 several thousand marines actually landed in Lebanon; their work was done swiftly and with little bloodshed. In Guatemala the United States arranged the overthrow of a left-wing government, and the CIA laid contingency plans for a refugee invasion of Cuba which later failed miserably. Approved aerial reconnaissance of the Soviet Union backfired when one of the spy planes was shot down just in time to wreck the proposed 1960 summit meeting. Nonetheless, until John Kennedy during the 1960 campaign raised the question of a "missile gap" and then as president embarked on various military adventures, the world for a time seemed at peace.

The 1950s at home

Raised in the Midwest at the beginning of this century, Dwight Eisenhower never gave up most of the economic and social verities of that region and time. Although the theater of World War II schooled him away from isolationism, his views on domestic issues underwent no such change and resembled those of another midwesterner—the conservative Senator Robert Taft of Ohio, his unsuccessful opponent for the 1952 Republican presidential nomination. As Eisenhower once remarked: "I laughed at [Taft] one day, and I said, 'How did you ever happen to be known as a conservative and me as a liberal?'"

The Eisenhower years at home have been characterized as a time of political and social stasis. If America did enjoy a rest during the fifties its duration was short-lived. The so-called placid decade began only after the end of the Korean War in 1953 and the Army-McCarthy hearings of 1954; and it seemed to close in 1957 with the Soviet achievements in space and discouraging economic recession at home.

THE ECONOMY OF THE 1950s

Business interests had favored Eisenhower's election, but the economic climate during his administration left something to be desired. Republicans still employed the rhetoric of classical economists, but now they also trusted in the Federal Reserve Board to regulate the economy with fiscal and monetary tools. The Board's efforts, halfhearted and tardy, could scarcely prevent three recessions from plaguing the Eisenhower years in 1953, 1957, and 1959. Even after their onset the administration reacted slowly; as a result high unemployment persisted throughout the decade, rising to more than 7 percent in 1958. Yet the president worried more about inflation than about the slow rate of economic growth and the resulting job scarcity. (The Soviet gross national product was increasing half again as fast as that of the United States.) Important social needs in health and other welfare areas required an active and growing economy— the kind that a business-dominated Republican party might have been expected to provide. Corporations, however, pre-

Theodore Roszak, Sea Sentinel
Collection of Whitney Museum of American
Art, New York

ferred a more limited and assured volume of sales, technically called the "administered price." Unionized craft workers found contentment in their own rising wages passed on to consumers in the form of higher prices. The poor suffered most by the absence of new investments and jobs. Blacks, Mexican Americans, Indians, and some old people, shut away in ghettos, migrant camps, or reservations, were "invisible." They lacked any political representation even in the Democratic party with its labor union base.

A major irony of the fifties was that the business-dominated Republicans appeared fearful of stimulating rapid economic growth, while the Democrats, especially in the political campaigns of 1958 and 1960, made it a central goal. Dwight Eisenhower was the first Republican president since Herbert Hoover; his party seemed to be recovering very slowly from the trauma of holding office during the Great Depression.

After twenty years of Democratic rule and virulent Republican criticisms, the nation might have expected some far-reaching changes in governmental operations. Few occurred. During his eight years as president, Eisenhower and his predominantly Democratic Congresses even extended many New Deal laws such as Social Security. By the end of the decade only a tiny minority of Americans seriously considered repealing the legislative work of the thirties.

The fifties, in fact, set in place the important groundwork for the Great Society legislation of the sixties. Laws were drafted; Congress held interminable hearings. Aid to public education, sponsored by Senator Taft, would have been passed but for controversy over issues of race and of church and state. The American Medical Association continued to prevent passage of any national health care programs, but endorsed broadly based private health plans subsidized by government. Toward the end of his second term the president vetoed housing and water pollution control bills. But Eisenhower and his "free market" Secretary of Agriculture Ezra Taft Benson could not reverse the entrenched farm subsidy programs; total government payments to farmers increased during the Republican administration.

SIGNS OF UNREST

America in the fifties lacked a political Left; the conservative administration could go its own way without having to accommodate itself to serious dissent. Many of Eisenhower's advisers, including Vice-President Nixon, urged more progressive domestic policies, but the president would rarely support such programs when threatened with congressional opposition. Although Eisenhower in 1956 won reelection against Stevenson by over 9 million votes, the 1958 congressional elections heralded a resurgence of Democratic strength. Throughout the decade the Democrats had kept control of the House of Representatives by a slim margin. But in 1958 they captured 65 percent of the seats. Many older Republican standpatters involuntarily retired from the Senate, their places taken by younger men less content with the status quo. The 1958 vote signaled dissatisfaction with the sluggish economy as well as the Russian coup in space. Eisenhower's great personal popularity never embraced his party.

The sociological dimension of the decade also reveals a turbulence beneath the thin crusts of conformity. To accommodate their burgeoning families and to benefit from generous tax breaks on mortgages, the middle class accelerated its flight to the suburbs in the 1950s, while many blacks, impoverished whites, and Hispanics moved cityward where they would become an important force in the next decade. These two movements, inward and outward from the cities, sharpened the contrasts by race and class between the core cities and suburban communities—and helped to precipitate the urban crises of the 1960s.

The standardized suburban housing and shopping centers of the fifties spawned a vast assortment of new subcultures. Without small-town leaders to enforce traditional values, the new suburban dweller—often moved by his corporation or the military from one end of the country to another—was thrown more upon his own professional skills for a sense of personal identity and status. "Packaging" in housing, leisure, and food compensated perhaps for some of the strain and flux. But the "roots" to which these mobile people had made reference in the past were rapidly vanishing.

The rising birth rate was perhaps another symptom of a striving for roots. For at least 150 years, the American birth rate had been declining, and since about the 1890s middle-class families of the towns and cities had been limiting the number of their children and investing heavily in each boy to fit him for the complicated tasks of business, management, or the professions. During the same period the urban lower class as well as countrydwellers of all stations produced large families from which the city factories drew much of their labor. No one has satisfactorily explained why in the middle of this century the trend among the middle classes was temporarily reversed. It may be that the United States was simply approaching a postindustrial economy in which economic decisions are determined more by the wishes of consumers than by the sterner logic of industrial needs. Whatever the reasons, the birth rate soared to levels approaching those of the under-developed world; at such a pace the population would double every thirty-five years. Then, during the 1960s, births abruptly declined.

As the surface consensus of the fifties broke apart, group after group began to assert its separate identity. In addition to the growing civil rights movement spurred by the Supreme Court school desegregation decision of 1954 a distinct group of adolescents appeared with values for the first time largely separate from those of the adult middle class. A small community of rebels, the "beats," pitted their devotion to poetry, drugs, jazz, and handicrafts against the temptations of Mammon. Another enclave, the "radical" Right, emerged chiefly from among southern Democrats and from Republican conservatives convinced that Eisenhower betrayed them by failing to repeal New Deal legislation and to confront communism more militantly. Working in tiny patriotic groups, these Americans promoted anti-communism in thousands of communities across the nation. Their interest in local, small-scale approaches as opposed to bureaucratic solutions for social problems, ironically became a characteristic of the New Left in the 1960s.

The social problems of the sixties by and large existed in the fifties as well. Not until toward the end of the Eisenhower years, however, did publicists begin the task of educating the public and promoting legislative action. In *The Affluent Society* John Kenneth Galbraith attacked a wealthy nation that disregarded public needs. One of the most influential works in the muckraking genre did not even appear in book form until 1962, Michael Harrington's *The Other America*. One of Harrington's special concerns was the exploited "Chicanos"—Mexican Americans—of the Western states.

Mexican Americans

Racial prejudice, together with the Anglos urge for profit and political power, left Mexican-Americans in poverty, a poverty which many quietly accepted. "I love to be poor," said Cleotas Vigil, a small rancher near San Cristobal, New Mexico, one summer in the early 1950s, "I am immune to being poor." Decay marred his village; empty houses and old machines littered the landscape. He spoke of a farmer's lifeline to markets, "Our road was dirt in my grandfather's day, it has not changed." Yet this life without material goods had its own compensations, rewards which explained a stubborn attachment to a land so hostile. Sociologists often spoke of commu-nality—that timeless sense of place, of roots—which pervaded the small villages in the Southwest. "In those days," Cleotas explained more simply, "everything, everybody was in harmony."

The sixties ended Chicano resignation. Many now lived in urban *barrios*, or ghettos, far from the comforting countryside. Then, too, second and third generation Mexican-Americans, now native-born citizens, realized that the United States, not Mexico, was their homeland. The suspicions of the 1950s, when anti-Communist hysteria equated alien with subversive, had blunted both reformist impulse and opportunity. Chicano writers spoke of the "decade of defense," when Anglo indifference forced the Chicano community to look inward. During the Kennedy-Johnson years, however, Americans could no longer ignore the Chicanos. The country's second largest minority now numbered some four million persons. New housing patterns—the result of the GI bill of rights and new industries—broke down the old *barrios*. Local leaders galvanized complacent Chicanos into a quest for equality.

The 1960s taught the Chicanos that redress lay in organization. Like other minorities, Mexican-Americans copied the often successful techniques of black protest. In 1968 students stalked out of Los Angeles schools where sub-standard education condemned many Chicanos to near illiteracy. In Texas and California, where they accounted for ten per cent or more of the population Mexican-Americans ran for local office, often forcing Democrats or Republicans to take up their cause or face defeat. National politicians, too, felt this pressure. John Kennedy in 1960 and Hubert Humphrey again in 1968 made a special effort to identify with local Chicano causes; one reason Humphrey carried Texas was overwhelming support from the *barrios*. Demonstrations against job discrimination and segregation created a sense of racial pride among Chicanos, who chanted "La Raza" much as blacks sung "We Shall Overcome." The Anglo community responded belatedly, especially in California where Governor Ronald Reagan blocked important open housing legislation and cut aid to local schools. President Johnson's war on poverty prompted rising expectations which a country beset by foreign war, white backlash, and economic deterioration could not fulfill.

Disillusionment fragmented Chicano protest during the 1970s. Leaders like Cesar Chavez turned to direct action aimed at improving economic conditions for a limited number of Chicano workers. Beginning as early as 1965, Chavez's union, the National Farm Workers Association (NFWA), had struck some of California's major vineyards. Many thought this crusade futile—no one had ever before organized field workers, especially in the face of agribusinessmen determined to break the union. But Chavez skillfully used the workers' racial pride and Catholic faith to cement union solidarity. At the same time, his nonviolent methods, the obvious needs of Chicano field hands, the ill-concealed excesses of local ranchers, all brought sympathy and financial support from liberals across the country. Chavez then appealed for a consumer boycott on wine, a threat which forced many vineyards to recognize the NFWA and negotiate fair wages. Understandably elated, Chavez used the same tactics against the table grape industry and the lettuce growers during the early 1970s. This time, unfortunately, a murky jurisdictional dispute with the Teamsters Union, the hostility of local Catholic bishops, and tensions between Mexican immigrants and Mexican-American citizens delayed a settlement for some seven years.

Other Chicano leaders, discouraged by the long strike, took up more militant solutions. Some, like Jose Gutierrez of San Antonio, Texas, turned toward racial politics. Early in 1970 he organized *La Raza Unida*, a party dedicated to electing Mexican-Americans to the school board and the city council. He convinced the city's Chicanos to vote as a bloc. After easy victories in the neighborhoods sometimes nearly seventy-five percent Mexican-

American, the newly elected officials initiated free breakfast and lunch programs, bilingual instructions, and Chicano studies courses. Other leaders, though, abandoned any pretense of working within the system. Corky Gonzales, a young, charismatic Chicano leader from Denver, argued that the Mexican-Americans must purify their own racial identity. Only separation from the Anglos, not integration, could insure that sense of pride necessary for social and economic advance. Still others, like Reies Lopez Tijerina, *El Tigre*, employed almost quixotic gestures—like "liberating" a national park in New Mexico—to unify the Chicanos around his vision of a return to the land. Despite this variety of voices, Mexican-Americans won limited but distinct successes throughout the 1960s and the 1970s.

The Warren court

The Supreme Court headed by Chief Justice Earl Warren, who served from 1953 to 1969, was notable for a series of dramatic decisions. During that time, increasing conflict over civil rights and in race relations prompted critics to accuse the Court of usurping legislative powers and involving itself in social transformation. Yet the involvement in social issues was neither new nor unusual. The Court can only rule on the issues which come before it, and those decisions historically memorable have always ruled on important social problems. Surely the Court's enunciation of the doctrine of "separate but equal" in *Plessy* v. *Ferguson* (1896) remains as political an act as the decision which overturned it, *Brown* v. *Board of Education* (1954).

Although the Court did not invent racial tensions or succeed in mitigating them, the Brown case, the first major decision of the Warren Court, served as a reference point throughout the civil rights crisis of the 1960s. The NAACP team of lawyers, headed by Thurgood Marshall, later to become the first black justice on the Court, had been attacking "separate but equal" for fifteen years and the Court had responded by tightening the promised equality provisions. Then the Warren Court unanimously held in the *Brown* case that "separate educational facilities are inherently unequal," and that implementation proceed "with all deliberate speed"—a vague phrase permitting another decade of inaction.

Some of the Warren Court's most controversial decisions came in the areas of criminal procedure and the rights of the accused. In a series of cases the liberal majority ruled that the principle of equality before the law, the heart of the *Brown* decision, covered almost every action of government and held that the constitutional guarantee of due process ensured citizens fair treatment from governmental agencies. In *Gideon* v. *Wainwright* (1963), the Court guaranteed in all felony cases the right to counsel in the courtroom. Clarence Earl Gideon, a poor white southerner with a long criminal

record, had been accused of breaking and entering a Florida poolroom and convicted at a trial in which he had had to defend himself without legal counsel. Three years later the guarantee of courtroom counsel was extended to the police station in *Miranda* v. *Arizona;* here the Court ruled that police interrogators must inform a suspect of his right to hire a lawyer (or have the state provide one), tell him of his right to remain silent, and warn him that any statement he made can be used against him.

The Court set off a religious furor when it again ruled on education in a number of cases in 1962–63 outlawing compulsory prayer and Bible reading in public schools. The Court upheld the rights of the individual student against the imposition of a particular morality and also the separation of church and state.

A group of obscenity convictions was set aside by the Court with the notable exception of *Ginzburg* v. *U.S.;* the sentence of Ralph Ginzburg, the publisher of some rather pretentious high-art erotica, was sustained. A direct political decision of the Warren Court also had individualist implications: the enunciation of the doctrine of "one man, one vote," which required that both houses of state legislatures reflect the actual distributions of population. The first such case, in 1962, was *Baker* v. *Carr.*

By the end of the 1960s, the "Warren majority" had begun to leave the Court; Warren's own retirement and Hugo Black's death removed two of the four central figures. Warren, who had come to the bench after two terms as governor of California and an unsuccessful bid for the vice-presidency in 1948, appeared to be a moderate Republican when appointed by President Eisenhower in 1953; at the time no one expected him to become a social engineer. Another Eisenhower appointee, William Brennan, proved to be a staunch defender of individual freedoms. Black, a Democratic senator from Alabama appointed to the Court by FDR, had been an honorary Klansman at the time; surprisingly, he staunchly and consistently defended civil liberties. William O. Douglas, the fourth judge who helped make the far-reaching social decisions, had worked as a Wall Street lawyer and headed the Securities and Exchange Commission; some feared when he was appointed in 1939 that he would be subservient to corporate wealth. Yet these men gave the Court its "liberal" cast, and they gained important votes from some of the justices appointed by Kennedy and Johnson during the 1960s.

John F. Kennedy

An assessment of John Kennedy's less-than-three-year presidential term remains difficult. His administration was marked by few concrete legislative accomplishments and not until his last year did he exercise any strong executive leadership on such critical domestic issues as the rights of black Americans. Instead, Kennedy preoccupied himself with international tensions and seemed almost to welcome foreign challenges; he clearly raised the stakes in Vietnam. On the other hand, the youngest man (at forty-three) ever elected president, he touched chords in American society which Eisenhower, for all his warm qualities, could not have hoped to sound. Kennedy's personal style reflected America's own transformation from the private pursuits of the fifties to the greater social awareness of the sixties. The unfulfilled promise of Kennedy's thousand days in office is nearly impossible to measure.

Former Ambassador to Great Britain Joseph Kennedy, Jr., taught his Irish Catholic children a gospel of competition and a distrust of the Soviet Union which he shared with his friend Senator Joe McCarthy. The boy John Kennedy displayed a bookish turn—his father published his senior thesis at Harvard as *Why England Slept*—and while serving in World War II won a purple heart in an authentic, lonely act of heroism. As Massachusetts congressman and senator in the late forties and fifties, John Kennedy charted a stern anti-Communist course in response to early cold war conditions. Yet he stood aloof from Senate cliques and liberal or conservative cabals; he had about him a sense of unpredictability. At times Kennedy's actions appeared the purest expedience—hospitalized during the vote to censure Joe McCarthy, he did not pair against him—but he was capable of forthright independent thinking. It was this complex man who, with the help of his father's money and his own charm, good looks, and intelligence, emerged the winner of the Democratic presidential nomination in 1960.

The election was bound to be close. No Roman Catholic had ever been president, but Kennedy carefully balanced his ticket with the Senate majority leader, Lyndon Johnson of Texas. The Republican nominee, Vice-President Richard Nixon, experienced bad luck and committed serious errors. Perhaps the worst of these was agreeing to face the younger and more photogenic Kennedy in a series of television debates. In a medium that subordinates the message, Kennedy outshone the tired-looking Nixon. Kennedy also employed the religious issue in an effective, if somewhat devious, way. He promised not to let his religion influence his decisions in the White House, and he specifically said he would oppose federal aid to parochial schools. Yet during the primaries he also implied that a vote for him would demonstrate a lack of religious bigotry. Kennedy probably lost more votes than he gained on account of his religion, but the factor helped him carry important states with large Catholic populations like Illinois. Kennedy won the election by a hair's breadth.

With no clear popular mandate, Kennedy moved cautiously. He retained such stalwarts as J. Edgar Hoover of the FBI and Allen Dulles of the CIA. Such decisions indicated not only a desire for governmental continuity, but also a patience with conservatism that unsettled his liberal supporters. The narrowness of his victory in enlarging the size of the obstructive House Rules

Lyndon and Lady Bird get mad
Stern

655

Committee reinforced his prudence. On civil rights Kennedy worked with special care, for Nixon had won almost half the votes of the South. The president lacked—or so he thought—an ideological majority in Congress.

CUBA

Unwilling to jeopardize his precarious popularity and hemmed in by various forces on domestic issues, Kennedy gave greatest attention to foreign policy. Here he inherited a number of serious problems from Eisenhower; the most pressing was Cuba, now in the hands of Fidel Castro. Unknown to Kennedy the presidential candidate, some thousand Cuban refugees had been trained high on a coffee *finca* in the Guatemalan mountains for an invasion of their homeland. It was a contingency plan, but one that generated its own momentum. Sensitive to the charge of weakness, Kennedy wanted to act firmly. So, with the encouragement of the CIA and the Joint Chiefs of Staff, and in the face of a noncommittal stance from Secretary of State Dean Rusk, he determined in April 1961 to go ahead. The result was a fiasco. The refugees landed at the well-defended Bay of Pigs with no escape route to the mountains in case of trouble. Their most important supplies went into a single boat, sunk because air cover was inadequate. But Kennedy must at least be credited with resisting the entreaties of his military advisers to employ American troops and massive bombing.

Why did Kennedy believe such an effort would destroy Castro? Bad advice and inexperience no doubt played a part. So did the hope of recapturing lost properties for American corporations. Hearing often from his family and church and on the floor of Congress about "liberating" Eastern European nations, he may even have been simply naive. If people living under communism yearned for freedom and if communism was evil, the oppressed masses of Cuba would surely revolt at the first opportunity. But such an analysis neglected, among other things, the wretched conditions of the peasantry under dictator Fulgencia Batista, whom Castro had replaced.

After the Bay of Pigs failure, Kennedy became all the more convinced that his administration faced an important testing period demanding great self-sacrifice. He urged and got from Congress more funds for military purposes. He then attended a summit meeting in the fall of 1961 with Soviet Premier Khrushchev in Vienna, but the two men, both in a bristling mood, got on badly. On his return Kennedy stepped up the draft and called for the building of bomb shelters. Accepting advice from former Secretary of State Dean Acheson, he probably overreacted when East Germany constructed the defensive Berlin Wall. In the spring of 1962 with various threats Kennedy followed the Soviet lead in resuming nuclear tests. A compromise of sorts was reached with the USSR over Laos, yet the American troop commitment in neighboring Vietnam grew from some nine hundred men in 1961 to over sixteen thousand two years later.

But the most dangerous and dramatic event of Kennedy's administration occurred closer to home in the fall of 1962. Reacting in part to a United States boycott of Cuban sugar, Fidel Castro decided to let the USSR place intermediate-range missiles in Cuba. When Kennedy finally discovered them, he interpreted the act as a blatant challenge to the existing world balance of power. Some advisers recommended another attack on Cuba, but his brother, Attorney General Robert Kennedy, argued that it was not in the American vein to bomb a small island as the Japanese had bombed Pearl Harbor. After rejecting a Soviet compromise calling for a reciprocal withdrawal of American missiles in Turkey, President Kennedy set up a naval quarantine against additional missile shipments. As the world watched breathlessly, a Soviet ship carrying technical equipment turned back. In exchange for the missile withdrawal, Kennedy pledged no further aggression against Castro. Before the nation Kennedy appeared courageous, and the episode helped the Democrats in the off-year elections. But he had carried the world to the brink of nuclear disaster.

After the trauma of the missile crisis Soviet-American relations underwent a thaw. A "hot line" assured emergency telephone communication between Washington and Moscow. The Test Ban Treaty of 1963 outlawed aboveground nuclear testing. Khrushchev rejected Chinese militance, reaffirming his belief in peaceful coexistence. America sold $250 million of surplus wheat to the Soviets, who had suffered crop failures. Kennedy, in a speech at American University, welcomed a new era of cooperation. Unfortunately, the widening war in Vietnam quickly put an end to this brief interlude of good feelings.

DOMESTIC PROBLEMS

The foreign crises of his administration diverted Kennedy from pressing domestic problems; even so, he seemed unwilling to proceed in these areas because of his thin electoral victory. In 1961, however, Congress passed administration bills for a Peace Corps, lower- and middle-income housing, a higher minimum wage, water pollution control, and area redevelopment which provided funds for retraining the unemployed. By 1963 the president seemed nervous about his poor record in domestic policy and at last awakened to the issue of civil rights He also emphasized the need for tax reform and tax reduction to stimulate spending.

Kennedy had treated large corporations well, and so in April 1962 when the head of United States Steel broke his promise not to raise prices, Kennedy became furious. Several government departments promptly canceled their steel orders, and the Justice Department hinted darkly of antitrust action. After Kennedy himself appeared on television to denounce the big steel interests, the increase was grudgingly rescinded. Many in the business community never forgave the president, although he signed a generous depreciation allowance for that year and reduced corporate income taxes by 20 percent in 1963. Kennedy's important tax-cut proposals for businesses and individuals went into effect in 1964 and, by stimulating the economy, helped to finance the social welfare programs of President Lyndon Johnson's Great Society.

ASSASSINATION

In Dallas, on November 22, 1963, Lee Harvey Oswald assassinated Kennedy. A tidal wave of grief and affection for the martyred president resulted in streets and schools and airports named for him, and millions transferred their affections to his younger brothers Robert and Edward. Congress finally passed most of JFK's programs. Among some scholars a reaction eventually set in against Kennedy, mostly for his aggressive foreign policy. It seems an indisputable point. But if it is generally hard to employ such labels as "liberal" and "conservative," it is difficult to think of Kennedy in this perspective. What can one say about the eager young Kennedy who excitedly denounced the labor boss James Hoffa on grounds that he had "no discrimination or taste or style"? He remains an enigmatic figure.

The civil rights movement

The movement for the equal rights of black people is embedded within the history of twentieth-century American liberalism. For years white liberals supported and worked in important civil rights organizations such as the NAACP and the Urban League. The liberal goal of integration presupposed the superiority of white institutions. In the mid-sixties the coming of black nationalism would challenge liberal values. But in the meantime—from about 1954 to 1965—the civil rights movement seemed to fly forward in a momentous effort to undo our entire history.

Even before the Supreme Court school desegregation decision of 1954, many events prepared the way for the movement: rising incomes and employment opportunities for blacks during World War II; President Truman's order desegregating the armed forces; the Democratic party's insistence on including in its 1948 platform a "fair employment" recommendation; the general drift toward economic security for middle-class blacks in a more urban, industrialized South; and a perceptible growth in social and legal safeguards for individual blacks, achieved through their power in the northern Democratic party. Yet the Court's decision in *Brown* v. *Board of Education* provided an essential catalyst, for it concerned the schooling of the young and threatened the traditional American belief in black inferiority. The case even raised the controversy of miscegenation—blacks marrying whites—after being thrown together in schools at an impressionable age.

Brown, in effect, was the culmination of a series of cases reversing the "separate-but-equal" doctrine set in *Plessy* v. *Ferguson* (1896), which upheld the legality of segregation in public accommodations—and therefore of all other forms of racial discrimination.

When the decision came, most of the South reacted predictably. Racist "White Citizens' Councils" sprang up. Politicians vowed defiance of the Supreme Court decision even though it allowed gradual accommodation with the law. But the courage of small black children—who defied local customs and attended previously all-white schools—inspired the entire black community.

THE GREAT EVENTS

The first great victory of the civil rights movement occurred not in the schools but on the buses of Montgomery, Alabama, in 1955. For more than sixty years Montgomery's black people had ridden in the back of the city's buses. Then, one evening Mrs. Rosa Parks, a handsome black seamstress in rimless glasses, took a seat near the front of the bus. When she refused the

Lunch counter sit-down protest, 1960, Portsmouth, Va.
James A. Walker, Jr.

driver's order to relinquish it to a white man and move to the crowded rear, she was arrested, jailed briefly, and ordered to trial. In response, the pastor of the Dexter Avenue Baptist Church, Martin Luther King, Jr., organized a bus boycott, which proved 90 percent effective. Day after day, blacks walked to and from work or joined in car pools. This Christian tactic of passive resistance troubled the white community—and the bus company almost went bankrupt. Nearly a year later the Supreme Court ruled bus segregation unconstitutional, forcing the city to concede defeat.

The next important episode in Little Rock, Arkansas, two years later put the federal government squarely behind the fledgling movement. Governor Orval Faubus posted National Guardsmen outside Central High School to prevent the attendance of black students. President Eisenhower, who lacked a moral feeling for the issue, at first backed off. Then, goaded by the governor's challenge to the supremacy of the federal government, the president determined to uphold the law. When a howling mob replaced the Guardsmen, he sent a thousand paratroopers to Little Rock to enforce the court order. Senator Russell of Georgia fulminated at "Hitler's storm troopers," but Congress in that year managed to pass a timid Civil Rights Act—the first in almost a century.

The movement then adopted a new method: nonviolent direct action. In Greensboro, North Carolina, early in 1960, two black college students sat down at a Woolworth's lunch counter and ordered coffee. Local lunch counters served one color only, but the blacks stayed seated at this white counter all afternoon. The next day sixteen fellow students joined in, and the following day fifty more repeated the tactic, including a few whites from the Women's College of North Carolina. By the end of the week the tactic had spread to other stores and then to other cities. The effect was electric. Many stores gave way, and—buoyed by the movement's genuine moral strength—the students searched for fresh antagonists.

So far the work seemed easy; the goals could be accomplished almost instantaneously. In a moment a cup of coffee could be served or a bus desegregated. Rarely in modern times has the commonplace had such dignity conferred upon it. By their simplicity these acts paralleled the drama and immediacy of Christian conversion: with such small gestures, a society might give signs of its regeneration. Blacks and whites could join hands and create an instant community singing "Deep in our hearts, we do believe, we shall overcome some day." But harder days lay ahead.

Attention shifted to the Deep South, especially to Mississippi and Alabama. In 1961 "freedom riders," black and white, daringly traveled together on interstate buses and integrated transportation facilities throughout the South. After numerous acts of violence, Attorney General Robert F. Kennedy sent federal marshals into Alabama to protect the riders and requested the Interstate Commerce Commission to ban segregation in bus depots and

March on Washington, 1963
UPI

airports. Then, in 1962, federal troops went to "Ole Miss"—the University of Mississippi—to stop serious rioting and to secure the enrollment of James Meredith, the school's first black student. The following year a confrontation over local issues in Birmingham, Alabama, sparked the use of police dogs, fire hoses, and mass arrests; that year the bombing of a black church killed four small girls. In 1964 three civil rights workers were brutally murdered in Mississippi. FBI men implicated the sheriff, his deputy, and sixteen others, but the local all-white jury would not convict them. Lower-class blacks, now involved in the movement for the first time, began to fight back. The period of urban rioting had begun.

Birmingham at last aroused President Kennedy to action. In a televised speech he spoke movingly to the nation and urged the enactment of a civil rights law that would end segregation in most places of public accommodation. The Democratic party had finally embraced the civil rights movement. The March on Washington of August 23, 1963, brought a gentle army of over two hundred thousand in support of federal legislation. But it took Kennedy's death to bring quick action; the first significant Civil Rights Act was passed in 1964. Further laws in 1965 and 1966 guaranteed voting rights and prohibited discrimination in housing. But in these same years rebellions broke out in urban ghettos. By 1966 the civil rights movement, once it had moved outside the South, was dead. Lower-class whites and blacks perceived even less community of interest than did their middle-class compeers. Instead, they confronted each other over economic matters, for the rising material expectations of both groups remained unfulfilled.

BLACK POWER

The new slogan "Black Power" seemed to promise more violence; it built upon the earlier civil rights movement while at the same time rejecting it. Between 1965 and 1968 large-scale riots took place in Detroit, Los Angeles, Newark, and Washington, D.C. The old moderate organizations like the NAACP gave way to Stokely Carmichael's militant following. "Black is beautiful" implied that assimilation into white society would no longer do. The Black Muslims, a small but growing nationalist sect that first gained nationwide attention in the 1960s, became exceedingly prominent even without its martyred leader, Malcolm X. In a new search for identity blacks dug into the African past, and the ghettos became quiet as they turned in upon themselves.

But the problems of blacks increased with the widening gap between expectations and reality. One young man, George Jackson, symbolized much of the despair. Born in poverty to a black family in 1941, he got in trouble with the police before he was sixteen. Permanently incarcerated since 1960, self-educated largely in solitary confinement, charged with the murder of a

John F. Kennedy
Magnum, Elliott Erwitt

prison guard in 1970—and author of a notable book that same year—he died violently in September 1971 in San Quentin Prison, an enigmatic and contradictory symbol to all Americans. To some he was an image of violence and lawlessness. He led others to violence in his wake: his own younger brother Jonathan died in a wild attempt to gain George's freedom by taking a judge hostage, his lawyer accused of smuggling a gun to him in prison. But to many champions of black power George Jackson symbolized man's indomitable will, particularly the black man's struggle to retain identity and force in the face of brutalizing circumstances. Many admired the brilliance of his untutored writing. To men and women on the Left the appeal lies in his revolutionary political philosophy; to ghetto dwellers he is the prisoner who never could be cowed into any submission: "He wasn't a good nigger, that's for sure," says his mother, "and that's the reason I'm proud of him." For all that he wrote and for all that has been written about him, we know

Fire-gutted buildings in Washington, D.C.
Wide World

almost nothing and understand even less about this permanent prisoner who, as he wrote, could "still smile sometimes."

Lyndon Johnson

In Lyndon Johnson heroic vision vied with petty willfulness. Born in rural Texas, he worked his way through college and then briefly taught poor people in a country school. Extremely ambitious, he was elected to Congress, first the House and then the Senate. There he worked for his native state's oil, natural gas, and aircraft industries; he was one Democrat who always remained in the good graces of businessmen. As Senate Democratic leader in the 1950s, he bent with the times, at first cooperating with Eisenhower and then deserting him as Democrats became more assertive late in the decade. Johnson found the vice-presidency under Kennedy a dull job, although it gave him a national position transcending his regional identity and brought him closer to the White House.

The office of president might have been especially designed for Lyndon Johnson, so readily did he embrace its manifold powers. Remembering the brevity of the 1933–35 New Deal coalition, he lost no time in pushing for the tax cut that would stimulate the economy and provide tax receipts for his myriad Great Society programs. Just six years before with the country in the midst of recession, Congress had overwhelmingly rejected a pump-priming cut; in 1964 it easily passed one. A year after corporate and personal taxes went down sharply, Treasury revenues from taxation actually increased.

During Johnson's presidency Congress passed more laws aiding minorities and the poor than during any comparable period in history. In part the national mood after Kennedy's assassination demanded their enactment. But even before his death a liberal coalition had begun to form that would provide the approving votes in Congress; it included organized labor, moderate southerners, blacks and other minorities, the poor, middle-class liberals, and even many businessmen. These groups allied with the master politician in the White House.

Johnson's favorite Great Society project was the Economic Opportunity Act of 1964—the basis for his "War on Poverty." A perfect issue for the fall campaign, the poverty program brought together and extended a number of laws passed under Kennedy: area redevelopment, retraining of the unemployed, public works, youth employment. Added to these were the Job Corps emphasizing vocational education; VISTA—Volunteers in Service to America, a domestic Peace Corps; and the community action agencies, which in some places sparked alternatives to decaying political machines. The twin goals of providing opportunity and eradicating poverty had wide appeal. In the election year a near-billion-dollar appropriation launched the new programs in grand style.

THE 1964 ELECTION

Johnson had set the stage for his election: government largesse to the poor, a civil rights bill, and a tax cut for the middle class and for corporations. What Republican candidate could hope to challenge the man who, in addition to all this, would campaign on a platform of atonement for the death of John Kennedy? The Republicans came up with a long shot: Senator Barry Goldwater of Arizona. A leader of the radical Right, Goldwater favored a return to modest government spending except for purposes of national defense. He hoped to attract working-class Democrats unhappy over "giveaways" to the poor and to the blacks. And perhaps even a hitherto invisible group of nonvoters would answer his call on election day.

Goldwater ran a unique campaign. At the convention, in tones of high-minded exclusion, he rejected those "who do not care for our cause." In impoverished West Virginia he condemned the poverty program; in Tennessee he stood by his earlier promise to sell parts of the Tennessee Valley Authority (TVA); in Florida he criticized Social Security. The Democrats eagerly publicized his offhand remark in the primaries about defoliating Vietnam jungles with tactical nuclear weapons. Using such statements, they easily portrayed Goldwater as a reckless man lacking true conservative principles. The president deflected attacks on his foreign policy by bombing North Vietnam for allegedly firing on an American destroyer in the Gulf of Tonkin. Johnson won by almost a two-to-one popular margin, an edge nearly as great as FDR's over Alf Landon in 1936.

THE JOHNSON COALITION

Liberal legislation that had not been passed before the election was rushed through Congress in the next session. Major new programs in 1965 included aid to public schools and Medicare (health insurance for the aged under Social Security). Other laws provided funds for model cities, regional health centers, and rent supplements for lower-income families. Big business especially welcomed programs such as job training, which provided skilled workers in areas of scarcity. During the Johnson years, corporations even loaned personnel to job-training centers—in fact a government subsidy to business. Public awareness of ecology lagged, however, and the Great Society appropriated little money to fight water, air, and noise pollution. This, perhaps, marked the limit beyond which businessmen would not go for fear of violating their own self-interest.

The Johnson coalition split apart during 1966. The Vietnam War demanded more and more of the national budget, cutting deeply into domestic appropriations. The president promised "guns *and* butter" but could not deliver both. Additional civil rights acts in 1965 and 1966 troubled the industrial workers in the Democratic party, for the movement had spread to the North, threatening white enclaves and de facto school segregation. The civil rights cause also became a scapegoat for major ghetto insurrections—in New York (1964), Los Angeles (1965), and Newark and Detroit (1967)—as well as the violent rhetoric of black power. No longer were blacks and union-oriented whites capable of easy coexistence within the Democratic party; and no political coalition can long survive unless its members live in reasonable harmony. The "white backlash" influenced several contests during the 1966 congressional elections. The Goldwater candidacy now appeared not so much hopeless as premature.

Vietnam

While the American interest in Southeast Asia goes back only a few decades, other Western countries with rival empires and ideologies began competing there more than a century ago. After the 1860s French colonialism in particular shaped the area's economic and social growth, producing a feudal political structure, a near-absence of industry, and agriculture polarized between subsistence farming and large-scale production of export crops. Not surprisingly, this exploitation prompted nationalist resistance almost from the start. After World War I, in response to French refusal to endorse moderate reforms, Vietnamese nationalists adopted more militant tactics. Under the leadership of the youthful Ho Chi Minh, nationalism and communism blended inseparably. Emerging as the strongest native leader at the end of World War II, he declared Vietnam's independence.

Still unwilling to relinquish their influence, France and Britain struggled to impose neocolonialism in Asia. Anglo-French occupation troops set up a puppet government in Vietnam while the French began a war of reconquest. With American military aid coming in 1950 after the fall of China to the Communists and the outbreak of hostilities in Korea, France lasted against Ho until the collapse of the major inland fortress of Dien Bien Phu in 1954. President Eisenhower resisted pressures from his advisers to intervene, while other conferees meeting at Geneva temporarily divided Vietnam to expedite military disengagement. Yet the Republican administration sabotaged the Geneva agreement to determine the country's future through free elections. By granting enormous sums of economic aid to Premier Ngo Dinh Diem, who in turn prevented meaningful elections, America committed itself to the establishment of a non-Communist South Vietnam. Progress made in the South from 1954 to 1957, however, could not offset indigenous Communist gains at the end of the decade. Eisenhower admitted to the incoming President Kennedy that foreign affairs were a "mess," particularly in Southeast Asia.

One of Kennedy's major campaign thrusts had been against the Republicans' reliance on nuclear weapons. Time and again, the new president stressed the need for flexible approaches to guerrilla fighting in "wars of national liberation." Vietnam was the ideal test of this flexibility. Kennedy began to provide artillery and fighter-bombers to bolster Premier Diem's personalist regime. More important, some sixteen thousand American "advisers" went to Vietnam in an attempt to do what Diem and his followers could not. Initially, these steps augured well; the Communist Vietcong lost territory in 1962. The Kennedy troop increment, following the pledges of the Eisenhower administration, was the second critical decision committing

Barry Goldwater wore glasses without lenses
UPI

the United States to victory in Vietnam. Kennedy agonized over these decisions. He knew that once additional troops went in, the logic of redeeming the investment with even more men would be compelling. Ultimately the Kennedy administration judged Diem a liability, and America withdrew support for him just before Kennedy's own assassination in 1963.

A BROADER WAR

When Lyndon Johnson assumed the presidency, a reversal of American policy in Vietnam might have meant political suicide. Johnson inherited not only the war itself and a shaky government in Saigon dependent on vast American aid, but also Kennedy's principal foreign policy advisers and a domestic political climate requiring that a Democratic president avoid "appeasement" in world affairs. A pretext to bomb North Vietnam came in August 1964 when its ships allegedly attacked at least one American destroyer some twenty miles out to sea. This prompted the Senate to pass, with only two dissenting votes—those of senators Wayne Morse of Oregon and Ernest Gruening of Alaska—the Gulf of Tonkin Resolution which granted the president extraordinary powers to pursue the war. During the last months of 1964, air attacks sought to improve morale in the South, but bombing never brought the settlement its leading proponents anticipated.

After the 1964 election, Johnson moved toward full-scale war. He took action, his memoirs report, "to protect our interests and keep our promises." More than the elusive hope for victory drove Johnson on. A steady, calculated American effort—so the constant refrain went—would convince the North it could not win. (The use of force in 1965 had prevented an alleged Communist takeover in the Dominican Republic.) This argument expanded into a philosophy embracing the entire Far East. The heightened American presence—exceeding five hundred thousand troops by 1967—would "contain" China and convince Communists elsewhere of America's intent to deter attack. Finally, so the reasoning went, a withdrawal would produce the "domino effect" Eisenhower had warned of in eastern Asia: if Vietnam became Communist, other nations would inevitably follow. At home, the Pentagon had developed scores of innovative military techniques that could now be tested. And further pressure came from the Pentagon's new constituency—corporations and labor unions from defense-industry areas who lobbied in Congress for larger and larger military budgets.

Attempts at negotiation failed as long as either side thought it held the upper hand. In 1964 U Thant, secretary general of the United Nations, persuaded most of the major powers to reconvene the Geneva Conference. Johnson demurred. His demand for a non-Communist government in Saigon precluded any hope for an early settlement. At the end of 1965 the president announced a thirty-seven-day bombing halt, a cynical maneuver to

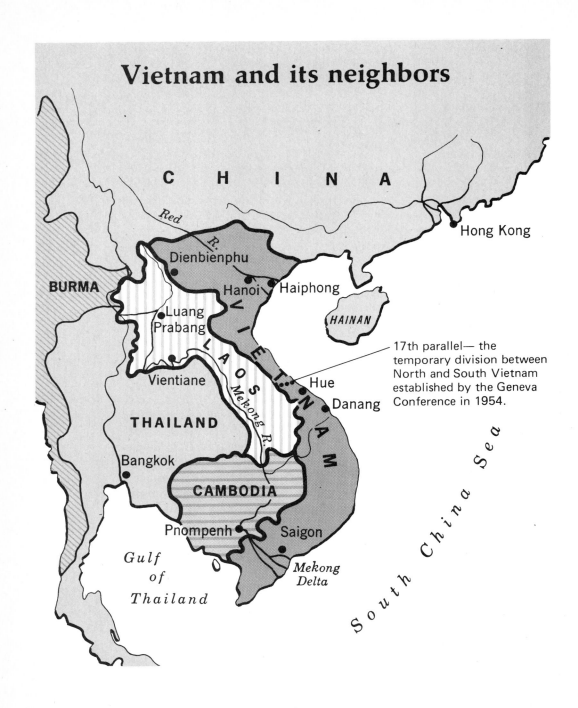

Vietnam and its neighbors

CHINA

Hong Kong

Red R.

Dienbienphu

Hanoi · Haiphong

BURMA

HAINAN

Luang Prabang

LAOS

VIETNAM

17th parallel— the temporary division between North and South Vietnam established by the Geneva Conference in 1954.

Vientiane

Mekong R.

Hue

Danang

THAILAND

Bangkok

CAMBODIA

Gulf of Thailand

Pnompenh

Saigon

Mekong Delta

South China Sea

silence war critics. Nothing came of his accompanying diplomatic flourishes; nothing was expected. Renewed air attacks concentrated on cutting the flow of supplies to the Vietcong. Another effort to rally American opinion in behalf of the war came in a February 1966 meeting between Johnson and the South Vietnamese regime at Honolulu. There President Thieu and Vice-President Ky promised economic reforms and democratic elections. But the Constituent Assembly that resulted remained captive to the same generals who ran the country.

THE ANTIWAR MOVEMENT

A growing antiwar movement in the United States questioned the purpose of the frustrating conflict (as did nearly all of our Western allies). Senator J. William Fulbright attacked the "arrogance of power," writing that "power tends to confuse itself with virtue." America's history of victory, strength, and prosperity made it self-righteous and ready to distort reality. Vietnam taught us, the senator argued, that our political institutions and methods of political bargaining could not flourish in an alien culture. Above all, young people and educators condemned the immorality of the war: the use of napalm which fastened to the skin and burned into the body; cluster bombs; the defoliation of the countryside. In October 1967 some two hundred thousand Americans demonstated in Washington against the war—and against President Johnson.

Growing doubts became convictions after the Tet "New Year" offensive of January–February 1968. Striking simultaneously at all the major cities of the South, the Vietcong inflicted severe casualties and seriously threatened Saigon itself. The American embassy underwent heavy attack. Hue, the ancient capital near the northern dividing line, became enemy territory for several weeks. The efficiency and secrecy of these maneuvers made plain the ineptness of the South Vietnamese troops. Although a bloody counteroffensive resecured the cities, the Vietcong had scored a notable propaganda victory by demonstrating their strength and determination. Tet also destroyed many American illusions about the effectiveness of a limited campaign of firepower from the air and "search-and-destroy" missions on the ground.

With military victory still not in sight and with the domestic economy in the grip of runaway inflation—the war was costing $30 billion annually—the Johnson administration resolved to try diplomacy. Rejecting the American commander General Westmoreland's request for still more troops, Johnson, after his relatively weak showing in the New Hampshire primary in late March 1968, announced that he would not seek reelection and would instead seek peace. Yet almost immediately he seemed to regret offering to meet with the Communists, who were unresponsive at meetings in Paris;

Mangrove forests in Vietnam before and after defoliation
UPI

maybe a little more pressure would, after all, bring success. The change in policy initiated by Johnson—sharply limited bombing, troop reduction, and "Vietnamization" of the war—determined the course of events during four subsequent years. Talks which began in Paris on May 10, 1968, stalled for five months as both sides made impossible demands. Just before the American elections an agreement came, but South Vietnam quickly renounced it. This disunity brought more complications, including a quarrel over the shape of the bargaining table; Johnson's need for even partial victory impeded his quest for peace.

From the outset the new Republican president, Richard Nixon, pursued the Johnsonian goal of limited victory. And the war dragged on. In June 1969, after a meeting with President Thieu in Guam, Nixon announced his "doctrine" that Asians would have to fight their own wars without the support of American ground troops. But in April 1970 American and South Vietnamese troops briefly invaded Cambodia to destroy enemy supplies and sanctuaries; in February 1971 a similar offensive was launched in Laos. The Senate demonstrated its changed mood by repealing the Tonkin Gulf Resolution, eighty-one to ten, and by threatening to impose a cutoff date on the presence in Vietnam of American troops. Then in June 1971 the *New York Times* began serial publication of a secret report commissioned by Secretary of Defense Robert McNamara in 1968; these exhaustive "Pentagon Papers," which traced the history of American involvement in the war, exposed the dubious assumptions and blunders of a generation of American leaders. The Nixon administration unsuccessfully attempted to halt their publication and prosecuted Daniel Ellsberg for releasing them. Another revelation concerning Vietnam was the unmitigated horror of the massacres at My Lai and Song My. In what has been called "a slaughter caused by mass psychosis," American soldiers killed scores of defenseless civilians in these towns. The killings, hushed up by superior officers, occurred in the early spring of 1968—just a short time after the frightening experience of Tet.

In 1972, while Nixon hoped for a quiet winding down of the war, North Vietnamese troops in the South attacked major northern cities. The war started up all over again, although fewer than fifty thousand American troops remained in Vietnam on June 30, 1972—a 90 percent reduction from 1968. Nixon mined North Vietnamese harbors including Haiphong's and bombed the North brutally. At the same time he promised to withdraw all American troops four months after the release of American prisoners of war. Peace talks became serious around election time, 1972, when Nixon and his foreign policy adviser Henry Kissinger sincerely believed a settlement was at hand. When they were disappointed, the president in December ordered the bombing of Hanoi; his planes hit a hospital and populated areas of the city. Heavy criticism, both at home and abroad, may have caused him to suspend the bombing; but the incident revealed his unpredictability. Whether the bombings had the desired effect is unclear. Perhaps in spite of them a truce finally came to Vietnam on January 27, 1973.

THE 1968 ELECTION

Johnson's popularity plummeted because of Vietnam. As the war raged interminably—bringing a cost in lives and money far out of proportion to any advantage that might accrue—a distrust for established institutions spread, particularly among young people. Momentarily, hopes rose for purgation of the Democratic party as Senator Eugene McCarthy of Minnesota and Senator Robert Kennedy of New York spoke out against the war. The dramatic Vietcong offensive early in 1968 during Tet (the Vietnamese lunar New Year) gave their message the tang of truth. McCarthy, with his white hair and handsome profile, looked a gallant man. His impressive showing against Johnson in the early New Hampshire primary probably contributed to the president's decision to withdraw from the coming election and to reduce the bombing of North Vietnam. But McCarthy lacked political savvy and could not compete with Kennedy, who attracted blacks and Mexican Americans—essential constituencies, he believed, for any Democratic presidential candidate. On the night of his victory in the all-important California primary, Robert Kennedy was killed by a Jordanian immigrant, Sirhan Sirhan, who thought him anti-Arab. With Martin Luther King's slaying by a white racist just weeks before, it all seemed a nightmarish reflection of the war itself.

The Republican candidate for president in 1968, Richard Nixon, had a long career of government service. He became nationally famous during the forties when his relentless prodding during congressional hearings revealed that an important figure in the Roosevelt administration, Alger Hiss, had probably been a Communist. Nixon coasted into the Senate following a 1950 California campaign in which he permitted his manager to characterize his female opponent as the "pink lady." (Some of her people called Nixon an anti-Semite.) With a voting record that alarmed neither Republican conservatives nor liberals, Nixon became Eisenhower's vice-president and then nearly defeated Kennedy in 1960. His second chance came in 1968.

The Democratic nominee turned out to be Vice-President Hubert Humphrey—not a man to chart an abrupt new course for his party. He had too consistently and vehemently supported President Johnson on Vietnam. The antiwar young turned out in force at the Chicago Democratic Convention to precipitate what an eminent study group later termed a "police riot." In the last weeks of his campaign Humphrey finally called for a halt to all bombing of North Vietnam and for immediate peace negotiations, but Nixon, too, had a "plan" for ending the war. Nixon also hit hard at the decisions of the Supreme Court under Chief Justice Earl Warren. In a "law-and-order" campaign the Court's decisions protecting the rights of suspected

Mrs. Coretta King in mourning.
Wide World

criminals were blamed for steeply rising crime rates. With Alabama Governor George Wallace's American party drawing conservatives away from Nixon, Humphrey almost won a victory in November. Wallace, employing antiblack and economic themes, received almost 10 million votes. But in an election a near-miss is as good as a mile, and Richard Nixon, elected with 43 percent of the vote, would make the critical decisions that lay ahead.

The social spectrum

Many Americans in the 1950s shared a mood of cultural exhaustion with the rest of the world, partly a matter of catching up on material things lost in depression and war, and partly a revulsion against the excesses of ideology. Communism and fascism alike seemed absurd romantic visions, vast over-simplifications to apply to a complex and varied society. The sociologist Daniel Bell proclaimed an "end to ideology." The managers and piecemeal reformers alone fit the new era.

Against the technicians' view of things—so naturally suited to the gradual and "sensible" steps in the escalation of the Vietnam War—sprang up a romantic temperament among the young of the middle and later 1960s. This inchoate counterculture grew in part from the adolescent styles of the 1950s, and especially the belief in young people as separate from the rest of society

675

rather than simply as apprentices to adult roles. The youth culture also grew because of its opposition to the conventional temper of bureaucracy. The young people in the civil rights movement had acquired a moral passion and communal vision incompatible with the routine impersonality of social institutions. University revolts came in part from the practicing of a virtue that universities have traditionally preached but perhaps too often strayed from: relentless and open inquiry even at the expense of breaking with established intellectual forms.

In the early sixties the youth movement was largely a phase of American reformism. A moderate peace movement, beginning in the 1961 Berlin crisis and ending in the 1963 signing of the nuclear test-ban treaty, worked through organizations of the old Left. Even the militant SNCC (Student Non-Violent Coordinating Committee) originated in and cooperated with the civil rights movement. Students for a Democratic Society, the radical SDS of the later sixties, also began on a standard liberal course with roots in older reformist groups. But SDS was reborn in 1962 at Port Huron, Michigan, where two University of Michigan graduate students drafted the "Port Huron Statement." Its call for the rehabilitation of existing institutions was familiar, but its tone—communal, antibureaucratic, student-oriented—anticipated the new styles and militance of the years ahead.

THE UNIVERSITIES

One of the places where radicals could exercise their own right of free speech was the university. Such schools as Wisconsin and Berkeley cherished a reform tradition and even in the fifties bred a bohemian radical fringe. But at Berkeley in the fall of 1964, after a raucous demonstration against a House Un-American Activities Committee hearing and a restriction on campus political recruiting, a full-scale student revolt threw the university into turmoil for months. Similar outbreaks occurred elsewhere, in protest against the Vietnam War, notably at Columbia in 1968 and at Harvard in 1969.

Put simply, the universities still depended on regulations imposed from above, while the student activists wanted participatory democracy. The administrators favored bureaucratic procedure through which to express grievances; faced with institutional inertia, students turned to demonstrations. Many faculty sympathized with the cry for more elective courses and varied curricula, which could rest on the traditional commitment to imaginative inquiry. But the demand to address social problems beyond the university distressed professors who wished to escape the burdens of outside involvement or who saw a conflict between them and liberal studies. Student power in fact raised the question of how much authority the faculty itself exercised. Universities such as Michigan State had cooperated on military intelligence projects of dubious academic value, and had even tolerated classified research for the federal government, violating the spirit of free inquiry.

DRUGS

A number of influences worked against the activists' political goals. Many students remained apathetic; for others, the world of drugs satisfied the urge to break with convention and created an air of comradely danger that drew a clear line against most adults. Smoking marijuana particularly created a feeling of community and, for many, seemed to blur the outlines of individual identity. Stronger "head" drugs—mescaline, LSD, STP, "speed"—enjoyed a more ephemeral popularity, presumably because of their occasional tendency to induce transient psychoses. The use of heroin spread, especially among the poor: its thoroughly addictive character fed a rising crime rate and disrupted social cohesion in large cities.

George Wallace
Richard Howard, Bethel

The centers of drug use—the famous hippie colony of Haight-Ashbury in San Francisco and the East Village in New York—rapidly fell prey to exploitive commerce or pervasive crime. Events such as the 1969 Woodstock rock festival in New York State, though tainted by middle-class adventure, caught some of the good commerce among the young. But only a year later, cat Altamont, California, a Hell's Angels motorcycle gang injured many people and committed a pointless murder during a Rolling Stones rock festival. Altamont was, in the phrasing of the young rock poet Don McLean, "the day the music died." The unwanted ingredient that apparently destroyed the counterculture was violence—so foreign to the life style the young attempted to practice and yet, in the words of black militant H. Rap Brown, "as American as cherry pie."

THE ARTS

Many of the American arts, nevertheless, reflected the pervasive influence of the youth culture. Folk music, which enjoyed a revival during the late fifties in Greenwich Village, especially adapted to political statement and was used by such performers as the young Bob Dylan, a conscious imitator of Woody Guthrie. Some of the early protest songs, sounding pastoral notes of innocence and pacifism, carried their listeners back over the fifties and Second World War to the Great Depression and the early labor movement. Rock 'n' roll music of the fifties, embodied in Elvis Presley, combined with folk to create folk rock. Hard rock curiously fused opposites: folkish melodies and the modern technology of electrical amplification. One group, the Who, experimented with rock opera; the musical *Hair* spawned a score of imitators; and Catholic churches conducted folk-rock masses.

Movies also catered to the young, for most moviegoers are under twenty-five. While slick films appeared more frequently than ever for the sole purpose of making money, the outstanding productions recalled the industry's great interwar achievements. Stanley Kubrick's *Doctor Strangelove* and *2001* with their mad fantasies and psychedelic visions, or Arthur Penn's *Bonnie and Clyde*, interspersing blandness and violence with the comic, especially captured some of the nation's darkest thoughts. *Alice's Restaurant* and *Zabriskie Point* seriously attempted to portray the shortcomings as well as the virtues of the counterculture. *Easy Rider* capitalized on a vicious stereotype of the South, while Norman Mailer and Andy Warhol brought new techniques of timing and subject matter to the experimental film world.

Drama as well as cinema fell victim to the pervasive interest in nudity. Some of the most interesting plays not only emphasized sexual freedom, such as *Dionysus in '69*, but also contributed lively innovations in staging and sometimes drew audiences into the play. But although off-Broadway theaters staged interesting works by such native talents as Edward Albee and Leroi Jones, foreign authors predominated.

In painting, a fresh new influence came into view in the fifties: Jackson Pollock practiced an impulsive yet purposeful style dubbed "action painting." He dripped paints onto a huge canvas, employing the motions of his whole body and aiming the colors with raw energy rather than carrying them on the tip of his brush. Pollock's radicalism concretely expressed the varied strains of the sixties. "Happenings" enjoyed a vogue, including a 1963 piece that gradually destroyed itself by burning, sawing, and beating itself to death. In his "pop" art Andy Warhol—who most successfully commandeered the media in the name of art—took inspiration from Roy Lichtenstein's cartoon parody: maddening rows of Brillo cartons, an eight-hour film of a man sleeping. Such names as Mark Rothko, Jasper Johns, and Frank Stella show the varied directions of modern American painting.

WOMEN'S LIBERATION

During World War II women had taken "men's jobs" and made some short-term economic gains, but generally by the fifties the force and conviction of the turn-of-the-century feminist movement had been forgotten. Time, transportation, and babysitting problems discouraged all but the most determined women from combining a socially mandatory marriage with professional training. In 1955, for instance, a smaller percentage of graduate students were women than thirty years before; and women in college took typically "feminine" courses in elementary education, home economics, or secretarial skills.

Although many men in the youth culture or radical movements of the mid-sixties rejected regular jobs, most women continued to perform the traditional chores. In the film *Alice's Restaurant* women appeared either as cooks or as sexual objects. Similarly, the world of rock music remained overwhelmingly a man's domain with women no better off than in middle-class culture. Janis Joplin for a long time worked for a group called Big Brother and the Holding Company, and females were notably present only in country-western or folk music and as black or "soul" singers.

Many women in the later 1960s rather suddenly concluded that their male counterparts had exploited them as cooks, secretaries, and bed partners. The new women activists of the late sixties sought no less than a transformation of their place and image in American society. One of the first major American books on the subject, Betty Friedan's *The Feminine Mystique* (1963) attacked the restrictions of domesticity. For too long the problems of suburban living, the child-centered philosophies of psychologists, and the pronouncements of Freudian analysts—the main subjects in women's magazines—had conspired to frustrate the independence and creativity of women caught up in an inflexible family structure. The year following publication of her book Friedan organized NOW, the National Organization for Women, which lobbied for equal pay for performing identical jobs, child care centers, and the reform of abortion laws. WITCH (originally the Women's International Terrorist Conspiracy from Hell), perhaps the most notorious of the women's liberation groups, swept into existence on Halloween 1968 in New York City. This group, with "covens" in major cities, demonstrated at the Bridal Fair held in Chicago in February 1969, asserting that the bridal industry and its magazines (edited principally by men) helped to perpetuate the myth that a woman's fulfillment is found only through a husband and children. At Atlantic City a year earlier, women had picketed the Miss America pageant. Miss America, they believed, represented "the degrading mindless-boob-girlie symbol" and was a walking commercial for the pageant's sponsors.

The psychological barriers between women and men are reinforced continually in the media. Advertising affects men as well as women, but women purchase 75 percent of consumer goods. Women's magazines are best sellers; they aim, say the feminists, only to make women buy material goods. Television soap operas, too, attempt to support women's role as superconsumers; the males are professionals and the women homemakers. Even children's

Roy Lichtenstein, Fastest Gun
Courtesy of Betty Asher

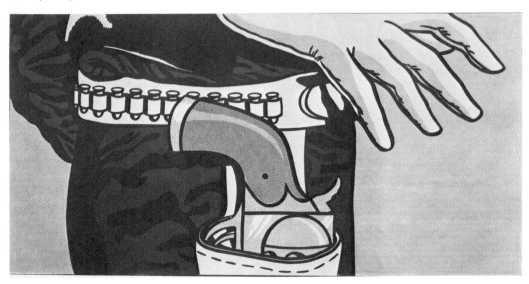

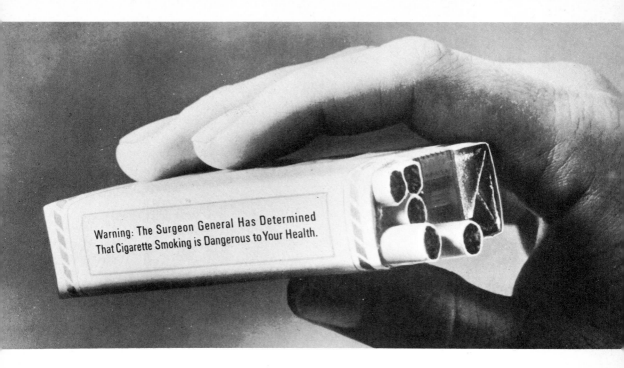

programs offer mostly stereotyped, passive females. Feminists argue that the so-called sexual revolution, glamorized by Hugh Hefner's *Playboy*, has not freed women but simply made them more available. They resent advertisements presenting women as "sexual objects," and especially ads that place women in sexual competition; nudity in movies, they hold, also reduces women to subjects of display.

Women began in the mid-sixties to meet in small groups for "consciousness raising," a frank and personal sharing of experiences. The reliance on personal contact makes those reached more militant and committed to the cause, for it exposes the indignities they encounter. An important part of the experience comes in breaking down the kinds of distrust bred by a system wherein the attachment to an individual man is expected to be the ultimate in a woman's experience.

Some of the literature by women on their freedom is philosophically akin to the radical Left in its assumption that only revolution against the capitalist system to produce socialism will bring about equality for women. Many radical feminists believe that a drastic change in our economic values must precede a turnabout in the traditional masculine view of women. They argue that equal pay for identical jobs performed by men and women is, by itself, tantamount to the "token" integration blacks have experienced in their efforts to win equal status within the social system.

681

Nixon's first term

At his 1968 inaugural Richard Nixon offered hope mainly for an improvement in foreign relations. "We are entering," he correctly noted, "an era of negotiation." A month after taking office he flew to Europe, where he encouraged West German leaders in their search for an easing of tensions with the East and also attempted to improve relations with Charles de Gaulle of France.

But Nixon's greatest ambition was an agreement with the Soviets on strategic arms limitation. Believing in negotiation from a position of strength, he first urged Congress to pass a $2.5 billion antiballistic missile (ABM) plan, which edged through the Senate in 1970 by a single vote. ABM sites already protected Moscow, which had also deployed sophisticated missiles with 25-megaton MIRV multiple-reentry warheads. As Nixon predicted, strategic arms–limitation talks (SALT) in Helsinki led to a treaty, signed during the president's visit to Russia in May 1972. Subsequently approved by the Senate, the settlement with Premier Kosygin also contained provisions for limiting certain offensive weapons.

Except for a resurgence of trouble in Vietnam during 1972 President Nixon seemed to be making headway against international tensions throughout the world. Major powers, following West German Chancellor Willy Brandt's lead, signed an important treaty in 1971 neutralizing Berlin and recognizing a Polish boundary claim. In Africa Nixon stayed clear of the Nigerian Civil War but afterward tried to provide food for secessionist Biafra and other areas. Developments went badly for the United States in Latin America; in the face of adverse events in Chile, Peru, and Ecuador, Nixon seemed ready to accept the desire there for economic and political independence, but "unofficial" trade pressures were exerted.

In the Middle East trouble continued unabated throughout Nixon's term. The Arab states demanded Israeli withdrawal from territory occupied during the Six-Day War of 1967. Israelis first wanted assurances of future security; some even wanted permanent possession of Jerusalem and the west bank of the Jordan River. Sporadic violations of the cease-fire occurred almost daily. In 1969 United Arab Republic President Nasser of Egypt proposed a plan embodying nonbelligerence and territorial integrity for all nations; on the same day Nixon accepted a French offer for Big Four talks at the United Nations. But Israel rejected Nasser's proposals and resisted American pressures to negotiate. In 1970 Secretary of State William Rogers finally arranged for a renewal of indirect talks. But Palestinian Arab guerrillas ignored the cease-fire and fighting broke out in Jordan. The Palestinians hijacked a total of four commercial jetliners, holding them hostage and then blowing up the empty vehicles. Secretary Rogers tried to maintain a middle ground against strong pro-Israeli groups in the United States; he backed Israel's desire not to relinquish territory before a settlement but also advocated a partial Israeli pullout in the Sinai peninsula and the reopening of the Suez Canal. No significant progress toward peace came about in the area.

A briefer conflict flared in Asia during 1971 as a result of a political and religious struggle between East and West Pakistan. Culminating in the defeat of West Pakistan, the short war led to the creation of the new nation of Bangla Desh in the area formerly known as East Pakistan. Ironically, the United States and the People's Republic of China found themselves both supporting the defeated West Pakistanis. In his State of the World message of February 1971, Nixon had already made the most explicit of a series of friendly overtures to China. In April an American table tennis team and three newsmen visited Peking; they were the first western visitors since the communist takeover. Prime Minister Chou En-lai stated that more newsmen would be welcome, and Nixon on the same day announced the end of certain trade restrictions against China. Then Henry Kissinger, Nixon's influential head of the National Security Council, secretly visited Peking in July 1971. Finally, in October, Communist China entered the United Nations and Taiwan (Nationalist China) was expelled.

From these salutory developments emerged President Nixon's stunning goodwill trip to China. He landed in Peking on February 20, 1972. At the end of five days of conferences Nixon and Chou En-lai issued a joint communiqué pledging peaceful coexistence and recognizing Taiwan as an "internal" Chinese issue. It was an amazing and, for most Americans, a welcome feat by the man who had become nationally prominent riding the crest of a pervasive anticommunism in the late forties and early fifties. The trip to China and the subsequent trip to the Soviet Union raised hopes for world peace.

LEGISLATIVE PROBLEMS

Nixon's domestic problems required something more than even his considerable political skill could provide. His worst difficulty was a dangerous inflationary spiral. The president's economic advisors, Paul McCracken and Arthur F. Burns, attempted to scale down the budget without precipitating severe recession. Johnson's Great Society programs suffered sharp cuts and defense spending declined, although enormous federal budget deficits persisted. "Tight money" (high interest rates)—accomplished by a raising of the Federal Reserve banks' rediscount rate—completed the first steps of Nixon's economic program. Congress by only a narrow margin refused support for Nixon's controversial and costly aircraft, the supersonic transport (SST),

Richard Nixon speaking extemporaneously, September 1968
UPI

which threatened harm to the environment. In 1971, a freeze on prices and wages intensified antiinflationary pressures. But as late as 1972, unemployment remained near 6 percent and inflation persisted.

Nixon also moved to balance the American trade deficit with foreign countries. When West Germany "floated" the mark to curtail the inflow of dollars, the United States in August 1971 took steps to devalue the dollar internationally, contingent upon reciprocal moves by strong-currency nations like Germany and Japan. A brief 10 percent surcharge on imports also helped to improve the balance of foreign trade and to force other countries to cooperate with Nixon's plans for the international economy.

The Republican administration proposed its own program of welfare reform. Under the proposal the Social Security Administration would provide each family of four with a minimum annual income of $1600, with the head of the household permitted to earn another $720 without reduction of the initial amount. Liberal Democrats found the program ungenerous but tended to see it as a step in the right direction. Nixon, however, never exerted his full influence for its passage, and partisan Democrats and conservative Republicans were obstructive.

Meanwhile, Nixon's antiwar critics found reductions of troop strength in Vietnam too gradual as well as disingenuous because of a greater reliance on air power. The expeditions into Cambodia sparked nationwide campus protests, and nervous National Guardsmen killed four demonstrating students at Kent State University, Ohio, in April 1970. Nixon apparently believed himself the victim of unfair coverage on these events by the "liberal" eastern press, a message Vice-President Agnew widely disseminated in an inimitable flowery rhetoric. In the 1970 campaign Agnew singled out war protesters for criticism, praised "law and order," and chided senators who had helped defeat the nominations of the southern judges Clement Haynesworth and G. Harrold Carswell to the Supreme Court. Voters did not respond, however, and Democrats retained control of both houses of Congress as they had since the 1950s.

Nixon's actions on such domestic problems as school desegregation and water and air pollution received both criticism and applause. This public reaction suggested that he took a moderate course on controversial domestic issues. The president's own rhetoric, however, revealed the innate conservatism of his administration. He could not help revealing his feelings against the Black Panthers on trial for conspiracy in New York; he denounced Charles Manson before a jury had found him guilty of murder; he stood behind Governor Nelson Rockefeller's use of force in the brutal quelling of an Attica, New York, prison riot; he also criticized that state's liberal abortion law.

Despite little progress in human relations, Americans landed on the moon during Nixon's administration. The historic landing of astronauts Neil Armstrong and Edwin Aldrin took place on July 20, 1969. The moon landing,

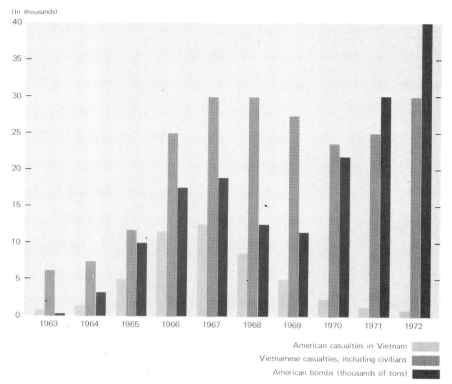

(In thousands)

American casualties in Vietnam
Vietnamese casualties, including civilians
American bombs (thousands of tons)

War in Vietnam, 1963–1972

Nixon's trips to China and Russia, and slowly returning prosperity late in 1972 all boded well for the president as the 1972 election approached. Moreover, Nixon had all the advantages of an incumbent. He raised an enormous campaign fund before a new law required disclosure of donors' names. He used his cabinet officers and Vice-President Agnew to wage the campaign while he remained above the fray in the White House. He managed not to get identified with an espionage scandal involving a break-in at Democratic National Headquarters in the Watergate, a large apartment complex in Washington, even though all the trails led to the White House staff; later it was shown that Attorney General John Mitchell knew of the dealings—and that Nixon or his staff, or both, had been directing widespread espionage and other activities reminiscent of similar acts in totalitarian states. And in domestic politics he found a decisive issue—not racism perhaps, but certainly race. Pollsters agreed that Nixon's unsympathic stance toward blacks was the key issue pulling normally Democratic ethnic voters toward him.

To the Democratic nominee George McGovern disaster came in his choice of Senator Thomas Eagleton of Missouri as vice-presidential candidate. Eagleton, despite his claim not to have any "skeletons in the closet," kept secret three periods of psychiatric treatment, two involving shock therapy, for severe mental depression. Statistically speaking, mental illness recurs, and the rest periods required to avoid it are not available in the presidency. Given also its control over nuclear weapons, the presidency is almost the only elected office to which a formerly mentally ill person should not aspire. The problem could not be solved by compassion, a fact which many of McGovern's supporters could not understand. When the disclosure came McGovern at first stood fast by his candidate; but when Eagleton would not gracefully withdraw he was forced off the ticket. This affair was a stroke of incredibly bad luck. McGovern never recovered from it. Because he backed

Senator George McGovern

down on supporting Eagleton, McGovern, while constantly facing the media in spontaneous situtations, received ruthless criticism for any inconsistency; President Nixon, safe in the White House, could avoid open meetings with the press entirely.

McGovern's moment of recognition about the campaign may have come on October 11 en route from Boston to Minneapolis. As the 727 jet sailed over oceans of clouds, he listened to a seven-minute tape given him that morning in Boston. It contained a Vietnam veteran's emotional recollections of the continuing war:

> I don't think the American people really, really understand war and what's going on. We went into villages after they dropped napalm and the human beings were fused together like pieces of metal that had been soldered. . . . We have jets that drop rockets and in the shells they have penny nails and those nails—one nail per square inch for about the size of a football field—you can't believe what they do to a human being. . . . And what bothers me is, when you're there you accept it. You rationalize it. You condone it. You say it's right because they are the enemy.

At that moment McGovern may have seen that his candidacy against the war and the president would be in vain. The American people, glad our troops were coming home, wanted to know nothing of the intensified air war that rained terror over Vietnam. Nixon won reelection by a 61 to 39 percent majority, yet Democrats actually increased their strength in the Senate and remained well ahead in the House.

Space

As American astronauts Neil Armstrong and Edwin "Buzz" Aldrin walked on the moon on July 20, 1969, an estimated quarter of humanity watched via communications satellites which beamed their images to earth. To some, the achievement represented an opportunity for international progress— "One small step for a man, one giant leap for mankind," as Armstrong put it. But to others, the landing of *Apollo XI* was simply the culmination of an overly expensive effort, undertaken at the cost of domestic and other scientific goals—a technological triumph which signified little.

The Apollo project, born of damaged American pride, reflected the effort to overcome an early Russian lead in the "space race." Russia launched the first artificial satellite, *Sputnik I*, in October 1957, an event which set off deep concern in America about the country's scientific and technological capacities. In fact, it was a time of significant international cooperation among scientists—the International Geophysical Year had begun that summer—but the political atmosphere was highly charged with troop movements in the Middle East and memories still strong of the Hungarian revolt the previous year. The Soviet challenge generated not only the space race but also an overall upsurge in domestic spending for scientific education. Although the United States readily responded with its *Explorer I* satellite in January 1958, confirming the existence of the Van Allen radiation belt, and with *Vanguard I,* in March, testing solar cells, the Russians remained ahead. Their *Sputnik II* (November 1957) had orbited a dog in space, making clear the possibility of manned flight. Yet Eisenhower's science advisers set no target date for a manned moon landing, maintaining that the prohibitive cost—$20 to $40 billion—would hardly be worth the limited scientific results. Nonetheless, Project Mercury, organized in October 1958, revealed plans to orbit and recover a manned craft and study the astronauts' reactions in space flight.

Then on April 12, 1961, Russian cosmonaut Yuri Gagarin orbited in space for nearly two hours, traveling once around the earth. Less than a month later, the United States responded with Alan Shepard's 15-minute suborbital flight. President Kennedy soon announced to Congress the American goal—to land a man on the moon and retrieve him safely by 1970. Yet as the decade wore on, American space efforts continued to be responses to Russian achievements. Russian cosmonaut Alexei Leonov became the first man to "walk" in space on March 18, 1965. Five days later, the National Aeronautics and Space Administration set up Project Gemini, a series of extended flights involving rendezvous, docking maneuvers, and controlled descents and landings; within three months, an American also "walked" in space.

Despite fatalities in both the Russian and American space programs in 1967, as well as the slackening of manned efforts by the Russians, the United States proceeded toward its goal, and in October 1968 began Project Apollo. As Apollo proceeded, the initial preoccupation with beating the Soviets to the moon diminished somewhat; a lead over the Russians in prolonged flight had been established by Gemini, and Vietnam steadily replaced all of the United States' other international concerns. Domestic discontent opened criticism about space program funding; the impressive technological mastery of outer space paled when ghetto rebellions highlighted pressing problems closer to home. Even scientists complained that the Apollo program took an excessive share of the government scientific budget, especially as funding leveled off in all but defense-related research at the height of the war.

As Eisenhower's advisers predicted, the effort to put a man on the moon cost over $25 billion. Meanwhile, the federal government continued to support a number of less glamorous but more potentially profitable space programs, such as the unmanned interplanetary explorations—Rangers and Surveyors to provide information about the moon, Mariners and Vikings to collect data on Mars and Venus. While Apollo got the publicity, Americans got accustomed to immediate transmission of television images around the world via satellite along with their evening weather reports. As these technological "spinoffs" became commonplace, as public opinion against government policy in Vietnam mounted, and as the ecology movement turned attention to the scarce resources of the earth, public interest in the manned space effort faded. Nearly everyone with access to television watched at least part of the first moon landing; the subsequent Apollo missions, whatever their scientific merit, fell flat as spectacle.

Nixon's second administration

Nixon's triumphal election victory renewed his sense of purpose. He moved to test his belief that state and local officials should take many burdens from a bloated federal bureaucracy. More private enterprise and fewer government controls would revive the lagging economy. The ballyhooed counterculture of the sixties, Nixon felt, destroyed America's true values: order, productivity, family life, self-reliance. "The work ethic," he said again and again, "must replace the welfare ethic." Buoyed by a vital response from Middle America, Nixon set about organizing "four more years." Yet the Watergate scandal soon tarnished his new hopes, and the man so exultant in early 1973 resigned in disgrace only eighteen months later.

VIETNAM, THE MIDDLE EAST, AND DETENTE

Nixon and Kissinger had pursued peace with honor in Vietnam for four years. The combatants, stalemated on the battlefield, sought victory at the bargaining table. When Kissinger returned to Paris for talks shortly after the American election, Le Duc Tho demanded a virtual capitulation: a radical, Marxist regime must replace Thieu's pro-West dictatorship. Angered, Nixon ordered an armada of B-52s to attack North Vietnam twenty-four hours a day "until they are ready to negotiate." The massive renewal of war stunned many people in the United States, but worried leaders in Hanoi yielded in early January 1973. (China and Russia, they feared, might look the other way while Nixon quite literally destroyed North Vietnam.) Both sides rapidly agreed to a cease-fire called the Paris Accords, which ended American involvement in Southeast Asia. The United States promised to withdraw fifty thousand GIs still in the region and dismantle its military installations there. In return, the North Vietnamese would release American POWs. An international conference, both sides anticipated, would neutralize all Indochina and impose coalition governments in Laos, Cambodia, and South

Vietnam. In this "peace with honor" the Paris Accords copied, almost exactly, the Geneva agreements of 1954. Even the cease-fire soon fell apart, the Communists renewing their attacks in the South when Thieu tried to regain disputed territory. By the middle of 1974 some forty-eight thousand more soldiers had died in South Vietnam, while guerrillas in Cambodia locked the pro-American regime of Lon Nol in its capital, Phnom Penh.

But Nixon and Kissinger, now secretary of state, took solace from their trials in Vietnam with new, sophisticated initiatives in the Middle East. On the Jewish holy day of Yom Kippur (October 1973), Egyptian and Syrian armies attacked Israel, apparently with Russia's tacit approval. Assured of diplomatic support from Washington, Israeli commander Moshe Dayan brilliantly parried the Arab assault, then surrounded Egypt's Third Army in the Sinai and drove rapidly toward Damascus, Syria's capital. Other Arab nations—principally Saudi Arabia, Libya, and the small states around the Persian Gulf—retaliated with an oil embargo against all those who supported Israel, especially the United States. But then escalation stopped: Moscow refused direct aid to its clients in the Middle East, and Nixon wisely rejected suggestions to break the embargo by force. Instead, he took up a bold plan conceived by Kissinger. In settling, or at least easing, the mosaic of hatreds in the Middle East, the United States could insure Israel's survival, end the oil embargo, and seize the diplomatic initiative from Russia. During a month of dramatic "shuttle diplomacy," the secretary played upon Egypt's disappointment with Soviet leaders and need for America's technology, reminded Israeli rulers of their dependence upon the United States for weapons, and pointed out the Arab's huge losses of oil revenue. The pieces to the complex puzzle came together in a cease-fire agreement which ended the embargo and changed American policy. Now neutral, rather than pro-Israeli, the United States quickly gained ascendancy in the Middle East.

Despite this success, Nixon and Kissinger knew that their nation's vital interests still centered in Europe. Diplomacy by small courtesy continued, but detente with the Soviet Union required substance, not congenial visits. The Strategic Arms Limitation Talks (SALT) bogged down amid nuclear technicalities and the opposition of military commanders on both sides. Eventually the negotiators agreed to an odd formula: each country could build the next generation of multiwarheaded missiles, but then they must stop the arms race. At most this only postponed hard decisions for a few more years. Trade betweeen the two superpowers also fell far short of earlier hopes. Detente, that mutual understanding to avoid war despite their differences, guaranteed tolerance, it seemed, but not amity. It also complicated America's relations with the rest of Europe, whose leaders, freed from the bugaboo of a hostile Soviet Union, more and more pursued an independent course.

DOMESTIC TROUBLES

Just as he aimed at restoring global balance, Nixon yearned to bring stability inside the United States. Never much interested in economics, the president took refuge in the classical clichés. Ending government "interference" with business could restore growth and halt inflation. So he canceled all government controls early in 1973, but prices shot upward rapidly. By mid-summer food shortages forced the administration to clamp down once again, but then in 1974 Nixon abandoned all regulations. The country had moved far from the simplicities of an earlier day, and as the oil embargo vividly showed, American leaders no longer enjoyed freedom of action. Then, as the Watergate scandals gradually unfolded, a besieged Nixon lost all interest in the economy, which drifted into double-digit inflation and the worst unemployment since the late 1930s. Economic woes did dampen the energies of the sixties, and more and more the nation turned away from reform toward more mundane pursuits. Americans now worried about their own jobs, and college students pushed to get into the right professional school. Ironically, Nixon achieved that quieting of voices he had asked for years before. But the new tone which settled over the country did not cloud interest in one of the greatest political dramas in the nation's history. For this conservative president was responsible for a constitutional upheaval and renewed divisions within American society.

Watergate

During the difficult days of 1970, Nixon and his White House staff thought themselves besieged by a hostile press while "radicals" threatened to undermine the country. To defend "national security," they resorted to illegal tactics. The president, for example, worried about leaks in his negotiations with the Vietnamese and the Russians. So when a former government researcher, Daniel Ellsberg, stole and published important records about the war, "The Pentagon Papers," Nixon organized an undercover effort to discredit him. Though the "plumbers" failed to stop leaks, the secret ring lived on, collecting information about the private lives of political opponents, hounding "enemies" of the administration, and organizing a "dirty tricks" campaign against Democratic candidates for the presidency. White House staff men John Ehrlichman and H. R. Haldeman supervised these activities from the White House and kept Nixon generally informed. During May 1972 John Mitchell, now director of the Committee to Re-elect the President (CREEP), agreed to a "plumbers" proposal for wiretaps to be planted in Democratic National Headquarters in the Watergate apartment complex. There, on the night of June 16, Washington police arrested five men for burglary.

Three days later Haldeman told Nixon about the episode. Clearly worried, both men immediately planned a cover-up: no one must ever reveal the politically explosive links between the White House and clandestine operations. Nixon approved huge sums to silence G. Gordon Liddy and E. Howard Hunt—the two "plumbers" who had set up the Watergate burglary—and outlined plans to foil an FBI investigation of the incident. Later Haldeman ordered the destruction of all memos and files about "Gemstone," code name for the burglary. For a while, the plan worked. Most citizens accepted White House denials of any involvement, and the FBI found its investigation at a dead end, lacking evidence and confronted with CIA pleas not to go further "for reasons of national security."

Though most voters forgot about the Watergate episode, the law did not. Following usual procedures, a grand jury indicted seven men: the five original burglars, led by James McCord, and the two White House "plumbers," Hunt and Liddy. When all seven pleaded guilty in federal district court, Judge John Sirica angrily told them, "Without a trial, the truth will never come out." He sentenced the seven to long prison terms but promised leniency if anyone volunteered more information. Then, in March, McCord wrote Sirica. He accused "the White House" of covering up the burglary and bribing him with offers of money and executive clemency. Suddenly, Watergate blazed across the front pages. Who, exactly, in the White House was guilty of such crimes? If Nixon, he must surely be removed from office, for obstruction of justice, bribery, and misuse of the CIA were "high crimes." Sirica called the Watergate grand jury back together for a thorough investigation. Democrats in the Senate assembled a special committee, chaired by Sam Ervin of North Carolina, for a public probe of possible White House complicity. Nixon, a lawyer, knew of his own guilt, so he responded with a desperate public relations gambit. Blaming "an excess of zeal among subordinates" for the Watergate break-in, the president dismissed Haldeman, Ehrlichman, and his attorney, John Dean, and appointed a special prosecutor, Archibald Cox, to investigate the affair. Once again, he disclaimed knowledge of or responsibility for the cover-up.

But the contrived plan soon backfired. Cox and his superior, Attorney General Elliot Richardson, not only focused on the Watergate scandal but also looked into Nixon's financial and tax records. John Dean told startled senators on the Ervin committee what he had already told the grand jury: Nixon was covering up the original cover-up! His complicated testimony confused more than it clarified, and in any case Dean offered no hard evidence. The question remained, as the loquacious Senator Howard Baker of Tennessee phrased it, "What did the President know and when did he start knowing it?" No one knew how to prove that until one morning in early July Ervin was questioning Arthur Butterfield, a middle-echelon member of the White House staff, about this nagging problem of evidence. Butterfield calmly answered, "Well, I suppose it would all be on the tapes."

The almost innocent answer stunned everyone, not the least President Nixon. For several years a complicated taping system had recorded most of his Oval Office conversations. Nixon had thought the tapes would ease his task of memoir writing later on, though his critics wondered whether he also had calculated their worth as political blackmail. Now, he realized, they would ruin his presidency, for the evidence of his earlier crimes were all there. Nixon knew that if he destroyed the tapes, he would only compound his troubles, for they were now evidence in a criminal case. If he allowed his own lawyers and staff to listen to the evidence, they might resign or, worse, make it public. So Nixon told no one about his guilt, not even his personal attorneys; instead, he "stonewalled it." For months he refused to turn over tapes to Cox's office, the grand jury, or the Ervin committee. Constitutional principle and long legal tradition backed up his claim to "executive privilege," the right of any president to withhold private papers from congressional inquiry. The country and the media split deeply between those who believed in Nixon's innocence, or that he had done nothing worse than his predecessors, and those who had long belittled "Tricky Dicky" or thought him a dangerous man.

After several months of virtual deadlock, Cox announced in late October that he would obtain a court order forcing Nixon to turn over all relevant tapes. Frightened, the president wanted to fire the dangerous prosecutor, but Richardson refused. So Nixon dismissed the attorney general and his deputy, William Ruckelshaus, and eventually Cox as well. This "Saturday Night Massacre" convinced perhaps a majority of Americans that Nixon really did have something to hide. Two days later, the House of Representatives ordered its Judiciary Committee to begin impeachment proceedings. Meanwhile, vice-president Spiro Agnew resigned under suspicion of taking bribes while a Maryland official.

Now cornered, Nixon could only wait. He essayed another public relations gambit, "Operation Candor," which soon proved self-defeating. (He told one shocked audience, for example, "Your President is not a crook!") Months of legal maneuvering began, Nixon and his lawyers arguing that executive privilege protected the tapes from public scrutiny while Leon Jaworski, Cox's successor, and the impeachment committee countered that the president could not judge his own case. In the meantime, the Judiciary Committee slowly retraced all the ground covered by the other Watergate investigations. Their effort was moderate, even-handed, and moved more by sadness than by retribution. Near the end, their hearings were televised, and Americans first realized the extent of Nixon's lawlessness. Public monies had gone into his estates in Florida and California; he had defrauded the government on his personal income taxes. He had recklessly used agencies like the CIA and FBI against his "enemies," and bent government regulations for his friends. He had flouted laws passed by Congress, refusing to spend certain appropriations and prolonging air attacks in Cambodia. The Watergate cover-up itself was a felony. In late July, a coalition of Democrats, moderate Republicans, and southern conservatives on the committee voted to impeach the president and recommend his removal from office for these "high crimes and misdemeanors." But still, no "smoking gun" of hard evidence implicated Nixon directly, and many thought likely a long, difficult struggle in the Senate.

But it was the courts, not the legislature, which finally destroyed Nixon's presidency. The Supreme Court ordered him to turn over all those tapes which Jaworski and the Judiciary Committee had subpoenaed. Nixon could only comply, for refusing to do so was itself an impeachable offense. Now the country knew what Nixon had known for months: that he was guilty of obstructing justice, of lying, of subverting the law. The conversation between Nixon and Haldeman three days after the break-in showed a conspiracy to obstruct justice by cloaking White House involvement. Here, at last, was the "smoking gun." Within two days, nearly all Senate Republicans had disavowed him, and most citizens clamored for his resignation. Bumper stickers taunted, "Honk if you think he's guilty."

On August 8, Nixon addressed the nation. He admitted only "errors of judgment," not criminal actions, and quit office "to spare the country a prolonged Constitutional crisis." His quiet, careful speech dwelled upon his achievements in foreign affairs and his obvious hopes to be remembered as a peacemaker. Near the end, he spoke of "the man in the arena," the person "who dares greatly in order to achieve greatly." But the next day, during a farewell speech to the White House staff, the private man revealed more about his feelings and his motives. Recalling his parents, he sobbed in shame at what he had done. He rambled, ironically mocking himself. "Never hate those who oppose you," Nixon said, "for you will end by destroying yourself." Many who heard him that morning thought him a driven, lonely man, one too tempted by the powers of his office, a personality too flawed by fears of inadequacy. But others, less sympathetic, believed Nixon a tyrant who consciously had used the presidency for mean, dishonorable purposes. Worse, they pointed out, he had almost gotten away with his crimes, for his successor Gerald Ford pardoned him, saying, "May the man who brought peace to millions find peace within himself."

Ford takes over

As Nixon jetted across the United States toward a haven in San Clemente, California, the drama of that week in August continued. The new president, Gerald R. Ford, took the oath of office but frankly admitted, "I am well aware that I have received the votes of no one." Despite the novelty of an appointed chief executive, most Americans hoped for stability from the

White House. Ford immediately picked up this theme, promising "a little straight talk among friends" and pledging an administration of "openness and candor." Nixon's aloof, almost imperial manner gave way to Ford's homespun folksiness. He toasted his own muffins for breakfast and admitted he could not always discipline his five children; mispronunciations dotted his speeches ("in my judg-a-ment" became something of a Ford trademark); the president and his family opened gifts around a Christmas tree much like that of any working person. He referred often to his days as a football player in college.

But this new, low-keyed presidency did not change the substance of Republican policy. Ford believed vigorously in a strong military establishment. America's commitment to detente continued, but American power must always command respect. Like Nixon, he wanted to cut federal bureaucracy and "return government to the people." He told a group of small businessmen that Washington could best help "by leaving you alone for a change." Free enterprise and competition, he thought, could restore prosperity. Ford's administrative style reminded many of Eisenhower. For many years a congressman from a safely Republican district in Michigan, Ford had risen slowly in party ranks, finally becoming House Minority Leader in 1965. Always a "man of the House," Ford thought of himself as a team player. (Curiously enough, several biographers have argued since that he delegated too much authority, that the team more often than not ran its leader.) Some critics questioned his intellectual capacity, recalling Johnson's cruel riposte, "Jerry Ford was hit in the head once too often while playing football." No one doubted the new president's sincerity or his honesty, but many wondered whether he could deal effectively with the wide array of problems which challenged the United States in late 1974.

DOMESTIC DILEMMAS

Although Ford reassured Americans, "Our long national nightmare is now behind us," Watergate still bedeviled the country. Nixon worried that he might be imprisoned for his crimes. The spectacle of a president in jail also troubled his successor. So Ford pardoned Nixon—in advance—for any felonies he had committed while in office. Critics smelled a deal: had Ford earlier promised Nixon a pardon to insure his own appointment as vice-president? Many Americans, shamed enough by their miscreant chief executive, welcomed Nixon's oblivion. Yet the scandals continued. A special Senate investigating committee concluded during 1975 that the Central Intelligence Agency had planned the assassination of foreign leaders, including Fidel Castro, and had spied illegally on American citizens. The senators also proved that for years the FBI gathered political intelligence for incumbent presidents and harassed groups or leaders they considered "too radical." Abuse of power, it seemed, extended far beyond one man.

Revelations about official misdeeds added to anxieties over inflation and high unemployment. At first Ford thought inflation the greater danger, for it boosted interest rates which in turn slowed business investment. So he organized the ill-starred WIN program, "Whip Inflation Now," calling upon Americans not to buy overpriced goods and cutting back federal projects. After a nationwide gasoline shortage early in 1975, the automobile industry, the nation's biggest, suffered a huge drop in demand for its gas-guzzlers. General Motors, Ford, and Chrysler laid off hundreds of thousands of workers, and a deep recession became worse. Declining demand closed more and more factories, idling more and more men and women. Ford now focused upon jobs. He projected a $60 billion budget deficit and wanted Congress to cut taxes. The Treasury forced interest rates down and higher unemployment benefits cushioned the effects of massive layoffs. Congress tried to prop up the housing industry with tax credits for new building. Despite these efforts to encourage demand, the economy remained sluggish. Many blamed the Federal Reserve system, that autonomous agency which followed a policy of "monetary restraint" throughout Ford's presidency. Arthur Burns of the Federal Reserve apparently considered inflation the greater enemy; the politicians thought joblessness more harmful. Action by both sides often canceled each other out, leaving the economy adrift in "stagflation."

Paralysis within the government itself hampered efforts to fight recession. The November 1974 congressional elections had returned sizeable Democratic majorities to each house. Liberal measures like national health insurance, direct federal jobs for the unemployed, and large-scale social reform programs repeatedly fell victim to the White House. National energy policy illustrated the stalemate dramatically. Ford and most conservatives thought higher prices for gasoline would limit energy use most effectively; the market, not bureaucrats, could automatically cut waste. Democrats countered with a plan to conserve oil by direct rationing; all Americans, not just the poor, should cut back. A compromise bill passed in late 1975 awkwardly postponed any decision. Once again, the nation drifted, and Americans gradually returned to their "fuelish" ways.

Despite these worries, nearly everyone celebrated the country's two hundredth year of independence, the Bicentennial in 1976. An epidemic of interest in colonial life styles swept across America: waiters bustled around restaurants in makeshift knee breeches and lace shirts; local fire companies reenacted famous Revolutionary War battles; every evening television audiences learned tidbits about "what happened two hundred years ago today." The fever peaked on July 4 when the media linked the nation into a vast community festival, bringing local celebrations national attention. In New York City, for example, thirty-four "tall ships"—replicas of nineteenth-century clipper ships from all over the world—cruised in the harbor while millions watched along the banks of the Hudson River. Everywhere, it seemed, not just in New York but in places like Wells, Vermont, where high-spirited paraders blocked a state highway for two hours with tractor-pulled floats and costumed marchers, Americans were happy, pleased with themselves and their country.

ON COURSE IN FOREIGN AFFAIRS

Even before his inauguration, Ford had promised to retain Henry Kissinger as secretary of state. The new president followed carefully the policies of America's famous diplomat, especially his emphasis upon global order. Ford, like his predecessor, junketed around the world, to China, Russia, Europe, and the Caribbean. Yet these face-to-face meetings lacked the drama of Nixon's earlier travels; the United States now sought to preserve, not innovate. The SALT talks, for example, bogged down amid suspicions of intentional Soviet violations of previous agreements. Kissinger postponed a scheduled negotiation in 1975, and military leaders in both countries stirred up old fears reminiscent of the cold war. The two superpowers did arrange a "wheat treaty" which regularized Soviet imports from the United States at some 7 million tons annually. But growing American influence in the Middle East, where Kissinger's tilt toward neutrality after the Yom Kippur War had gained plaudits from the Egyptians and a measure of security for Israel, soured Russian-American relations. Neither country, though, abandoned detente, that mutual understanding to avoid nuclear war.

In Southeast Asia the 1973 ceasefire had broken down almost immediately. Both Vietcong rebels and Thieu's generals determined upon a violent, final end to a war now nearly thirty years long. The increasingly harsh Saigon regime bolstered its control around the capital and in the Mekong River delta region further south, often driving peasants off their land and packing millions into already congested cities. During the early spring of 1975 the Communists launched a coordinated attack all across the country. North Vietnamese troops rushed toward Saigon, creating massive crowds of refugees. Thieu's disillusioned armies disappeared into the jungle or fought civilians for transportation out of the combat zone. Ford asked for $1.2 billion "to give South Vietnam a chance to save itself," but Congress refused. On April 30, North Vietnamese and Vietcong troops captured Saigon itself, now christened "Ho Chi Minh City," and reunified Vietnam. Only days later radical Khmer Rouge guerrillas in neighboring Cambodia destroyed the pro-West regime of Lon Nol. Overzealous soldiers, apparently without authority, seized a United States merchant ship, the *Mayaguez*, on May 12. Ford quickly sent a force of airborne marines to free the captive crew. This grandiose rescue mission sustained many casualties, and most observers scored Ford for not trying diplomacy first. But even hawks wanted no more forays into gunboat diplomacy; America had had enough of Indochina.

The unpredictable presidential election of 1976 refashioned American politics. New laws limited campaign expenses, while nearly thirty states held party primaries. Republicans and Democrats alike fought for their party's nomination in unusually open, unusually close races. Politicians sensed that many Americans were almost apolitical now, discouraged by economic adversity and Watergate. Could anyone solve those problems of runaway complexity which challenged America's future? Worried by talk about a post-industrial society of technological uniformity, many voters looked anxiously toward old values and to an end of "permissiveness."

A former governor of California, Ronald Reagan, challenged Ford for the Republican nomination. Reagan used his oratorical flair and good looks—together with the earnest intensity of his supporters—to launch a media campaign which nearly defeated the president. Government spending must go down, Reagan insisted, and the bureaucrats must stop interfering with business and local customs. His stock "anti-Washington" speech always drew cheers, especially when he spoke out against "welfare cheats" or condemned busing for "destroying neighborhood schools." Ford countered with an energetic tour, promising tax cuts and a new energy policy based upon more business investment. He also relied heavily upon the regalia of the presidency itself. The race between these two conservative Republicans remained close until the very end. Meeting in Kansas City, the GOP convention picked Ford on the first ballot, though Reaganites had come within some fifty votes of victory. The heated contest had divided the party (Reagan refused to appear on the convention podium with Ford), and Ford's choice of the conservative Senator Robert Dole of Kansas as his running mate did little to attract votes in the urban East or the South.

The prospect of a divided GOP, together with memories of the Watergate scandals and the stumbling economy, had convinced many Democrats long before that their party's standard bearer would certainly become the next president. A year before the election, ten men, mostly senators, had entered the race. (The Democrats' sentimental favorite, Edward M. Kennedy, declined to run.) Early primaries quickly pared this field. Jimmy Carter, former governor of Georgia, won a psychologically important caucus victory in Iowa and swept the New Hampshire primary in March. The surprising dark horse frontrunner was a different type of politician. Representing the "New South," especially its willingness to accept the social reforms of the 1960s, the Baptist Carter spoke often of brotherhood and the need for love. He wanted to return government to the people, to end the imperial presidency and an isolated bureaucracy. Carefully cultivating the image of a moderate reformer who could make things work, the Georgian overwhelmed a succession of challengers. Carter gradually won over more and more of the South from the more radical and racist George Wallace. A victory against liberal favorite Representative Morris Udall in Wisconsin, capped by yet another win in Pennsylvania over Senator Henry Jackson, left Carter a convincing centrist candidate. A "stop Carter" movement coalesced around former presidential candidate Hubert Humphrey, but poor health forced him to stay out of the race. By the time the Democrats convened for the convention in New York City, Carter had corralled enough votes for a first-ballot victory. His vice-presidential choice, Senator Walter Mondale of Minnesota, indicated the Democrats' campaign strategy: unite the South with the urban, liberal states of the North.

Though early polls showed Carter far in the lead, the race proved very close. Ford's earnest campaigning avoided controversy, and his careful speeches emphasized a plucky, underdog style. In contrast, Carter stumbled badly at first. He vowed to pardon draft evaders and told *Playboy* magazine about his "mental lust" for women. Both incidents seemed gratuitously naive, and both lost him stature among voters. (The Ford team suffered from its own gaffes, particularly when Secretary of Agriculture Earl Butz maligned blacks.) Three times the two candidates debated national policy face-to-face on television. Carter seemed competent enough, knowledgeable about economics and foreign affairs. Ford, however, often appeared nervous, and the old image of "a nice guy in over his head" came back. During the last debate, the president insisted that the Soviet Union did not "dominate" Eastern Europe, a slip of the tongue which alienated many ethnic voters in urban areas. By election day, "the campaign of mistakes" had probably not changed very many minds. Carter triumphed throughout the South, but not until early the next morning did victories in Ohio, Pennsylvania, and New York give him the presidency. (The later electoral college count was Carter 297, Ford 242, Reagan 1.) Ford graciously accepted defeat, providing one of the smoothest transitions of power in American history. Then on January 20, 1977, a ritual nearly two hundred years old was repeated once again: a newly inaugurated president spoke of his hopes for the American people. The future, as always, concealed both problems and opportunities.

An interregnum: from republican to democrat

Carter had promised an aggressive refashioning of government, but his campaign had avoided specific remedies. During the three months between the election and his inauguration on January 20, 1977, a small, young staff took charge of the two most important tasks, formulating an economic recovery program and selecting some two thousand presidential appointments. Carter asked for suggestions from political leaders and some seventy-five other influential Americans, ranging from the president of Notre Dame University, Father Hesburgh, to gossip columnist Ann Landers. The new cabinet secretaries would run their own departments, he told reporters, without interference from the White House staff. Meanwhile, Carter himself concentrated on economics: taxes, inflation, unemployment, and the government's budget.

Carter's major appointments reflected an unusual mixture of tradition and venturesome hints of reform. Secretary of State-designate Cyrus R. Vance, for example, had worked as a government lawyer during the Kennedy-Johnson years, especially on Vietnam negotiations. An Atlanta banker known for his conservative fiscal philosophy, Thomas B. Lance, became director of the Office of Budget and Management. However, he later resigned when questionable banking practices were uncovered. Michael Blumenthal, President of the Bendix Corporation, took over at the Treasury Department. An international economist, Blumenthal opposed the Humphrey-Hawkins full employment bill as "too much bureaucracy." Carter asked another executive, Harold Brown, President of the California Institute of Technology, to run the Department of Defense; Brown was one of the Pentagon's "whiz kids" during McNamara's tenure there. If such appointments forecast a business-as-usual administration, others broke with the past. Civil rights activist Andrew Young became Ambassador to the United Nations. "Once we get on the right side of moral issues in this world," Young told a press conference, "then we can have an orderly approach to its problems." Carter selected a black woman, Patricia Harris, as Secretary of Housing and Urban Development. As his personal assistant for national security affairs—Kissinger's old post—he picked Zbigniew Brzezinski, a professor of international politics from Columbia University. Brzezinski had criticized detente for "bipolarizing" United States foreign policy, that is, for mistakenly excluding the third world and downgrading relations with America's allies in Europe.

Economics preoccupied the new President. Any cure for inflation called for decisive action, perhaps even wage and price controls. Though Carter repeatedly denied any such plans, many businesses raised prices as a precaution. Industrial leaders and most Republicans favored tax cuts to stimulate consumer buying and business investment; labor unions and many Democrats, in contrast, thought large-scale public works a more certain and socially beneficial method for restoring prosperity. Then, too, as higher energy costs fueled retail price hikes, economic solutions collided with the energy puzzle. An unusually severe winter in the Midwest and East strained reserves of natural gas. Many factories closed, and unemployment shot up to 8.1 percent by January.

Jimmy Carter and the new presidency

Despite these problems, most citizens responded favorably to Carter's nonchalant style. Determined to scrap the "imperial presidency," he opened the office to public scrutiny. Numerous press conferences signaled this change, but few expected his dramatic gestures of reconciliation. Beginning his inaugural address with a graceful thank-you to Ford "for all you have done to heal our land," the first president from the deep South in 128 years called for "a new spirit of unity." Attired in a business suit, Carter walked down Pennsylvania Avenue rather than ride in a limousine. (Later he canceled all chauffeured cars for his staff.) In February the President spoke on national television wearing a cardigan sweater and sitting before a fire. He followed up this "fireside chat" six weeks later with a novel "phone-in": Carter answered calls personally from citizens for about two hours. A few days later, he spoke at a town meeting in the village of Clinton, Massachusetts. Even in his frequent formal reports to the nation about energy and foreign policy, the President insisted, "America's strength lies in the strength of our people."

But this new presidency, however accessible to the public, still encountered old problems. Some, Carter solved with dispatch, as when he pardoned draft evaders. In foreign policy he moved with fresh purpose, rededicating America to a defense of human rights and calling for actual disarmament instead of the future restraints of the Vladivostok Accord. Both steps angered the Russians—and some of America's allies as well—but liberals at home and western Europeans generally approved Carter's pledge for greater morality and less realpolitik in foreign affairs. On those issues which most troubled the people, energy and the economy, the new President moved more methodically. Still studying his options, Carter waited until April to unveil recovery proposals designed, as he had vowed in his inaugural address, to restore "a fresh faith in the old dream." After suddenly dropping plans for a tax rebate, the administration concentrated upon providing government-financed jobs for the unemployed. Larger standard deductions for those taxpayers not filing itemized returns generated a small increase in purchasing power among lower income groups. Budget deficits, continuing from the Nixon-Ford years, maintained a high level of government spending, though Carter promised to balance the budget by 1981. The economy perked up: housing starts and automobile sales posted record gains, and unemployment declined slightly. During a dramatic speech on nationwide television in mid-April, Carter spoke of "the brutal facts about the energy crisis." Convinced that American demand would soon exceed its supplies, he urged conservation measures and more reliance on the country's inexhaustible coal reserves. Plans to tax "gas-guzzling" cars, as well as gasoline itself, encountered opposition from legislators and the car companies; environmentalists attacked the

702

use of polluting coal; public utilities balked at Carter's ban on breeder reactors. Congress, always more responsive to special interests, seemed likely to revamp such proposals considerably.

Still, the country moved ahead. Everywhere, not just in the booming Southwest, construction picked up as did consumer spending. Carter devoted much time to his plans for a reorganization of the executive branch. New York City survived another financial crisis. College professors remarked on the new docility of their students, now more interested in jobs than in protest. Even Nixon's self-serving television memoir about the Watergate scandal raised little comment. The 1970s continued to seem a respite from the public energy of the vivid preceding decade.

President Jimmy Carter
White House Photo

Things to think about: 1953–1977

To what extent did Kennedy influence his country? Compare Eisenhower's foreign policy to Kennedy's. See Eisenhower's memoirs *The White House Years* (2 vols., 1963 and 1965), and Emmet John Hughes, *The Ordeal of Power* (1963). On Eisenhower's successor read Arthur Schlesinger, Jr., *A Thousand Days: John F. Kennedy in the White House* (1965), and the essays in Aida DiPace Donald, ed., *John F. Kennedy and the New Frontier* (1966). For social history of the 1950s see the model suggested in David Riesman, *The Lonely Crowd* (1950), and the controversial essays in Daniel Bell, ed., *The New American Right* (rev. ed., 1963).

Why did the civil rights movement give way to black power? Compare James Baldwin, *The Fire Next Time* (1963), to Theodore Draper, *The Rediscovery of Black Nationalism* (1970), and Harold Cruse, *Rebellion or Revolution?* (1968).

Compare Lyndon Johnson's record in foreign versus domestic policy. Why did we get involved in Vietnam? On domestic history see James L. Sundquist, *Politics and Policy: The Eisenhower, Kennedy, and Johnson Years* (1968), Doris Kearns, *Lyndon Johnson and the American Dream* (1976), and *Vantage Point* (1971), the memoirs of Lyndon Johnson. Henry Brandon discusses the background of the Vietnam War under three presidents in *Anatomy of Error: The Inside Story of the Asian War on the Potomac, 1954–1969* (1969); Frances Fitzgerald, *Fire in the Lake* (1973), offers a splendid historical background. Townsend Hoopes helped shape the decision to deescalate the war and tells the story in *The Limits of Intervention* (1969). See also David Halberstane's fascinating *The Best and the Brightest* (1972).

Was Barry Goldwater a radical? See the candidate's own *Conscience of a Conservative* (1960) and the more cautious *Where I Stand* (1964), and the critical essays on Goldwater in Richard Hofstadter, *The Paranoid Style in American Politics* (1965). Excellent books centering on the mid-1960s are Alexander Bickel, *The Supreme Court and the Idea of Progress* (1970), and Theodore J. Lowi, *The End of Liberalism* (1967).

Why did women's liberation become an important social movement in the late 1960s? See Betty Friedan's *The Feminine Mystique* (1963), a precursor of the movement, and William H. Chafe, *The American Woman* (1972). On the youth culture of the 1960s see the important work of Theodore Roszak, *The Making of a Counter Culture* (1969), and that of Philip Slater, *The Pursuit of Loneliness* (1970), and Kirkpatrick Sale, *SDS* (1973).

What manner of man was Richard Nixon? Garry Wills, *Nixon Agonistes* (1970), and Theodore White, *The Making of the President, 1972* (1973). Arthur M. Schlesinger, Jr., *The Imperial Presidency* (1973), Jonathan Schell, *The Time of Illusion* (1976), and Carl Bernstein and Robert Woodward, *All the President's Men* (1974).

Abolition The demand for immediate end to black slavery without compensation to slave-owners.

Armistice A truce, usually between two military opponents. Its declaration often indicates a negotiated settlement is likely.

Artisan A small-scale, self-employed handi-craftsman, such as a blacksmith, wheelwright, or carpenter.

Balance of Payments The difference between the total value of goods, services, and capital exported from a nation and the total value of its imports. If exports are more than imports, the balance is positive; if exports are fewer than imports, the balance is negative.

Banknotes Paper currency issued by privately owned banks and backed only by their individual assets, rather than by legal guarantee or government reserves.

Barnburners The radical Jacksonian faction of the Democratic party in New York State, led by Martin Van Buren. The group refused to acquiesce in the more conservative, elitist views of the party and, as a result, preferred to "burn the barn down" rather than live in it.

Bear Market A period of consistently falling prices on stock or commodity markets.

Black Nationalism The philosophy and practice that blacks should not seek integration or equality with the white community but rather assert their own economic and cultural independence.

Bloody Shirt A post-Civil War campaign tactic used by the Republicans which obscured real issues in preference for condemning the Democrats as the party of treason and urging citizens to vote as they had fought, for the Union and for the GOP.

Border States Those states geographically between the South and North—Delaware, Maryland, Kentucky, and Missouri—with legalized slavery but without a plantation society based upon large-scale agriculture.

Brains Trust In New Deal history, a group of informal presidential advisors drawn from universities.

Bullion Pure gold held as reserves to back paper currency.

Bull Market Consistently rising prices on stock or commodity markets, often accompanied by extensive speculation with borrowed money.

Capitalism An economic system based upon production for private profit and dependent upon the central role of the person who controls capital for further expansion.

Cash Crops Agricultural crops, such as corn, wheat, and cotton, grown to be sold on a commercial market rather than consumed by the farmer.

Charter In American history, a legal document which grants property and sets up a government for a new colony.

Civil Liberties (Civil Rights) Those privileges of American citizens which limit government powers over the individual and guarantee his right to participate in the political process, to benefit from social services, and to legal equality. Black Rights The effort to secure those civil liberties denied to black citizens because of racial prejudice.

Closed Shop An arrangement whereby potential employees are required to join a union as a condition of employment.

Coastal Trade Seaborne commerce wholly within the coastal waters of the United States and not with foreign ports.

Collective Security A diplomatic device in which all major powers agree to oppose, collectively, any aggressive action by one nation which might disrupt world peace.

Currency Supply The total amount of paper money and specie in circulation at a given time. (Some economists would also include bank deposits and/or credit.) An increase in the supply of currency usually boosts prices and lowers interest rates; a decrease reverses both tendencies.

Dark Horse A presidential candidate who unexpectedly wins his party's nomination despite unfavorable odds.

Deflation A rapid decrease in commodity prices and investment values, usually because of a decline in consumer demand or because of a reduction in the supply of currency and available credit.

Depression An economic crisis characterized by severe unemployment, rapid deflation, agricultural overproduction, and industrial stagnation.

Devaluation A legal reduction in the gold value of a currency. When adopted, the device stimulates exports and discourages imports, thus easing an adverse balance of payments.

Electoral College Those people, selected by the citizens of every state, who formally cast each state's allotted votes in a presidental election. Their ballots are tabulated by the House of Representatives.

Enlightenment An eighteenth-century philosophical movement which emphasized man's rationality and his ability to impose order upon the material universe.

Faction A group of men loyal to a particular man or who come together briefly for a specific purpose, in contrast to a political party which unites a much larger group of people around a broad ideology for a longer period of time.

Farm Bloc A nonpartisan group in Congress which votes as a unit to secure laws favorable to their farmer constituents. These legislators from the Middle West often combine with southerners for mutual benefit.

Fire-eaters Southern extremists who advocated secession even if it resulted in civil war.

Fishing Rights Privileges granted to fish in a nation's territorial waters and to dry the catch on its uninhabited islands.

Freeholders In American colonial history, people who owned land or property worth a certain amount and thus qualified for citzenship, especially the right to vote and hold office.

Free Soil A political doctrine that Congress should prohibit slavery in the territories of the United States, so that only "free men" would farm the land.

Free Trade The doctrine that governments should not impose any tariffs. In classical economic theory, this would increase world production, as each nation would specialize in what it manufactured most efficiently, thus guaranteeing the lowest possible prices.

Frontier In American history, the westernmost fringe of permanent settlement.

Fundamentalism A movement within twentieth-century Protestantism which emphasized the literal truth of the Bible.

Gentry The colonial upper class which dominated politics through their social prestige and whose wealth permitted time for intellectual pursuits and government.

Gold Standard An international monetary system under which a government maintains the value of its currency in terms of a certain weight of pure gold by buying and selling bullion. This limits the amount of paper money in circulation and establishes the relative worth of all currencies.

Gospel of Wealth A moralistic justification for the concentration of riches in the hands of a few. A wealthy person must be superior; government should not interfere with its operations, since to do so would subvert "natural laws." (See Social Darwinism) Yet wisdom compelled the rich man to improve his community, primarily by helping people to help themselves.

Great Plains That area from the Dakotas to Texas, last to be settled, which is relatively arid and dependent upon wheat production.

Greenbacks Paper money issued by the federal government to finance the Civil War. Since this currency could not be redeemed for gold, it depreciated rapidly.

Holding Company A method of business consolidation, organized by bankers, to secure economic stability within a given industry by rigid controls over prices.

Home Rule Popular municipal reform, particularly during the Progressive era, which seeks local or city self-government without interference from the state.

Impeachment The Constitutional process to remove a president from office. The House of Representatives must first charge the chief executive with "high crimes and misdemeanors" and the Senate must then convict him. In each case, the vote requires a two-thirds majority.

Imperialism The policy and practice of extending the dominion of one nation, usually by direct territorial acquisition or indirect economic control over other areas.

Imperial Preference Economic arrangements between a mother country and its colonies which guarantee mutually favorable tariff treatment and discriminate against countries outside the empire.

Impressment The illegal seizure of American sailors by British naval officers for service in the Royal Fleet.

Industrialization The utilization of machine power to increase man's productivity. In its broader sense, the economic and social consequences of the nineteenth-century technological revolution which created rapid transportation, new materials, and huge business combinations.

Inflation A rapid increase in commodity prices, usually because of an increase in consumer demand without a parallel increase in industrial production or because of an increase in the amount of currency in circulation and available credit.

Initiative A political device, prominent in western states, which permits voters to originate, and then adopt, laws at special elections.

Injunction A court order, issued by a federal or local judge, which prohibits certain action until an investigation determines the legality of its probable consequences.

Internal Improvements Federally financed enterprises to build roads, canals, harbors, and other large-scale projects which would promote the industrial development of the United States.

Internationalism The belief that national interests are best served by political and economic cooperation with other countries in pursuit of the common good.

Isolationism A traditional American foreign policy which seeks to capitalize upon the nation's geographical remoteness, and consequent military advantages, by avoiding active participation in world affairs.

Jim Crow System Those practices and laws which enforced racial separation and, in effect, created a caste system. (See segregation)

Judiciary The judges which compose the court system of any country.

Laissez-Faire An economic doctrine which asserts that government must not intervene in the free functioning of the market or with individual enterprise.

Lame Duck The name given to an incumbent Congress and president after the election of a new government and before its inauguration some time later.

Legal Tender Any form of money which a government declares acceptable in payment of public taxes and private debts.

Loyalists Colonists, often called tories, who remained loyal to Britain during the American Revolution and who often later emigrated to Canada.

Manifest Destiny The belief that America's rightful, natural fate was to expand and dominate the western hemisphere, thus spreading the "empire for freedom."

Monopoly Exclusive control over the supply of a commodity which enables a businessman to determine its price.

Monroe Doctrine A diplomatic device, first spelled out by President James Madison, which promises America's noninvolvement in European affairs provided the colonial powers make no attempt to extend their empires in the New World.

Muckrakers Early twentieth-century journalists who probed the dark corners of American life, especially the decline of representative government, economic exploitation, and social inequality, in newspapers and mass circulation magazines such as McClure's and Collier's.

Nationalism A conscious effort to exalt one political or cultural state as superior to all others.

Natural Rights The eighteenth-century belief that man has certain privileges, particularly against arbitrary government, which no political authority can deny.

Naval Stores Raw materials, particularly pitchblend for caulking and trees for masts and hulls, necessary to maintain trading ships and naval vessels.

Navigation Acts A series of Parliamentary laws during the seventeenth century which sought to monopolize colonial trade for England's benefit.

Neutrality A diplomatic strategy whereby a nation avoids specific commitment to any country involved in a dispute with another and pledges to treat both nations equally, without favoring either one, according to international law.

Neutral Rights Those privileges and responsibilities which international law grants to countries not involved in a dispute; usually identified in American history with freedom of the seas and equal trading opportunities.

New Freedom A theory of political economy advocated by Woodrow Wilson which would break up business concentrations in an effort to restore competition and small, individual enterprise and so alleviate the social consequences of industrialization.

New Nationalism A theory of political economy advocated by Theodore Roosevelt which, while accepting big corporations, would have regulated such combinations in the public interest. The federal government would protect individuals from any adverse consequences of such an economic system.

Nonentanglement An American diplomatic tenet which proscribed United States participation in foreign affairs in an effort to avoid overseas troubles.

Nullification The theory that a state, acting under its "ultimate sovereignity," may set aside federal laws.

Old Guard That faction within the Republican party which did not want to reform machine politics or ameliorate the consequences of industrialization.

Open Door Policy A major tenet in American diplomacy which opposes exclusive or imperial privileges in order to insure equal access to overseas markets by all nations. This approach favors America's economic interests as an advanced industrial power.

Open Shop A business establishment which does not require membership in a labor union as a condition of employment.

Panic A brief financial emergency usually confined to the banking community. A "panic" often occurs during periods of tight money when institutions cannot easily borrow short-term funds to meet unexpected deposit withdrawals.

Patronage The power to make appointments to government jobs on a basis other than merit alone.

Populism, The Populists A western and southern political and social movement of the late nineteenth century which sought to restore government responsive to its citizens and restructure capitalism in the interests of the common people.

Predestination The Calvinist doctrine that God's omnipresence in past and future permits his knowledge of a person's ultimate fate. Thus God, but not man, knows whether he will end in heaven or hell.

Progressivism A loosely coordinated political reform movement in early twentieth-century America which sought to break up monopoly capitalism, thus restoring the individual's control over his economic future, and to remold corrupt, machine-ridden government, making it responsive to the social needs of the people.

Prohibition Outlawry of the sale, manufacture, or transportation of alcoholic beverage in the United States between 1920 and 1933. This Progressive-oriented reform reflected their belief in the usefulness of law to accomplish fundamental social change.

Public Works Construction projects, such as schools, roads, or dams, financed by government to facilitate economic activity or to promote public recreation.

Racism A belief that one race is superior to all others, which are themselves innately inferior.

Radical Reconstruction That period, roughly from 1866 to 1870, when radical Republicans attempted to recast Southern politics and Southern society toward a two-party system and racial equality.

Recall A Populist reform which permits the people to oust government officials at a special election held after a small number of voters petition for his removal.

Recession A relatively short period—technically at least two quarters of economic decline—of mild unemployment, reduced investment, and production cutbacks.

Reciprocity Mutual reductions of tariffs between two countries on goods of specific interest to each. For example, the United States might lower its duties against Cuban sugar if Cuba reduced its tariffs on American automobiles.

Redeemers Those conservative whites who took over state government in the South after Reconstruction and quickly dismantled the effort to establish racial equality and economic democracy.

Referendum A political tool, first adopted in western states, which allows the people to vote on proposed legislation before it becomes law.

Remonstrance Formal objections about the Crown's administration addressed to the British Parliament by an American colony.

Reparations Goods and money demanded of Germany by the European victors in World War I. Economic crises during the early 1920s and again in the 1930s interrupted payments and finally destroyed the effort to collect as much as $22 billion.

Republic Representative government which does not share its authority or power with a king or an aristocracy.

Restoration The return of monarchical government to England in 1660 when Charles II came to the throne, superseding Oliver Cromwell's Puritan republic.

Royalists Those who favor monarchical government or the supremacy of king over Parliament.

Saints In Calvinist doctrine, those people (the "elect") whom God knows will be saved and go to heaven. (See Predestination)

Secession In American history, the theory that a state has a right to leave the Union and resume its sovereign status.

Sedition Any verbal or other nonviolent incitement to resist government authority.

Segregation A system of race relations characterized by its attempt to minimize interracial contact and insure the social predominance of whites over blacks.

Silver Block Six western states—Idaho, Montana, Nevada, Utah, Colorado, and Arizona—whose representatives in Congress usually voted as a unit in order to secure legislation beneficial to the mining interests which dominated state politics. In particular, they sought to make silver legal tender or to increase its price on commodity markets.

Slave Codes A series of state laws which locked the slave into a rigid caste system and prevented his self-improvement.

Specie Gold or silver coins which derive their value exclusively from the value of their metal content rather than from law as in paper currency. (See Hard Money)

Social Darwinism The belief that, like Charles Darwin's theories about animal evolution, struggle and the survival of the fittest characterize human society and economic relationships. Since the strong survived because they were superior, government intervention was necessarily futile and undesirable.

Social Gospel A humanitarian movement in American Protestantism which sought a ameliorate the abuses of industrialism.

Socialism In its classic, nineteenth-century meaning, socialism meant government owneship of the "means of distribution," such as railroads and banks. Since World War I, the term more often suggests government moderation of the social consequences of capitalist industrialization, particularly business regulation, and the provision of minimal, basic welfare services.

Subtreasury Plan The effort to establish a federally financed commodity loan system so that farmers could borrow against their crops.

Tariffs A tax levied on foreign goods imported into the United States. Protective tariff Artificially high tariffs designed to boost the prices of foreign goods, thus "protecting" domestic industries from overseas competition. Revenue tariff Low tariffs which encourage commerce, and thus maximize government revenues from import taxes.

Tenancy An agricultural practice, particularly widespread in the South, under which an absentee owner rents his land to a tenant in return for a percentage of the crop.

Third World Those predominately nonwhite, underdeveloped, recently independent countries who do not adopt a foreign policy or economic system favorable either to the capitalist United States or the communist Soviet Union.

Trust An extralegal arrangement to consolidate a particular industry organized directly by manufacturers. A trust usually pools properties, thereby achieving a monopoly.

Welfare State The result when government guarantees certain minimal levels of social and economic well-being to its citizens. All advanced, industrial states have adopted this goal, to varying degrees, as unrestrained capitalism simultaneously creates the need for, and the money to provide, such services as education, health care, and unemployment compensation.

Yellow Journalism Sensational, often highly exaggerated news stories consciously published to increase circulation. William Randolph Hearst's New York Journal developed the practice during the 1890s.

Yeoman Farmer An independent, self-sufficient farmer. Thomas Jefferson and other founding fathers hoped that the United States would become an agrarian society based upon small landowners.

The Declaration of Independence

When in the course of human events it becomes necessary for one people to dissolve the political bands which have connected them with another and to assume, among the powers of the earth, the separate and equal station to which the laws of nature and of nature's God entitle them, a decent respect to the opinions of mankind requires that they should declare the causes which impel them to the separation.

We hold these truths to be self-evident, that all men are created equal; that they are endowed by their Creator with certain unalienable rights; that among these are life, liberty, and the pursuit of happiness. That, to secure these rights, governments are instituted among men, deriving their just powers from the consent of the governed; that, whenever any form of government becomes destructive of these ends, it is the right of the people to alter or to abolish it, and to institute a new government, laying its foundation on such principles, and organizing its powers in such form, as to them shall seem most likely to effect their safety and happiness. Prudence, indeed, will dictate that governments long established should not be changed for light and transient causes; and, accordingly, all experience hath shown that mankind are more disposed to suffer, while evils are sufferable, than to right themselves by abolishing the forms to which they are accustomed. But when a long train of abuses and usurpations, pursuing invariably the same object evinces a design to reduce them under absolute despotism, it is their right, it is their duty, to throw off such government and to provide new guards for their future security. Such has been the patient sufference of these colonies, and such is now the necessity which constrains them to alter their former systems of government. The history of the present King of Great Britain is a history of repeated injuries and usurpations, all having, in direct object, the establishment of an absolute tyranny over these States. To prove this, let facts be submitted to a candid world:

He has refused his assent to laws the most wholesome and necessary for the public good.

He has forbidden his governors to pass laws of immediate and pressing importance, unless suspended in their operation till his assent should be obtained; and, when so suspended, he has utterly neglected to attend to them.

He has refused to pass other laws for the accommodation of large districts of people, unless those people would relinquish the right of representation in the legislature: a right inestimable to them and formidable to tyrants only.

He has called together legislative bodies at places unusual, uncomfortable, and distant from the depository of their public records, for the sole purpose of fatiguing them into compliance with his measures.

He has dissolved representative houses, repeatedly for opposing, with manly firmness, his invasions on the rights of the people.

He has refused, for a long time after such dissolutions, to cause others to be elected; whereby the legislative powers, incapable of annihilation, have returned to the people at large for their exercise; the state remaining, in the meantime, exposed to all the danger of invasion from without and convulsions within.

He has endeavored to prevent the population of these States; for that purpose, obstructing the laws for naturalization of foreigners, refusing to pass others to encourage their migration hither, and raising the conditions of new appropriations of lands.

He has obstructed the administration of justice by refusing his assent to laws for establishing judiciary powers.

He has made judges dependent on his will alone for the tenure of their offices and the amount and payment of their salaries.

He has erected a multitude of new offices and sent hither swarms of officers to harass our people and eat out their substance.

He has kept among us, in time of peace, standing armies, without the consent of our legislatures.

He has affected to render the military independent of, and superior to, the civil power.

He has combined with others to subject us to a jurisdiction foreign to our Constitution and unacknowledged by our laws, giving his assent to their acts of pretended legislation—

For quartering large bodies of armed troops among us;

For protecting them by a mock trial from punishment for any murders which they should commit on the inhabitants of these States;

For cutting off our trade with all parts of the world;

For imposing taxes on us without our consent;

For depriving us, in many cases, of the benefit of trial by jury;

For transporting us beyond seas to be tried for pretended offences;

For abolishing the free system of English laws in a neighboring province, establishing therein an arbitrary government, and enlarging its boundaries, so as to render it at once an example and fit instrument for introducing the same absolute rule into these colonies;

For taking away our charters, abolishing our most valuable laws, and altering, fundamentally, the powers of our governments;

For suspending our own legislatures and declaring themselves invested with power to legislate for us in all cases whatsoever.

He has abdicated government here by declaring us out of his protection and waging war against us.

He has plundered our seas, ravaged our coasts, burnt our towns, and destroyed the lives of our people.

He is, at this time, transporting large armies of foreign mercenaries to complete the works of death, desolation, and tyranny already begun with circumstances of cruelty and perfidy scarcely paralleled in the most barbarous ages, and totally unworthy the head of a civilized nation.

He has constrained our fellow citizens, taken captive on the high seas, to bear arms against their country, to become the executioners of their friends and brethren, or to fall themselves by their hands.

He has excited domestic insurrections amongst us and has endeavored to bring on the inhabitants of our frontiers, the merciless Indian savages, whose known rule of warfare is an undistinguished destruction of all ages, sexes, and conditions.

In every stage of these oppressions, we have petitioned for redress in the most humble terms; our repeated petitions have been answered only by repeated injury. A prince whose character is thus marked by every act which may define a tyrant is unfit to be the ruler of a free people.

Nor have we been wanting in attention to our British brethren. We have warned them, from time to time, of attempts made by their legislature to extend an unwarrantable jurisdiction over us. We have reminded them of the circumstances of our emigration and settlement here. We have appealed to their native justice and magnanimity, and we have conjured them, by the ties of our common kindred, to disavow these usurpations, which would inevitably interrupt our connections and correspondence. They, too, have been deaf to the voice of justice and consanguinity. We must, therefore, acquiesce in the necessity which denounces our separation, and hold them, as we hold the rest of mankind, enemies in war, in peace, friends.

We, therefore, the representatives of the United States of America, in general Congress assembled, appealing to the Supreme Judge of the world for the rectitude of our intentions, do, in the name and by the authority of the good people of these colonies, solemnly publish and declare, that these united colonies are, and of right ought to be, free and independent states: that they are absolved from all allegiance to the British Crown, and that all political connection between them and the state of Great Britain is, and ought to be, totally dissolved; and that, as free and independent states, they have full power to levy war, conclude peace, contract alliances, establish commerce, and to all other acts and things which independent states may of right do. And, for the support of this declaration, with a firm reliance on the protection of Devine Providence, we mutually pledge to each other our lives, our fortunes, and our sacred honor.

The Constitution of the United States of America

We the people of the United States, in order to form a more perfect union, establish justice, insure domestic tranquillity, provide for the common defense, promote the general welfare, and secure the blessings of liberty to ourselves and our posterity, do ordain and establish this Constitution for the United States of America.

ARTICLE 1

SECTION 1. All legislative powers herein

granted shall be vested in a Congress of the United States, which shall consist of a Senate and House of Representatives.

SECTION 2. 1. The House of Representatives shall be composed of members chosen every second year by the people of the several States, and the electors in each State shall have the qualifications requisite for electors of the most numerous branch of the State legislature.

2. No person shall be a representative who shall not have attained to the age of twenty-five years, and been seven years a citizen of the United States, and who shall not, when elected, be an inhabitant of that State in which he shall be chosen.

3. Representatives and direct taxes[1] shall be apportioned among the several States which may be included within this Union, according to their respective numbers, which shall be determined by adding to the whole number of free persons, including those bound to service for a term of years, and excluding Indians not taxed, three fifths of all other persons.[2] The actual enumeration shall be made within three years after the first meeting of the Congress of the United States, and within every subsequent term of ten years, in such manner as they shall by law direct. The number of representatives shall not exceed one for every thirty thousand, but each State shall have at least one representative; and until such enumeration shall be made, the State of New Hampshire shall be entitled to choose three, Massachusetts eight, Rhode Island and Providence Plantations one, Connecticut five, New York six, New Jersey four, Pennsylvania eight, Delaware one, Maryland six; Virginia ten, North Carolina five, South Carolina five, and Georgia three.

4. When vacancies happen in the representation from any State, the executive authority thereof shall issue writs of election to fill such vacancies.

5. The House of Representatives shall choose their speaker and other officers; and shall have the sole power of impeachment.

SECTION 3. 1. The Senate of the United States shall be composed of two senators from each State, chosen by the legislature thereof,[3] for six years; and each senator shall have one vote.

2. Immediately after they shall be assembled in consequence of the first election, they shall be divided as equally as may be into three clas-

ses. The seats of the senators of the first class shall be vacated at the expiration of the second year, of the second class at the expiration of the fourth year, and of the third class at the expiration of the sixth year, so that one third may be chosen every second year; and if vacancies happen by resignation, or otherwise, during the recess of the legislature of any State, the executive thereof may make temporary appointments, until the next meeting of the legislature, which shall then fill such vacancies.[4]

3. No person shall be a senator who shall not have attained to the age of thirty years, and been nine years a citizen of the United States, and who shall not, when elected, be an inhabitant of that State for which he shall be chosen.

4. The Vice President of the United States shall be President of the Senate, but shall have no vote, unless they be equally divided.

5. The Senate shall choose their other officers, and also a president pro tempore, in the absence of the Vice President, or when he shall exercise the office of the President of the United States.

6. The Senate shall have the sole power to try all impeachments. When sitting for that purpose, they shall be on oath or affirmation. When the President of the United States is tried, the chief justice shall preside: and no person shall be convicted without the concurrence of two thirds of the members present.

7. Judgment in cases of impeachment shall not extend further than to removal from office, and disqualifications to hold and enjoy any office of honor, trust or profit under the United States: but the party convicted shall nevertheless be liable and subject to indictment, trial, judgment and punishment, according to law.

SECTION 4. 1. The times, places, and manner of holding elections for senators and representatives, shall be prescribed in each State by the legislature thereof; but the Congress may at any time by law make or alter such regulations, except as to the places of choosing senators.

2. The Congress shall assemble at least once in every year, and such meeting shall be on the first Monday in December, unless they shall by law appoint a different day.

SECTION 5. 1. Each House shall be the judge of the elections, returns and qualifications of its

[1] See the Sixteenth Amendment.
[2] See the Fourteenth Amendment.
[3] See the Seventeenth Amendment.

[4] See the Seventeenth Amendment.

own members, and a majority of each shall constitute a quorum to do business; but a small number may adjourn from day to day, and may be authorized to compel the attendance of absent members, in such manner, and under such penalties as each House may provide.

2. Each House may determine the rules of its proceedings, punish its members for disorderly behavior, and, with the concurrence of two thirds, expel a member.

3. Each House shall keep a journal of its proceedings, and from time to time publish the same, excepting such parts as may in their judgment require secrecy; and the yeas and nays of the members of either House on any question shall, at the desire of one fifth of those present, be entered on the journal.

4. Neither House, during the session of Congress, shall, without the consent of the other, adjourn for more than three days, nor to any other place than that in which the two Houses shall be sitting.

SECTION 6. 1. The senators and representatives shall receive a compensation for their services, to be ascertained by law, and paid out of the Treasury of the United States. They shall in all cases, except treason, felony, and breach of the peace, be privileged from arrest during their attendance at the session of their respective Houses, and in going to and returning from the same; and for any speech or debate in either House, they shall not be questioned in any other place.

2. No senator or representative shall, during the time for which he was elected, be appointed to any civil office under the authority of the United States, which shall have been created, or the emoluments whereof shall have been increased, during such time; and no person holding any office under the United States shall be a member of either House during his continuance in office.

SECTION 7. 1. All bills for raising revenue shall originate in the House of Representatives; but the Senate may propose or concur with amendments as on other bills.

2. Every bill which shall have passed the House of Representatives and the Senate, shall, before it becomes a law, be presented to the President of the United States; If he approves he shall sign it, but if not he shall return it, with his objections, to that House in which it shall have originated, who shall enter the objections at large on their journal, and proceed to reconsider it. If after such reconsideration two thirds of that House shall agree to pass the bill, it shall be sent, together with the objections, to the other House, by which it shall likewise be reconsidered, and if approved by two thirds of that House, it shall become a law. But in all such cases the votes of both Houses shall be determined by yeas and nays, and the names of the persons voting for and against the bill shall be entered on the journal of each House respectively. If any bill shall not be returned by the President within ten days (Sundays excepted) after it shall have been presented to him, the same shall be a law, in like manner as if he had signed it, unless the Congress by their adjournment prevent its return, in which case it shall not be a law.

3. Every order, resolution, or vote to which the concurrence of the Senate and the House of Representatives may be necessary (except on a question of adjournment) shall be presented to the President of the United States; and before the same shall take effect, shall be approved by him, or being disapproved by him, shall be repassed by two thirds of the Senate and House of Representatives, according to the rules and limitations prescribed in the case of a bill.

SECTION 8. The Congress shall have the power

1. To lay and collect taxes, duties, imposts, and excises, to pay the debts and provide for the common defense and general welfare of the United States; but all duties, imposts, and excises shall be uniform throughout the United States;

2. To borrow money on the credit of the United States;

3. To regulate commerce with foreign nations, and among the several States, and with the Indian tribes;

4. To establish an uniform rule of naturalization, and uniform laws on the subject of bankruptcies throughout the United States;

5. To coin money, regulate the value thereof, and of foreign coin, and fix the standard of weights and measures;

6. To provide for the punishment of counterfeiting the securities and current coin of the United States;

7. To establish post offices and post roads;

8. To promote the progress of science and useful arts, by securing for limited times to authors and inventors the exclusive right to their respective writings and discoveries;

9. To constitute tribunals inferior to the Supreme Court;

10. To define and punish piracies and felon-

ies commited on the high seas, and offenses against the law of nations;

11. To declare war, grant letters of marque and reprisal, and make rules concerning captures on land and water;

12. To raise and support armies, but no appropriation of money to that use shall be for a longer term than two years;

13. To provide and maintain a navy;

14. To make rules for the government and regulation of the land and naval forces;

15. To provide for calling forth the militia to execute the laws of the Union, suppress insurrections and repel invasions;

16. To provide for organizing, arming, and disciplining the militia, and for governing such part of them as may be employed in the service of the United States, reserving to the States respectively, the appointment of the officers, and the authority of training the militia according to the discipline prescribed by Congress;

17. To exercise exclusive legislation in all cases whatsoever, over such district (not exceeding ten miles square) as may, by cession of particular States, and the acceptance of Congress, become the seat of the government of the United States, and to exercise like authority over all places purchased by the consent of the legislature of the State in which the same shall be, for the erection of forts, magazines, arsenals, dockyards, and other needful buildings; and

18. To make all laws which shall be necessary and proper for carrying into execution the foregoing powers, and all other powers vested by this Constitution in the government of the United States, or any department or officer thereof.

SECTION 9. 1. The migration or importation of such persons as any of the States now existing shall think proper to admit, shall not be prohibited by the Congress prior to the year one thousand eight hundred and eight, but a tax or duty may be imposed on such importation, not exceeding ten dollars for each person.

2. The privilege of the writ of habeas corpus shall not be suspended, unless when in cases of rebellion or invasion the public safety may require it.

3. No bill of attainder or ex post facto law shall be passed.

4. No capitation, or other direct, tax shall be laid, unless in proportion to the census or enumeration hereinbefore directed to be taken.[5]

[5] See the Sixteenth Amendment.

5. No tax or duty shall be laid on articles exported from any State.

6. No preference shall be given by any regulation of commerce or revenue to the ports of one State over those of another: nor shall vessels bound to, or from, one State be obliged to enter, clear, or pay duties in another.

7. No money shall be drawn from the treasury, but in consequence of appropriations made by law; and a regular statement and account of the receipts and expenditures of all public money shall be published from time to time.

8. No title of nobility shall be granted by the United States: and no person holding any office or profit or trust under them, shall, without the consent of the Congress, accept of any present, emolument, office, or title, of any kind whatever, from any king, prince, or foreign State.

SECTION 10. 1. No State shall enter into any treaty, alliance, or confederation; grant letters of marque and reprisal; coin money; emit bills of credit; make any thing but gold and silver coin a tender in payment of debts; pass any bill of attainder, ex post facto law, or law impairing the obligation of contracts, or grant any title of nobility.

2. No State shall, without the consent of the Congress, lay any imposts or duties on imports or exports, except what may be absolutely necessary for executing its inspection laws: and the net produce of all duties and imposts laid by any State on imports or exports, shall be for the use of the treasury of the United States; and all such laws shall be subject to the revision and control of the Congress.

3. No State shall, without the consent of the Congress, lay any duty of tonnage, keep troops, or ships of war in time of peace, enter into any agreement or compact with another State, or with a foreign power, or engage in war, unless actually invaded, or in such imminent danger as will not admit of delay.

ARTICLE II

SECTION 1. 1. The executive power shall be vested in a President of the United States of America. He shall hold his office during the term of four years, and, together with the Vice President, chosen for the same term, be elected, as follows:

2. Each State shall appoint, in such manner as the legislature thereof may direct, a number of electors, equal to the whole number of senators and representatives to which the State may

be entitled in the Congress: but no senator or representative, or person holding an office of trust or profit under the United States, shall be appointed an elector.

The electors shall meet in their respective States, and vote by ballot for two persons, of whom one at least shall not be an inhabitant of the same State with themselves. And they shall make a list of all the persons voted for, and of the number of votes for each; which list they shall sign and certify, and transmit sealed to the seat of the government of the United States, directed to the president of the Senate. The president of the Senate shall, in the presence of the Senate and House of Representatives, open all the certificates, and the votes shall then be counted. The person having the greatest number of votes shall be the President, if such number be a majority of the whole number of electors appointed; and if there be more than one who have such majority, and have an equal number of votes, then the House of Representatives shall immediately choose by ballot one of them for President; and if no person have a majority, then from the five highest on the list the said House shall in like manner choose the President. But in choosing the President, the votes shall be taken by States, the representation from each State having one vote; a quorum for this purpose shall consist of a member or members from two thirds of the States, and a majority of all the States shall be necessary to a choice. In every case, after the choice of the President, the person having the greatest number of votes of the electors shall be the Vice President. But if there should remain two or more who have equal votes, the Senate shall choose from them by ballot the Vice President.[6]

3. The Congress may determine the time of choosing the electors, and the day on which they shall give their votes; which day shall be the same throughout the United States.

4. No person except a natural born citizen, or a citizen of the United States, at the time of the adoption of this Constitution, shall be eligible to the office of President; neither shall any person be eligible to that office who shall not have attained to the age of thirty-five years, and been fourteen years a resident within the United States.

5. In case of the removal of the President from office, or of his death, resignation, or inability to discharge the powers and duties of the said office, the same shall devolve on the Vice President, and the Congress may be law provide for the case of removal, death, resignation or inability, both of the President and Vice President, declaring what officer shall then act as President, and such officer shall act accordingly, until the disability be removed, or a President shall be elected.

6. The President shall, at stated times, receive for his services a compensation, which shall neither be increased nor diminished during the period for which he shall have been elected, and he shall not receive within that period any other emolument from the United States, or any of them.

7. Before he enter on the execution of his office, he shall take the following oath or affirmation:—"I do solemnly swear (or affirm) that I will faithfully execute the office of President of the United States, and will to the best of my ability, preserve, protect and defend the Constitution of the United States."

SECTION 2. 1. The President shall be commander in chief of the army and navy of the United States, and of the militia of the several States, when called into the actual service of the United States; he may require the opinion, in writing, of the principal officer in each of the executive departments, upon any subject relating to the duties of their respective offices, and he shall have power to grant reprieves and pardons for offenses against the United States, except in cases of impeachment.

2. He shall have power, by and with the advice and consent of the Senate, to make treaties, provided two thirds of the senators present concur; and he shall nominate, and by and with the advice and consent of the Senate, shall appoint ambassadors, other public ministers and consuls, judges of the Supreme Court, and all other officers of the United States, whose appointments are not herein otherwise provided for, and which shall be established by law: but the Congress may by law vest the appointment of such inferior officers, as they think proper, in the President alone, in the courts of law, or in the heads of departments.

3. The President shall have power to fill up all vacancies that may happen during the recess of the Senate, by granting commissions which shall expire at the end of their next session.

SECTION 3. He shall from time to time give to the Congress information of the state of the Union, and recommend to their consideration such measures as he shall judge necessary and

[6] Superseded by the Twelfth Amendment.

expedient; he may, on extra-ordinary occasions, convene both Houses, or either of them, and in case of disagreement between them with respect to the time of adjournment, he may adjourn them to such time as he shall think proper; he shall receive ambassadors and other public ministers; he shall take care that the laws be faithfully executed, and shall commission all the officers of the United States.

SECTION 4. The President, Vice President, and all civil officers of the United States, shall be removed from office on impeachment for, and conviction of, treason, bribery, or other high crimes and misdemeanors.

ARTICLE III

SECTION 1. The judicial power of the United States shall be vested in one Supreme Court, and in such inferior courts as the Congress may from time to time ordain and establish. The judges, both of the Supreme and inferior courts, shall hold their offices during good behavior, and shall, at stated times, receive for their services, a compensation, which shall not be diminished during their continuance in office.

SECTION 2. 1. The judicial power shall extend to all cases, in law and equity, arising under this Constitution, the laws of the United States, and treaties made, or which shall be made, under their authority;—to all cases affecting ambassadors, other public ministers and consuls;—to all cases of admiralty and maritime jurisdiction;—to controversies to which the United States shall be a party;[7]—to controversies between two or more States;—between a State and citizens of another State;—between citizens of different States;—between citizens of the same State claiming lands under grants of different States, and between a State, or the citizens thereof, and foreign States, citizens or subjects.

2. In all cases affecting ambassadors, other public ministers and consuls, and those in which a State shall be party, the Supreme Court shall have original jurisdiction. In all the other cases before mentioned, the Supreme Court shall have appellate jurisdiction, both as to law and fact, with such exceptions, and under such regulations as the Congress shall make.

3. The trial of all crimes, except in cases of impeachment, shall be by jury; and such trial shall be held in the State where the said crimes shall have been committed; but when not committed within any State, the trial shall be at such place or places as the Congress may by law have directed.

SECTION 3. 1. Treason against the United States shall consist only in levying war against them, or in adhering to their enemies, giving them aid and comfort. No person shall be convicted of treason unless on the testimony of two witnesses to the same overt act, or on confession in open court.

2. The Congress shall have power to declare the punishment of treason, but no attainder of treason shall work corruption of blood, or forfeiture except during the life of the person attainted.

ARTICLE IV

SECTION 1. Full faith and credit shall be given in each State to the public acts, records, and judicial proceedings of every other State. And the Congress may by general laws prescribe the manner in which such acts, records and proceedings shall be proved, and the effect thereof.

SECTION 2. 1. The citizens of each State shall be entitled to all privileges and immunities of citizens in the several States.[8]

2. A person charged in any State with treason, felony, or other crime, who shall flee from justice, and be found in another State, shall on demand of the executive authority of the State from which he fled, be delivered up to be removed to the State having jurisdiction of the crime.

3. No person held to service or labor in one State under the laws thereof, escaping into another, shall, in consequence of any law or regulation therein, be discharged from such service or labor, but shall be delivered up on claim of the party to whom such service or labor may be due.[9]

SECTION 3. 1. New States may be admitted by the Congress into this Union; but no new State shall be formed or erected within the jurisdiction of any other State; nor any State be formed by the junction of two or more States, or parts of States, without the consent of the legislatures of the States concerned as well as of the Congress.

2. The Congress shall have power to dispose of and make all needful rules and regulations respecting the territory or other property belonging to the United States; and nothing in this Constitution shall be so construed as to pre-

---

[7] See the Eleventh Amendment.

[8] See the Fourteenth Amendment, Sec. 1.
[9] See the Thirteenth Amendment.

judice any claims of the United States, or of any particular State.

SECTION 4. The United States shall guarantee to every State in this Union a republican form of government, and shall protect each of them against invasion; and on application of the legislature, or of the executive (when the legislature cannot be convened) against domestic violence.

ARTICLE V

The Congress, whenever two thirds of both Houses shall deem it necessary, shall propose amendments to this Constitution, or, on the application of the legislatures of two thirds of the several States, shall call a convention for proposing amendments, which in either case, shall be valid to all intents and purposes, as part of this Constitution, when ratified by the legislatures of three fourths of the several States, or by conventions in three fourths thereof, as the one or the other mode of ratification may be proposed by the Congress; Provided that no amendment which may be made prior to the year one thousand eight hundred and eight shall in any manner affect the first and fourth clauses in the ninth section of the first article; and that no State, without its consent, shall be deprived of its equal suffrage in the Senate.

ARTICLE VI

1. All debts contracted and engagements entered into, before the adoption of this Constitution, shall be as valid against the United States under this Constitution, as under the Confederation.[10]

2. This Constitution, and the laws of the United States which shall be made in pursuance thereof; and all treaties made, or which shall be made, under the authority of the United States, shall be the supreme law of the land; and the judges in every State shall be bound thereby, any thing in the Constitution or laws of any State to the contrary notwithstanding.

3. The senators and representatives before mentioned, and the members of the several State legislatures, and all executive and judicial officers, both of the United States and of the several States, shall be bound by oath or affirmation to support this Constitution; but no religious test shall ever be required as a qualification to any office or public trust under the United States.

---

[10] See the Fourteenth Amendment, Sec. 4.

ARTICLE VII

The ratification of the conventions of nine States shall be sufficient for the establishment of this Constitution between the States so ratifying the same.

Done in Convention by the unanimous consent of the States present the seventeenth day of September in the year of our Lord one thousand seven hundred and eighty-seven, and of the independence of the United States of America the twelfth. In witness whereof we have hereunto subscribed our names.

[Names omitted]

Articles in addition to, and amendment of, the Constitution of the United States of America, proposed by Congress, and ratified by the legislatures of the several States, pursuant to the fifth article of the original Constitution.

AMENDMENT I [FIRST TEN AMENDMENTS RATIFIED DECEMBER 15, 1791]

Congress shall make no law respecting an establishment of religion, or prohibiting the free exercise thereof; or abridging the freedom of speech, or of the press; or the right of the people peaceably to assemble, and to petition the government for a redress of grievances.

AMENDMENT II

A well regulated militial, being necessary to the security of a free State, the right of the people to keep and bear arms, shall not be infringed.

AMENDMENT III

No soldier shall, in time of peace be quartered in any house, without the consent of the owner, nor in time of war, but in a manner to be prescribed by law.

AMENDMENT IV

The right of the people to secure in their persons, houses, papers, and effects, against unreasonable searches and seizures, shall not be violated, and no warrants shall issue, but upon probable cause, supported by oath or affirmation, and particularly describing the place to be searched, and the persons or things to be seized.

AMENDMENT V

No person shall be held to answer for a capital, or otherwise infamous crime, unless on a presentment or indictment of a grand jury, except in cases arising in the land or naval forces, or in the militia, when in actual service in time of war or public danger; nor shall any person be subject for the same offense to be twice put in jeopardy of life or limb; nor shall be compelled in any criminal case to be a witness against himself, nor be deprived of life, liberty, or property, without due process of law; nor shall private property be taken for public use, without just compensation.

AMENDMENT VI

In all criminal prosecutions, the accused shall enjoy the right to a speedy and public trial, by an impartial jury of the State and district wherein the crime shall have been committed, which district shall have been previously ascertained by law, and to be informed of the nature and cause of the accusation; to be confronted with the witnesses against him; to have compulsory process for obtaining witnesses in his favor, and to have the assistance of counsel for his defense.

AMENDMENT VII

In suits at common law, where the value in controversy shall exceed twenty dollars, the right of trial by jury shall be preserved, and no fact tried by a jury shall be otherwise reëxamined in any court of the United States, than according to the rules of the common law.

AMENDMENT VIII

Excessive bail shall not be required, nor excessive fines imposed, nor cruel and unusual punishments inflicted.

AMENDMENT IX

The enumeration in the Constitution of certain rights shall not be construed to deny or disparage others retained by the people.

AMENDMENT X

The powers not delegated to the United States by the Constitution, nor prohibited by it to the States, are reserved to the States respectively, or to the people.

AMENDMENT XI [JANUARY 8, 1798]

The judicial power of the United States shall not be construed to extend to any suit in law or equity, commenced or prosecuted against one of the United States by citizens of another State, or by citizens or subjects of any foreign State.

AMENDMENT XII [SEPTEMBER 25, 1804]

The electors shall meet in their respective States, and vote by ballot for President and Vice President, one of whom, at least, shall not be an inhabitant of the same State with themselves; they shall name in their ballots the person voted for as President, and in distinct ballots, the person voted for as Vice President, and they shall make distinct lists of all persons voted for as President and of all persons voted for as Vice President, and of the number of votes for each, which lists they shall sign and certify, and transmit sealed to the seat of the government of the United States, directed to the President of the Senate;—The President of the Senate shall, in the presence of the Senate and House of Representatives, open all the certificates and the votes shall then be counted;— The person having the greatest number of votes for President, shall be the President, if such number be a majority of the whole number of electors appointed; and if no person have such majority, then from the persons having the highest numbers not exceeding three on the list of those voted for as President, the House of Representatives shall choose immediately, by ballot, the President. But in choosing the President, the votes shall be taken by States, the representation from each State having one vote; a quorum for this purpose shall consist of a member or members from two thirds of the States, and a majority of all the States shall be necessary to a choice. And if the House of Representatives shall not choose a President whenever the right of choice shall devolve upon them, before the fourth day of March next following, then the Vice President shall act as President, as in the case of the death or other constitutional disability of the President. The person having the greatest number of votes as Vice President shall be the Vice President, if such number be a majority of the whole number of electors appointed, and if no person have a majority, then from the two highest numbers on the list, the Senate shall choose the Vice President; a quorum for the purpose shall consist of two thirds of the whole number of Senators, and a majority of the whole number shall be necessary to a choice. But no person constitutionally ineligible to the office of President shall be eligible to that of Vice President of the United States.

AMENDMENT XIII [DECEMBER 18, 1865]

SECTION 1. Neither slavery nor involuntary

servitude, except as a punishment for crime whereof the party shall have been duly convicted, shall exist within the United States, or any place subject to their jurisdiction.

SECTION 2. Congress shall have power to enforce this article by appropriate legislation.

AMENDMENT XIV [JULY 28, 1868]

SECTION 1. All persons born or naturalized in the United States, and subject to the jurisdiction thereof, are citizens of the United States and of the State wherein they reside. No State shall make or enforce any law which shall abridge the privileges or immunities of citizens of the United States; nor shall any State deprive any person of life, liberty, or property, without due process of law; nor deny to any person within its jurisdiction the equal protection of the laws.

SECTION 2. Representatives shall be apportioned among the several States according to their respective numbers, counting the whole number of persons in each State, excluding Indians not taxed. But when the right to vote at any election for the choice of electors for President and Vice President of the United States, representatives in Congress, the executive and judicial officers of a State, or the members of the legislature thereof, is denied to any of the male inhabitants of such State, being twenty-one years of age, and citizens of the United States, or in any way abridged, except for participating in rebellion, or other crime, the basis of representation therein shall be reduced in the proportion which the number of such male citizens shall bear to the whole number of male citizens twenty-one years of age in such State.

SECTION 3. No person shall be a senator or representative in Congress, or elector of President and Vice President, or hold any office, civil or military, under the United States, or under any State, who having previously taken an oath, as a member of Congress, or as an officer of the United States, or as a member of any State legislature, or as an executive or judicial officer of any State, to support the Constitution of the United States, shall have engaged in insurrection or rebellion against the same, or given aid or comfort to the enemies thereof. But Congress may by a vote of two thirds of each House, remove such disability.

SECTION 4. The validity of the public debt of the United States, authorized by law, including debts incurred for payment of pensions and bounties for services in suppressing insurrection or rebellion, shall not be questioned. But neither the United States nor any State shall assume or pay any debt or obligation incurred in aid of insurrection or rebellion against the United States, or any claim for the loss or emancipation of any slave; but all such debts, obligations, and claims shall be held illegal and void.

SECTION 5. The Congress shall have power to enforce, by appropriate legislation, the provisions of this article.

AMENDMENT XV [MARCH 30, 1870]

SECTION 1. The right of citizens of the United States to vote shall not be denied or abridged by the United States or by any State on account of race, color, or previous condition of servitude.

SECTION 2. The Congress shall have power to enforce this article by appropriate legislation.

AMENDMENT XVI [FEBRUARY 25, 1913]

The Congress shall have power to lay and collect taxes on incomes, from whatever source derived, without apportionment among the several States, and without regard to any census or enumeration.

AMENDMENT XVII [MAY 31, 1913]

The Senate of the United States shall be composed of two senators from each State, elected by the people thereof, for six years; and each senator shall have one vote. The electors in each State shall have the qualifications requisite for electors of the most numerous branch of the State legislature.

When vacancies happen in the representation of any State in the Senate, the executive authority of such State shall issue writs of election to fill such vacancies: *Provided*, That the legislature of any State may empower the executive thereof to make temporary appointments until the people fill the vacancies by election as the legislature may direct.

This amendment shall not be so construed as to affect the election or term of any senator chosen before it becomes valid as part of the Constitution.

AMENDMENT XVIII[11] [JANUARY 29, 1919]

After one year from the ratification of this article, the manufacture, sale, or transportation of intoxicating liquors within, the importation thereof into, or the exportation thereof from

[11] Repealed by the Twenty-first Amendment.

719

the United States and all territory subject to the jurisdiction thereof for beverage purposes is thereby prohibited.

The Congress and the several States shall have concurrent power to enforce this article by appropriate legislation.

This article shall be inoperative unless it shall have been ratified as an amendment to the Constitution by the legislatures of the several States, as provided in the Constitution, within seven years from the date of the submission hereof to the States by Congress.

AMENDMENT XIX [AUGUST 26, 1920]

The right of citizens of the United States to vote shall not be denied or abridged by the United States or by any State on account of sex.

Congress shall have the power to enforce this article by appropriate legislation.

AMENDMENT XX [JANUARY 23, 1933]

SECTION 1. The terms of the President and Vice President shall end at noon on the 20th day of January, and the terms of Senators and Representatives at noon on the 3d day of January, of the years in which such terms would have ended if this article had not been ratified; and the terms of their successors shall then begin.

SECTION 2. The Congress shall assemble at least once in every year, and such meeting shall begin at noon on the 3d day of January, unless they shall by law appoint a different day.

SECTION 3. If, at the time fixed for the beginning of the term of President, the President-elect shall have died, the Vice President-elect shall become President. If a President shall not have been chosen before the time fixed for the beginning of his term, or if the President-elect shall have failed to qualify, then the Vice President-elect shall act as President until a President shall have qualified; and the Congress may by law provide for the case wherein neither a President-elect nor a Vice President-elect shall have qualified, declaring who shall then act as President, or the manner in which one who is to act shall be selected, and such person shall act accordingly until a President or Vice President shall have qualified.

SECTION 4. The Congress may by law provide for the case of the death of any of the persons from whom the House of Representatives may choose a President whenever the right of choice shall have devolved upon them, and for the case of the death of any of the persons from whom the Senate may choose a Vice President when-

ever the right of choice shall have devolved upon them.

SECTION 5. Sections 1 and 2 shall take effect on the 15th day of October following the ratification of this article.

SECTION 6. This article shall be inoperative unless it shall have been ratified as an amendment to the Constitution by the legislatures of three-fourths of the several States within seven years from the date of its submission.

AMENDMENT XXI [DECEMBER 5, 1933]

SECTION 1. The Eighteenth Article of amendment to the Constitution of the United States is hereby repealed.

SECTION 2. The transportation of importation into any State, Territory, or possession of the United States for delivery or use therein of intoxicating liquors in violation of the laws thereof, is hereby prohibited.

SECTION 3. This article shall be inoperative unless it shall have been ratified as an amendment to the Constitution by conventions in the several States, as provided in the Constitution, within seven years from the date of the submission thereof to the States by the Congress.

AMENDMENT XXII [MARCH 1, 1951]

No person shall be elected to the office of the President more than twice, and no person who had held the office of President, or acted as President, for more than two years of a term to which some other person was elected President shall be elected to the office of the President more than once.

But this article shall not apply to any person holding the office of President when this article was proposed by the Congress, and shall not prevent any person who may be holding the office of President, or acting as President, during the term within which this article becomes operative from holding the office of President or acting as President during the remainder of such term.

This article shall be inoperative unless it shall have been ratified as an amendment to the Constitution by the legislatures of three-fourths of the several States within seven years from the date of its submission to the States by the Congress.

AMENDMENT XXIII [MARCH 29, 1961]

SECTION 1. The District constituting the seat of Government of the United States shall appoint in such manner as the Congress may direct:

A number of electors of President and Vice President equal to the whole number of Senators and Representatives in Congress to which the District would be entitled if it were a State, but in no event more than the least populous State; they shall be in addition to those appointed by the States, but they shall be considered, for the purposes of the election of President and Vice President, to be electors appointed by a State; and they shall meet in the District and perform such duties as provided by the twelfth article of amendment.

SECTION 2. The Congress shall have power to enforce this article by appropriate legislation.

AMENDMENT XXIV [JANUARY 23, 1964]

SECTION 1. The right of citizens of the United States to vote in any primary or other election for President of Vice President, for electors for President or Vice President, or for Senator or Representative in Congress, shall not be denied or abridged by the United States or any State by reason of failure to pay any poll tax or other tax.

SECTION 2. The Congress shall have power to enforce this article by appropriate legislation.

AMENDMENT XXV [FEBRUARY 10, 1967]

SECTION 1. In case of the removal of the President from office or of his death or resignation, the Vice President shall become President.

SECTION 2. Whenever there is a vacancy in the office of the Vice President, the President shall nominate a Vice President who shall take office upon confirmation by a majority vote of both Houses of Congress.

SECTION 3. Whenever the President transmits to the President pro tempore of the Senate and the Speaker of the House of Representatives his written declaration that he is unable to discharge the powers and duties of his office, and until he transmits to them a written declaration to the contrary, such powers and duties shall be discharged by the Vice President as Acting President.

SECTION 4. Whenever the Vice President and a majority of either the principal officers of the executive departments or of such other body as Congress may by law provide, transmit to the President pro tempore of the Senate and the Speaker of the House of Representatives their written declaration that the President is unable to discharge the powers and duties of his office, the Vice President shall immediately assume the powers and duties of the office as Acting President.

Thereafter, when the President transmits to the President pro tempore of the Senate and the Speaker of the House of Representatives his written declaration that no inability exists, he shall resume the powers and duties of his office unless the Vice President and a majority of either the principal officers of the executive departments or of such other body as Congress may by law provide, transmit within four days to the President pro tempore of the Senate and the Speaker of the House of Representatives their written declaration that the President is unable to discharge the powers and duties of his office. Thereupon Congress shall decide the issue, assembling within forty-eight hours for that purpose if not in session. If the Congress, within twenty-one days after receipt of the latter written declaration, or, if Congress is not in session, within twenty-one days after Congress is required to assemble, determines by two-thirds vote of both Houses that the President is unable to discharge the powers and duties of his office, the Vice President shall continue to discharge the same as Acting President; otherwise, the President shall resume the powers and duties of his office.

AMENDMENT XXVI [JUNE 30, 1971]

SECTION 1. The right of citizens of the United States who are eighteen years of age or older to vote shall not be denied or abridged by the United States or by any State on account of age.

SECTION 2. The Congress shall have power to enforce this article by appropriate legislation.

PRESIDENTS, VICE-PRESIDENTS, AND CABINET MEMBERS, 1789–1881

President		Vice-President		Secretary of State		Secretary of Treasury	
1. George Washington	1789	John Adams	1789	T. Jefferson	1789	Alex. Hamilton	1789
				E. Randolph	1794	Oliver Wolcott	1795
				T. Pickering	1795		
2. John Adams	1797	Thomas Jefferson	1797	T. Pickering	1797	Oliver Wolcott	1797
Federalist		Democratic-Republican		John Marshall	1800	Samuel Dexter	1801
3. Thomas Jefferson	1801	Aaron Burr	1801	James Madison	1801	Samuel Dexter	1801
Democratic-Republican		Democratic-Republican				Albert Gallatin	1801
		George Clinton	1805				
		Democratic-Republican					
4. James Madison	1809	George Clinton	1809	Robert Smith	1809	Albert Gallatin	1809
Democratic-Republican		Independent-Republican		James Monroe	1811	H. W. Campbell	1814
						A. J. Dallas	1814
		Elbridge Gerry	1813			W. H. Crawford	1816
		Democratic-Republican					
5. James Monroe	1817	D. D. Thompkins	1817	John Q. Adams	1817	W. H. Crawford	1817
Democratic-Republican		Democratic-Republican					
6. John Q. Adams		John C. Calhoun	1825	Henry Clay	1825	Richard Rush	1825
*		*					
7. Andrew Jackson	1829	John C. Calhoun	1829	E. Van Buren	1829	Sam D. Ingham	1829
Democrat		Democrat		E. Livingston	1831	Louis McLane	1831
		Martin Van Buren	1833	Louis McLane	1833	W. J. Duane	1833
		Democrat		John Forsyth	1834	Roger B. Taney	1833
						Levi Woodbury	1834
8. Martin Van Buren	1837	Richard M. Johnson	1837	John Forsyth	1837	Levi Woodbury	1837
Democrat		Democrat					
9. William H. Harrison	1841	John Tyler	1841	Daniel Webster	1841	Thos. Ewing	1841
Whig		Whig					
10. John Tyler	1841			Daniel Webster	1841	Thos. Ewing	1841
Whig and				Hugh S. Legare	1843	Walter Forward	1841
Democrat				Abel P. Upshur	1843	John C. Spencer	1843
				John C. Calhoun	1844	Geo. M. Bibb	1844
11. James K. Polk	1845	George M. Dallas	1845	James Buchanan	1845	Robt. J. Walker	1845
Democrat		Democrat					
12. Zachary Taylor	1849	Millard Fillmore	1849	John M. Clayton	1849	Wm. M. Meredith	1849
Whig		Whig					
13. Millard Fillmore	1850			Daniel Webster	1850	Thomas Corwin	1850
Whig				Edward Everett	1852		
14. Franklin Pierce	1853	William R. D. King	1853	W. L. Marcy	1853	James Guthrie	1853
Democrat		Democrat					
15. James Buchanan	1857	John C. Breckinridge	1857	Lewis Cass	1857	Howell Cobb	1857
Democrat		Democrat		J. S. Black	1860	Philip F. Thomas	1860
						John A. Dix	1861
16. Abraham Lincoln	1861	Hannibal Hamlin	1861	W. H. Seward	1861	Salmon P. Chase	1861
Republican		Republican				W. P. Fessenden	1864
		Andrew Johnson	1865			Hugh McCulloch	1865
		Unionist					
17. Andrew Johnson	1865			W. H. Seward	1865	Hugh McCulloch	1865
Unionist							
18. Ulysses S. Grant	1869	Schuyler Colfax	1869	E. B. Washburne	1869	Geo. S. Boutwell	1869
Republican		Republican		Hamilton Fish	1869	W. A. Richardson	1873
		Henry Wilson	1873			Benj. H. Bristow	1874
		Republican				Lot M. Morrill	1876
19. Rutherford B. Hayes	1877	William A. Wheeler	1877	W. M. Evarts	1877	John Sherman	1877
Republican		Republican					

*No distinct party designations.

Secretary of War		Attorney-General		Postmaster-General†		Secretary of Navy		Secretary of Interior	
						Established April 30, 1798.		Established March 3, 1849.	
Henry Knox	1789	E. Randolph	1789	Samuel Osgood	1789				
T. Pickering	1795	Wm. Bradford	1794	Tim. Pickering	1791				
Jas. McHenry	1796	Charles Lee	1795	Jos. Habersham	1795				
Jas McHenry	1797	Charles Lee	1797	Jos. Habersham	1797	Benj. Stoddert	1798		
John Marshall	1800	Theo. Parsons	1801						
Sam'l Dexter	1800								
R. Griswold	1801								
H. Dearborn	1801	Levi Lincoln	1801	Jos. Habersham	1801	Benj. Stoddert	1801		
		Robert Smith	1805	Gideon Granger	1801	Robert Smith	1801		
		J. Breckinridge	1805			J. Crowninshield	1805		
		C. A. Rodney	1807						
Wm. Eustis	1809	C. A. Rodney	1809	Gideon Granger	1809	Paul Hamilton	1809		
J. Armstrong	1813	Wm. Pinkney	1811	R. J. Meigs, Jr.	1814	William Jones	1813		
James Monroe	1814	Richard Rush	1814			B. W. Crownin-			
W. H. Crawford	1815					shield	1814		
Isaac Shelby	1817	Richard Rush	1817	R. J. Meigs, Jr.	1817	B. W. Crownin-			
Geo. Graham	1817	William Wirt	1817	John McLean	1823	shield	1817		
J. C. Calhoun	1817					Smith Thompson	1818		
						S. L. Southard	1823		
Jas. Barbour	1825	William Wirt	1825	John McLean	1825	S. L. Southard	1825		
Peter B. Porter	1828								
John H. Eaton	1829	John M. Berrien	1829	Wm. T. Barry	1829	John Branch	1829		
Lewis Cass	1831	Roger B. Taney	1831	Amos Kendall	1835	Levi Woodbury	1831		
B. F. Butler	1837	B. F. Butler	1833			Mahlon Dickerson	1834		
Joel R. Poinsett	1837	B. F. Butler	1837	Amos Kendall	1837	Mahlon Dickerson	1837		
		Felix Grundy	1838	John M. Niles	1840	Jas. K. Paulding	1838		
		H. D. Gilpin	1840						
John Bell	1841	J. J. Crittenden	1841	Francis Granger	1841	George E. Badger	1841		
John Bell	1841	J. J. Crittenden	1841	Francis Granger	1841	George E. Badger	1841		
John McLean	1841	Hugh S. Legare	1841	C. A. Wickliffe	1841	Abel P. Upshur	1841		
J. C. Spencer	1841	John Nelson	1843			David Henshaw	1843		
Jas. M. Porter	1843					Thos. W. Gilmer	1844		
Wm. Wilkins	1844					John Y. Mason	1844		
Wm. L. Marcy	1845	John Y. Mason	1845	Cave Johnson	1845	George Bancroft	1845		
		Nathan Clifford	1846			John Y. Mason	1846		
		Isaac Toucey	1848						
G. W. Crawford	1849	Reverdy Johnson	1849			Jacob Collamer	1849	Wm. B. Preston	1849
		Thomas Ewing							1849
C. M. Conrad	1850	J. J. Crittenden	1850	Nathan K. Hall	1850	Wm. A. Graham	1850	A. H. Stuart	1850
				Sam. D. Hubbard	1852	John P. Kennedy	1852		
Jefferson Davis	1853	Caleb Cushing	1853	James Campbell	1853	James C. Dobbin	1853	Robert McClelland	1853
John B. Floyd	1857	J. S. Black	1857	Aaron V. Brown	1857	Isaac Toucey	1857	Jacob Thompson	1857
Joseph Holt	1861	Edw. M. Santon	1860	Joseph Holt	1859				
S. Cameron	1861	Edward Bates	1861	Horatio King	1861	Gideon Wells	1861	Caleb B. Smith	1861
E. M. Stanton	1862	Titian J. Coffey	1863	M'tgomery Blair	1861			John P. Usher	1863
		James Speed	1864	Wm. Dennison	1864				
E. M. Stanton	1865	James Speed	1865	Wm. Dennison	1865	Gideon Wells	1865	John P. Usher	1865
U. S. Grant	1867	Henry Stanbery	1866	A. W. Randall	1866			James Harlan	1865
L. Thomas	1868	Wm. M. Evarts	1868					O. H. Browning	1866
J. M. Schofield	1868								
J. A. Rawlins	1869	E. R. Hoar	1869	J. A. J. Creswell	1869	Adolph E. Borie	1869	Jacob D. Cox	1869
W. T. Sherman	1869	A. T. Ackerman	1870	Jas. W. Marshall	1874	Geo. M. Robeson	1869	C. Delano	1870
W. W. Belknap	1869	Geo. H. Williams	1871	Marshall Jewell	1874			Zach. Chandler	1875
Alphonso Taft	1876	Edw. Pierrepont	1875	James N. Tyner	1876				
J. D. Cameron	1876	Alphonso Taft	1876						
G. W. McCrary	1877	Chas. Devens	1877	David M. Key	1877	R. W. Thompson	1877	Carl Schurz	1877
Alex. Ramsey	1879			Horace Maynard	1880	Nathan Goff, Jr.	1881		

†Not in Cabinet until 1829.

PRESIDENTS, VICE-PRESIDENTS, AND CABINET MEMBERS, 1881–1977

President	Vice-President	Secretary of State	Secretary of Treasury	Secretary of War*
20. J. A. Garfield 1881 Republican	C. A. Arthur 1881 Republican	James G. Blaine 1881	Wm. Windom 1881	R. T. Lincoln 1881
21. Chester A. 1881 Arthur Republican		F. T. Frelinghuysen 1881	Chas. J. Folger 1881 W. O. Gresham 1884 H. McCulloch 1884	R. T. Lincoln 1881
22. G. Cleveland 1885 Democrat	T. A. Hendricks 1885 Democrat	Thos. F. Bayard 1885	Daniel Manning 1885 Chas. S. Fairchild 1887	W. C. Endicott 1885
23. Benjamin 1889 Harrison Republican	Levi P. Morton 1889 Republican	James G. Blaine 1889 John W. Foster 1892	Wm. Windom 1889 Charles Foster 1891	R. Proctor 1889 S. B. Elkins 1891
24. G. Cleveland 1893 Democrat	A. E. Stevenson 1893 Democrat	W. Q. Gresham 1893 Richard Olney 1895	John G. Carlisle 1893	D. A. Lamont 1893
25. William 1897 McKinley Republican	Garret A. Hobart 1897 Republican Theo. Roosevelt 1901 Republican	John Sherman 1897 Wm. R. Day 1897 John Hay 1898	Lyman J. Gage 1897	R. A. Alger 1897 Elihu Root 1899
26. Theodore Roosevelt 1901 Republican	Chas. W. 1905 Fairbanks Republican	John Hay 1901 Elihu Root 1905 Robert Bacon 1909	Lyman J. Gage 1901 Leslie M. Shaw 1902 G. B. Cortelyou 1907	Elihu Root 1901 Wm. H. Taft 1904 Luke E. Wright 1908
27. W. H. Taft 1909 Republican	J. S. Sherman 1909 Republican	P. C. Knox 1909	F. MacVeagh 1909	J. M. Dickinson 1909 H. L. Stimson 1911
28. Woodrow 1913 Wilson Democrat	T. R. Marshall 1913 Democrat	Wm. J. Bryan 1913 Robert Lansing 1915 Bainbridge Colby 1920	W. G. McAdoo 1913 Carter Glass 1918 D. F. Houston 1920	L. M. Garrison 1913 N. D. Baker 1916
29. Warren G. Harding 1921 Republican	Calvin Coolidge 1921 Republican	Chas. E. Hughes 1921	Andrew W. Mellon 1921	John W. Weeks 1921
30. Calvin 1923 Coolidge Republican	Chas. G. Dawes 1925 Republican	Chas. E. Hughes 1923 Frank B. Kellogg 1925	Andrew W. Mellon 1923	John W. Weeks 1923 Dwight F. Davis 1925
31. Herb. Hoover 1929 Republican	Charles Curtis 1929 Republican	Henry L. Stimson 1929	Andrew W. Mellon 1929 Ogden L. Mills 1932	James W. Good 1929 Pat. J. Hurley 1929
32. Franklin D. Roosevelt 1933 Democrat	J. Nance Garner 1933 Democrat H. A. Wallace 1941 Democrat H. S. Truman 1945 Democrat	Cordell Hull 1933 E. R. Stettinius, Jr. 1944	Wm. H. Woodin 1933 Henry Morgenthau, Jr. 1934	Geo. H. Dern 1933 H. A. Woodring 1936 H. L. Stimson 1940
33. Harry S. 1945 Truman Democrat	Alben W. Barkley 1949 Democrat	James F. Byrnes 1945 Geo. C. Marshall 1947 Dean G. Acheson 1949	Fred M. Vinson 1945 John W. Snyder 1946	R. H. Patterson 1945 K. C. Royall 1947
34. Dwight D. 1953 Eisenhower Republican	Richard M. Nixon 1953 Republican	J. Foster Dulles 1953 Christian A. Herter 1959	George C. Humphrey 1953 Robert B. Anderson 1957	*Sec'y of Defense* Est. July 26, 1947 J. V. Forrestal 1947 L. A. Johnson 1949 G. C. Marshall 1950
35. John F. Kennedy 1961 Democrat	Lyndon B. Johnson 1961 Democrat	Dean Rusk 1961	C. Douglas Dillon 1961	R. A. Lovett 1951 C. E. Wilson 1953 N. H. McElroy 1957 T. S. Gates, Jr. 1959
36. Lyndon B. Johnson 1963 Democrat	Hubert H. Humphrey 1963 Democrat	Dean Rusk 1963	G. Douglas Dillon 1963 Henry H. Fowler 1965 Joseph W. Barr 1968	R. S. McNamara 1961 C. M. Clifford 1968 M. R. Laird 1969 Elliot Richardson 1973 James Schlesinger 1973
37. Richard M. Nixon 1969 Republican	Spiro T. Agnew 1969 Republican Gerald R. Ford 1973 Republican	William P. Rogers 1969 Henry A. Kissinger 1973	David M. Kennedy 1969 John B. Connally 1971 George P. Schultz 1972	

*Lost cabinet status in 1947.

Attorney-General	Postmaster-General	Secretary of Navy†	Secretary of Interior	Secretary of Agriculture‡
W. MacVeagh 1881	T. L. James 1881	W. H. Hunt 1881	S. J. Kirkwood 1881	
B. H. Brewster 1881	T. O. Howe 1881 W. Q. Gresham 1883 Frank Hatton 1884	W. E. Chandler 1881	Henry M. Teller 1881	
A. H. Garland 1885	Wm. F. Vilas 1885 D. M. Dickinson 1888	W. C. Whitney 1885	L. Q. C. Lamar 1885 Wm. F. Vilas 1888	N. J. Colman 1889
W. H. H. Miller 1889	J. Wanamaker 1889	Benj. F. Tracy 1889	John W. Noble 1889	J. M. Rusk 1889
R. Olney 1893 J. Harmon 1895	W. S. Bissell 1893 W. L. Wilson 1895	Hilary A. Herbert 1893	Hoke Smith 1893 D. R. Francis 1896	J.S. Morton 1983
J. McKenna 1897 J. W. Griggs 1897 P. C. Knox 1901	James A. Gary 1897 Chas. E. Smith 1898	John D. Long 1897	C. N. Bliss 1897 E. A. Hitchcock 1899	James Wilson 1897
P. C. Knox 1901 W. H. Moody 1904 C. J. Bonaparte 1907	Chas. E. Smith 1901 Henry C. Payne 1902 Robt. J. Wynne 1904 G. B. Cortelyou 1905 G. von L. Meyer 1907	John D. Long 1901 Wm. H. Moody 1902 Paul Morton 1904 C. J. Bonaparte 1905 V. H. Metcalf 1907 T. H. Newberry 1908	E. A. Hitchcock 1901 J. R. Garfield 1907	James Wilson 1901
G. W. Wickersham 1909	F. H. Hitchcock 1909	G. von L. Meyer 1909	R. A. Ballinger 1909 W. L. Fisher 1911	James Wilson 1909
J. C. McReynolds 1913 Thos. W. Gregory 1914 A. M. Palmer 1919	A. S. Burleson 1913	Josephus Daniels 1913	F. K. Lane 1913 J. B. Payne 1920	D. F. Houston 1913 E. T. Meredith 1920
H. M. Daugherty 1921	Will H. Hays 1921 Hubert Work 1922 Harry S. New 1923	Edwin Denby 1921	Albert B. Fall 1921 Hubert Work 1923	H. C. Wallace 1921
H. M. Daugherty 1923 Harlan F. Stone 1924 John G. Sargent 1925	Harry S. New 1923	Edwin Denby 1923 Curtis W. Wilbur 1924	Hubert Work 1923 Roy O. West 1928	H. M. Gore 1924 W. M. Jardine 1925
Wm. D. Mitchell 1929	Walter F. Brown 1929	Chas. F. Adams 1929	Ray L. Wilbur 1929	Arthur M. Hyde 1929
H. S. Cummings 1933 Frank Murphy 1939 Robt. H. Jackson 1940 Francis Biddle 1941	James A. Farley 1933 Frank C. Walker 1940	Claude A. Swanson 1933 Chas. Edison 1940 Frank Knox 1940 James V. Forrestal 1944	Harold L. Ickes 1933	H. A. Wallace 1933 C. R. Wickard 1940
Tom C. Clark 1945 J. H. McGrath 1949 J. P. McGranery 1952	R. E. Hannegan 1945 J. L. Donaldson 1947	James V. Forrestal 1945	H. L. Ickes 1945 Julius A. Krug 1946 O. L. Chapman 1951	C. P. Anderson 1945 C. F. Brannan 1948
Herbert Brownell, Jr. 1953 W. P. Rogers 1957	Arthur E. Summerfield 1953	*Sec'y of Health Educ. & Welfare* Est. April 1, 1953 O. C. Hobby 1953 M. B. Folsom 1955 A. S. Flemming 1958	Douglas McKay 1953 Fred Seaton 1956	Ezra T. Benson 1953
Robt. F. Kennedy 1961	J. Edward Day 1961 John A. Gronouski 1963	Abraham A. Ribicoff 1961 A. Celebrezze 1962	Stewart L. Udall 1961	Orville L. Freeman 1961
Robt. F. Kennedy 1963 Nicholas deB. Katzenbach 1965 Ramsey Clark 1967	John A. Gronouski 1963 Lawrence F. O'Brien 1965 Marvin Watson 1968	A. Celebrezze 1963 John W. Gardner 1965 Wilbur J. Cohen 1968	Stewart L. Udall 1963	Orville L. Freeman 1963
John N. Mitchell 1969 Richard Kleindienst 1972 Elliot Richardson 1973	Winton M. Blount 1969	Robert H. Finch 1969 Elliot L. Richardson 1970 Casper W. Weinberger 1973	Walter J. Hickel 1969 Rogers C. B. Morton 1971	Clifford M. Hardin 1969 E. L. Butz 1971

Other Members

Sec'y of Commerce and Labor Est. Feb. 14, 1903
- G. B. Cortelyou 1903
- V. H. Metcalf 1904
- O. S. Straus 1907
- Chas. Nagel 1909
- (Dept. divided, 1913)

Sec'y of Commerce Est. March 4, 1913
- W. C. Redfield 1913
- J. W. Alexander 1919
- H. C. Hoover 1921
- H. C. Hoover 1925
- W. F. Whiting 1928
- R. P. Lamont 1929
- R. D. Chapin 1932
- D. C. Roper 1933
- H. L. Hopkins 1939
- Jesse Jones 1940
- Henry A. Wallace 1945
- W. A. Harriman 1946
- C. W. Sawyer 1948
- S. Weeks 1953
- L. L. Strauss 1958
- F. H. Mueller 1959
- L. H. Hodges 1961
- L. H. Hodges 1963
- John T. Conner 1965
- A. B. Trowbridge 1967
- C. R. Smith 1968
- M. H. Stans 1969
- Peter G. Peterson 1972
- Frederick B. Dent 1973

Sec'y of Labor Est. March 4, 1913
- W. B. Wilson 1913
- J. J. Davis 1921
- W. N. Doak 1930
- Frances Perkins 1933
- L. B. Schwellenbach 1945
- M. J. Tobin 1948
- M. P. Durkin 1953
- J. P. Mitchell 1953
- A. J. Goldberg 1961
- W. Willard Wirtz 1962
- G. P. Schutlz 1969
- J. D. Hodgson 1970
- Peter Brennan 1973

Sec'y of Housing and Urban Development Est. Sept. 9, 1965
- Robt. C. Weaver 1966
- George W. Romney 1969
- James T. Lynn 1973

Sec'y of Transporation Est. Oct. 15, 1966
- Alan S. Boyd 1967
- John A. Volpe 1969
- Claude S. Brinegar 1973

†*Lost cabinet status in 1937.*   ‡*Cabinet status since 1889.*

PRESIDENTIAL ELECTIONS, 1789–1856

Year	Number of States	Candidates	Party	Popular Vote*	Electoral Vote†	Percentage of Popular Vote
1789	11	George Washington	No party designations		69	
		John Adams			34	
		Other Candidates			35	
1792	15	George Washington	No party designations		132	
		John Adams			77	
		George Clinton			50	
		Other Candidates			5	
1796	16	John Adams	Federalist		71	
		Thomas Jefferson	Democratic-Republican		68	
		Thomas Pinckney	Federalist		59	
		Aaron Burr	Democratic-Republican		30	
		Other Candidates			48	
1800	16	Thomas Jefferson	Democratic-Republican		73	
		Aaron Burr	Democratic-Republican		73	
		John Adams	Federalist		65	
		Charles C. Pinckney	Federalist		64	
		John Jay	Federalist		1	
1804	17	Thomas Jefferson	Democratic-Republican		162	
		Charles C. Pinckney	Federalist		14	
1808	17	James Madison	Democratic-Republican		122	
		Charles C. Pinckney	Federalist		47	
		George Clinton	Democratic-Republican		6	
1812	18	James Madison	Democratic-Republican		128	
		DeWitt Clinton	Federalist		89	
1816	19	James Monroe	Democratic-Republican		183	
		Rufus King	Federalist		34	
1820	24	James Monroe	Democratic-Republican		231	
		John Quincy Adams	Independent Republican		1	
1824	24	John Quincy Adams		108,740	84	30.5
		Andrew Jackson		153,544	99	43.1
		William H. Crawford		46,618	41	13.1
		Henry Clay		47,136	37	13.2
1828	24	Andrew Jackson	Democrat	647,268	178	56.0
		John Quincy Adams	National Republican	508,064	83	44.0
1832	24	Andrew Jackson	Democrat	687,502	219	55.0
		Henry Clay	National Republican ⎫	530,189	49	42.4
		William Wirt	Anti-Masonic ⎬	33,108	7	2.6
		John Floyd	National Republican ⎭		11	
1836	26	Martin Van Buren	Democrat	765,483	170	50.9
		William H. Harrison	Whig		73	
		Hugh L. White	Whig ⎫		26	49.1
		Daniel Webster	Whig ⎬	739,795	14	
		W. P. Mangum	Whig ⎭		11	
1840	26	William H. Harrison	Whig	1,274,624	234	53.1
		Martin Van Buren	Democrat	1,127,781	60	46.9
1844	26	James K. Polk	Democrat	1,338,464	170	49.6
		Henry Clay	Whig	1,300,097	105	48.1
		James G. Birney	Liberty	62,300		2.3
1848	30	Zachary Taylor	Whig	1,360,967	163	47.4
		Lewis Cass	Democrat	1,222,342	127	42.5
		Martin Van Buren	Free Soil	291,263		10.1
1852	31	Franklin Pierce	Democrat	1,601,117	254	50.9
		Winfield Scott	Whig	1,385,453	42	44.1
		John P. Hale	Free Soil	155,825		5.0
1856	31	James Buchanan	Democrat	1,832,955	174	45.3
		John C. Fremont	Republican	1,339,932	114	33.1
		Millard Fillmore	American	871,731	8	21.6

*Percentage of popular vote given for any election year may not total 100 percent because candidates receiving less than 1 percent of the popular vote have been omitted.

†Prior to the passage of the Twelfth Amendment in 1804, the electoral college voted for two presidential candidates; the runner-up became Vice-President. Data from Historical Statistics of the United States, Colonial Times to 1957 (1961), pp. 582–683, and The World Almanac.

PRESIDENTIAL ELECTIONS, 1860–1932

Year	Number of States	Candidates	Party	Popular Vote	Electoral Vote	Percentage of Popular Vote
1860	33	Abraham Lincoln	Republican	1,865,593	180	39.8
		Stephen A. Douglas	Democrat	1,382,713	12	29.5
		John C. Breckinridge	Democrat	848,356	72	18.1
		John Bell	Constitutional Union	592,906	39	12.6
1864	36	Abraham Lincoln	Republican	2,206,938	212	55.0
		George B. McClellan	Democrat	1,803,787	21	45.0
1868	37	Ulysses S. Grant	Republican	3,013,421	214	52.7
		Horatio Seymour	Democrat	2,706,829	80	47.3
1872	37	Ulysses S. Grant	Republican	3,596,745	286	55.6
		Horace Greeley	Democrat	2,843,446	*	43.9
1876	38	Rutherford B. Hayes	Republican	4,036,572	185	48.0
		Samuel J. Tilden	Democrat	4,284,020	184	51.0
1880	38	James A. Garfield	Republican	4,453,295	214	48.5
		Winfield S. Hancock	Democrat	4,414,082	155	48.1
		James B. Weaver	Greenback-Labor	308,578		3.4
1884	38	Grover Cleveland	Democrat	4,879,507	219	48.5
		James G. Blaine	Republican	4,850,293	182	48.2
		Benjamin F. Butler	Greenback-Labor	175,370		1.8
		John P. St. John	Prohibition	150,369		1.5
1888	38	Benjamin Harrison	Republican	5,447,129	233	47.9
		Grover Cleveland	Democrat	5,537,857	168	48.6
		Clinton B. Fisk	Prohibition	249,506		2.2
		Anson J. Streeter	Union Labor	146,935		1.3
1892	44	Grover Cleveland	Democrat	5,555,426	277	46.1
		Benjamin Harrison	Republican	5,182,690	145	43.0
		James B. Weaver	People's	1,029,846	22	8.5
		John Bidwell	Prohibition	264,133		2.2
1896	45	William McKinley	Republican	7,102,246	271	51.1
		William J. Bryan	Democrat	6,492,559	176	47.7
1900	45	William McKinley	Republican	7,218,491	292	51.7
		William J. Bryan	Democrat; Populist	6,356,734	155	45.5
		John C. Woolley	Prohibition	208,914		1.5
1904	45	Theodore Roosevelt	Republican	7,628,461	336	57.4
		Alton B. Parker	Democrat	5,084,223	140	37.6
		Eugene V. Debs	Socialist	402,283		3.0
		Silas C. Swallow	Prohibition	258,536		1.9
1908	46	William H. Taft	Republican	7,675,320	321	51.6
		William J. Bryan	Democrat	6,412,294	162	43.1
		Eugene V. Debs	Socialist	420,793		2.8
		Eugene W. Chafin	Prohibition	253,840		1.7
1912	48	Woodrow Wilson	Democrat	6,296,547	435	41.9
		Theodore Roosevelt	Progressive	4,118,571	88	27.4
		William H. Taft	Republican	3,486,720	8	23.2
		Eugene V. Debs	Socialist	900,672		6.0
		Eugene W. Chafin	Prohibition	206,275		1.4
1916	48	Woodrow Wilson	Democrat	9,127,695	277	49.4
		Charles E. Hughes	Republican	8,533,507	254	46.2
		A. L. Benson	Socialist	585,113		3.2
		J. Frank Hanly	Prohibition	220,506		1.2
1920	48	Warren G. Harding	Republican	16,143,407	404	60.4
		James M. Cox	Democrat	9,130,328	127	34.2
		Eugene V. Debs	Socialist	919,799		3.4
		P. P. Christensen	Farmer-Labor	265,411		1.0
1924	48	Calvin Coolidge	Republican	15,718,211	382	54.0
		John W. Davis	Democrat	8,385,283	136	28.8
		Robert M. La Follette	Progressive	4,821,289	13	16.6
1928	48	Herbert C. Hoover	Republican	21,391,993	444	58.2
		Alfred E. Smith	Democrat	15,016,169	87	40.9
1932	48	Franklin D. Roosevelt	Democrat	22,809,638	472	57.4
		Herbert C. Hoover	Republican	15,758,901	59	39.7
		Norman Thomas	Socialist	881,951		2.2

*Because of the death of Greeley, Democratic electors scattered their votes.

PRESIDENTIAL ELECTIONS, 1936–1976

Year	Number of States	Candidates	Party	Popular Vote*	Electoral Vote†	Percentage of Popular Vote
1936	48	Franklin D. Roosevelt	Democrat	27,752,869	523	60.8
		Alfred M. Landon	Republican	16,674,665	8	36.5
		William Lemke	Union	882,479		1.9
1940	48	Franklin D. Roosevelt	Democrat	27,307,819	449	54.8
		Wendell L. Wilkie	Republican	22,321,018	82	44.8
1944	48	Franklin D. Roosevelt	Democrat	25,606,585	432	53.5
		Thomas E. Dewey	Republican	22,014,745	99	46.0
1948	48	Harry S. Truman	Democrat	24,105,812	303	49.5
		Thomas E. Dewey	Republican	21,970,065	189	45.1
		J. Strom Thurmond	States' Rights	1,169,063	39	2.4
		Henry A. Wallace	Progressive	1,157,172		2.4
1952	48	Dwight D. Eisenhower	Republican	33,936,234	442	55.1
		Adlai E. Stevenson	Democrat	27,314,992	89	44.4
1956	48	Dwight D. Eisenhower	Republican	35,590,472	457‡	57.6
		Adlai E. Stevenson	Democrat	26,022,752	73	42.1
1960	50	John F. Kennedy	Democrat	34,227,096	303§	49.9
		Richard M. Nixon	Republican	34,108,546	219	49.6
1964	50	Lyndon B. Johnson	Democrat	42,676,220	486	61.3
		Barry M. Goldwater	Republican	26,860,314	52	38.5
1968	50	Richard M. Nixon	Republican	31,785,480	301	43.4
		Hubert H. Humphrey	Democrat	31,275,165	191	42.7
		George C. Wallace	American Independent	9,906,473	46	13.5
1972	50	Richard M. Nixon	Republican	45,767,218	521	61.0
		George S. McGovern	Democrat	28,357,668	17	38.0
1976	50	Jimmy Carter	Democrat	40,276,040	297	51.1
		Gerald R. Ford	Republican	38,532,630	241	48.9

*Percentage of popular vote given for any election year may not total 100 percent because candidates receiving less than 1 percent of the popular vote have been omitted.
†Prior to the passage of the Twelfth Amendment in 1804, the electoral college voted for two presidential candidates; the runner-up became Vice-President. Data from Historical Statistics of the United States, Colonial Times to 1957 (1961). pp. 682–683, and The World Almanac.
‡Walter B. Jones received 1 electoral vote   §Harry F. Byrd received 15 electoral votes.

JUSTICES OF THE UNITED STATES SUPREME COURT, 1789–1977

Name (Chief Justices in Italics)	Service (Terms)	(Years)	Name (Chief Justices in Italics)	Service (Terms)	(Years)
John Jay (N.Y.)	1789–1795	6	George Shiras, Jr. (Pa.)	1892–1903	11
John Rutledge (S.C.)	1789–1791	2	Howell E. Jackson (Tenn.)	1893–1895	2
William Cushing (Mass.)	1789–1810	21	Edward D. White (La.)	1894–1910	16
James Wilson (Pa.)	1789–1798	9	Rufus W. Peckham (N.Y.)	1895–1909	14
John Blair (Va.)	1789–1796	7	Joseph McKenna (Calif.)	1898–1925	25
James Iredell (N.C.)	1790–1799	9	Oliver W. Holmes (Mass.)	1902–1932	30
Thomas Johnson (Md.)	1792–1793	½	William R. Day (Ohio)	1903–1922	19
William Paterson (N.J.)	1793–1806	13	William H. Moody (Mass.)	1906–1910	4
John Rutledge (S.C.)*	1795–1795		Horace H. Lurton (Tenn.)	1910–1914	4
Samuel Chase (Md.)	1796–1811	15	*Edward D. White* (La.)	1910–1921	11
Oliver Ellsworth (Conn.)	1796–1800	4	Charles E. Hughes (N.Y.)	1910–1916	6
Bushrod Washington (Va.)	1798–1892	31	Willis Van Devanter (Wyo.)	1911–1937	26
Alfred Moore (N.C.)	1800–1804	4	Joseph R. Lamar (Ga.)	1911–1916	5
John Marshall (Va.)	1801–1835	34	Mahlon Pitney (N.J.)	1912–1922	10
William Johnson (S.C.)	1804–1834	30	James C. McReynolds (Tenn.)	1914–1941	27
Brock. Livingston (N.Y.)	1806–1823	17	Louis D. Brandeis (Mass.)	1916–1939	23
Thomas Todd (Ky.)	1807–1826	19	John H. Clarke (Ohio)	1916–1922	6
Joseph Story (Mass.)	1811–1845	34	*William H. Taft* (Conn.)	1921–1930	9
Gabriel Duval (Md.)	1811–1835	24	George Sutherland (Utah)	1922–1938	16
Smith Thompson (N.Y.)	1823–1843	20	Pierce Butler (Minn.)	1923–1939	16
Robert Trimble (Ky.)	1826–1828	2	Edward T. Sanford (Tenn.)	1923–1930	7
John McLean (Ohio)	1829–1861	32	Harlan F. Stone (N.Y.)	1925–1941	16
Henry Baldwin (Pa.)	1830–1844	14	*Charles E. Hughes* (N.Y.)	1930–1941	11
James M. Wayne (Ga.)	1835–1867	32	Owen J. Roberts (Pa.)	1930–1945	15
Roger B. Taney (Md.)	1836–1864	28	Benjamin N. Cardozo (N.Y.)	1932–1938	6
Philip P. Barbour (Va.)	1836–1841	5	Hugo L. Black (Ala.)	1937–1971	34
John Catron (Tenn.)	1837–1865	28	Stanley F. Reed (Ky.)	1938–1957	19
John McKinley (Ala.)	1837–1852	15	Felix Frankfurter (Mass.)	1939–1962	23
Peter V. Daniel (Va.)	1841–1860	19	William O. Douglas (Conn.)	1939–	
Samuel Nelson (N.Y.)	1845–1872	27	Frank Murphy (Mich.)	1940–1949	9
Levi Woodbury (N.H.)	1845–1851	6	*Harlan F. Stone* (N.Y.)	1941–1946	5
Robert C. Grier (Pa.)	1846–1870	24	James F. Byrnes (S.C.)	1941–1942	1
Benjamin R. Curtis (Mass.)	1851–1857	6	Robert H. Jackson (N.Y.)	1941–1945	13
John A. Campbell (Ala.)	1853–1861	8	Wiley B. Rutledge (Iowa)	1943–1949	6
Nathan Clifford (Maine)	1858–1881	23	Harold H. Burton (Ohio)	1945–1958	13
Noah H. Swayne (Ohio)	1862–1881	19	*Fred M. Vinson* (Ky.)	1946–1953	7
Samuel F. Miller (Iowa)	1862–1890	28	Tom C. Clark (Tex.)	1949–1967	18
David Davis (Ill.)	1862–1877	15	Sherman Minton (Ind.)	1949–1956	7
Stephen J. Field (Calif.)	1863–1897	34	*Earl Warren* (Calif.)	1953–1969	16
Salmon P. Chase (Ohio)	1864–1873	9	John M. Harlan (N.Y.)	1955–1971	16
William Strong (Pa.)	1870–1880	10	William J. Brennan (N.J.)	1956–	
Joseph P. Bradley (N.J.)	1870–1892	22	Charles E. Whittaker (Mo.)	1957–1962	5
Ward Hunt (N.Y.)	1872–1882	10	Potter Stewart (Ohio)	1958–	
Morrison R. Waite (Ohio)	1874–1888	14	Byron R. White (Colo.)	1962–	
John M. Harlan (Ky.)	1877–1911	34	Arthur J. Goldberg (Ill.)	1962–1965	3
William B. Woods (Ga.)	1880–1887	7	Abe Fortas (Tenn.)	1965–1969	4
Stanley Matthews (Ohio)	1881–1889	8	Thurgood Marshall (Md.)	1967–	
Horace Gray (Mass.)	1881–1902	21	*Warren E. Burger* (Minn.)	1969–	
Samuel Blatchford (N.Y.)	1882–1893	11	Harry A. Blackmun (Minn.)	1970–	
Lucius Q. Lamar (Miss.)	1888–1893	5	Lewis F. Powell, Jr. (Va.)	1971–	
Melville W. Fuller (Ill.)	1888–1910	22	William H. Rehnquist (Ariz.)	1971–	
David J. Brewer (Kans.)	1889–1910	21	John P. Stevens (Mich.)	1975–	
Henry B. Brown (Mich.)	1890–1906	16			

*Appointed and served one term, but not confirmed by the Senate.

INDEX

Brisbane, Albert, 226
Brook Farm, 228
Brown, Harold, 701
Brown, John, 293, 297–98
Brown, Joseph, 317
Brown v. Board of Education (1954), 651, 658–59
Bryan, William Jennings, 416–19, 479, 517–18
Brzezinski, Zbigniew, 701
Buchanan, James, 293, 311
Bull-Moose Campaign, 465–67
Bunker Hill, 98
Burgoyne, John, 103
Burns, Arthur, 697
Burr, Aaron, 149, 155
Business: in late nineteenth century, 369–77
Butler, Pierce (South Carolinian), 291
Butterfield, Arthur, 693

Cabot, John, 2–5
Cagney, James, 571
Calhoun, John C., 188–89, 227–38, 246, 276, 286
California, 270, 281–82, 286–87, 615
Calvert, Sir George, 24, 26, 49
Calvin, John, 27
Canada, 165, 274–76
Canning, George, 182
Cannon, Joe, 464
Capone, Al, 492–95
Cardenas, Lazaro, 554
Carnegie, Andrew, 376–77
Carolina, colony of, 44, 61
Caroline affair, 275
Carranza, Venustiano, 480
Carter, Jimmy, 699–703
Cartwright, Peter, 225
Casablanca Conference, 598
Cass, Lewis, 283
Castro, Fidel, 656–57
Cathay Company, 19
Century of Dishonor, A (1881), 365
Chambers, Whitaker, 632
Chancellorsville, 322
Chase, Salmon P., 282–83
Chase, Samuel, 151–52
Chautauqua, 394
Chavez, Cesar, 650
Cherokee, 185
Chesapeake, 164
Chicanos, 649–51
Chief Joseph, 354–57
China, 435–36, 625, 627, 669, 683. *See also* Chiang Kai-shek
Chinese Exclusion Act (1882), 359
Chinese immigration, 358
Churchill, Winston, 592–605 *passim*, 609
CIO, 562, 577
Cities: in ante-bellum period, 260–64; in late nineteenth century, 380–87; in Progressive Era, 449–52
City-manager, 450
Civil liberties, in Civil War, 336–38
Civil Rights Act: of 1866, 343; of 1875, 349; of 1964, 1965, and 1966, 662
Civil Rights Movement, 638–46, 658–65
Civil War, 311–32
Civilian Conservation Corps (CCC), 546–47
Clark, J. Reuben, 553
Clark Memorandum, 553
Clay, Henry, 181, 183, 188–89, 191, 196, 198, 201–4, 211, 246, 274, 276, 285–86

Clay, Lucius D., 626
Clayton Antitrust Act (1914), 469
Cleveland, Grover, 391, 402, 407, 411–15, 426–27
Clinton, DeWitt, 210
Clinton, George, 118, 143, 193
Coal strike (1902), 459–60
Cobb, Howard, 316
Cold War, 604–9, 624–36
Collier, John, 578
Colonial government, 55–59
Columbus, Christopher, 2, 4, 6, 14
Committee for Industrial Organization, 563
Committee on Public Information, 489, 496
Committees of Correspondence, 98
Common Sense, 84, 111
Communitarianism, 226–28
"Compromise of 1850," 286–87
"Compromise of 1877," 359–60
Confederacy, The, 306–34 *passim*
Congress of Industrial Organizations, 562, 577
Congress of Racial Equality (CORE), 616
Connecticut Compromise, 119
Conservation, 460–61
Constitution of the United States, 118–24
Continental Congresses, 98–100, 102
Cooke, Jay, 358
Coolidge, Calvin, 507–9, 528
Cooper, James Fenimore, 213
Cornwallis, Charles, 104, 133
Coronado, Vásquez de, 17
Cortés, Herran, 14–15
Cotton, 157–58, 202–3, 266–67, 270
Cotton gin, 126–29
Coughlin, Father Charles, 557
Cowboys, 360–61
Cox, Archibald, 693–94
Cox, James, 505
Coxey, Jacob S., 398–401
Crawford, William H., 188, 191
Creel, George, 489
Crime of '73, 406
"Critical Period," 112
Crittenden, John J., 311
Cromwell, Oliver, 33, 41
Crusade in Europe, 642
Cuba, 289, 431–33, 554, 656–57
Cuban revolution, 427
Culpepper's rebellion, 49
Currency, *See* Bryan, William Jennings; Specie Circular; Populism
Currency Act of 1764, 90; of 1873, 406
Custer, George A., 363–64
Czolgosz, Leon, 456

Dale, Sir Thomas, 22
Darrow, Clarence, 518, 551
Davis, Jefferson, 316–17
Davis, John W., 508
Dawes Act, 365–66
Dayan, Moshe, 691
Dean, John, 693
Deane, Silas, 134
Debs, Eugene, 411, 413–14, 467, 498
Declaration of Independence, 101
Declaratory Act, 93
de Gaulle, Charles, 596–98, 682
De Lôme, Dupuy de, 429
Democracy in America (1832), 212
Depression: of 1819, 202; of 1837 and 1839, 204–5; of 1870s, 358–59; of 1894, 412; of 1929, 543–80
De Soto, Hernando, 17

De Tocqueville, Alexis, 212, 368
Dewey, George, 431
Dewey, John, 448
Dewey, Thomas E., 602, 621–23, 642
Diaz, Porfirio, 479
Dickens, Charles, 253
Dickinson, John, 93, 100
Diem, Ngo Dinh, 667, 669
Dien Bien Phu, 667
Direct primary, 455
Dix, Dorothea, 232
"Dixiecrats," 622–24
"Dollar Diplomacy," 463
Dominican Republic, 669
Dominion of New England, 51–52
Doubleday, Abner, 264
Douglas, Stephen A., 284, 286, 290, 296–99
Douglass, Frederick, 229, 244, 267, 332, 348
Dow, Neal, 229
Drake, Sir Francis, 18
Dred Scott v. Sandford, 294
Dreiser, Theodore, 449
Drugs, in youth culture, 677
Drummond, William, 49
Dubinsky, David, 562
Du Bois, W. E. B., 472–74
Dulles, Allen, 654
Dulles, John Foster, 643–44
Dumbarton Oaks, 603
Dupuy de Lôme, 429
Dylan, Bob, 678

Eagleton, Thomas, 687
East India Company, 96–98
Economic Opportunity Act (1964), 665
Edison, Thomas, 382
Education: colonial, 71–73; higher, 393–94; nineteenth century, 230
Edwards, Jonathan, 38–40, 77
Ehrlichman, John, 692–93
Eisenhower, Dwight D., 599, 635–36, 641–47, 660
Election: of 1800, 149–50; of 1824, 191–93; of 1828, 195–98; of 1840, 199; of 1860, 298–99; of 1876, 351; of 1896, 415–19; of 1912, 465–67; of 1936, 562–63; of 1948, 621–24; of 1968, 674–75; of 1976, 699–700
Eliot, Charles W., 394
Elizabeth I (Queen of England), 19
Ellis Island, 451–52
Ellsberg, Daniel, 673
Emancipation Proclamation (1863), 321, 330, 340
Embargo, 167
Emergency Banking Relief Act, 546
Emerson, Ralph Waldo, 213–15
End Poverty in California (EPIC), 555
England, in the New World, 18–35. *See* Great Britain
Era of Good Feelings, 193–95
Ericson, Leif, 11
Erie Canal, 210
Ervin, Sam, 693
Evangelism, nineteenth century, 221–26
Explorers. *See* Cortes, Pizarro, Ponce de Leon, Coronado, de Soto, La Salle, Frobisher, Columbus, Hakluyt

Fair Deal, 623ff.
Fair Employment Practices Commission (FEPC), 616
Fair Employment Standards Act (1938), 561